THE MANY FACES OF
ALEXANDER HAMILTON

THE LIFE & LEGACY OF
AMERICA'S MOST *Elusive* FOUNDING FATHER

Edited by

DOUGLAS AMBROSE & ROBERT W. T. MARTIN

New York University Press

NEW YORK & LONDON

NEW YORK UNIVERSITY PRESS
New York and London
www.nyupress.org

Library of Congress Cataloging-in-Publication Data
The many faces of Alexander Hamilton : the life and legacy of America's
most elusive founding father / edited by Douglas Ambrose and Robert W.
T. Martin.

p. cm.
Includes bibliographical references and index.
ISBN–13: 978–0–8147–0714–2 (cloth : alk. paper)
ISBN–10: 0–8147–0714–9 (cloth : alk. paper)
1. Hamilton, Alexander, 1757–1804—Congresses.   2. Statesman—United
States—Biography—Congresses.   3. United States—Politics and govern-
ment—1783–1809—Congresses.   I. Ambrose, Douglas, 1957–   II. Mar-
tin, Robert W. T. (Robert William Thomas), 1967–
                    E302.6.H2M36   2006
            973.4'092—dc22   2005026120

New York University Press books are printed on acid-free paper,
and their binding materials are chosen for strength and durability.

Manufactured in the United States of America
10 9 8 7 6 5 4 3 2 1

For

Carl & Menges

in gratitude

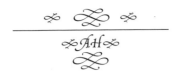

Contents

Acknowledgments

THROUGHOUT his life and especially as the prime mover behind the *Federalist Papers*, Alexander Hamilton was well aware that publication—unlike the often solitary work of writing—is always a collective endeavor that relies on many contributions, great and small. This book is no exception. The most obvious contributions here are those of the scholars who enrich the following pages. We greatly appreciate their careful research, good natures, and, not least, punctuality.

The chapters all began as papers at a working conference at Hamilton College honoring its namesake (and early trustee), Alexander Hamilton. The success of the conference owes much to the contributions and comments of other attending scholars besides our authors. We therefore thank Lance Banning, Richard Brookhiser, Doug Egerton, Eugene Genovese, John Steele Gordon, Graham Hodges, Dan Littlefield, Paul Rahe, and Robert Scigliano. We are also grateful for the conference work of our colleagues Frank Anechiarico, Maurice Isserman, Phil Klinkner, Bob Paquette, and Carl Rubino, as well as Sharon Rippey and Dannelle Parker.

None of these efforts, however, nor even the conference itself, would have been possible without the vision, initiative, and generous support of Carl Menges, a Hamilton College alumnus and Life Trustee, as well as a serious student of American history. We dedicate this book to Carl in honor of his contributions.

The book itself owes a great deal to the encouragement, advice, and support (not to mention patience) of our editor, Debbie Gershenowitz. We also appreciate the work of her colleagues at New York University Press, especially Salwa Jabado and Despina Papazoglou Gimbel. At Hamilton, the book has benefited from the careful eyes of Dawn Woodward and Andrew Graves. And we thank our dean, David Paris, for his support.

We also gratefully acknowledge publishers who agreed to allow previously published works to be included here. A version of Colleen Sheehan's essay first appeared in the *American Political Science Review* 98 (2004): 405–424 and is reprinted with the permission of Cambridge University Press. Robert Martin's essay first appeared in *The Journal of the Early Republic* 25 (2005): 21–46 (copyright © 2005 Society for Historians of the Early American Republic) and is reprinted by permission of the University of Pennsylvania Press.

Finally, we remain—as always—grateful for and indebted to the advice, support, and inexplicable forbearance of our long-suffering spouses, Sheila O'Connor-Ambrose and Gretchen Herringer.

DOUG AMBROSE
ROB MARTIN

CHAPTER 1

Introduction
The Life and Many Faces of Alexander Hamilton

DOUGLAS AMBROSE

*E*VERYONE knows the face. It gazes out from the ten-dollar bill, confident, strong, thoughtful. Most Americans know the face of Alexander Hamilton from that ten-dollar bill, and most would probably acknowledge that he rightly occupies a place among the pantheon of those we call "the founders." But of all those founders, Hamilton remains the most elusive. For as much as Americans may recognize the face on the bill, few really know the man. And many who think they know him find it hard to embrace him with the same enthusiasm that they do a Washington, a Jefferson, a Madison, an Adams. Hamilton remains both enigmatic and suspect; important, yes, but somewhat tarnished by his supposed lack of idealism, his crass realism regarding economics, finance, military power, and national authority.

Scholars and commentators have not neglected Alexander Hamilton. From before his death in 1804 to the present, historians, political scientists, economists, and others have explored the ways in which Hamilton contributed to the course of American history. And those accounts demonstrate that Hamilton has always functioned as a lightning rod. During his life he embroiled himself in nearly every major political development from the Revolution through the election of 1800. He did so as an active public servant, serving as military officer, delegate to the Constitutional Convention, and first Secretary of the Treasury, and, especially, through his writing. His prolificacy staggers the imagination: at his death at the age of 49 he had produced enough material to fill 27 volumes.[1] Hamilton produced much of that voluminous writing in the contentious debates over everything from the treatment of the Continental Army to the electoral

1

crisis of 1800 when Thomas Jefferson and Aaron Burr received the same number of electoral votes and the House of Representatives had to choose who would become president. Hamilton, as most of his biographers have noted, neither shied away from confrontation nor always acted as discreetly as he might have.[2] As a result, he made many enemies who accused him of being everything from a monarchist to an embezzler. John Adams's famous characterization of Hamilton as "a bastard Bratt of a Scotch Pedlar" aptly captures how acid could be the perception of Hamilton by his political and personal enemies. Yet others, notably but not exclusively his Federalist friends such as Fisher Ames and John Marshall, found Hamilton to be not only brilliant, but dedicated to the nation he helped found and a man of high moral character.[3]

But if Hamilton was a figure who aroused strong feelings among his contemporaries, he has been no less so for scholars. As Stephen Knott demonstrates in his essay in this volume and in his book *Alexander Hamilton and the Persistence of Myth,* those who have written about Hamilton, like his contemporaries, have provided us with portraits that range from damning to hagiographic.[4] This volume offers a variety of portraits and perspectives that reflect, in part, the persisting enigmatic character of Hamilton. But the essays below also demonstrate that whatever the disagreements about who Hamilton was and what his influence may have been, he remains a central figure in our continuing effort to understand both the founding era and its legacy on subsequent American history. He demands to be studied because his actions, his motives, and his achievements indelibly shaped his world and ours.

Hamilton's Life

Hamilton had, most certainly, one of the most unusual personal histories of the founders. His lineage, as Adams suggested in his biting quip, did not foretell greatness. He was born on January 11, 1755, on the British island colony of Nevis to Rachel Faucett Lavien and James Hamilton. Five years prior to Alexander's birth, Lavien, who came from a respectable family, had walked out of an unhappy marriage to Johann Michael Lavien, leaving behind both her husband and their young son, Peter. By 1752 she was living with James Hamilton. Through James Hamilton, the fourth son of a Scottish nobleman, Alexander could—and did—claim a distinguished bloodline. But by the time James Hamilton began cohabiting with Rachel

Faucett Lavien, he had little more than that bloodline left. He had come to the British West Indies in 1741 as a 23–year-old seeking his fortune. He never found it. What he did find was a meager if not impoverished life as a merchant, a life marked by "too large a portion of indolence," as his son Alexander put it.[5] James and Rachel had two children, James Jr. born in 1753 and Alexander born in 1755. When Alexander was 10 years old, his family migrated from Nevis to the nearby island of St. Croix. James Hamilton then abandoned his family; he would never return. Three years later, Rachel died. Her son Peter Lavien inherited all she had, leaving James Jr. and 13–year-old Alexander with nothing. A probate court placed them under the guardianship of their cousin Peter Lytton. An unstable individual, Lytton committed suicide less than a year after taking the boys in.[6]

Young Alexander Hamilton somehow managed to overcome the volatility of his childhood. Although he received little formal schooling, he became a voracious reader and fluent in French while his mother was still alive. His intellectual abilities attracted the attention of two merchants, David Beckman and Nicholas Cruger, who employed him as a clerk in their firm in Christiansted, the main city on St. Croix. Hamilton quickly assumed more and more responsibilities for the firm of Beckman & Cruger; as a 16–year-old he ran the operation for several months while Beckman and Cruger were traveling on business. But it was the appearance in St. Croix of Hugh Knox, a Scotch-Irish Presbyterian minister, that changed Hamilton's life forever. Knox recognized that Hamilton's talents extended well beyond mercantile affairs. He cultivated Hamilton's intellectual faculties as best he could, but soon realized that his library could not satisfy Hamilton's appetite. Hamilton's precocious abilities gained wider attention in 1772 when a local newspaper published his vivid description of a hurricane that ravished St. Croix. Knox soon began to collect funds to send 17–year-old Hamilton to the mainland colonies for a formal education.

Soon after arriving at Boston, Hamilton found his way to the Elizabethtown Academy in New Jersey. Here he prepared for admission to the College of New Jersey, today known as Princeton, by mastering Latin and Greek. The trustees of Princeton, however, denied Hamilton's request that he be admitted with permission to advance as quickly as he could. He turned to King's College, today's Columbia, and enrolled in 1774, just as the imperial crisis reached a boiling point. Hamilton combined his studies with political writing, producing his first significant pamphlet, *A Full Vindication of the Measures of Congress,* in late 1774. More political writings followed in 1775 and Hamilton joined the New York provincial militia that same year. When New York's Provincial Congress ordered the establishment of an artillery company in 1776, it appointed the 21–year-old Hamilton to be its commander with the rank of captain. Although military service cut short his academic career, leaving him without a degree, he embraced his new responsibilities and soon saw considerable action in the battles in New York and New Jersey in 1776 and early 1777, including George Washington's surprise attack on Trenton and the subsequent Battle of Princeton.

Just as Hugh Knox had recognized Hamilton's talents, so too did Washington. On March 1, 1777, Washington appointed Hamilton his aide-de-camp and promoted him to lieutenant colonel in the Continental Army. For the next four years, Hamilton would be at Washington's side; for the rest of his life, Hamilton would be a force in American public life. From 1777 to 1781 he functioned as Washington's primary secretary, drafting letters and reports. He served with him in the field at Brandywine Creek and Monmouth Court House. He wintered with him at Valley Forge and Morristown. He accompanied him to West Point just as Benedict Arnold's treasonous plot unfolded. Yet as vital as Hamilton's services were to Washington, Hamilton yearned to return to a field command. After Washington rejected several requests, Hamilton finally provoked a confrontation in 1781 that led to his resignation from Washington's staff. He soon thereafter received an appointment as commander of a New York infantry battalion, and in October 1781 led a successful assault on the British fortifications at Yorktown.

Military service did not monopolize Hamilton's life between 1777 and 1781. In 1780 he courted and married Elizabeth Schuyler, daughter of one of New York's most prestigious families. They would have eight children together; the first, Philip, was born in January 1782. Hamilton also remained active in political debates, primarily through essays and letters to newspapers. As early as 1780, Hamilton determined that the new national government under the Articles of Confederation required strengthening, and he even called for a national bank and a convention to revise the Articles. Upon leaving active service in late 1781 and returning to New York, Hamilton commenced both the study of law and an active political career, receiving an appointment in 1782 from the New York legislature to serve as delegate to Congress. In Congress he first met and worked with James Madison. Although he left Congress in 1783, his brief experience there further convinced him that the government under the Articles needed revision.

Hamilton then embarked on a legal career, moving to New York City and opening a law office. Through both his legal career and his pen, Hamilton remained deeply engaged in the politics of his state and country. In a series of pamphlets he criticized New York laws that punished Loyalists, and he defended Loyalists in court against suits based on those laws.[7] In 1784 he helped establish the Bank of New York and became one of its directors, and in 1785 he helped found the Society for Promoting the Manumission of Slaves. He returned to active political life in 1786 when he was elected to the New York assembly for the following year. Before his term began, the assembly in 1786 appointed him as a delegate to the Annapolis Convention, which met to discuss the problems of interstate commerce under the Articles of Confederation. Although only a few states sent delegates and the convention resolved no problems, it did adopt a resolution, drafted by Hamilton, that urged that another convention assemble in Philadelphia in 1787 and that it focus on broad constitutional changes. In 1787 the New York legislature appointed Hamilton to be one of three delegates to the Philadelphia Convention. His two fellow delegates, Robert Yates and Robert Lansing Jr., opposed creating a strong central government. Since the convention decided that each state would have one vote, Hamilton could not get his state to vote for proposals he favored. Although he delivered several speeches before the convention, including his infamous June 18 speech in which he praised the British government and proposed a government modeled after it, he left Philadelphia in late June and only occasionally attended sessions during the rest of the summer. He returned to the convention in early September and signed the final document later that month, even though he had deep reservations about its final form. Notwithstanding those reservations, he returned to New York and within a month had published his first *Federalist* essay.[8]

Hamilton conceived the *Federalist* essays as a tactical measure to sway New York opinion in favor of ratifying the new Constitution. He recruited fellow New Yorker John Jay and James Madison to the cause. Between October 1787 and March 1788, 77 essays, all published under the pseudonym "Publius," appeared in New York newspapers. The essays also appeared in bound form in two volumes. Volume 1 included the first 36 essays and appeared in March of 1788. The second volume, published in May 1788, included the remaining 31 articles and 8 essays that had not yet appeared in the newspapers. Hamilton probably wrote 51 of the 85 *Federalist Papers,* Madison 29, and Jay 5.[9] In the spring of 1788, soon after the first volume of *Federalist Papers* appeared, Hamilton gained election to the

New York ratifying convention, which met in Poughkeepsie in June. Hamilton and his fellow Federalist supporters of the Constitution found themselves outnumbered by its Antifederalist opponents, but once word arrived at the convention that Virginia had become the ninth state to ratify the Constitution, the tide turned in the Federalists' favor and the convention approved unconditional ratification. Although the *Federalist Papers* had not accomplished Hamilton's immediate goal of changing New York's position on the Constitution, the collection quickly became *the* authoritative text on America's federal government.[10]

Only fourteen months after New York's ratification of the Constitution, President George Washington nominated and the Senate confirmed Hamilton to be the first secretary of the newly created department of the Treasury. He faced an imposing task. National finances were in disarray, America's credit among lender nations was weak, the country lacked a stable currency, states quarreled over trade relations, and debt plagued both the state and central governments. Within three months of assuming his new position, Hamilton produced his "Report on Public Credit." His ambitious plan called for both the funding of the $54 million national debt and the assumption of $25 million of state debts by the federal government. Both aspects of the plan aroused controversy. Hamilton sought to have the holders of old Continental securities exchange the now-depreciated notes for new bonds at face value; critics, led by former ally James Madison, favored discriminating between the original holders of the securities, many of whom were Revolutionary War veterans, and those who later purchased them at a fraction of their face value. Madison's discrimination proposal failed in the House of Representatives, and Hamilton's funding plan went forward. His plan to have the federal government assume the debts of the states, however, failed in its initial vote in the House. Some states, including Madison's Virginia, argued that the assumption plan punished those states that had paid off much of their war debt by forcing them to pay for the debts of less responsible states. In the famous dinner compromise of 1790, Hamilton, Madison, and Secretary of State Thomas Jefferson hammered out a solution wherein Virginia and other Southern states accepted assumption in return for the establishment of the permanent national capital at a location on the Potomac River.[11]

At the end of 1790 Hamilton submitted another report to the House that called for the chartering of a national bank. Once again, Madison and others opposed the proposal, arguing that the Constitution did not authorize such a measure. Although both the House and Senate approved a bill establishing the Bank of the United States in early 1791, President George Washington solicited written opinions from several cabinet members, including Jefferson, who agreed with Madison, before deciding whether or not to sign the bill. Hamilton responded to these objections with a passionate defense of a broad interpretation of the Constitution and especially of the "necessary and proper" clause (Article One, Section VIII, Clause 18). Washington signed the Bank bill. Late in 1791 Hamilton submitted his third famous report to the House. The "Report on Manufactures," which detailed an ambitious plan to establish a strong manufacturing sector of the economy through government subsidies and protective tariffs, proved unsuccessful. Critics objected to Hamilton's proposals on both constitutional and pragmatic grounds, and Congress never acted on the report's recommendations. Hamilton himself, however, remained committed to industrial development. In 1791 he helped form the Society for the Encouragement of Useful Manufactures, which established a site in Paterson, New Jersey. Hamilton hoped that similar private ventures would stimulate the growth of domestic industry.[12]

Hamilton's bold vision and proposals during his first 18 months as Treasury Secretary helped stimulate the development of America's first political parties. By 1792, Jefferson and Madison mobilized those opposed to Hamilton's policies in Congress and launched a vigorous newspaper campaign that criticized Hamilton and his program. Hamilton and his supporters responded with articles in sympathetic newspapers. Soon, Jefferson, Madison, and their allies became known as Republicans, Hamilton and his supporters continued to label themselves Federalists, and the first American party system emerged.[13] The divisions within Washington's cabinet, and the country, grew deeper after revolutionary France declared war on Great Britain in 1793. Washington declared U.S. neutrality and determined that the 1778 alliance with France did not require the United States to support France. Republicans objected and argued that only Congress had the constitutional authority to interpret treaties and declare neutrality. Hamilton published several essays defending Washington's actions, and Madison responded with essays supporting the Republican position. Hamilton continued to attack the French Revolution and its American supporters in 1793 and 1794.

One of Hamilton's last major public acts before he resigned as Treasury Secretary in January 1795 concerned the 1794 Whiskey Rebellion. Prompted by a Hamilton-sponsored excise tax on whiskey, farmers in western Pennsylvania took up arms in protest. Hamilton urged, both in newspaper essays and in the cabinet, decisive military action, in part as a way of demonstrating the resolve of the federal government. Washington agreed, and he and Hamilton led a force of 10,000 militia against the insurgents.[14]

Although Hamilton left the cabinet in 1795 and never returned to public service, he continued to exert significant political influence until his death in 1804. He vigorously defended fellow Federalist John Jay and the 1795 treaty with Great Britain that bore his name, writing more than a score of newspaper articles and withstanding insults and even physical abuse at a public meeting in New York City. He continued to work closely with Washington, advising him and helping him write his famous farewell address in 1796. In 1797 Hamilton wrote a series of essays criticizing French seizures of American ships trading with Britain, and as the crisis with France deepened in 1798 with the infamous "XYZ Affair," he advocated a military buildup in case of war. President John Adams responded to the crisis by conducting an undeclared naval war with France and by asking George Washington to assume command of the newly enlarged U.S. Army. Washington insisted that Hamilton be appointed inspector general. Adams complied, and in July 1798 Hamilton received a commission as major general. He worked to strengthen domestic fortifications and to reorganize nearly every aspect of the army, from tactics to uniforms. Adams appointed Hamilton as second in command of the army, but when Washington died in December 1799, Adams refused to elevate Hamilton to commander in chief. As relations with France improved by mid-1800, Adams demobilized the enlarged army, and Hamilton ended his military service in June 1800.[15]

Hamilton's relations with Adams, which had never been good, worsened during the course of Adams's term. Hamilton resented not being appointed commander in chief and objected to Adams's diplomacy with France, believing him to be too accommodating to the French. Adams, in turn, rightly suspected that Hamilton used his influence with several members of Adams's own cabinet to thwart Adams's leadership. By 1800, Hamilton was actively working against Adams and lobbying for Charles Cotesworth Pinckney to be the Federalist candidate for president in the election of 1800. In October 1800, just weeks before the election, Republican newspapers published a pamphlet Hamilton had written that viciously attacked Adams. Hamilton had intended to circulate the pamphlet privately among Federalists, but its widespread publication revealed the deep divisions among Federalists and irreparably damaged Hamilton's standing among many in his party. The election of 1800 resulted in Republicans Thomas Jefferson and Aaron Burr both receiving the same number of electoral votes as there was then no way of indicating Burr as the vice-presidential choice. The House of Representatives thus had to decide the election, and Hamilton wrote to a number of Federalists and urged them to support Jefferson over Burr. In February 1801, after a tense week of debate, the House elected Jefferson president.[16]

With the Republicans in power, Hamilton concentrated on his legal practice and family concerns, but he managed to find plenty of time to remain politically active. He continued working for the New York Society for Promoting the Manumission of Slaves, which he had helped establish back in 1785. Hamilton's contributions to the Manumission Society reflected his lifelong abhorrence of slavery and his efforts to eradicate it from New York. In 1799, the New York legislature passed a gradual emancipation law that put slavery in the state on the road to a slow but sure extinction.[17] He helped found a newspaper, the *New York Evening Post,* and used its pages to keep up a running attack on Jefferson and his administration. Hamilton also experienced profound personal tragedy when his oldest son, Philip, died in late 1801 from wounds received in a duel with a Republican lawyer named George Eacker. Philip's death devastated Hamilton and, combined with the Republican triumph at all levels of the federal government, led him to the edge of despair. In a famous 1802 letter to old friend Gouverneur Morris, Hamilton lamented, "Mine is an odd destiny. Perhaps no man in the UStates has sacrificed or done more for the present Constitution than myself—and contrary to all my anticipations of its fate . . . I am still labouring to prop the frail and worthless fabric. Yet I have the murmurs of its friends no less than the curses of its foes for my reward. What can I do better than withdraw from the Scene? Every day proves to me more and more that this American world was not made for me."[18]

But Hamilton did not "withdraw from the scene," and he did not abandon the American world even if he believed it was abandoning him. He worked on drafting what would, in somewhat modified form, become the Twelfth Amendment to the Constitution, which required separate balloting by presidential electors for president and vice-president. Although Hamilton continued to attack the Jefferson administration, he was one of the few Federalists who supported Jefferson's Louisiana Purchase. And some of Hamilton's legal work had profound implications. One of his last major cases, which he argued before the New York supreme court in February 1804, five months before his death, was that of Harry Croswell.

Croswell edited a Federalist newspaper and was charged with seditious libel for publishing articles accusing Thomas Jefferson of having paid James T. Callender to print harsh attacks on George Washington, John Adams, and others. Hamilton argued against the common-law tradition that held the truth of a libelous claim was no defense; all the New York attorney general, Jeffersonian Ambrose Spencer, had to prove was that Croswell had published the defamatory articles. Croswell was convicted, and Hamilton appeared before the state supreme court to argue for a new trial and for the admission of truth as a defense in libel cases. Although he lost the case before a Republican-dominated court, most of the New York legislature attended the session in which Hamilton made his argument. The legislature promptly began debate on revising the state's libel law and passed a statute incorporating Hamilton's position in April 1805. Hamilton, of course, did not live to see it.[19]

Hamilton's continued involvement in state and local politics led to his death. Long suspicious of Aaron Burr, Hamilton grew alarmed when Burr decided to run for governor of New York. Many disgruntled northeastern Federalists, convinced that Jeffersonian domination would only get worse over time, contemplated secession and the creation of a separate republic. Most who entertained such a notion believed that New York's inclusion in the new republic was vital, and they believed that Burr as governor would aid their efforts. Hamilton was appalled. He worked vigorously to convince Federalists to support the other Republican candidate for governor, Morgan Lewis (there was no Federalist candidate). Lewis won the April 1804 election. In June, Burr initiated contact with Hamilton and demanded that he explain certain remarks that a letter printed in an Albany newspaper attributed to Hamilton. According to one source, Hamilton labeled Burr "a dangerous man, and one who ought not to be trusted with the reins of government." Even more offensive to Burr was the source's claim that Hamilton had expressed "a still more despicable opinion" of Burr.[20] As was usual with such "affairs of honor," negotiations between the two parties lasted for over a week, and Burr, unsatisfied by Hamilton's actions, challenged him to a duel. Hamilton accepted, and two weeks later, on the morning of July 11, 1804, Hamilton and Burr faced each other on a field in Weehawken, New Jersey, not far from where Philip Hamilton received his mortal wound three years earlier. Burr's shot struck Hamilton, passed through his liver, and lodged in his spine. Hamilton's aides brought him back to Manhattan, where he survived until midafternoon on July 12, giving him time to say goodbye to his wife Eliza and their children. A well-attended public funeral followed on July 14, and Hamilton was buried in the graveyard of Trinity Church in lower Manhattan.[21]

Even this brief review of Hamilton's life demonstrates his centrality to the history of the founding era. No serious student of that era, including the authors of the essays in this volume, denies that Hamilton played a vital role in some of the most important questions of national politics, public policy, and economic development. But scholars have debated fiercely the meaning and consequences of Hamilton's life. His legacies remain contested: Was he a closet monarchist or a sincere republican? A victim of partisan politics or one of its most active promoters? A lackey for British interests or a foreign policy mastermind? An economic genius or a shill for special interests? The father of a vigorous national government or the destroyer of genuine federalism? A defender of governmental authority or a dangerous militarist? The essays below testify to the continuing debates over both the effects of Hamilton's efforts during his life and the diverse and competing legacies of those efforts and effects in the two centuries since his death. Although the essays will not end those debates, they remind us that in attempting to understand Hamilton and his legacies, we grapple with the vexing and important questions about the nature and meaning of republicanism, federalism, and freedom that Americans have faced not only during the founding era but through all of American history.

This book's contents reflect the conflict and debate among historians and political scientists regarding Hamilton and his legacies. The essays also reveal common threads that suggest that, notwithstanding important differences, some consensus about Hamilton exists among modern scholars. All of the essays, to varying degrees, demonstrate Hamilton's recognition that his life would have a lasting legacy, that his actions would shape and influence posterity. The notion of fame that Douglass Adair long ago identified as one of the distinguishing characteristics of the founders, informed nearly all of Hamilton's public actions. Hamilton fit Adair's definition of an individual who desired fame, a person who sought "never to be forgotten by those later generations that will be born into a world his actions helped to shape."[22] But Hamilton's legacies have not necessarily been those that he intended, nor do scholars agree on what, exactly, those legacies have been. To what extent do we live in "Hamilton's republic"?[23] Was Hamilton, as a recent major exhibition at the New-York Historical Society claimed, "The Man Who Made Modern America"?[24] How, if at all, did Hamilton, as Stephen Knott argues in his essay, "make us what we are"? The essays in this volume, both individually and collectively, powerfully demonstrate that Hamilton remains a compelling subject, one that prompts scholars to engage in innovative and important work about the man, the era, and the legacies we still struggle to understand.

Stephen Knott's opening essay provides a sweeping examination of Hamilton's image from his own era through the middle of the twentieth century. Americans, Knott argues, have almost always evaluated Hamilton alongside Thomas Jefferson, and for much of American history Hamilton has suffered from the comparison. Knott questions whether the relative positions of Jefferson and Hamilton in American memory should persist, of whether the credit "given the poet should exceed that given the architect and engineer of the founding." The "predominant impression of Hamilton in the American mind," Knott suggests, remains that of Jeffersonian newspaper editor Philip Freneau, who in the 1790s portrayed Hamilton as "monocrat, Anglophile, and enemy of liberty." Hamilton's reputation reached its nadir, according to Knott, in the 1930s as Progressive historians, especially Claude G. Bowers, extended Freneau's negative portrayal. "By the end of the New Deal," Knott writes, "the Hamiltonian image in the American mind was something akin to a hybrid mix of Ebenezer Scrooge and Benito Mussolini." Even though recent scholarship has improved Hamilton's image by contrasting his role as founder of the New York Society for the Manumission of Slaves with his rival Jefferson's attitudes and actions concerning slavery, and even though some American liberals in the 1950s and 1960s gravitated toward Hamilton's "support for national power" as they increasingly viewed "Jefferson's states' rights doctrine as camouflage for Jim Crow," Knott argues that Americans still resist embracing Hamilton. Part of that resistance, Knott explains, results from the misleading but persistent image we have inherited from Jefferson and his descendants.

As Knott demonstrates, scholars have long contrasted Hamilton with his fellow founders, and with good reason. The essays by Robert M. S. McDonald and James Read show that Hamilton's life and legacy have been bound up with his collaborators and enemies, especially Thomas Jefferson and James Madison. McDonald argues that Hamilton's biting attacks on Jefferson, attacks motivated by Hamilton's conviction that Jefferson sought personal glory over the public good, actually helped make Jefferson a prominent national political figure. As McDonald argues, "At the same time that Hamilton worked to destroy Jefferson's reputation, he promoted Jefferson's image as the opposition's chief leader and unintentionally stimulated the development of a Republican press that would rush to Jefferson's defense." McDonald's point here, that Hamilton "unintentionally" helped "thrust [Jefferson] to the forefront of Americans' political consciousness," helps us see how some of Hamilton's legacies have been more than a bit ironic. In trying to destroy Jefferson, Hamilton actually strengthened Jeffersonianism. As Madison and other Jeffersonians came to Jefferson's defense, they forged the reputation most Americans, as Knott argues, still have of him: the people's defender against the aristocratic Hamiltonian Federalists.

James Read also looks at the Hamilton-Jefferson relation. Read detects a strange asymmetry in the often heated conflict between them. Jefferson, he maintains, presented Hamilton not as an individual but as a representative of monarchism, corruption, and subversion of republican government. Hamilton, on the other hand, though he opposed Jefferson's policies, did not accuse Jefferson of subversion or disloyalty. Instead, Hamilton directed his fiercest attacks against what he saw as Jefferson's "devious and mischievous character" and Jefferson's attempts to harm him personally. When there were great public issues at stake, Read argues, Hamilton's view of Jefferson was moderate and balanced; his view of Jefferson was most vitriolic when responding to a perceived personal attack. Read thus concludes that one of the central conflicts of the 1790s—that between the Federalist Hamilton and the Republican Jefferson—was, at least from Hamilton's perspective, driven more by offended reputation than by ideology. Although Read argues, in seeming contrast to McDonald, that Hamilton "made no serious effort to build a party or an ideology on the basis of a demonized archetypal image of Jefferson," Read's analysis of the Jefferson-Hamilton feud ultimately complements McDonald's essay. As Read states, although Hamilton may not have tried to build the Federalist Party on his personal critique of Jefferson, that critique, as McDonald points out, encouraged Republican mobilization and counterattack that focused not only on Hamilton, but on the policies and principles Republicans associated with him. Federalists then responded in kind, escalating the conflict into a full-blown struggle between rival parties. Like McDonald, Read acknowledges the unforeseen consequences, the unintended legacies, of Hamilton's conflict with Jefferson.

The next three essays all grapple with Hamilton's relation to the complex and contentious notion of "republicanism" in early American political thinking. Robert W. T. Martin's essay explores Hamilton's "reconceptualization of republicanism" in the 1780s and 1790s. This new theory of republicanism, Martin argues, led Hamilton to develop a "nuanced conception of citizenship" that contrasted sharply with other contemporary notions of the role of citizens in a republic, which tended to be considerably more egalitarian and participatory. Early national politics thus witnessed a battle between two "competing visions of the proper virtue of republican citizens." Hamilton's republicanism emphasized that "the people's virtue lay not in vigilance, but confidence." Citizens of Hamilton's republic exercised their political responsibilities by electing the "better sort." Citizens were then to express "confidence" in those they had elected. In Hamilton's view, "ambitious men could be trusted with power because their historical reputations would so clearly depend on truly serving the public good." The problems of a republic, Hamilton believed, derived less from the ambitions of the elite than from the people's malleability, their susceptibility to demagoguery. Martin's close examination of Hamilton's views on representation and press liberty reveals that Hamilton believed that "the solution to classic problems of republicanism was not a closer connection to the *demos,* but a greater reliance on the ambitions of the elite." Martin concludes that Hamilton's "elitist republicanism" attempted to reformulate "received wisdom" and adapt it "to novel circumstances" so that "wise guides" could lead the new American republic while enjoying the "public confidence" of those who elected them and recognized their authority.

The scholarly debate over "republicanism" has devoted much attention, as Martin's essay demonstrates, to the meaning and role of "virtue" in the early republic. Barry Alan Shain's essay investigates the diverse uses of virtue in *The Federalist Papers.* Shain favors viewing "Publius" as a single rather than as a multiple author.[25] Whatever differences Hamilton and Madison had after *The Federalist*—and the essays by McDonald, Read, Martin, and Sheehan testify to the magnitude of those differences—Shain believes that in *The Federalist* Madison, Hamilton, and Jay spoke with one voice. And that voice, Shain argues, expresses a "consistent and powerful liberal theory of government," one that sought to channel "men's selfish natures rather than [encourage] self-limiting virtue." Publius addressed two audiences, a modern Federalist one that denied that virtue could be the basis of a republic, and a traditional Antifederalist audience that believed that political virtue was necessary to republican government. Although Shain acknowledges that Publius occasionally appealed to virtue, Publius did so only in a rhetorical fashion, to satisfy his traditional audience. Far more frequently, Shain asserts, Publius insisted that "good government was possible without a politically virtuous people or a truly virtuous government." Much like Martin's notion of Hamilton's "elitist republicanism," Shain argues that Publius devised a "new foundation" for republicanism: "the desire for fame and honor of each individual office holder." In placing confidence not in virtue but in the "selfish quest for fame in those who would govern," Publius, Shain maintains, "aligned himself with progressive liberal thought" by abandoning "traditional republican remedies," such as "a virtuous and selfless leadership or on frequent electoral recurrence to the people." Shain concludes that, as many Antifederalists argued, the "government defended by Publius was one that had taken Montesquieu's essence of monarchical government, a striving for honor and recognition, and had transformed it into a foundation for a new kind of popular system with republican form and monarchical essence." In an important and underappreciated way, Shain asserts, Publius attempted to recover the essence of monarchy by dressing it in the new clothes of republican rhetoric and forms.

Although Shain believes that Hamilton and Madison spoke with one voice as Publius, Colleen Sheehan emphasizes the fundamental differences between them in the post–*Federalist Papers* years. Examining Hamilton and Madison's acrimonious battle in the early 1790s, she posits that the conflict arose from their profoundly differing beliefs regarding "the nature and role of public opinion in a republic." Hamilton and Madison both "sought to cultivate and form public opinion," but their "competing visions about the mode of its formation, the character of its composition, and the extent of its influence on government" reflected opposing "philosophic conceptions of republicanism." Sheehan agrees with Shain that Hamilton believed that a successful republic had to channel "men's selfish passions and interests" rather than rely on people's virtuous dedication to the public good. Much like Martin, she contends that Hamilton advocated a rather "submissive role for the citizenry," essentially consisting of electing the "better sort to political office and supporting the government they had chosen." The "wise republican statesman" would cultivate "opinions of confidence by promoting measures that gratify the average citizen's passion for material gain." Hamilton's conception of public opinion as "the confidence and esteem" of the people in their leaders contrasts sharply, Sheehan argues, with Madison's understanding of public opinion as the active and ongoing sovereign authority in republican government. Rejecting Shain's view that Madison as Publius shared Hamilton's "vision of a modern commercial republic composed of diverse rival economic interests actuated by the untutored passion of acquisitiveness," she asserts that Madison "was a more unhesitating democrat than is generally believed." Unlike Hamilton, Madison believed that the duties of the citizens were not limited to participation in elections, but were "substantial and ongoing." His conception of the role of the statesman and educated elite in a republic, Sheehan argues, was not to "inspire respect and confidence" in their own abilities, but rather to exercise "a kind of civic leadership that aspired to cultivate civic understanding, refine mores and manners, and educate the people for their indispensable role in a self-governing republic." Sheehan concludes that Hamilton vigorously resisted the Madisonian and Republican democratization of the politics of public opinion in the 1790s and throughout the remainder of his life, which has contributed in no small way to the legacy of his aristocratic tendencies and sympathies.

One of the ironies that Sheehan notes is that although Hamilton resisted the "new politics of public opinion," he undoubtedly was "the chief American theorist of the modern commercial republic." And if there is one legacy of Hamilton that approaches consensus it is that of the economic genius whose farsighted policies paved the way for American economic development. Carey Roberts in his essay argues that this one rather clear and undisputed image we have of Hamilton misunderstands Hamilton's influence on the 1790s' economy. Roberts maintains that "Hamilton was neither a defender of an aristocracy of wealth nor was he the architect of America's economic 'take-off.'" Hamilton's inflationary policies, Roberts shows, contributed to an "artificial boom" that suggested that the economy was stronger than it actually was and prompted investors to envision a long era of economic growth. When busts came in 1792 and 1796, those disappointed investors—the very aristocracy of wealth that most people assume Hamilton carried around in his back pocket—concluded that Hamilton and his policies either caused the busts or failed to protect their investments. Not until the late 1790s, well after Hamilton left office, did the economy significantly improve, and its improvement may well have been due to policies antithetical to Hamilton's. Roberts thus concludes that Hamilton's policies not only promoted an unstable economy during most of the 1790s but also seriously damaged the Federalist Party's political fortunes. Again noting the contrast between the legacy of Hamilton and his actual experiences, Roberts notes that Hamilton's policies proved unable to win over the "monied interests" to the Federalist cause.

If Roberts helps question the legacy of Hamilton as the brilliantly successful Secretary of the Treasury, Daniel Lang seeks to draw attention to one of Hamilton's less familiar legacies: that of an early proponent of what international relations theorists label as "realism" in foreign affairs. Lang analyzes closely Hamilton's attitudes and policies regarding the "strategic and human rights issues" that the dramatic slave revolution in Saint-Domingue posed to America in the 1790s. In doing so, he demonstrates much about Hamilton's geopolitical imagination and the principles that informed that imagination. Lang notes that although "Hamilton's opposition to slavery was clear and long-standing," the United States' "alliance commitments" and "financial debt to France" limited Hamilton and the United States' ability to "affect events" as France's richest colony revolted and fought a 13–year struggle that eventually resulted in the creation of the independent nation of Haiti. Nonetheless, as Lang points out, Hamilton's actions and thoughts reveal both his suspicions of revolutionary France and his indirect efforts to aid the creation of an independent Haiti. Lang also concludes that Hamilton's behavior toward the Saint-Domingue revolution, including his recommendation that Haiti adopt a lifelong executive and a military government, "makes clear that enthusiasm for republican government . . . must be tempered by knowledge that it may not be appropriate in all circumstances." Hamilton's "realist" approach to the Saint-Domingue revolution, Lang notes, ought to be one of the Hamiltonian legacies with which modern diplomats and politicians grapple as they ponder America's role in international affairs.

While Lang suggests that foreign policy specialists could benefit from an engagement with Hamilton's foreign policy legacy, Peter McNamara's essay directly confronts the ways twentieth- and twenty-first-century policy makers have attempted to use other aspects of Hamilton's legacy. He critically examines Herbert Croly's influential book *The Promise of American Life* (1909) and contrasts Croly's Hamilton with Hamilton himself. Croly believed that Hamilton's great insight was the notion of a "national principle." Hamilton perceived how an energetic national government could, through legislation and policy, address vital national interests. But Croly, according to McNamara, criticized Hamilton for fearing democracy and for focusing on "institutional" devices to secure republicanism rather than concentrating on, as McNamara puts it, "the deeper political task of shaping the characters of citizens." McNamara argues that Croly's public philosophy proposed "to revive the idea of cultivating civic virtue as the central goal of political life." Croly thus envisioned a public philosophy that could utilize "Hamiltonian means to Jeffersonian ends." A democratized but energetic national government, Croly believed, could advance the cause of progressive politics. McNamara demonstrates, however, that "Croly too hastily assumed that Hamiltonian methods or means might be decoupled from Hamiltonian ends or goals." Along the same lines as Shain and Sheehan, McNamara argues that Hamilton rejected the idea that virtue could provide a sufficient basis for modern republicanism. Instead, like Martin, McNamara points out that Hamilton chiefly sought to cultivate the people's confidence, not their virtue. And since Hamilton stated that the "people's confidence in and obedience to government" were directly proportional to the "goodness or badness of its administration," the key to a successful national government was not how democratic it was but how effectively it identified the common good and acted in pursuit of it. Croly, and other twentieth-century progressives, McNamara contends, failed to recognize that "Hamilton's 'national principle' encompassed within it both ends and means, and thus Hamiltonian means are not simply extendable or transferable to non-Hamiltonian ends." McNamara concludes by suggesting that the dramatic twentieth-century expansion of government programs—an example of utilizing "Hamiltonian means"—has led the "public to question the effectiveness of government" and to lose confidence in it, the antithesis of "Hamiltonian ends." Attempts like Croly's to use Hamilton's legacy require policy makers to consider "precisely the very idea of Hamiltonian 'means' as well as the original ends to which they were directed." Only then can we determine how "Hamiltonianism" might still function as an American public philosophy.

In the book's epilogue, John Patrick Diggins contemplates the legacy of Hamilton for one profoundly influential American: Abraham Lincoln. Diggins challenges the long-held tendency to identify Abraham Lincoln with Thomas Jefferson and Jeffersonian doctrines. Instead, Diggins argues, "Lincoln's political mind and the values he stood for . . . place him closer to Alexander Hamilton and the values he expressed and the vision he had for America." Both Hamilton and Lincoln emerged from poor backgrounds, "were nationalists at periods in American history when most loyalties were local and regional," and abhorred slavery. Their mutual abhorrence of slavery derived from both their shared vision of "an economic system open to all" and their understanding that man was "an economic creature and a social animal, determined by interest and desiring distinction." Hamilton and Lincoln "both looked to ambition as the driving force that makes a difference in life," and they sought to help shape a society and government that rewarded healthy ambition even as it checked overweening ambition that threatened stability and opportunity. Lincoln, Diggins contends, "shared Hamilton's dream of a republic of workers and entrepreneurs, a culture that rewarded ambition and extended to people of all colors the right to rise." In their commitment to a society that allowed all to rise as both of them had, Hamilton and Lincoln looked forward to and encouraged the development of modern, capitalist America. And in "upholding the authority of the nation-state against the doctrine of state sovereignty and secession," Lincoln, Diggins concludes, boldly took "his stand with Hamilton against Jefferson and the Jeffersonian tradition." Lincoln, Diggins suggests, helped extend and expand Hamilton's legacy and, by doing so, made America more firmly "Hamilton's republic."

The essays in this volume do not resolve all the debates that surround Hamilton and his legacies. Nor do they clear away all the shadows that obscure the face of our most elusive founder. Scholars will continue to contest the nature of Hamilton's republicanism, the extent of his elitism, his commitment to equality, and his legacies to the new nation. But these excellent essays do help us both see the man more clearly and appreciate his centrality to any understanding of the nature of the Founding Era. Hamilton's life and legacies, as much as those of any other founder, make us ponder what America was, is, and should be. And that is the legacy of which he would be proudest. This volume powerfully demonstrates that we can benefit from his legacy only by trying to see him clearly and by engaging critically his still compelling thoughts about the nature and meaning of the republic to which he devoted his life.

NOTES

1. Harold C. Syrett et al., ed. *The Papers of Alexander Hamilton,* 27 vols. (New York: Columbia University Press, 1961–87), hereinafter *PAH.* The *PAH* do not include Hamilton's legal papers. They are located in Julius Goebel, Jr., and Joseph H. Smith, eds., *The Law Practice of Alexander Hamilton,* 5 vols. (New York: Columbia University Press for William Nelson Cromwell Foundation, 1964–81).

2. The biographical literature on Hamilton is enormous. For thoroughness, see Broadus Mitchell's two-volume study, *Alexander Hamilton: Youth to Maturity, 1755–1788* (New York: Macmillan, 1957), and *Alexander Hamilton: The National Adventure, 1788–1804* (New York: Macmillan, 1962), and Ron Chernow, *Alexander*

Hamilton (New York: Penguin Press, 2004). Other important biographies include John C. Miller, *Alexander Hamilton: Portrait in Paradox* (New York: Harper and Brothers, 1959), Forrest McDonald, *Alexander Hamilton: A Biography* (New York: W. W. Norton, 1979), and Richard Brookhiser, *Alexander Hamilton: American* (New York: Free Press, 1999).

3. For Adams's comment, see Adams to Thomas Jefferson, 12 July 1813 in Lester J. Cappon, ed., *The Adams-Jefferson Letters* (Chapel Hill: University of North Carolina Press, 1959), 354. For Ames, see his eulogy of Hamilton, "A Sketch of the Character of Alexander Hamilton," in Seth Ames, ed., *Works of Fisher Ames*, 2 vols. (Boston, 1854; reprint, edited and enlarged by W. B. Allen, Indianapolis: Liberty Fund, 1984), I, 510–519.

4. Stephen F. Knott, *Alexander Hamilton and the Persistence of Myth* (Lawrence: University Press of Kansas, 2002).

5. *PAH*, 25:89, letter to William Jackson, 26 August 1800. This fascinating letter constitutes Hamilton's most extensive commentary on his family background.

6. The most recent and judicious discussion of Hamilton's youth is Chernow, *Hamilton*, 7–40.

7. Hamilton focused especially on arguing against the Trespass Act, which permitted individuals who had fled New York City when the British captured it to sue Loyalists who had occupied their property during the period of British control.

8. For more on Hamilton's role in the Annapolis and Philadelphia conventions, see Mitchell, *Hamilton: Youth to Maturity*, 356–413; and Chernow, *Hamilton*, 222–242.

9. The authorship of a number of the *Federalist Papers* remains in dispute. For the latest effort to determine who wrote which numbers, see Robert Scigliano's introduction to The Modern Library's edition of *The Federalist* (New York: Random House, 2000).

10. On Hamilton's role in the creation of the *Federalist Papers,* see Mitchell, *Hamilton: Youth to Maturity*, 414–425; and Chernow, *Hamilton*, 243–269. See also the essay by Barry Shain in this volume.

11. The best discussion of Hamilton's career as Secretary of the Treasury is McDonald, *Hamilton*. On the dinner compromise, see Jacob E. Cooke, "The Compromise of 1790," *William and Mary Quarterly* 28 (1971), 629–648, and Joseph J. Ellis, *Founding Brothers: The Revolutionary Generation* (New York: Alfred A. Knopf, 2000), 48–80.

12. On Hamilton and the Society for the Establishment of Useful Manufactures, see Chernow, *Hamilton*, 370–388. Although the society failed during Hamilton's life, Paterson did become a center of early American manufacturing by the 1840s.

13. There exists a voluminous secondary literature on the first American party system. See Stanley Elkins and Eric McKitrick, *The Age of Federalism: The Early American Republic, 1788–1800* (New York: Oxford University Press, 1994), 257–488,

for a thorough overview. See also the essays by James Read, Robert McDonald, Colleen Sheehan, and Robert W. T. Martin in this volume.

14. On the Whiskey Rebellion, see Thomas Slaughter, *The Whiskey Rebellion: Frontier Epilogue to the American Revolution* (New York: Oxford University Press, 1988). On Hamilton's role, see Chernow, *Hamilton*, 468–481.

15. On the political and military developments of the later 1790s and Hamilton's relation to them, see Chernow, *Hamilton*, 546–602; and Mitchell, *Hamilton: The National Adventure*, 423–487.

16. On the Hamilton/Adams feud, see Chernow, *Hamilton*, 592–629; and David McCullough, *John Adams* (New York: Simon and Schuster, 2001), 549–552. Hamilton's efforts to influence the House vote for president proved futile. Federalists continued to support Burr over Jefferson. See Elkins and McKitrick, *Age of Federalism*, 746–750.

17. On Hamilton and slavery, see James Oliver Horton, "Alexander Hamilton: Slavery and Race in a Revolutionary Generation," *New-York Journal of American History* 65 (Spring 2004), 16–24; and Chernow, *Hamilton*, 210–216.

18. Hamilton to Gouverneur Morris, 29 February 1802, *PAH* 25: 544. For more on Philip Hamilton's death, see Chernow, *Hamilton*, 650–655. Hamilton's daughter Angelica suffered a mental breakdown following her brother's death and never recovered.

19. On Hamilton and the Croswell case, see Goebel, ed., *Law Practice of Hamilton*, 1:775ff; Chernow, *Hamilton*, 667–671; and Robert W. T. Martin's essay in this volume. Many praised Hamilton's argument before the Supreme Court as one of his greatest feats of oratory and legal reasoning. For more on early American libel law, see Robert W. T. Martin, *The Free and Open Press: The Founding of American Democratic Press Liberty, 1640–1800* (New York: New York University Press, 2001).

20. The remarks attributed to Hamilton derived from a letter from Charles D. Cooper that appeared in the April 24, 1804, edition of the *Albany Register*. Burr included Cooper's letter in a June 18, 1804, letter to Hamilton that initiated the correspondence that led to the duel. For that letter see Joanne Freeman, ed., *Alexander Hamilton: Writings* (New York: Library of America, 2001), 1008–1010.

21. The Burr-Hamilton duel has produced a vast literature. See Joanne Freeman, *Affairs of Honor: National Politics in the New Republic* (New Haven: Yale University Press, 2001), 159–198; Freeman, "Dueling as Politics: Reinterpreting the Burr-Hamilton Duel," *William and Mary Quarterly* 53 (April 1996), 289–318; and W. J. Rorabaugh, "The Political Duel in the Early Republic: Burr v. Hamilton," *Journal of the Early Republic* 15 (1995), 1–23. For more on the relations between Burr and Hamilton, see Thomas Fleming, *Duel: Alexander Hamilton, Aaron Burr, and the Future of America* (New York: Basic Books, 2000), and Arnold A. Rogow, *A Fatal Friendship: Alexander Hamilton and Aaron Burr* (New York: Hill and Wang, 1999).

22. Douglass Adair, "Fame and the Founding Fathers," in Trevor Colbourn, ed.,

Fame and the Founding Fathers: Essays by Douglass Adair (New York: W. W. Norton, 1974), 3–36, quotation from 14.

23. Michael Lind, *Hamilton's Republic: Readings in the American Democratic Nationalist Tradition* (New York: Free Press, 1997).

24. The exhibit, and its title, elicited criticism, as does anything regarding Hamilton. See Edward Rothstein, "Our Father the Modernist," *New York Times,* September 10, 2004; and Mike Wallace, "That Hamilton Man," *New York Review of Books* 52 (February 10, 2005).

25. On the question of whether one should treat Publius as a single author, see George W. Carey, "Publius—A Split Personality?" *Review of Politics* 46 (January 1984), 5–22; and Alpheus Thomas Mason, "The Federalist: A Split Personality," *American Historical Review* 57 (April 1952), 625–643.

PART I

The Contest with Jefferson

CHAPTER 2

"Opposed in Death as in Life"
Hamilton and Jefferson in American Memory

STEPHEN KNOTT

*T*HE division between Thomas Jefferson and Alexander Hamilton has, in many ways, permeated the consciousness and self-understanding of Americans. As recently as 1987, President Ronald Reagan, speaking at a bicentennial celebration, could capture and express perfectly the prevailing national sentiment with the simple affirmation that "we're still Jefferson's children." But Reagan might well have added these comments from his friend George Will: "There is an elegant memorial in Washington to Jefferson, but none to Hamilton. However, if you seek Hamilton's monument, look around. You are living in it. We honor Jefferson, but live in Hamilton's country."[1] While George Washington, Thomas Jefferson, and Abraham Lincoln have eclipsed him in the American mind, it was Alexander Hamilton who made the twentieth century "the American century." Clearly, the more immediate sources of American power in that century were traceable to the actions of Lincoln, in preserving the nation, and to the two Roosevelts, Woodrow Wilson, and many of the Cold War presidents. But the foundation of America's superpower status was laid in the early days of the republic when Alexander Hamilton, who had a vision of American greatness, battled with forces fearful of the concentrated political, economic, and military power necessary to achieve that greatness.

All of Hamilton's endeavors were directed toward establishing the United States as a formidable nation, efforts which ultimately came to fruition. The Hamiltonian blueprint for America, which lay in considerable tension with Jefferson's hopes for the new nation, consisted in the following: the creation of an integrated economy eventually capable of surpassing that of the European powers in manufacturing; a federal judiciary with adequate powers to protect property and liberties from democratic excess; the establishment of a professional army and navy; and an energetic chief executive with commander in chief powers that would enable him to repel foreign attacks and suppress domestic insurrections.

While much of Hamilton's vision came to pass, he has never won the affection of many of his countrymen, in part because of his tendency to insult our democratic sensibilities with alleged impolitic comments about the character of the people. Ironically, despite years of scathing criticism directed against his hated rival, President Jefferson was in many ways a distinctly Hamiltonian executive—but his charge that Hamilton was un-American echoes to this day.[2] Hamilton's reputation has no doubt also been hurt by the fact that he was less of a Renaissance man than Jefferson. To borrow from the latter's biographer Gilbert Chinard, Hamilton had no interest in playing the violin, dancing the minuet, or designing farm implements. Our neglect of Hamilton can also be attributed to the fact that he made us what we are, while Jefferson's malleable legacy appeals to visionaries seeking a new and better world. Jefferson's dream of an America constantly remaking itself and shedding the shackles of the past captures the American imagination, for dreams are frequently more appealing than reality, and it is easier to celebrate what might be than to defend what is. Jefferson was the poet of the American founding, while Hamilton was the nation builder who infused the essential elements of permanence and stability in the American system. It is not unusual for poets to portray themselves as somehow above the fray, disdaining or at best taking for granted the "petty" practical matters that make civil society possible, such as a sturdy framework of laws backed by viable government institutions. But Hamilton's public life was dedicated to erecting such a structure, and the question remains whether the credit given the poet should exceed that given the architect and engineer of the founding.

The battle over interpreting Hamilton's role in the founding of the nation began within days after he was buried. President Thomas Jefferson and his supporters reacted with silence in public and, in some cases, private concern that the emotional reaction to Hamilton's death might impair their party's political prospects in the 1804 elections. Upon hearing the news of the duel, the Sage of Monticello was his usual Sphinxlike self, offering little comment other than noting in a letter to his daughter, "I presume Mr. Randolph's newspapers will inform him of the death of Colo. Hamilton, which took place on the 12th." The next day he sent his friend

Philip Mazzei a letter mentioning various "remarkable deaths lately," including Samuel Adams, who had died months earlier, Jefferson's own daughter, Maria; and Alexander Hamilton. There may have been some repressed feelings of relief that this "Colossus" had finally been done in, and, of all things, by the vice-president of the United States.[3] A nineteenth-century Oliver Stone would have reveled in this scenario, vulnerable as it was to a conspiratorial interpretation, for in one act, two of Jefferson's political rivals were no longer threats to his power.

At the time of Hamilton's death the confrontation between the two men had receded as Hamilton and his party were overwhelmed by a popular and successful Jefferson presidency. Hamilton's premature demise and Jefferson's longevity (1743–1826) provided the latter with twenty-two years in which to portray their confrontation in a most favorable light without fear of rebuttal. Jefferson attributed to Hamilton an affinity for Caesar that was probably untrue, and sought to undermine Hamilton's "Americanism" by labeling him as something akin to a British agent. Their confrontation began during the period when Jefferson was Secretary of State (March 1790–December 1793) and Hamilton was Secretary of the Treasury. Questions over commerce and banking, constitutional interpretation, federalism, and American policy toward Great Britain and France drove the two men apart.

Jefferson often dealt with unpleasant situations like his relationship with Hamilton in an indirect manner, usually through the use of surrogates. He shied from direct confrontation, unlike Hamilton, who often clumsily chose a frontal assault when a flanking maneuver would have sufficed. Hamilton's sense of honor inclined him toward open confrontation; Jefferson's aversion to coercion, as well as his shyness, led him to seek circuitous routes to achieve his ends. James Madison and James Monroe were Jefferson's point men in his struggles with Hamilton, and anonymous leaks to journalists or congressional allies often served as their preferred method of attack. While Hamilton also engaged in such tactics, Jefferson habitually resorted to these devices both out of character and out of necessity, due to his covert role as the opposition leader of the administration to which he belonged.

Only in private letters or in later works such as the *Anas* did Jefferson candidly reveal his thoughts on Hamilton. The *Anas* was a loose collection of anecdotes based on notes jotted down during his years in power and was designed to counter John Marshall's *Life of Washington*, that "five volume libel" which portrayed Jefferson and his adherents in a less than flattering light. Jefferson wrote a preface to the *Anas* on February 4, 1818, and withheld publication of the collection until after his death.[4] Though Jefferson cleansed the record to remove the more embarrassing entries, expressions of contempt for Hamilton and his policies remained intact. Hamilton's financial system was a "machine for the corruption of the legislature," for Hamilton "was not only a monarchist, but for a monarchy bottomed on corruption." This "singular character" possessed some virtues, among which was his acute understanding and his "disinterested, honest, and honorable [conduct] in all private transactions." However, Hamilton's corrupt machinations were the result of his being "bewitched and perverted by the British example." Jefferson cited a report in the *Anas* describing a toast to King George III at a New York City dinner party in which "Hamilton started up on his feet, and insisted on a bumper and three cheers." Much of the *Anas* contains unsubstantiated gossip from sources like John Beckley (who played a key role in the effort to destroy Hamilton in 1797 by leaking information to the press on the "Reynolds Affair") passing on reports of Hamilton's efforts on behalf of "the paper and stock-jobbing interest." Convinced that Hamilton had aided and abetted corruption as Treasury Secretary, one of Jefferson's first acts as president was to order his Secretary of the Treasury, Albert Gallatin (1761–1849), to search the department's files for incriminating evidence. When none was found, Jefferson saw this not as an exoneration of Hamilton but as further evidence of his skill at deceit.[5]

Jefferson's attitude toward Hamilton was partly the result of his preference for men who would defer to him. He preferred associates who saw themselves as part of his extended family, a family that did not quarrel but reached consensus through the benign, oblique guidance of the Sage himself. (He regarded his slaves, for instance, as part of his "family" at Monticello.) The younger (fourteen years) Hamilton did not defer; moreover, his exemplary military record was a constant reminder to the revolutionary Virginian that only one of them had ever directly faced hostile fire from British soldiers. When the yellow fever epidemic ravaged Philadelphia in 1793, Jefferson mocked Hamilton's fear of the disease and questioned his bravery. He wrote Madison, "A man as timid as he is on the water, as timid on horseback, as timid in sickness, would be a phaenomenon if the courage of which he has the reputation in military occasions were genuine."[6]

At bottom, Jefferson could not countenance the fact that an immigrant upstart without the appropriate pedigree had dared challenge him. In a letter to President Washington, Jefferson stated that he would not let his reputation be "clouded by the slanders of a man whose history, from the moment at which history can stoop to notice him, is a tissue of machinations against the liberty of the country which has not only recieved [*sic*] and given him bread, but heaped it's [*sic*] honors on his head." Gilbert Chinard (1881–1972), a sympathetic biographer of Jefferson, said of this letter to Washington, "In one sentence he [Jefferson] had expressed not only condemnation of Hamilton's policies but all the scorn of a Virginian, of the old stock, for the immigrant of doubtful birth, who was almost an alien. He knew full well the weight such a consideration might have on the mind of Washington; it was a subtle but potent appeal to the solidarity of the old Americans against the newcomer."[7] It was the first of many attacks questioning Hamilton's "Americanism."

Jefferson's animus toward Hamilton persisted until Jefferson's death in 1826. Future president Martin Van Buren related this account of a visit he made to Monticello twenty years after Hamilton's passing:

> In all my conversations with him [Jefferson] in 1824, when he spoke of the course pursued by the Federal party, [he] invariably personified it by saying 'Hamilton' did or insisted thus; and, on the other hand, 'the Republicans' held or claimed so and so; and that upon my calling his attention to the peculiarity of his expression, he smiled and attributed his habit to the universal conviction of the Republicans that Hamilton directed every thing.[8]

This is classic Jefferson, reluctant to portray himself wielding power. The Republican "family" worked as a collegial body while the more hierarchical Federalists had their "strong man" issuing directives from above.

One of the more successful purveyors of misinformation regarding Hamilton was the Jeffersonian propagandist Philip Freneau. Handpicked by Jefferson and Madison to edit the *National Gazette* in 1791, Freneau initially praised Hamilton's financial measures, but quickly shifted his position on cue from the Virginians. The shift occurred in the wake of three essays written by Madison warning of the evils of the British system. From that point on Freneau was unrelenting in describing every proposal of Hamilton's as a covert attempt, as Donald Stewart put it, to "fasten a crown upon America." It was class politics at its worst, for Hamilton was accused of selling the Union to foreign and domestic speculators at the expense of "the industrious mechanic, the laborious farmer, and generally the poorer class of people." Jefferson was very satisfied with Freneau for having "saved our Constitution which was galloping fast into monarchy,"[9] and the image of Hamilton as monocrat, Anglophile, and enemy of liberty, first promulgated by Freneau at Jefferson's behest, remains the predominant impression of Hamilton in the American mind.

Hamilton's adversaries often referred to his June 18, 1787, speech at the Constitutional Convention to bolster their case that Hamilton was "un-American." The notion that he was an Englishman at heart was a caricature derived from Hamilton's statement that the British government was "the best in the world," and, despite its defects, provided a suitable model in some respects for the new American Constitution. Critics also seized upon his advocacy of the election of a president for life (assuming good behavior) and his preference for an elected Senate with lifetime tenure. What is often ignored in accounts portraying Hamilton as hostile to popular rule was his proposal for a House of Representatives elected by universal male suffrage, a proposal more democratic than that which ultimately emerged under the new government. It is true that Hamilton sought a stable national government capable of "vigorous execution" and "good administration," and while he believed that the institutions of government should be rooted in popular consent, he also thought they must be able to resist popular whims.[10] It requires a leap of the imagination to find monarchical inclinations in his comments or actions, but curiously, it is a leap that many Americans are still inclined to take.

Thomas Jefferson's campaign against Alexander Hamilton persisted long after Hamilton's death. The memory of a dead Hamilton was seen as a threat to Jeffersonianism, perhaps even more of a threat than a living Hamilton whose tactical political skills were somewhat wanting. Jefferson and his lieutenants succeeded in burying Hamilton and Federalism in what has to be considered one of the most effective and resilient campaigns in the history of American politics. Jefferson's success is partly attributable to the fact that both he and Madison outlived Hamilton by decades and were better able to influence the historical record. Jefferson attempted to gloss over and explain some of his more outlandish statements regarding the French Revolution, for instance, while Hamilton's record was presented to the world without the influence of any sober second thoughts. His alleged comments reported by Jefferson (twenty years after the fact) that the greatest man in the history of the world was Julius Caesar is but one instance of Jefferson's effort to "spin" history. Hamilton, of course, was long dead when Jefferson reported this tale.

Jefferson won the battle for the hearts and minds of most Americans, although he briefly lost the struggle within the scholarly community during the latter half of the nineteenth century. In the twentieth century, Jeffersonians wrote the histories, and outside of a small cadre of Republican politicians and conservative academics and a few American businessmen, Hamiltonianism was commonly perceived as not quite "American." The image of Hamilton fashioned by Jefferson and his allies has endured and flourished, and the Hamilton of American memory is a Hamilton who championed privilege and was a foe of liberty. Never has such a resilient description of a political figure, based on so little evidence, been circulated and accepted by so many.

As the founding generation passed on, a second generation of American political leaders emerged to carry on the struggle begun by Jefferson and Hamilton. While the Federalist "party" was dead, remnants of Hamiltonian thought could be found in such statesmen as Daniel Webster, Henry Clay, John Marshall, and ironically John Quincy Adams, all of whom would be subjected to many of the same allegations of elitist designs directed against Hamilton. The popular image of Hamilton as an un-American monarchist was solidified during the Jacksonian era in part because American politics, at least presidential politics, was dominated by men (Andrew Jackson, Martin Van Buren, John Tyler, James K. Polk) who were inclined, in most instances, to champion the Jeffersonian platform of states rights, agrarianism, expansion of suffrage, strict constitutional interpretation, and to oppose internal improvements and government intervention in the economy. Although they certainly shared and perhaps even expanded on Hamilton's notion of an energetic executive, at least in the cases of Jackson and Polk, they remained faithful to Jeffersonian principles. Hamilton's name was frequently invoked by these men and their followers, for as Marvin Meyers has observed, "for most of the country the Federalist conservatism of Hamilton or John Adams was stone dead: its ghost walked only in the speeches of Jacksonians trying to frighten honest citizens out of their opposition."[11]

Andrew Jackson's (1767–1845) contempt for Hamilton was evident during the warm reception he provided for Hamilton's killer in May 1805. Aaron Burr stayed with Jackson for several days, and his arrival in Nashville produced an outpouring of support, with cannons firing salutes and dinners given in his honor. As Jackson's biographer Robert Remini observed, Burr's killing of Hamilton "restored Burr's standing in the

Republican party as far as westerners were concerned." Jackson's contempt for Hamilton and Federalism stemmed from his "political creed," which was formed, as he put it, "in the old republican school" committed to states' rights. Jacksonianism was by definition a refutation of the principles of Federalism, as Jackson clearly stated in his first presidential address to Congress. The foremost principle of the American experiment, he contended, was that "the majority is to govern," and in fundamental disagreement with Hamilton's arguments for the beneficial filtering effects of representation, he maintained that "as few impediments as possible should exist to the free operation of the public will." He once wrote his private secretary, "The people are the government, administering it by their agents; they are the Government, the sovereign power."[12]

During his brief tenure as a member of the House of Representatives in 1796–1797, Jackson opposed an effort to issue a farewell address praising outgoing President George Washington, in part due to his disdain for Hamilton's financial policies. Referring to Washington, he once observed the "Executive of the Union" had "been Grasping after power, and in many instances, Exercised powers, that he was not Constitutionally invested with." The type of strong central government favored by Hamilton was "calculated to raise around the administration a moneyed aristocracy dangerous to the liberties of the country." When John Quincy Adams and Henry Clay took the presidency away from him in 1824 with their "corrupt bargain," the event was seen by Jacksonians as an attempt to, as Remini characterized it, "steal the government in order to reassert Hamiltonian doctrines."[13]

Jackson was determined to avenge this injustice in the election of 1828. The party's de facto strategist, Martin Van Buren, couched that election as a showdown between the Hamiltonianism of Adams and Clay and the Jeffersonian Republicanism of Jackson and John C. Calhoun, and it is fair to say that the movement begun by Jefferson in the "Revolution of 1800" reached its climax with Andrew Jackson's election in 1828. Whatever misgivings Jefferson had about Jackson, and he had some, there was no denying that Jackson was a natural outgrowth of Jefferson's efforts to champion the common man and to move the American polity in a more populist direction.[14]

During the age of Jackson, Hamilton served as a useful foil for Democrats committed to tarring their opponents, particularly Whigs, as "elitists" corruptly allied with the Second Bank of the United States (BUS). Criticism of and opposition to the BUS formed an ideological center of those critical of Hamilton and his political aims. The BUS was an insult to Jacksonian first principles, an elitist East Coast institution that corruptly benefited its friends and ignored the interests of the people. It was frequently referred to as a "monster" by Jacksonians, for it "carried the bad seed of Hamilton's first monster, matured all the old evils, and created some new ones" including "constitutional impiety, consolidated national power, aristocratic privilege, and plutocratic corruption."[15] Jackson believed that the Bank had promoted "aristocratical tendencies" and that it was his solemn duty to "restrain the sinister aspirations of wealth, and to check the growth of an authority so unfriendly to . . . the just rights of the people." The threat to the "mass of the people" emanated from "combinations of the wealthy and professional classes—from an aristocracy which thro' the influence of riches and talents, insidiously employed, sometimes succeeds . . . in establishing the most odious and oppressive Government under the form of a free institution."[16]

Jackson's campaign against the BUS was a continuation of the kind of politics that had been so effective against Hamilton and the Federalists. (Ironically, one of Hamilton's sons, James, was an ally of Jackson's in the Bank war and helped to draft a message to Congress urging that the Bank's charter not be renewed.)[17] It was, as Daniel Webster put it, an attempt by the president to "influence the poor against the rich. It wantonly attacks whole classes of the people, for the purpose of turning against them the prejudices and resentments of other classes."[18]

By the mid-nineteenth century, the debate over a national bank was overshadowed by the more volatile issue of the status of slavery in the newly acquired American territories. The Civil War ushered in an era that saw Alexander Hamilton eclipse Thomas Jefferson as a revered figure in the minds of most Americans, at least in the North. Jefferson's reputation suffered on the two major issues at stake: defenders of the union condemned his authorship of the secessionist Kentucky Resolutions of 1798, while his notoriety as one of the largest slaveholders in Virginia repelled those who saw the war as a struggle for abolition. For many Northern observers, America's bloodiest war vindicated Hamilton: the advocate of a strong national government that eclipsed in importance the particular states seemed to many to have foreseen the turmoil and bloodshed that had pulled the nation apart.

A number of Union soldiers who went on to become leaders of the Republican Party during the Gilded Age greatly admired Hamilton, with Ohio Republican James Garfield perhaps his foremost promoter. During his campaign for president in 1880 he delivered an address at Republican headquarters in New York City praising the accomplishments of Hamilton. Rutherford B. Hayes (1822–1893), James G. Blaine (1830–1893), Benjamin Harrison (1833–1901), and even Democrat Grover Cleveland (1837–1908) had, if not admiration for Hamilton, a deep interest in his life and works. Harrison said of Hamilton that he was a "conspicuous statesman" whose "great work in the Treasury Department" ensured that "the liberties wrested by arms from the British crown were made secure." Blaine, who served as Garfield and Benjamin Harrison's Secretary of State and was a repeated candidate for president, described "all Mr. Hamilton's work" as having "a remarkable value and a singular application in the developments of subsequent years," particularly his "mastery of finance which gave Mr. Hamilton his enduring fame."[19]

By the end of the nineteenth century, Hamilton was a revered figure among Ivy League–educated New England scholars. One such admirer was John Torrey Morse (1840–1937), whose *The Life of Alexander Hamilton* was harshly critical of Jefferson, while its portrayal of Hamilton led one to believe that the latter could do no wrong. Morse contended that Hamilton, while partly responsible for the rift between himself and Jefferson, was the victim of a broad-based assault on his character. Jefferson behaved "most unhandsomely by Hamilton in the way of gratuitous calumny." The preferred technique of this "untrustworthy moralist" was the "subtle *letter poison*" designed to "inculcate a strong prejudice and to create a sort of flavor of dishonesty." Hamilton's affair with Mrs. Reynolds was in some way the latter's fault, as Hamilton was unfortunate enough "to be led into an intrigue" with a woman of "some personal attractions" but little education and "no generous traits to be set off against her want of chastity."

Morse viewed Jefferson as the inspiration for the secessionist doctrines of John C. Calhoun and Jefferson Davis, while Hamilton championed Union and sound foreign and economic policies. According to Morse, the mourning produced by Hamilton's death was comparable to that of Lincoln's, and he cited favorably Chancellor Kent's claim that if Hamilton had lived "he would have rivaled Socrates or Bacon." Morse's *Life* was generally well received and became something of a standard text on its subject, though some critics such as *The Nation* viewed it as a "frank panegyric" marked by an indecorous manner.[20]

Needless to say, the Harvard-educated Morse had little regard for Jeffersonian and Jacksonian politicians. As the editor of the popular and influential *American Statesmen Series* published between 1882 and 1900, Morse had a penchant for selecting fellow New Englanders to write for his series. It was to one of those contributors, his cousin Henry Cabot Lodge (1850–1924), that Morse wrote in 1881, "Let the Jeffersonians and the Jacksonians beware! I will poison the popular mind!!"[21]

John T. Morse asked his cousin to write for the *American Statesmen Series* in February 1881, and his first contribution was *Alexander Hamilton* (1882). Henry Cabot Lodge had been a student of Henry Adams at Harvard, and later at *The North American Review* he served as an assistant editor to Adams. It was in this capacity that Lodge wrote a review of Morse's biography, which he criticized for its tendency to "to consider Hamilton as always in the right" and its "fatal tone of the lawyer pleading for the criminal" when dealing with indefensible aspects of Hamilton's career.[22]

The tone of Lodge's *Alexander Hamilton* was set in John T. Morse's preface, where he claimed that "Hamilton's fame indicates the unformulated but full appreciation of the unquestionable historic fact that he was the real maker of the government of the United States." Lodge argued that the democratic principles of Jefferson and the nationalist principles of Hamilton dominated the history of the United States, but he found that

> the great Federalist has the advantage. The democratic system of Jefferson is administered in the form and on the principles of Hamilton; and while the former went with the current and fell in with the dominant forces of the time, Hamilton established his now accepted principles, and carried his program to completion in the face of relentless opposition, and against the mistaken wishes of a large part of the people.[23]

Jefferson was portrayed far more gently by Lodge in comparison to Morse's account, and Lodge was willing to acknowledge certain character defects in Hamilton, including the "strength of his passions, which sometimes overmastered his reason" and his inability to manage men "wherein his great rival Jefferson stood supreme." It was Hamilton's "uncurbed passion" that led him into a "low intrigue with a worthless woman." Lodge rejected Chancellor Kent's claim that had Hamilton lived longer he would have rivaled Socrates or Bacon for "his work was done" at the time of the duel. Nevertheless, Hamilton was that rare statesman who represented "great ideas." He embodied the principle of "nationality," which was "the very breath of his public life." At a time when "American nationality meant nothing, he grasped the great conception in all its fullness, and gave all he had of will and intellect to make its realization possible. He and Washington alone perceived the destiny which was in store for the republic."[24]

Lodge's interest in Hamilton did not end with the publication of *Alexander Hamilton,* for he went on to edit nine volumes of *The Works of Alexander Hamilton* published in 1885–1886 and reissued in 1904. In his preface to *The Works,* Lodge reiterated the Gilded Age theme that Hamilton championed nationalism while Jefferson promoted the idea that the Union "was a confederacy" and that the conflict between those "opposing forces . . . culminated in the Civil War." By 1907, Senator Lodge boasted that his *Alexander Hamilton* had sold thirty-five thousand copies, and it would go on to sell for fifty years after it was published. Throughout his life, Lodge's devotion to Hamilton never wavered. Shortly before his death he wrote that Hamilton was "the greatest constructive mind in all our history and I should come pretty near saying . . . in the history of modern statesmen in any country."[25]

Lodge's high regard for Hamilton probably did not please his mentor Henry Adams (1838–1918), who had written him in 1876 that

> You do not of course expect me to acquiesce entirely in your view of A.H. . . . I dislike Hamilton because I always feel the adventurer in him. The very cause of your admiration is the cause of my distrust; he was equally ready to support a system he utterly disbelieved in as one that he liked. From the first to the last words he wrote, I read always the same Napoleonic kind of adventuredom . . . future political crises all through Hamilton's life were always in his mind about to make him commander-in-chief.

While Lodge and Adams differed in their estimation of Hamilton, both understood that Hamilton's reputation had come full circle from the early decades of the century when his name and his principles were under constant attack. By the latter half of the nineteenth century, as Adams told Lodge, it was "always safe to abuse Jefferson."[26]

One prominent American who would have agreed with this assessment was Theodore Roosevelt. Roosevelt (1858–1919) was probably the most zealous admirer of Alexander Hamilton ever to inhabit the White House. TR believed that Hamilton was "the most brilliant American statesman who ever lived, possessing the loftiest and keenest intellect of his time." Hamilton was a man of "singularly noble and lofty character" and "brilliant audacity and genius" which equipped him for the "giant tasks of constructive statesmanship with which he successfully grappled." Roosevelt's discussion of Hamilton and his opponents in his book *New York* (1891) probably reflected TR's view of the political divisions in his own time between urban eastern Republicans and rural Democrats. Roosevelt claimed that Hamilton's effort to ratify the Constitution in New York State was truly heroic, for he faced a popular governor, George Clinton, who knew how to capitalize on the "cold, suspicious temper of small country freeholders" with their "narrow" jealousies. Hamilton had the advantage of being supported by "townsmen" who were "quicker witted, and politically more far-sighted and less narrow-minded than the average country folk of that day."[27]

Upon the recommendation of his friend Henry Cabot Lodge, Roosevelt wrote two volumes for John Morse's *American Statesmen* series. In 1887 he completed *Gouverneur Morris* and later told Morris's great-grandson that Morris and Hamilton "embodied what was best in the Federalist Party . . . they both of them had in them the touch of the heroic, the touch of the purple, the touch of the gallant." Both Roosevelt and Lodge adored Hamilton, and on a trip to London in 1886 Roosevelt could not wait to inform Lodge that James Bryce was "especially complimentary about your Hamilton." Years later, President Roosevelt wrote to his old friend Senator Lodge from the White House, "the more I study Jefferson the more profoundly I distrust him and his influence, taken as a whole." In another letter to Lodge in 1906 TR stated that he was looking for a Supreme Court appointee who would be a "follower of Hamilton and Marshall and not a follower of Jefferson and Calhoun."[28]

The problem with Jefferson, according to TR, was that he led a party that sought to "restrict the powers of the central government even to the point of impotence." Jefferson was guilty, along with Madison, of "criminal folly" in neglecting the American military in the years leading up to the War of 1812. Jefferson, he added, was "perhaps the most incapable executive that ever filled the presidential chair." While serving as one of Jefferson's successors, Roosevelt wrote to Frederick Scott Oliver, the author of a 1906 biography on Hamilton, "I have never hesitated to criticize Jefferson; he was infinitely below Hamilton. I think the worship of Jefferson a discredit to my country . . . I think Jefferson on the whole did harm in public life."[29]

TR did praise Jefferson for teaching his "one great truth"—that an American statesman should trust the people, a lesson lost on Hamilton and the Federalists. "I have not much sympathy with Hamilton's distrust of the democracy," TR observed, and he judged Lincoln to be "superior to Hamilton just because he was a politician and was a genuine democrat." Hamilton was also unsuccessful as a party leader, TR claimed, because he was "too impatient and dictatorial, too heedless of the small arts and unwearied, intelligent industry of the party manager."[30]

A number of factors contributed to Roosevelt's reverence for Hamilton. Growing up in New York City in a family with ancestral links to Hamilton probably sparked his youthful curiosity, as did Hamilton's war record. The influence of his friend Henry Cabot Lodge and his education at Harvard acquired during the apogee of New England reverence for Hamilton completed the process. TR's curiosity about Hamilton never waned, even during his busy years in the White House. He read English author Frederick Scott Oliver's *Alexander Hamilton, An Essay on American Union,* published in 1906 and pronounced it "the best life of Alexander Hamilton that has ever been written." TR strongly recommended the book to Secretary of State Elihu Root, Senator Lodge, and the U.S. ambassador to Great Britain, Whitelaw Reid.[31]

Theodore Roosevelt's political views lurched farther to the left after his departure from the White House. While his reverence for Hamilton continued, his criticism of his lack of faith in the people became more strident. In fact, throughout most of his political career TR kept his admiration for Hamilton confined to private communications, a probable political concession to the fact that Hamilton remained something of a controversial figure. He was able to merge elements of Hamiltonian and Jeffersonian (or as TR would have preferred to call it, Lincolnian) thought in his "Bull Moose" effort to recapture the White House in 1912. He did this by embracing the principles espoused by Herbert Croly (1869–1930) in *The Promise of American Life* (1909). Judge Learned Hand acted, as Croly put it, as "the instrument that forged the bond" between TR and Croly. Hand urged Roosevelt to read the book (TR's friend Henry Cabot Lodge had sent him a copy as well) and noted that it addressed a "set of political ideas which can fairly be described as neo-Hamiltonian, and whose promise is due more to you, as I believe, than to anyone else." Roosevelt read the book and agreed with its recommendations, though it would be a mistake to overstate Croly's influence on Roosevelt as the latter had already independently arrived at many of the same conclusions. Croly himself acknowledged this when he wrote to Judge Hand in 1910, "He (TR) is the original and supreme Hamiltonian revivalist." Nonetheless, according to Walter Lippmann, Croly "made articulate for Roosevelt his aspiration to combine the social and political reforms initiated by Bryan and La Follette with a Hamiltonian affection for a strong national government." Roosevelt described *The Promise of American Life* as "the most powerful and illuminating study of our national conditions which has appeared for many years."[32]

Running in 1912 on a platform with the tag line the "New Nationalism," TR proposed a far more interventionist federal government along the lines proposed by Croly. The gist of Croly's argument was that "neither the Jeffersonian nor the Hamiltonian doctrine was entirely adequate" to "our contemporary national problems." On the whole, Croly's preferred Hamilton over Jefferson, for "he was the sound thinker, the constructive statesman, the candid and honorable, if erring, gentleman." The existence of the Union was due only to the Herculean efforts of a few Federalists, "of whom Hamilton and Washington were the most important." An "efficient" government appeared to be Croly's Holy Grail, and the Jeffersonians in their distaste for the national government were primarily responsible for restraining its power. Hamilton was also partly to blame for this—by distrusting the people he in turn made the people distrust his new creation. Instead of seeking a "sufficiently broad, popular basis" for his ideas, he relied on the "the interested motives of a minority of well-to-do citizens" and thereby confirmed in the people's view that the rich were "the peculiar beneficiaries of the American Federal organization."

Jefferson's one saving grace was his boundless faith in the American people. Unfortunately this was tainted by his "meager, narrow, and self-contradictory" conception of democracy, which generated far more serious damage for the long-term interests of the United States than any of Hamilton's acts. Jeffersonian policy was the policy of "drift," while Hamilton's policy was "one of energetic and intelligent assertion of the national good." Nonetheless, Jefferson's creed profoundly influenced Americans because of his "ability to formulate popular opinions, prejudices, and interests" and led to a situation where any independent leadership was suspect. Jefferson's powerful legacy mandated that future generations of American leaders would have to "flatter and obey" the people.

Croly was somewhat optimistic that the days of drift and inefficiency were coming to an end. The promise of salvation appeared in the form of Teddy Roosevelt, who had revived the "Hamiltonian ideal of constructive national legislation" without the undemocratic trappings of Hamilton. In essence, both Croly and TR's progressivism sought to "give a democratic meaning and purpose to the Hamiltonian tradition and method," while both men possessed, as Croly put it, "a frank and full confidence in an efficient national organization as the necessary agent of the national interest and purpose."[33]

Herbert Croly had observed the rise of Woodrow Wilson (1856–1924) with some trepidation, for he believed Wilson was far too enamored with Jeffersonian individualism and feeble government. The twenty-eighth president's academic interests had repeatedly drawn him back to the American founding, where he found an Alexander Hamilton that both repelled and attracted him.

Wilson's friend and brother-in-law Stockton Axson said that early in his life Wilson "believed in a considerable degree of centralization, called himself a federalist, paid his devoir to Alexander Hamilton. It was long before he rightly appreciated Thomas Jefferson." Wilson read his future nemesis Henry Cabot Lodge's *Alexander Hamilton* in 1882 and noted in the margins of the book that Hamilton's effort to enlist the support of propertied interests was similar to the Republican Party's effort in the 1880 election to portray themselves as the party of financial stability and the Democrats as dangerous "innovators and experimenters." Wilson's early writings reflected his desire to model the American system of government along the lines of the British cabinet system. He lamented the absence of American statesmen in the 1880s, arguing that "not since the revolution has there gone by an age so poor as this in such fine talents as those which crowned the head of Hamilton." In his book *Congressional Government: A Study in American Politics* (1885) Wilson observed that Hamilton "had inherited warm blood and a bold sagacity, while in the other (Jefferson) a negative philosophy ran suitably through cool veins."[34]

However, as he began to emerge as a political figure in New Jersey and around the nation, Wilson appeared determined to disassociate himself from Hamiltonianism. In 1909, as his candidacy for governor of New Jersey loomed, he stated that "some of us are Jeffersonians, not Hamiltonians, in political creed and principle," though he still referred to Hamilton as a "great statesman." In a speech to Philadelphia Democrats in 1911 he described Hamilton as "one of the greatest statesman that this country has ever had" but added that he was a statesman "with whose fundamental tenets of government we must most of us dissent." He reiterated this position in remarks made in the spring of 1911, when he proclaimed, "I am a Democrat because I dissent from the Hamiltonian theory." After he emerged as the Democratic nominee for president in 1912, his rhetoric grew harsher. The directors of the Standard Oil Company "control(led)" the Government of the United States," a situation endorsed by the Republican Party. The Republicans accepted "the theory of Hamilton" that "the only safe guides in public policies are those persons who have the largest material stake in the prosperity of the country." It was Wilson's belief that the Republicans were adhering to Hamiltonian principles in their defense of privilege. More than once in the 1912 election he stated that Taft's party "linked the government of the United States up with men who control the big finances of the United States . . . the first man, the first great man, who avowed that theory in the United States was Alexander Hamilton."[35]

Wilson won the White House and would later privately tell his aide Colonel Edward M. House that Alexander Hamilton was the ablest of the founders. But publicly he continued to state that Hamilton's notion of enlisting the creditor interests of society in his scheme of government made him uncomfortable. In his bid for reelection in 1916, it all came together in remarks he made to the noted muckraker Ida M. Tarbell (1857–1944): "Hamilton was never an American. He never believed there was such a thing as the wisdom of the masses. He was a great conservative genius, and we needed that at the moment."[36] In his campaign for a second term, Wilson sought to win the progressive vote, and despite running against reform-minded Republican candidate Charles Evans Hughes, he succeeded to some extent in tarring him with the brush of privilege. For the bulk of his presidency, Wilson continued the practice begun by TR of implementing the Croly thesis—that Hamiltonian means be used for Jeffersonian ends. In so doing, he alleviated Croly's initial concerns to the point where one commentator observed that *The New Republic* "became virtually the house organ for the Wilson administration."[37]

During his long career, Woodrow Wilson expressed misgivings about Hamilton's "Americanism" and his alleged efforts to protect the interests of the wealthy. Nevertheless, there were elements of Hamilton's principles and practices that Wilson applauded. In contrast, his young assistant secretary of the navy and his Democratic successor in the Oval Office came to see Hamilton as something comparable to a cancer on the founding. While Wilson understood that labeling Republicans as Hamiltonian defenders of privilege was an effective tactic, Franklin Roosevelt (1882–1945) utilized this technique with greater frequency and far more success. Perhaps FDR's Harvard education and New York patrician background lent more "credibility" to his attacks in the minds of northerners.

FDR's New Deal coalition of southern Jeffersonians and northern progressives brought to fruition the dream of Herbert Croly and others to pursue Jeffersonian ends with Hamiltonian means. While the First World War sidetracked Woodrow Wilson's reform efforts, Franklin Roosevelt, assisted by the trauma of the Great Depression, completed the task of building a powerful progressive coalition. It was no easy chore, and it was a testament to FDR's political genius that he succeeded. That this member of the Hudson River gentry appealed to the likes of countless populists was a testament to FDR's political acumen. He effectively exploited the widespread animus among southerners toward northern Hamiltonian "plutocrats." One spectator at a rally for a southern gubernatorial candidate in the early 1920s witnessed this animus. The candidate's speech "could be digested into one sentence: a horrible gang of bandits, led by a man named Alexander Hamilton, is now gathering and probably arming in a place called Wall Street, preparatory to coming down and plundering the poor farmers unless I am elected." The observer added, "He was elected."[38] While some northern New Dealers originally admired Hamilton for his advocacy of a well-administered national government, as time wore on the rhetoric and the honors paid to Jefferson were akin to those emanating from their southern brethren.

One of the more significant contributors to the New Deal's critique of Hamilton was Claude G. Bowers (1878–1958). Bowers was an influential partisan "historian" and journalist who in his prime helped to shape the opinions of countless Americans, perhaps including Franklin D. Roosevelt. Born in Hamilton County, Indiana, Bowers initially admired Hamilton, but after wading through the latter's papers he decided that "my instincts were opposed to the philosophy of my hero." Unsuccessful in a race for Congress in 1904, Bowers then turned to journalism, eventually becoming an editorial writer for *The New York World* and *The New York Journal.* Bowers viewed the American experience as a perpetual struggle between the forces of light and darkness. The dark side consisted of defenders of plutocracy, who often acted on the basis of principle but were nonetheless contemptuous of their fellow citizens, particularly farmers. The plutocrats originated with Hamilton and the Federalists and went on to include such fellow travelers as Henry Clay, Daniel Webster, and the "Radical Republicans" of the Reconstruction era. The forces of light were led by Thomas Jefferson ("the greatest of all Americans"), Andrew Jackson, Andrew Johnson, Franklin D. Roosevelt, and Harry S. Truman. Bowers was the favorite historian of the New Deal and had no reservations about mixing his journalistic and scholarly endeavors with his role as a

Democratic Party activist and propagandist. As one biographer of Bowers observed, he never met a Democrat he didn't like.[39]

In *Jefferson and Hamilton: The Struggle for Democracy in America,* Bowers declared that Hamilton was a genius, a man of integrity, and possessed of great moral courage; but he also found him "dictatorial," contended that he used Christianity to further his ends, and "thought of himself of the race of military masters." The confrontation between Jefferson and Hamilton was clearly the latter's fault, for Jefferson "long sought to get along with Hamilton." Hamilton viewed himself as the prime minister of Washington's administration, and Jefferson resented the "dictatorial airs" of his younger cabinet colleague. Making matters worse was the corruption that was starting to seep into the social life of the Federalist-dominated capital, a social scene that was "idolatrous of money and distinctions" and where few were "capable of discriminating between anarchy and democracy." In this hostile atmosphere, Jefferson would fight for the masses, a fight that "still stalks the ways of men."[40]

A number of scholars and journalists recoiled from Bowers's simplistic tale of good versus evil, but many did not. Dumas Malone (1892–1986), who would eventually displace Bowers as Jefferson's foremost twentieth-century promoter, wrote an enthusiastic review of *Jefferson and Hamilton.* Bowers's book inspired Malone to undertake his own Jefferson biography. Historian Samuel Flagg Bemis argued that *Jefferson and Hamilton* was "most interesting" and though the author "must be a Democrat," the pro-Jefferson bias that appeared in the book served as a "good antidote to the several recent studies extolling the marvels of Federalism and glorifying too exclusively the genius of Hamilton." Political scientist Arthur N. Holcombe disliked the fact that George Washington appeared as a minor character in Bowers's account but believed that the general reader would welcome a "delightfully fresh and stimulating" story that would counter the "one-sided productions of Hamiltonian hero-worshippers." William E. Dodd, whom FDR would later appoint as his ambassador to Germany, described *Jefferson and Hamilton* as "a marvel of interest, a portrait gallery unsurpassed," while *The Nation* selected it along with only four other books for its Honor Roll of 1926.[41]

Although Republicans won in a landslide in the 1928 election, it was the last hurrah for the "old order." Events were about to turn in favor of the Democrats, and the siren call from Claude Bowers warning of greedy plutocrats soon appeared quite prophetic. One associate of Franklin Roosevelt later compared Bowers's attraction to Democrats with Harriet Beecher Stowe's appeal to the early abolitionists. FDR thought it would be particularly useful if Bowers's *The Tragic Era* (1929), a racist portrayal of the "Radical Republicans" and Reconstruction, was widely read throughout the South.

Franklin Roosevelt agreed with much of Bowers's assessment of Reconstruction, writing him that "the period from 1865 to 1876 should be known as America's Dark Ages." As a reward for Bowers's yeoman service to the Democratic Party, Roosevelt appointed him ambassador to Spain. FDR's aide Raymond Moley told Bowers that he was doing "the greatest kind of work for liberalism and democracy through your books." Bowers was later appointed ambassador to Chile and served there into the Truman years. He retained the deepest affection for Roosevelt, who was "the greatest human being I had ever known, and one of the greatest in all our time."[42]

To the day he died, Claude Bowers was profoundly moved by the fact that the only book review ever written by Franklin Roosevelt was of his *Jefferson and Hamilton*. Bowers wrote to FDR after the review appeared: "I wish I could tell you how delighted I am at the revelations of yourself that appear in the review. . . . I wrote the book really to recall the party of Jefferson to the real meaning of Jeffersonian Democracy, and you have brought it out." The review appeared in the *New York Evening World* on December 3, 1925, and was written by a Franklin Roosevelt eager to return to political life. It probably occurred to Roosevelt that a glowing review of a book written by an editorial writer for the *World* might be of some assistance in his race for governor in 1928. The review was entitled "Is There a Jefferson on the Horizon?" As a rallying cry for a Democratic politician eager to return to the fray, it was first rate; as an analysis of the founding, it was somewhat simplistic. Roosevelt began by noting that he "felt like saying "At Last" as I read Mr. Claude G. Bowers's thrilling 'Jefferson and Hamilton'" and exclaimed "I have longed to write this very book." He stated that he was "fed up" with the "romantic cult" surrounding Hamilton that began with the publication of Gertrude Atherton's *The Conqueror*. While Roosevelt found Hamilton a fascinating figure and acknowledged his financial prowess, his fondness for "Chambers of Commerce" and his "contempt for the opinion of the masses" meant that if the Federalists had triumphed over Jefferson, darkness would have descended on America. "I have a breathless feeling as I lay down this book—a picture of escape after escape which this Nation passed through in those first ten years; a picture of what might have been if the Republic had been finally organized as Alexander Hamilton sought." These same forces of darkness were present in the 1920s, and the question was whether there was a Jefferson on the horizon to fend them off.[43]

Franklin Roosevelt had not always viewed Hamilton or the Federalists negatively. He had written an essay as a Harvard undergraduate that one biographer characterized as "full of hero worship." Roosevelt believed that it was "because of his (Hamilton's) insistence" that the Constitutional Convention convened in 1787 and that his success in winning the ratification of the Constitution in New York was "the greatest moment in the life of Alexander Hamilton, now thirty one years old. And yet there were other moments." George Washington appointed him to "the greatest of the Cabinet offices" where Hamilton "ordered the finances of the country" and "removed for all time the risk of disintegration of the States." In 1921, when asked by Arthur Vandenberg to name the greatest American, FDR named Hamilton's fellow Federalist, George Washington. FDR's conversion to Jeffersonianism appears to have occurred sometime in the mid-1920s. Perhaps he was influenced by Claude Bowers's book, although he had written to Democratic leaders in December 1924 suggesting that Jeffersonian principles were applicable to contemporary America, months prior to the release of Bowers's book. In a private letter written shortly after publication of his book review, FDR argued that America in the mid-1920s was approaching

> a period similar to that from 1790–1800 when Alexander Hamilton ran the federal government for the primary good of the chambers of commerce, the speculators and the inside ring of the national government. He was a fundamental believer in an aristocracy of wealth and power—Jefferson brought the government back to the hands of the average voter, through insistence on fundamental principles and the education of the average voter. We need a similar campaign of education today, and perhaps we shall find another Jefferson.[44]

It is unclear whether FDR experienced a genuine conversion to Jeffersonianism based on principle or came to realize that political expediency required it. Nonetheless, his transformation was complete by the time of his presidency.

In his campaign for the White House in 1932, Roosevelt attacked Herbert Hoover and his administration for their "Hamiltonian" disdain for the interests of the common man. The Republican administration was more concerned with dispelling the Depression-era fears of the "strong," that is, big business, than the "weak." This concern was, Roosevelt contended, "spoken in the true Hamiltonian tradition . . . the allaying of it (fear) must proceed from the strong to the weak." One of FDR's more notable addresses was delivered at the Commonwealth Club in San Francisco in September of that year. Hamilton and the Federalists were described by FDR as believing that "popular Government was essentially dangerous and essentially unworkable." Hamilton was "the most brilliant, honest and able exponent of this point of view" who "believed that the safety of the Republic lay in the autocratic strength of its Government" and that the "destiny of individuals was to serve that government." The theme of Jefferson and Andrew Jackson combating the forces of privilege permeated FDR's speeches, particularly those delivered at gatherings of the party faithful. At one event in 1938, Roosevelt compared his struggle to that of his Democratic predecessors Jefferson and Jackson. Jefferson contested Federalists who were "in favor of control by the few" while Jackson struggled against the Bank of the United States. Jackson opposed the "same evil Jefferson fought—the control of government by a small minority instead of by a popular opinion duly heeded by the Congress, the Courts and the President." In a 1940 address at the University of Pennsylvania, FDR claimed that Hamilton's desire for a government by "a small group of public-spirited and usually wealthy citizens" would have developed over time "into Government by selfishness or Government for personal gain or Government by class."[45]

One of Roosevelt's goals was to elevate Jefferson above the partisan fray to the status of a national hero on par with Washington and Lincoln. This was a rank the Virginian had not been accorded prior to the New Deal. The erection of a permanent memorial in the nation's capital to Thomas Jefferson would go far toward achieving this goal. Roosevelt first became involved in efforts of this sort when he actively participated in the campaign to preserve Jefferson's estate at Monticello, becoming a member of the Board of Governors of the Thomas Jefferson Memorial Foundation in 1930. As the nation's chief executive, Roosevelt was the driving force behind the creation of the impressive Jefferson Memorial on the Tidal Basin in Washington. After years of fits and starts, Roosevelt declared in November 1938 that "when the Democratic Administration came back in 1933, we all decided to have a memorial to Thomas Jefferson," and he would not allow "the worst case of flim flamming this dear old capital of ours has been subject to" to stand in the way. In his speech laying the cornerstone for the memorial, FDR argued that the nation was "adding the name of Thomas Jefferson to the names of George Washington and Abraham Lincoln." While not intended to honor "the founder of a party," FDR couldn't resist noting that Jefferson "lived, as we live, in the midst of a struggle between rule by the self-chosen individual or the self-appointed few and rule by the franchise and approval of the many." Jefferson's shrine was dedicated by Roosevelt on April 13, 1943, the two-hundredth anniversary of his birth. The new memorial signified, in the words of Dumas Malone, Jefferson's "recognition as a member of our Trinity of immortals."[46]

Since the 1790s, Jefferson and his adherents had portrayed their struggle with Hamilton as a contest between the apostle of freedom and a scheming monocrat (later "plutocrat")—with the monocrat having the added peculiarity of foreign birth. By the end of the New Deal, the Hamilton image in the American mind was something akin to a hybrid mix of Ebenezer Scrooge and Benito Mussolini. The atmosphere was so hostile that even Charles Beard complained in 1948 that Hamilton's name aroused "choking emotions in the bosoms of all 'right thinkers' who confine their knowledge and thinking to the Anti-federalist tradition."[47] When Franklin Roosevelt succeeded in elevating Thomas Jefferson into the American Pantheon, Hamilton was, in a sense, "airbrushed" out of the founding.

Franklin Roosevelt's promotion of all things Jeffersonian was a remarkably astute political tactic, particularly in light of his conflict with the Supreme Court, where FDR's actions recalled Jefferson's and Jackson's clashes with that institution. His appeal to Jeffersonian principles in support of an "Economic Bill of Rights" was also a deft political stroke. Hamilton's reputation reached its nadir during the New Deal primarily due to the accusation that he lacked compassion for those at the bottom of the economic ladder. Appeals to economic equality proved a potent weapon in the hands of New Dealers, yet the ticking time bomb threatening Jefferson's reputation—one shortly to explode—was the equally compelling principle of racial equality.

Toward the end of the twentieth century and at the dawn of the new millennium, race relations emerged as the most vexing domestic issue confronting the United States. Jefferson's authorship of the controversial *Notes on the State of Virginia* and his role as one of the largest slaveholders in that state, coupled with credible evidence of an intimate relationship with one of his slaves, began to erode his reputation. Hamilton's immigrant status, and his founding role in the New York Society for Promoting the Manumission of Slaves, presented a compelling alternative. Additionally, Hamilton's support for national power drew the praise of American liberals who tended to view Jefferson's states' rights doctrine as camouflage for Jim Crow. Nevertheless, it was difficult to predict if the American public would abandon entirely the old myths regarding Hamilton and Jefferson. Much was at stake for the Democratic Party, for economic populists, and for Virginia boosters in celebrating Jefferson. Any transformation was likely to be slow, but it appeared that the cult of Jefferson was dying. While Jefferson's authorship of the Declaration of Independence has forever secured his place in the nation's pantheon, Americans seemed ready to reassess him. At the very least there was the realization that the twentieth-century celebration of Jefferson was excessive.

In 1960, historian Merrill Peterson observed that "the spacious grandeur of Monticello" stood in stark contrast to the "shabby disrepair and virtual anonymity" of the Hamilton Grange in crowded Harlem. It was, he said, a "true reflection of the two rivals' contemporary reputations."[48] For decades, Monticello served as a Potemkin Village where evidence of the existence of Jefferson's slaves was hidden from visitors. Monticello was, in a larger sense, emblematic of the twentieth-century airbrushing of history by Jeffersonian politicians and scholars. The crowded, slighted Grange, in the midst of New York's poverty and in the shadow of its great wealth, is the appropriate destination for Americans seeking the truth about their country's mixed record of triumph and failure.

In the future, a more diverse nation is apt to continue to focus on race as the crucial issue in the American experience. Race has always been Jefferson's Achilles' heel, and in the twenty-first century it could well be his undoing. If the past holds any lessons, then Hamilton's standing should continue to improve, for it appears to be an iron law that as one falls, the other rises. Jefferson and the Jeffersonians would have it no other way; as the Sage himself once put it, "opposed in death as in life."[49]

NOTES

1. Hugh Sidey, "We're Still Jefferson's Children," *Time*, 13 July 1987, 14, and George F. Will, *Restoration: Congress, Term Limits, and the Recovery of Deliberative Democracy* (New York: Free Press, 1992), 167.

2. Consider, for instance, Jefferson's actions against the Barbary pirates (and his careful and selective reporting of those actions to Congress) and his implementation of the stringent embargo of 1807–8 to halt trade between the United States and European belligerents.

3. Dumas Malone, *Jefferson the President, First Term, 1801–1805* (Boston: Little, Brown and Company, 1970), 425. The "Mr. Randolph" Jefferson refers to is his son-in-law, Thomas Mann Randolph, Jr. Philip Mazzei was the recipient of the famous Jefferson letter written in the spring of 1796 that appeared to accuse George Washington of abandoning his principles while under the spell of the "harlot England."

4. Merrill D. Peterson, *The Jefferson Image in the American Mind* (New York: Oxford University Press, 1960), 33, and Thomas Jefferson, *Writings,* ed. Merrill Peterson (New York: Library of America, 1984), 1530.

5. *The Writings of Thomas Jefferson,* ed. Andrew A. Lipscomb (Washington, DC: Thomas Jefferson Memorial Association, 1903), vol. 1, 271, 278–79, 311, 347, 432–33; John C. Miller, *Alexander Hamilton: Portrait in Paradox* (New York: Harper and Brothers, 1959), 534. Ironically, Albert Gallatin is buried a short distance from Hamilton in the Trinity Church graveyard in Manhattan.

6. *The Papers of Thomas Jefferson,* ed. John Catanzariti (Princeton, NJ: Princeton University Press, 1950–), vol. 27, 1 September to 31 December 1793, 62.

7. *Papers of Thomas Jefferson,* vol. 24, 1 June to 31 December 1792, 358; Gilbert Chinard, *Thomas Jefferson: The Apostle of Americanism* (Boston, MA: Little, Brown, 1929), 270.

8. Martin Van Buren, *Inquiry into the Origin and Course of Political Parties in the United States* (New York: Augustus M. Kelly, 1967), 116–17.

9. Donald H. Stewart, *The Opposition Press of the Federalist Period* (Albany: State University of New York Press, 1969), 487–89, 538–41; Forrest McDonald, *Alexander Hamilton* (New York: W. W. Norton, 1982), 239–41. Also, Emory Elliott, *Revolutionary Writers: Literature and Authority in the New Republic, 1725–1810* (New York: Oxford University Press, 1982), 133.

10. See *The Papers of Alexander Hamilton,* ed. Harold Syrett (New York: Columbia University Press, 1962), vol. 4, 178–211; see especially 192–95 and also 213. There are five different versions of Hamilton's June 18 speech, including Hamilton's own notes as well as those of James Madison, Robert Yates, John Lansing, Jr., and Rufus King. See also McDonald, *Alexander Hamilton,* 99–105, for a helpful discussion of Hamilton's speech.

11. Marvin Meyers, *The Jacksonian Persuasion: Politics and Belief* (Stanford, CA: Stanford University Press, 1957), 7.

12. Robert V. Remini, *Andrew Jackson and the Course of American Empire, 1767–1821* (New York: Harper and Row, 1977), 145; idem, *Andrew Jackson and the Course of American Freedom, 1822–1832* (New York: Harper and Row, 1981), 32; *A Compilation of the Messages and Papers of the Presidents, 1789–1897,* ed. James D. Richardson (Washington, DC: Government Printing Office, 1896), vol. 2, 448; Robert V. Remini, *Daniel Webster: The Man and His Time* (New York: W. W. Norton, 1997), 353n.26.

13. Remini, *Andrew Jackson and the Course of American Empire,* 92–94; William Graham Sumner, *Andrew Jackson* (Boston: Houghton, Mifflin, 1899), 13–14; Remini, *Andrew Jackson and the Course of American Freedom,* 33, 100, 114.

14. Jefferson's biographer Dumas Malone writes that Jefferson was on "the best of personal terms" with General Jackson and had approved of Jackson controversial operations in Florida that almost ignited a war with Great Britain. However, Malone also notes that "two Adams" men, Daniel Webster and George Ticknor, both reported conversations with Jefferson in which he stated that Jackson was a man of violent passions temperamentally unsuited to be president. Dumas Malone, *Jefferson and His Time: The Sage of Monticello* (Boston: Little, Brown, 1981), 436–37, 437n.42.

15. Marvin Meyers, *The Jacksonian Persuasion*, 10–11.

16. Robert V. Remini, *Andrew Jackson and the Course of American Democracy, 1833–1845* (New York: Harper and Row, 1984), 98.

17. Whatever attributes Jackson may have possessed, knowledge of the founding fathers was not one of them. He told James Hamilton that the latter's father "was not in favor of the Bank of the United States," although perhaps one must allow for the possibility that Jackson saw Nicholas Biddle's bank as a mutant offspring of the one founded by Hamilton. See Robert V. Remini, *Andrew Jackson and the Bank War: A Study in the Growth of Presidential Power* (New York: W. W. Norton, 1967), 49, 61–64.

18. Quoted in Arthur M. Schlesinger, Jr., "An Impressive Mandate and the Meaning of Jacksonianism," in *Andrew Jackson: A Profile*, ed. Charles Sellers (New York: Hill and Wang, 1971), 135.

19. *The Diary of James A. Garfield*, ed. Harry James Brown and Frederick D. Williams (Lansing: Michigan State University Press, 1981), vol. 4, 1878–1881, 436–37 and 437n.223; Benjamin Harrison, *This Country of Ours* (New York: Charles Scribner's Sons, 1897), 85, 208–9; James G. Blaine, *Twenty Years of Congress from Lincoln to Garfield, With a Review of the Events Which Led to the Political Revolution of 1860* (Norwich, CT: Henry Bill Publishing, 1884), vol. 1, 186, 483. See also George F. Parker, *Recollections of Grover Cleveland* (New York: Century Co., 1909), 286–87; *Diary and Letters of Rutherford Birchard Hayes, Nineteenth President of the United States*, ed. Charles Richard Williams (Ohio State Archaeological Society, 1922–1926), vol. 1, 1834–1860, 156, 160–161; vol. 4, 1881–1893, 164.

20. John T. Morse, Jr., *The Life of Alexander Hamilton* (Boston: Little, Brown, 1876), vol. 2, 19, 221, 274, 331–32, 336, 344, 371. Also, David Alan Lincove, "John T. Morse, Jr. (1840–1937)" in Clyde N. Wilson, ed., *American Historians, 1866–1912* (Detroit: Gale Research, 1986), 185.

21. David Alan Lincove, "John T. Morse, Jr.," 183–92.

22. John A. Garraty, *Henry Cabot Lodge: A Biography* (New York: Alfred A. Knopf, 1953), 38–39, 56–59, 58n.1; Henry Cabot Lodge, "The Life of Alexander Hamilton," *North American Review* 123 (July 1876): 113–44. Also, William C. Widenor, "Henry Cabot Lodge (1850–1924)," in Clyde N. Wilson, ed., *American Historians, 1866–1912*, 157–162.

23. Henry Cabot Lodge, *Alexander Hamilton* (Boston: Houghton Mifflin, 1882), vii, 280.

24. Lodge, *Alexander Hamilton*, 273–79. Lodge's admiration for Hamilton's nationalism is apparent throughout his biography. At one point he noted that Hamilton's fame as a writer rested in good measure on his contributions to *The Federalist*, which "has been turned to as an authority by the leading minds of Germany intent on the formation of the Germanic empire"; see p. 67.

25. Garraty, *Henry Cabot Lodge*, 56; William C. Widenor, *Henry Cabot Lodge and the Search for an American Foreign Policy* (Berkeley: University of California Press, 1980), 28.

26. *Letters of Henry Adams* (1858–1891), ed. Worthington Chauncey Ford (Boston: Houghton Mifflin, 1930), 284–84; William C. Widenor, "Henry Cabot Lodge (1850–1924)," in Clyde N. Wilson, ed., *American Historians, 1866–1912*, 160.

27. Theodore Roosevelt, *New York* (New York: Charles Scribner's Sons, 1924), 362–67; *Speeches, Correspondence and Political Papers of Carl Schurz*, ed. Frederic Bancroft (New York: G. P. Putnam's Sons, 1913), vol. 4, July 20, 1880–September 15, 1888, 241–42; J. W. Cooke, "Theodore Roosevelt (1858–1919)," in Clyde N. Wilson, ed., *American Historians, 1866–1912*, 242–49. In light of TR's love for Hamilton, it is ironic that Hamilton's grandson and biographer Dr. Allan McLane Hamilton wrote an essay in the pages of the *New York Times* in 1912 questioning Roosevelt's sanity along with the sanity of other progressive politicians. See "The Peril of an Insane Administration," *New York Times*, 12 May 1912, part 5, 2.

28. Theodore Roosevelt, *Gouverneur Morris* (Boston: Houghton, Mifflin, 1898), preface; *The Letters of Theodore Roosevelt*, ed. Elting E. Morison (Cambridge, MA: Harvard University Press, 1951–54), vol. 5, *The Big Stick, 1905–1907*, 407, and vol. 7, *The Days of Armageddon, 1909–1914*, 175. Also, *Selections from the Correspondence of Theodore Roosevelt and Henry Cabot Lodge, 1884–1918*, ed. Henry Cabot Lodge (New York: Charles Scribner's Sons, 1925), vol. 1, 50, and vol. 2, 282. TR's other volume in the American Statesman series was *Thomas Hart Benton* (Boston: Houghton, Mifflin, 1886).

29. Theodore Roosevelt, *New York*, 366; Carleton Putnam, *Theodore Roosevelt*, 224; Joseph Bucklin Bishop, *Theodore Roosevelt and His Time, Shown in His Own Letters* (New York: Charles Scribner's Sons, 1926), vol. 2, 27–28.

30. Theodore Roosevelt, *Gouverneur Morris*, 119; Bishop, *Theodore Roosevelt and His Time*, vol. 2, 27–28; Theodore Roosevelt, *New York*, 367.

31. *The Letters of Theodore Roosevelt*, vol. 5, *The Big Stick, 1905–1907*, 349, 368, 693; *Correspondence of Theodore Roosevelt and Henry Cabot Lodge*, vol. 2, 225.

32. Charles Forcey, *The Crossroads of Liberalism: Croly, Weyl, Lippmann, and the Progressive Era, 1900–1925* (New York: Oxford University Press, 1961), xxviii, 123, and 129; Nathan Miller, *Theodore Roosevelt: A Life* (New York: William Morrow, 1992), 514; Walter Lippmann, "Notes for a Biography," *New Republic* 63 (16

July 1930): 250–51. Also, Arthur M. Schlesinger, Jr.'s introduction in Herbert Croly, *The Promise of American Life* (Cambridge, MA: Belknap Press of Harvard University Press, 1965), xxiii.

33. Theodore Roosevelt, *The New Nationalism*, 3–33; Croly, *The Promise of American Life*, ch. 2, and 53, 168–69. Croly repeated his preference for Hamilton over Jefferson in later writings, arguing that "the nationalism of Hamilton, with all its aristocratic leaning, was more democratic, because more constructively social, than the indiscriminate individualism of Jefferson." See Herbert Croly, *Progressive Democracy* (New York: Macmillan, 1915), 54–55.

34. Clements, *The Presidency of Woodrow Wilson*, 15; Stockton Axson, *"Brother Woodrow": A Memoir of Woodrow Wilson*, ed. Arthur S. Link (Princeton, NJ: Princeton University Press, 1993), 71–72; *The Papers of Woodrow Wilson*, ed. Arthur S. Link (Princeton, NJ: Princeton University Press, 1966–1993), vol. 2, 150, 228; Henry Wilkinson Bragdon, *Woodrow Wilson: The Academic Years* (Cambridge, MA: Belknap Press of Harvard University Press, 1967), 126.

35. *The Papers of Woodrow Wilson*, ed. Link, vol. 19, 377, 467; vol. 22, 444; vol. 23, 108; vol. 24, 374; vol. 25, 83–84.

36. *The Papers*, ed. Link, vol. 29, 448; vol. 38, 326.

37. Sidney A. Pearson, Jr., "Herbert Croly and Liberal Democracy," *Society* 35 (July/August 1998): 67.

38. Francis Pendleton Gaines, *Southern Oratory: A Study in Idealism* (Huntsville: University of Alabama Press, 1946), 12–13.

39. Claude Bowers, *My Life: The Memoirs of Claude Bowers* (New York: Simon and Schuster, 1962), 1, 39; "Jefferson: Third President Relives in New Book by Bowers," *News-Week* (5 September 1936): 25; Michael Bordelon, "Claude G. Bowers," in Clyde N. Wilson, ed., *Twentieth-Century American Historians*, 86–92.

40. Claude Bowers, *Jefferson and Hamilton: The Struggle for Democracy in America* (Boston: Houghton Mifflin, 1925), 23, 33–35, 41, 69, 109, 135, 511.

41. Merrill D. Peterson, "Dumas Malone: An Appreciation," *William and Mary Quarterly*, 3rd series, 45, no. 2 (April 1988): 239, 249; Samuel Flagg Bemis, review of *Jefferson and Hamilton: The Struggle for Democracy in America* by Claude Bowers, *American Historical Review* 31, no. 3 (April 1926): 543–45; Arthur N. Holcombe, review of *Jefferson and Hamilton: The Struggle for Democracy in America* by Claude Bowers, *American Political Science Review* 20, no. 1 (February 1926): 215–17; Claude Bowers, *The Founders of the Republic* (Chicago: American Library Association, 1927), 7.

42. Bowers, *My Life*, 250, 260, 297, 303, 316.

43. Bowers, *My Life*, 127; Daniel R. Fusfeld, *The Economic Thought of Franklin D. Roosevelt and the Origins of the New Deal* (New York: Columbia University Press, 1956), 85–86; *The Roosevelt Reader: Selected Speeches, Messages, Press Conferences, and Letters of Franklin D. Roosevelt*, ed. Basil Rauch (New York: Rinehart and Co., 1957), 43–47. Bowers editorialized on FDR's behalf after the review appeared, although he probably would have been on Roosevelt's bandwagon

regardless of the review. Newly elected Governor Roosevelt wrote Bowers in 1929, "please let me tell you how very grateful I am for all the splendid editorials in the *Evening World*. They are a bulwark of strength." Claude Bowers, *My Life*, 250.

44. Frank Freidel, *Franklin D. Roosevelt: The Apprenticeship* (Boston: Little, Brown, 1952), 61n.56; Arthur Schlesinger, Jr., *The Age of Roosevelt: The Crisis of the Old Order, 1919–1933* (Boston: Houghton Mifflin, 1957), 102–3; Frank Freidel, *Franklin D. Roosevelt: The Ordeal* (Boston: Little, Brown, 1954), 205–6 and 206n. See the skeptical reaction in *The New Republic* to FDR's proposal to "recover and realize the Jeffersonian idea" in "The Great Jefferson Joke," 47 (9 June 1926): 73–74.

45. *The Public Papers and Addresses of Franklin D. Roosevelt*, ed. Samuel I. Rosenman, vol. 1, *The Genesis of the New Deal, 1928–1932* (New York: Random House, 1938), 631–32, 745; *The Public Papers*, ed. Rosenman, 1938 volume, *The Continuing Struggle for Liberalism* (New York: Macmillan, 1941), 40; *The Public Papers*, ed. Rosenman, 1940 volume, *War—and Aid to Democracies* (New York: Macmillan, 1941), 435–37.

46. Merrill Peterson, *The Jefferson Image in the American Mind*, 360, 377, 430; *The Public Papers*, ed. Rosenman, *War—and Neutrality* (New York: Macmillan, 1941), 1939 volume, 577–79; Dumas Malone, "The Jefferson Faith," *Saturday Review*, 17 April 1943, 4. Merrill Peterson documents the many efforts undertaken by FDR to memorialize Jefferson, including the issuance of postage stamps and the Jefferson nickel. See *The Jefferson Image in the American Mind*, 360–63.

47. Charles Beard quoted in Saul K. Padover, *The Genius of America: Men Whose Ideas Shaped Our Civilization* (New York: McGraw-Hill, 1960), 69.

48. Peterson, *The Jefferson Image*, 347.

49. Jefferson's comment was made in response to his placement of busts of Hamilton and himself facing each other in the entrance hall at Monticello. See www.monticello.org/jefferson/entrance/home.html.

CHAPTER 3

The Hamiltonian Invention of
Thomas Jefferson

ROBERT M. S. McDONALD

*T*HOMAS Jefferson claimed to crave neither power nor popularity. "Public service and private misery," he contended, are "inseparably linked together."[1] As he noted after two particularly difficult years as Virginia's governor, office-holding required "constant sacrifice of time" as well as "labour, loss," and dereliction of "parental and friendly duties." In 1782, when James Monroe prodded him to return to Richmond as a member of the House of Delegates, he replied that the idea left him "mortified."[2] But calls to public service continued to harry Jefferson, who agreed to serve in the Confederation Congress in 1783 and 1784 before embarking for France, where he worked briefly as a trade commissioner and then remained as minister plenipotentiary until 1789. He found the demands of diplomatic office more agreeable. "My little transactions are not made for public detail," he explained. "They are best in the shade: the light of the picture is justly occupied by others. To glide unnoticed thro' a silent execution of duty, is the only ambition which becomes me, and it is the sincere desire of my heart."[3]

Alexander Hamilton believed otherwise. By 1792, two years after Jefferson had obeyed, "with real regret," President George Washington's call to serve as Secretary of State, Hamilton, the Treasury Secretary, viewed him not only as a rival but also as a liar. Bad enough, Hamilton thought, that Jefferson opposed his financial programs; his motivations for doing so were far worse. Contrary to Jefferson's repeated avowals, Hamilton considered him vain and treacherous, a schemer willing to sacrifice national interest for personal glory.

More than any other single factor, Jefferson's rise to national prominence resulted from the scorn of Hamilton, who, tirelessly and almost sin-
gle-handedly, in 1792 and 1793 savaged his character in printed attacks that
James H. Read, elsewhere in this volume, aptly describes as "scorching" in
their tone.[4] While Read analyzes the factors that caused Hamilton's view of
Jefferson to evolve over the course of the decade to follow, this essay
focuses on Hamilton's earliest public critiques and their effect. In response
to Hamilton's assault, James Madison and other Republicans rushed to
Jefferson's defense. They picked up their pens and, in essays that appeared
in newspapers across the nation, developed Jefferson's reputation as a foe
of aristocracy, a champion of liberty, and a friend of the people. In short,
Hamilton's eagerness to discredit the Secretary of State brought about the
invention of a public figure whose popular appeal would eventually contribute to the Federalist faction's demise.

In March of 1790, when Jefferson arrived in New York, the temporary
American capital, his career as a diplomat had not yet ended. As Secretary
of State, of course, his responsibilities included the supervision of negotiations between representatives of the United States and foreign powers. But
Jefferson also agreed to serve as a peacemaking intermediary between
Hamilton and the loose band of congressmen who balked at his financial
programs. For more than two months, the House of Representatives had
been embroiled in controversy over the New Yorker's "First Report on the
Public Credit," which proposed measures such as the federal assumption
of states' unpaid Revolutionary War debts. Hamilton's supporters argued
that the program would affirm American honor, assuage foreign fears of
an uncreditworthy United States, and guarantee interest payments to
patriots who bought bonds and lent credit when the new nation needed
quick cash. Madison, however, organized a group of congressmen who
believed that the plan would unfairly benefit wealthy speculators who had
purchased bond issues and other credit certificates from their original
holders at significantly deflated prices. His coalition also argued that the
measure would wrongfully increase the payment burden of citizens in
states such as Virginia, which had already begun to pay its creditors, while
diminishing the obligations of taxpayers in debt-ridden Massachusetts
and South Carolina.[5]

Jefferson worked behind the scenes to resolve the dispute. At the urging
of the Treasury chief and emboldened by the belief that "men of sound
heads and honest views needed nothing more than explanation and

mutual understanding to enable them to unite," he arranged to host a meeting of Hamilton and Madison at his dinner table. The three men deliberated, and days later Hamilton emerged victorious from the debt-funding debate. At the same time, Virginia received a congressional commitment to locate the nation's permanent capital on the Potomac.[6]

Yet any hopes that Jefferson may have harbored for permanent reconciliation soon collapsed. At the end of April, he unwittingly helped to set off the opening salvo of an intensely public battle that would vault him to prominence as opposition leader. Through Madison, Jefferson received John Beckley's copy of the first volume of Thomas Paine's *Rights of Man*, a barbed rejoinder to Edmund Burke's recently published condemnation of the French Revolution. Beckley, clerk of the House of Representatives, had already arranged for the publication in America of Paine's polemic. He pressed Jefferson to forward the pamphlet directly to a Philadelphia printer. The Secretary of State complied, dashing off a letter that explained how he had come into possession of the work. "To take off a little of the dryness of the note," as he later told Madison, he informed the printer that he was "extremely pleased to find that it will be re-printed" in America, "and that something is at length to be publicly said against the political heresies which have sprung up among us." He followed this thinly veiled reference to a series of political essays ("Discourses on Davila") by Vice-President John Adams in the *Gazette of the United States,* which he thought revealed Adams's monarchical leanings, with the remark that he had "no doubt our citizens will rally a second time round the standard of Common sense." Seizing upon Jefferson's private letter as a public endorsement, the printer included it as a foreword to Paine's book, the American publication of which, he implied in an editorial note, Jefferson himself had masterminded.[7]

The discovery that his note prefaced the *Rights of Man* left Jefferson "thunderstruck," as he told the offended vice-president. To Madison he expressed "astonishment" and regret concerning both the letter and the publicity it had generated. "I tell [Adams] freely that he is a heretic," he asserted, "but certainly never meant to step into a public newspaper with that in my mouth." Not only did the printer's indiscretion wound Adams's ego, but it also strained Jefferson's relationship with Hamilton. The Treasury Secretary, Jefferson reported to Madison, was "open mouthed against me."[8]

The *Rights of Man* controversy reverberated through the public prints. Under the pseudonym "Publicola," John Quincy Adams, the vice-president's son, authored eleven essays, printed first in Boston's *Columbian Centinel* and then republished in other gazettes, that led the attack on Jefferson. The Secretary of State's "political heresies" remark proved that he possessed little tolerance for differing opinions, according to "Publicola." Moreover, the author of *The Rights of Man* insisted that only a "a general convention elected for the purpose" could rightfully alter a constitution; Jefferson's apparent concurrence with this idea exposed his opposition to America's founding charter, which granted amending powers to the Congress and state legislatures. Jefferson was a subversive demagogue, Publicola implied, and he implored his readers to "remain immovably fixed at the banners of our constitutional freedom, and not desert the impregnable fortress of our liberties, for the insubstantial fabrick of visionary politicians."[9]

If claims about Jefferson's supposed hostility to the Constitution characterized Adams's attack on the surface, anxiety over the propriety of his behavior emanated from its core. As Jefferson himself believed, open battle between two cabinet officers was an act of "indecency." It made the executive branch appear weak and divided, as Washington noted a year later when he called for conciliation between the feuding members of his administration.[10] Still worse, Jefferson's apparent endorsement of Paine's treatise brazenly dispensed with the customary cloak of pseudonymity, behind which nearly every office-holding polemicist retreated. Although the rules of republican discourse permitted public servants to promote ideas, this prevailing etiquette did not allow them to promote themselves. As a result, charges of demagoguery could fall on those who signed their names to political publications, the practice of which Jefferson seemed guilty. Nonetheless, Madison pointed out to his embarrassed friend, he had crossed no lines not already trodden upon by Adams himself. "Since he has been the 2d. Magistrate in the new Republic," Madison observed, "his pen has constantly been at work." While Adams's "name has not been prefixed to his antirepublican discourses, the author has been well known as if that formality had been observed. Surely if it be innocent and decent in one servant of the public thus to write attacks against its Government," Madison maintained, "it can not be very criminal or indecent in another to patronize a written defense of the principles on which that Government is founded."[11]

The emerging Federalist faction saw matters differently. Jefferson's repeated disavowals of any role in the appearance of his note at the front of Paine's book failed to convince this group, which came to believe that his endorsement represented political posturing, perhaps in preparation for a bid for higher office. "Mr. J[efferson] appears to have shown rather too much of a disposition to cultivate vulgar prejudices," Oliver Wolcott believed; "accordingly he will become popular in ale houses, and will do much mischief to his country by exciting apprehensions" against the government. "It is thought rather early for Electioneering," Adams dryly remarked to Secretary of War Henry Knox. A subsequent pamphlet made the same allegation: Jefferson, eager to succeed Washington as president, would trample the character not only of Adams, but also of Hamilton in order to prevail. This sort of self-promotion could not be taken lightly, Jefferson's opponents agreed. As Adams asserted in his "Discourses," the darkest force confronting republicanism was "the *passion for distinction*" —the desire of men to rise through the ranks of politics and society. The purpose of government, Adams contended, was "to regulate this passion" and to make it "an instrument of order and subordination." For Americans who agreed with Adams, Jefferson's alleged ambitions and apparent behavior could only appear to fly in the face of propriety.[12]

Jefferson attempted to prove his critics wrong. While "a host of writers" defended him, he resolved "to be utterly silent" in the skirmish, "except so far as verbal explanations could be made." He then offered the olive branch to Adams, assuring him that he still valued their friendship. He said that he had played no part in having "our names thrown on the public stage as public antagonists," and he issued a similar assurance to the president.[13]

But his opponents thought that his words had little connection with his deeds. At the same time as the *Rights of Man* controversy, Jefferson journeyed with Madison through New York and New England. The trip compounded suspicions that the two men stood at the head of a partisan vanguard. While they characterized their expedition as a vacation, members of the emerging Federalist faction thought otherwise. Nathaniel Hazard, a New York City merchant, held that Jefferson and Madison "scouted silently thro' the Country, shunning the Gentry, communing with & pitying the Shayites" who a decade earlier had rebelled against the government of Massachusetts.[14]

Hamilton's hostility for Jefferson already exceeded his enmity for Madison, in no small part because his more charitable attitude toward the congressman reflected both "*personal & political*" disillusionment after a healthy and lengthy relationship. The two had collaborated in the constitutional ratification debate; they had also cooperated on public matters, such as debt funding and assumption, as their respective responsibilities within the new government began to crystallize. How could he explain the fact that his former ally, from whom he had expected support and with whom he shared political views that "had formerly so much the *same point of departure,* should now diverge so widely in our opinions of the measures which are proper to be pursued"? Two explanations existed. He either had badly mistaken Madison's original intentions, or Madison had now fallen under the pernicious spell of Jefferson, who had been absent during the springtime of their partnership but had since returned to break it apart. Not surprisingly, Hamilton gravitated toward the second possibility. Jefferson, the real leader of the faction opposed to him, had duped Madison, who "had always entertained an exalted opinion" of his neighbor's "talents, knowledge and virtues."[15]

Jefferson's unseemly involvement in a dubious endeavor with Philip Freneau, his political appointee, lent credence to Hamilton's theory. Like his inadvertent public condemnation of Adams's "Davila" essays, which exposed him to charges that his alleged desire for distinction led him to fracture the administration that he had sworn to serve, Hamilton viewed Jefferson's nearly simultaneous grant of a state department post to Freneau, a Republican newspaperman, as a case of unpardonable partisanship. It also provided ample justification for a flurry of anti-Jefferson opprobrium. If the first offense seemed merely improper, the second appeared corrupt and left Jefferson singularly exposed to criticism. Since November of 1791, when a correspondent of Hamilton's unfurled a plan to target Jefferson, there existed an itch among Federalists to attack their nemesis within the administration. Hamilton waited, however, until May 1792. By then, he had suffered not only from Jefferson's alienation of Madison, his former friend, but also from persistent abuse on the pages of the *National Gazette,* which Freneau edited. Enraged, bitter, and thoroughly convinced that Jefferson was the malevolent source of all his problems, Hamilton lashed back.[16]

In a letter to Edward Carrington that constituted his first extended critique of Jefferson's character, Hamilton drew up a list of charges that would color Jefferson's image throughout his long career. The Secretary of State had long evinced hostility toward the Constitution, Hamilton claimed; he was also an ambitious demagogue, servile to France and subversive to American government. He amounted to a "visionary" philosopher and an atheist, Hamilton added, and he beguiled his supporters with remarkable cunning and intentional deceit. Jefferson's most "ardent desire," Hamilton thought, was to win for himself "the Presidential Chair." His "true colors," Hamilton concluded, must "be told."[17]

Seizing upon Jefferson's support of Freneau as an issue through which to discredit his cabinet colleague, in August Hamilton unleashed a series of essays, soon reprinted throughout the nation, in John Fenno's *Gazette of the United States.* Reiterating the charges that he had first outlined to Carrington, they amounted to a torrent of animus and provided his allies with a vocabulary of anti-Jefferson opprobrium. By then his hostility toward Jefferson had turned into outright hatred. He had surmised that the Secretary of State, in a letter to the president, sharply criticized his financial system as foolhardy, corrupt, and monarchical. At the same time, however, that Hamilton worked to destroy Jefferson's reputation, he promoted Jefferson's image as the opposition's chief leader and unintentionally stimulated the development of a Republican press that would rush to Jefferson's defense.[18]

Compared to the vicious mudslinging of 1792, previous partisan newspaper skirmishes must have seemed restrained. The year brought new methods of attack as criticism of Jefferson became increasingly frequent and personal. Federalist newspapers, led by Fenno's *Gazette,* assailed the Secretary of State. He abused the powers of office, conspired against the Constitution, and undermined Washington's government, all the while deviously concealing his immoral ambitions as he kowtowed to the common man like a brazen sycophant. As they attempted to rekindle the old anxieties concerning corruption, interestedness, licentiousness, and demagoguery that had pushed Americans toward revolution fifteen years earlier, Jefferson's detractors employed the language of civic virtue in an attempt to discredit the Republicans and clear the pathway toward the consolidation of federal power.

Republicans, of course, did more than participate in this frenzied politicization of print; through their establishment of a party organ, they helped to precipitate it. More than a year before Hamilton's entrance as a polemicist into the anti-Jefferson crusade, the Secretary of State had joined with Madison in a search for a popular and decidedly Republican alternative to Fenno's influential journal. At first, Jefferson assisted Benjamin Franklin Bache in efforts to bolster the faltering *General Advertiser.* By the summer of 1791, however, the continued success of *Gazette of the United States* caused him to seek a more effective alternative.[19]

Alongside Madison, he approached Revolutionary War poet Philip Freneau with the notion of establishing a national newspaper. After some initial indecision, Freneau finally agreed to set up shop in the temporary capital of Philadelphia and to commence publication of the *National Gazette*. Believing that the monarchist threat loomed larger than ever, Jefferson provided Freneau not only with foreign intelligence and a State Department printing contract, but also lent his assistance in enlisting subscribers and—to help put the enterprise on firm financial footing—a $250–a–year job as the State Department's clerk for foreign languages.[20]

While Jefferson made no secret of his support for the *National Gazette*, the Treasury Secretary cloaked himself under various pseudonyms to assert that Jefferson's patronage of Freneau, as well as the contents of the paper, revealed his corrupt nature.[21] As Jefferson's partner in the venture, Madison did not escape censure. But because Hamilton failed in his efforts to find firm evidence of the congressional leader's involvement in the affair, only Jefferson could be charged with serious violations of the public trust. "The late northern papers are replete with the abuse of Mr. Jefferson as the patron of Freneau's gazette," Henry Lee informed Madison. "You are introduced without being directly named."[22]

Writing as "An American," in Fenno's paper Hamilton fumed that his cabinet rival had purchased Freneau's loyalty. The "connection . . . between the *editor of a newspaper* and the head of a department of government," he argued, "is *indelicate* and *unfit*." He labeled Jefferson as both a hypocrite and an influence peddler in the worst of British traditions. The Secretary of State acted as an American Walpole, he claimed, procuring Freneau's favors with the federal purse. Although he understood that Madison worked hand-in-hand with Jefferson to encourage the poet-turned-newspaperman, Hamilton could point to no similar financial relationship between Freneau and his former friend. Accepting his own theory that Madison merely acted as Jefferson's disciple and hoping, no doubt, to wound all of his Republican opponents, Hamilton for the first time publicly labeled Jefferson as "the head of a party." The *National Gazette* amounted to a party organ, printed by Jefferson's subordinate, and bolstered by funds that flowed from the federal treasury. Freneau was Jefferson's "faithful and devoted servant," Hamilton asserted, and "the whole complexion of his paper is an exact copy of the politics of his employer." John Quincy Adams agreed. Jefferson, he implied in a letter to his brother, was the "Great man," while Freneau eked out an existence as "his parasite."[23]

Hamilton did not stop after charging Jefferson with corruption; he contended that his opponent aimed to use his ill-gotten influence to subvert the government and malign its leaders. Hamilton claimed "that Mr. Jefferson was in the origin opposed to the present Constitution of the United States." Writing under the pseudonym "Catullus," Hamilton reiterated that the Secretary of State sought to undermine the Constitution, "which it is the evident object of the National Gazette to discredit." In addition, he charged that Jefferson sought to use the *Gazette* to criticize the president, whose position he coveted. The Secretary of State burned with "ambitious ardor to dislodge" Washington and assume the presidency himself, contended a pamphlet written anonymously by South Carolina congressman William Loughton Smith, a fervent Hamiltonian. If there lived any Americans not impressed by these accusations of corruption, anticonstitutionalism, and impropriety, Jefferson's alleged support of attacks on Washington, whom citizens had elevated to demigod status, must have raised their ire.[24]

The harangues portrayed Jefferson's support for the *National Gazette* not only as corrupt and contemptuous of President Washington and the Constitution, but also as atheistic. One autumn, 1792 attack by the Treasury Secretary on the faith of the former minister to France held that, in Freneau's paper, "the clergy of our country [are] vilified, and religion [is] constantly ridiculed." The Republican sheet "must afford a rich repair to Infidels and Free-thinkers." Here, as elsewhere, Hamilton cast widely his net of persuasion. He made the charge sufficiently vague so as to cultivate the concern of all Americans who considered themselves religious—no small number in the revolutionary republic, especially in New England, where he might expect to consolidate alliances with pious, commercially connected citizens.[25]

But the virulence of his critique reflected his anxiety about the Jeffersonians' expanding popularity, a phenomenon that several of his polemics implicitly addressed. One noted the "affected appeals" made by the opposition to the "great body of the yeomanry." Another hoped that Americans had "too much discernment to be dupes of hollow and ostentatious pretensions" and "that the citizens of the United States know how to distinguish the men who *serve* them, from those who merely *flatter* them."[26]

Despite his self-assured avowals that Americans would rebuff the Republicans, to read between the lines of his defensive essays is to discern the rise of Jefferson in the eyes of his countrymen, especially the upstarts, the industrious middling class of mechanics and farmers. By directing his entreaties at the mass of the population, moreover, Hamilton assisted in the gradual creation of more popular, more broadly based public discourse. At the very least, he conceded to it. A few years earlier, while penning "The Federalist" with John Jay and Madison, Hamilton had joined with his partners to write as "Publius," a pseudonym that suggested singular authorship. But now he assumed at least four personas—"T.L.," "Catullus," "An American," and "Metellus," and worked in concert with Congressman Smith, who, writing as "Scourge," constituted a fifth—in an apparent effort to conjure an appearance of consensus.[27] With elections for the House and Senate fast approaching, this strategy seemed both logical and necessary. It did not, however, yield sufficient results. The votes of 1792, Jefferson gloated, produced "a decided majority in favor of the republican interest."[28]

Unlike his cabinet rival, Jefferson refused to contribute substantively to the polemics of 1792. While Hamilton, on the Federalist side, and Republicans such as Madison, James Monroe, and Edmund Randolph authored pseudonymous polemics, the stage-shy Secretary of State held fast to his "resolution" to never "write in a public paper without subscribing my name, and to engage openly an adversary who does not let himself be seen." He claimed to be revolted by "the indecency" of open "squabbling between two public ministers." The allegations against him were false, he contended, "and can be proved so; and perhaps will be one day." But he insisted that the defense of his character rested in the hands of others and not his own.[29]

Even so, Jefferson's loud refusal to fire the rhetorical cannons of the Republican press did not prevent him from quietly supplying his compatriots with ammunition and encouragement. In October, for example, he provided Madison and Monroe with notes concerning a 1786 letter he had written to Jay, knowing that the information would prove useful in their production of newspaper essays rebutting Hamilton's aspersions.[30] These men also published excerpts from a number of other letters that Jefferson in the late 1780s had sent to Madison revealing, contrary to the Treasury Secretary's claims, his general support for ratification of the Constitution. In an unsigned note introducing these documents, Madison and Monroe insisted that Jefferson's permission to print them had "neither been asked nor attained." Similarly, Jefferson reported to Washington that "not a word" of the enterprise "had ever been communicated to me."[31] At best, these statements stretched the truth, for the trio kept in close contact during the entire episode, and Monroe, more than a week before Jefferson professed to the president his surprise on seeing his words in print, sent through Madison a packet of papers regarding the letters "to return" to their mutual friend.[32]

Jefferson's concern for what he viewed as the national welfare, which often coalesced with his attentive regard for his own reputation, also moved him to urge allies to take action. In 1793, for example, when Hamilton, writing as "Pacificus," called for the end of America's alliance with France, Jefferson asked Madison to retaliate. "For god's sake," he implored, "pick up your pen, select the most striking heresies, and cut him to pieces in the face of the public." Although he never, as he pointedly insisted, lifted his own pen for Freneau's paper, he aided Madison in such endeavors by circumnavigating his self-imposed rules, deleting words and phrases from the congressman's pieces prior to publication, and offering admission to his extensive library so that anti-Federalist articles might be fully grounded in republican texts.[33]

In this light, Jefferson's encouragement of the *National Gazette* can be viewed as a provision for self-defense by proxy. He maintained, of course, that his support for Freneau's paper stemmed merely from his early "desire of seeing a purely republican vehicle of news established between the seat of government and all it's [*sic*] parts"—from his insistence on a truthful reporting of events.[34] The *Gazette,* however, propagated republicanism and truth as he and his allies saw them. He recognized that, in their version of reality, he was not a villain to be purged but a victim to be assisted.

Jefferson's avowals of innocence in the newspaper war seem no less disingenuous than his critics claimed,[35] but they reflect nonetheless an earnest, if clumsy, attempt to adapt the traditional standards of civic virtue to the new dynamics of popular national politics. He sought to model his conduct after that of men such as Washington, the paragon of republicanism who contemporaries compared to Cincinnatus. Like the famed Roman patriot, the president had secured his reputation by answering his country's call to military service and then, with victory in the Revolution secured, by trading sword for plow and returning to Mount Vernon. Washington, moreover, accepted civilian posts with professions of reluctance, and only after he had received assurances that his nation could not succeed without him. In addition, he maintained a strict separation between his private finances and public duties. As a result, throughout his long career, Washington assiduously avoided giving the impression that he wished to promote either his political or personal fortunes.[36]

Jefferson's attempt to secure for himself a reputation for disinterested-ness proved less successful, if only because the position in which he found himself became more complicated. He viewed his struggle against Hamil-ton as a reprise of the Revolution, a war to defend American liberty against British-style corruption and monarchy. But it was a guerrilla confl-ict with ill-defined battle lines, and it took place largely behind the scenes of American government. He understood that what he viewed as patriotic service could be taken by others as interestedness and factionalism. To publicly defend himself—or to pseudonymously defend himself and risk being identified—might only provide his opponents with ammunition in their campaign to portray him as a self-promoter.[37] Given his sincere dis-like of controversy and conflict, moreover, the decision to entrust his rep-utation to Madison, Monroe, and other friends came naturally.

But it did not come without consequences, and these he must have understood. His continuing patronage of Freneau further entangled him in the partisan dispute, making him an easy target for Hamilton's vitriol. The *National Gazette*, like Jefferson, grew increasingly hostile to Washing-ton, thus confirming Hamilton's fears that the Secretary of State aimed to topple the government.[38] If, as Hamilton claimed, Jefferson wished to be brought forward as a major figure in American politics, he could only conclude that agitating the vociferous New Yorker, with whom he battled at cabinet meetings, would yield sure results.[39] Finally, his resolve to let others uphold his honor—to lavish him with praise, describe his talents, and testify to his virtue—in no small way galvanized Republican opinion leaders around the notion that he personified their movement.

There existed no shortage of writers willing to answer Hamilton's asper-sions against the Secretary of State. Although Republican polemicists made scant reference to Jefferson during the first eight months of 1792, by September his name appeared frequently on the pages of the *National Gazette* and like-minded journals, where essayists responded to the Trea-sury Secretary's election-season offensive. Even though he was not a can-didate for office, steadfast assurances of Jefferson's virtue, genius, and sturdy record of service dominated opposition newspapers. As a conse-quence, the five men nominated to challenge Adams for the vice-presi-dency—Madison among them—received little attention from writers as Jefferson became the most heralded member of his fledgling faction. "The attacks which your enemies in administration have made upon you," New York statesman Robert R. Livingston assured his embattled friend, "have excited the public attention and served to convince those who were not acquaintd [*sic*] with your character of your attachment to the Liberties of your country."[40]

If an image of Jefferson as corrupt, subversive, irreligious, and crafty coalesced in the minds of his adversaries, patrons of Republican publications viewed him differently. One *National Gazette* essay, appearing during the second week of September, ridiculed the Hamiltonians' "shamefully and glaringly false" charges and described the Secretary of State as an "illustrious Patriot, statesman, and Philosopher" who possessed "a virtuous and dignified conduct." Shortly thereafter, "A Republican" writing in the same paper claimed that the "reputation of Mr. *Jefferson* [is] too well known to need any panegyric, he having filled with honor, the most important public offices both at home and abroad."[41]

Far from being a subversive, Jefferson espoused the defense and expansion of American liberty, Republican newspaper writers claimed. The Hamiltonians—not Jefferson—were corrupt, hostile to the Constitution, jealous of the president, and motivated by mad ambition. They maligned the Secretary of State, one of his allies contended, for his refusal to "sacrifice his judgment, his character, his fidelity, his oath, to measures and views adopted by his colleagues." As a result, his oppositional stance within the administration revealed not vice but virtue, not political opportunism but steady attachment to principle. He displayed a commendable "independence of character," according to an essay in *Dunlap's American Daily Advertiser,* and held firm to the views "that he possessed before he commenced the career of public trust." Jefferson's patriotism thus surpassed that of his cabinet colleagues. As one penman remarked, "such an unfeigned and benevolent regard for mankind in all their classes; such an anxious solicitude for their welfare, and vigilant attention to their rights, are rarely to be found united in any one person." According to a writer who called himself "Justice," in Jefferson "we see a mind highly illuminated by the science of government, a heart warmly devoted to the liberty of mankind; and a dutiful life to his country, withal, that must kindle an affectionate sympathy in every disinterested breast." Put simply, he excelled as the steadfast champion of liberty and all who aspired to it.[42] His opposition to Hamiltonian finance revealed his support of freedom, not faction; the only interest that he advocated was that of the vast majority. "Mr. J[efferson] does not suppress his dislike of any measures of the government," opined another writer. "But does it follow that he is an enemy to the government? If it does, then nine-tenths of the people are enemies."[43]

The contention that Jefferson's views concurred with those held by the great mass of Americans, one of the Republicans' most cherished beliefs, proved tactically useful, for it allowed them to assert that their opposition reflected the majority view. Consequently, Jefferson rose in the eyes of his countrymen not so much as the head of a faction but as a popular leader. "On the republican side," claimed a *National Gazette* contributor, "the superiority of numbers is so great, their sentiments are so decided, and the practice of making a common cause . . . is so well understood, that no temperate observer of human affairs will be surprised" if Hamilton's policies "should be reversed, and the government be administered in the spirit and form approved by the great body of the people." Another essayist argued that Federalist attacks against Jefferson's reputation displayed the "desperation of the Aristocratic junto" at the erosion of its public support. By the end of October, the *Gazette* reported that "the publications against Mr. Jefferson . . . are more like the ravings of guilt in despair, than like the reasonings of a man in his sober senses."[44]

> Even so, Federalist barbs could not be taken lightly. To a large extent, the image of Jefferson and the image of the Republican movement had merged together. "If a person of his note . . . could be destroyed in the public confidence," wrote Madison and Monroe in the first of their newspaper essays, "the cause would be humbled, and the friends of monarchy would triumph. An attack, therefore, upon this gentleman, must be deemed a direct but artful one upon principles, and in this view it becomes a matter of public concern, and merits particular attention."[45]

Hamilton failed to discredit his nemesis. Instead, by focusing on Jefferson's conduct and character, he thrust him to the forefront of Americans' political consciousness. By September 1792, less than a month after the Secretary of the Treasury commenced his "American" essays, John Beckley noted that citizens regarded Jefferson "as the head of the republican party." Arch-Federalist Fisher Ames certainly did, bragging of his own "anti Jefferson principles," calling the chief Republican newspaper "Mr. Jefferson's Press," and criticizing the Secretary of State for "the *factions* he has originated." Jefferson's new status even found expression in a 1793 etching by an unknown New York artist. Entitled a "Peep into the Antifederal Club," it depicts Jefferson perched on a soapbox, surrounded by a dissolute gang of anarchists, Jacobins, and criminals, as well as a black-faced "Citizen Mungo" (exclaiming "Our turn nex"), and the Devil himself.

Wielding a gavel to bring order to the pandemonium, Jefferson declares his intention to "Contrive some means of knocking down a Government and in its ruins raise myself to Eminence."[46]

Like Hamilton's attempts to ruin Jefferson's image, his efforts to drive the Secretary of State from office backfired. Concern for his reputation convinced Jefferson to delay his plans to retire at the conclusion of Washington's first term. The Secretary of State's resignation was the aim of the Federalist press, as his friends pointed out and as he understood. "Retiring just when I had been attacked in the public papers, would injure me in the eyes of the public," Jefferson explained to his daughter. Americans "would suppose I either withdrew from investigation, or had not the tone of mind sufficient to meet slander." Avoiding these two potential suspicions proved difficult, and he admitted the correctness of the second. Jefferson, who confessed to Washington an urgent desire to surround himself with people friendly to his views and to himself, as a member of the cabinet had "to move always exactly in the circle which I know to bear me peculiar hatred." Nonetheless, he persevered, remaining in office until the final day of 1793.[47]

When Jefferson returned to his little mountain at the edge of the Blue Ridge, he resolved to remain there for good. "The length of my tether is now fixed for life between Monticello and Richmond," he confided to a friend. But the sentiments that his stormy tenure as Secretary of State had helped to stir conspired against his plans. So did the message that his retirement conveyed, the recognition that the Federalists, who cast him as an ambitious office-seeker, had been wrong.[48] As the partisan conflict continued, he became fixed in the minds of countless Americans as a disinterested friend of liberty.[49] Despite his desire to live out his days at Monticello, his supporters had another vision. Writing to Jefferson in 1793, merchant Stephen Cathalan conveyed the desire of more than a few Republicans: "I hope Some days or other, you will be Placed by the unanimous votes to the most eminent Post in the united States."[50]

Assuredly, such sympathies ran counter to what Alexander Hamilton and his allies had hoped their assaults would produce. Instead of pushing Jefferson to the margins of early national politics, alienating him from the mass of the people, they had thrust him center stage in a drama that Republican penmen relentlessly characterized as a struggle between aristocrats and republicans, between Hamiltonians who sought to consolidate power in the hands of the few and Jeffersonians who wanted to diffuse it among the many. Not all Americans believed the Secretary of State's defenders; Jefferson's enemies represented all classes, especially in New England, where Federalist currents ran strongest. But Republican rhetoric possessed great appeal for a large and growing number of middling citizens, who came to see Jefferson as his allies portrayed him. He stood as a martyr—a surrogate for his nation—who suffered at the hands of Hamiltonians so that liberty and equality, the two-pronged promise of the Revolution, might one day be more fully secured.[51] Madison, who in 1796 coordinated a drive to elect his friend president, admitted that, of all Republicans, "Jefferson alone" could "be started with hope of success."[52]

By the closing days of Jefferson's tenure as Secretary of State, his public persona, although not yet fully developed, had been defined. To be sure, friends and foes refined it over the course of subsequent years, which saw new foreign policy crises and fresh Federalist initiatives. These years also witnessed Jefferson, however reluctantly, return to the public arena, where allies such as Madison—and enemies such as Hamilton—added color and detail to his image.

NOTES

1. Jefferson to James Monroe, 20 May 1782, in Julian P. Boyd, ed., *The Papers of Thomas Jefferson* (31 vols. to date; Princeton, 1950–), 6: 186.

2. Dumas Malone, *Jefferson and His Time* (6 vols.; Boston, 1948–81), 1: 314–16, 319–22, 349–51, 353, 361–66, 394–96; Jefferson to Monroe, 20 May 1782, in Boyd, ed., *Papers of Jefferson*, 6: 184–85.

3. Jefferson to John Paradise, 5 July 1789, in Boyd, ed., *Papers of Jefferson*, 15: 242. See also Jefferson to Alexander Donald, 2 Feb. 1788, ibid., *Papers of Jefferson*, 12: 572.

4. James H. Read, "Alexander Hamilton's View of Thomas Jefferson's Ideology and Character," in this volume, p. 77–106.

5. Malone, *Jefferson and His Time*, 2: 292–94; Joseph J. Ellis, *Founding Brothers: The Revolutionary Generation* (New York, 2001), chap. 2.

6. Ellis, *Founding Brothers*; Noble E. Cunningham, Jr., *The Jeffersonian Republicans: The Formation of a Party Organization, 1789–1801* (Chapel Hill, N.C., 1957), 4–5; Jefferson, "The Real History of the Assumption" [Feb. 1793], in Paul Leicester Ford, ed., *The Writings of Thomas Jefferson* (10 vols.; New York, 1892–99), 6: 172–74; Herbert E. Sloan, *Principle and Interest: Thomas Jefferson and the Problem of Debt* (New York, 1995), 148–50.

7. Jefferson to Madison, 9 May 1791, in Boyd, ed., *Papers of Jefferson*, 20: 293; Jefferson to Jonathan B. Smith, 26 Apr. 1791, ibid., 20: 290. See editorial note, ibid., 20: 268–73.

8. Jefferson to Adams, 17 July 1791, ibid., 20: 302; Jefferson to Madison, 9 May 1791, ibid., 20: 293–94. For a deft discussion of Adams's insecurity and sensitivity, see Peter Shaw, *The Character of John Adams* (Chapel Hill, N.C., 1976), esp. 240–44.

9. "Publicola," as quoted in "Rights of Man: The 'Contest of Burke and Paine . . . in America'" [editorial note], in Boyd, ed., *Papers of Jefferson*, 20: 280–82. Most people at the time thought that Publicola's words had sprung from the pen of John Quincy Adams's father, the vice-president. For Paine's view on the alteration of constitutions, see Paine, *The Rights of Man*, Part I, in Bruce Kuklick, ed., *Thomas Paine: Political Writings* (New York, 1989), 83.

10. Jefferson to Edmund Randolph, 17 Sept. 1792, in Boyd, ed., *Papers of Jefferson*, 24: 387; Washington to Hamilton, 29 July and 6 Aug. 1792, in Harold C. Syrett, ed., *The Papers of Alexander Hamilton* (27 vols.; New York, 1961–87), 12: 129–34, 276–77; Washington to Jefferson, 23 Aug. 1792, in Boyd, ed., *Papers of Jefferson*, 24: 317.

11. Madison to Jefferson, 12 May 1791, in Boyd, ed., *Papers of Jefferson*, 20: 294. On the use of pseudonyms in political writing, see Michael Warner, *The Letters of the Republic: Publication and the Public Sphere in Eighteenth-Century America* (Cambridge, Mass., 1990), 42–43, 66, 84–85, 96, 113; Jay Fliegelman, *Declaring Independence: Jefferson, Natural Language, and the Culture of Performance* (Stanford, Calif., 1993), 104–6, 150–51, 160–61; and Robert M. S. McDonald, "Thomas Jefferson's Changing Reputation as Author of the Declaration of Independence: The First Fifty Years, 1776–1826," *Journal of the Early Republic* 19 (Summer 1999): esp. 171–77.

12. Oliver Wolcott Jr. to Oliver Wolcott Sr., 14 Feb. 1792, in George Gibbs, ed., *Memoirs of the Administrations of Washington and John Adams, Edited from the Papers of Oliver Wolcott, Secretary of the Treasury* (2 vols.; New York, 1846), 1: 73; Adams to Henry Knox, 19 June 1791, as cited in "Rights of Man: The 'Contest of Burke and Paine . . . in America'" [editorial note], in Boyd, ed., *Papers of Jefferson*, 20: 278; [William Loughton Smith], *The Politicks and Views of a Certain Party, Displayed* (n.p., 1792), 27–31; Adams, "Discourses on Davila," [1790], in Charles Francis Adams, ed., *The Works of John Adams, Second President of the United States* (10 vols.; Boston, 1856), 6: 232–34.

13. Jefferson to Thomas Mann Randolph, Jr., 3 July 1791, in Boyd, ed., *Papers of Jefferson*, 20: 296; Jefferson to Adams, 17 July 1791, ibid., 20: 302; Jefferson to Washington, 8 May 1791, ibid., 20: 291–92.

14. Madison to Jefferson, 12 May 1791, ibid., 20: 295; Nathaniel Hazard to Hamilton, 25 Nov. 1791, in Syrett, ed., *Papers of Hamilton*, 9: 534; Robert Troup to Hamilton, 15 June 1791, ibid., 8: 478.

15. Hamilton to Carrington, 26 May 1792, ibid., 11: 427–29, 431–32, 435, 437–38, 440. Hamilton also surmised that Jefferson had influenced Andrew Brown, printer of *The Federal Gazette* and *Philadelphia Daily Advertiser*, who "was originally a

zealous federalist and personally friendly to me" but whose paper now "was equally bitter and unfriendly to me & to the Government." See Syrett, ed., *Papers of Hamilton,* 431. The notion that Jefferson manipulated Madison was first suggested by Gouverneur Morris; see Morris to Hamilton, 24 Dec. 1792, ibid., 13: 377. William Loughton Smith, a close ally of the Treasury chief, agreed, and noted relative political harmony in America "previous to the arrival into this Country of a certain Personage from a foreign Country." Madison, who once "ardently" promoted a long list of "measures calculated to give Tone and Energy to the Government, and even gave conditional approval to a National Bank plan," now followed the dictates of Jefferson, "for whose political dogmas" he "entertains the most unbounded veneration" and "in whose political steps he is always proud to tread." See [Smith], *The Politics and Views of a Certain Party, Displayed,* 3, 25.

16. Hamilton to Carrington, 26 May 1792, in Syrett, ed., *Papers of Hamilton,* 11: 430–31, 435–36; Hazard to Hamilton, 25 Nov. 1791, ibid., 9: 533.

17. Hamilton to Carrington, 26 May 1792, ibid., 11: 429, 431, 437, 438, 439–41, 442, 444. For an astute analysis of this letter as a blueprint for all of Hamilton's subsequent attacks, see James Arthur Mumper, "The Jefferson Image in the Federalist Mind, 1801–1809: Jefferson's Administration from the Federalist Point of View" (Ph.D. diss., University of Virginia, 1966), esp. i–vii.

18. See Mumper, "The Jefferson Image," iv–v; and Stanley Elkins and Eric McKitrick, *The Age of Federalism* (New York, 1993), 288. For Jefferson's letter, see Jefferson to Washington, 23 May 1792, in Boyd, ed., *Papers of Jefferson,* 23: 535–40. For the text that suggested Jefferson's criticisms, see Washington to Hamilton, 29 July 1792, in Syrett, ed., *Papers of Hamilton,* 12: 129–34.

19. Jefferson to Benjamin Franklin Bache, 22 Apr. 1791, in Boyd, ed., *Papers of Jefferson,* 20: 246; Jefferson to William Short, 28 July 1791, ibid., 20: 692–93; Donald H. Stewart, *The Opposition Press of the Federalist Period* (Albany, N.Y., 1969), 7–9, 19; Michael Lienesch, "Thomas Jefferson and the Democratic Experience: The Origins of the Partisan Press, Popular Political Parties, and Public Opinion," in Peter S. Onuf, ed., *Jeffersonian Legacies* (Charlottesville, Va., 1993), 318–21.

20. *Jeffersonian Legacies,* ed. Onuf, 319–21; Jefferson to Thomas Bell, 16 Mar. 1792, in Boyd, ed., *Papers of Jefferson,* 20: 759; Jefferson to Thomas Mann Randolph, Jr., 20 Nov. 1791, ibid., 22: 310.

21. Madison took care to preserve his anonymity as well, not only before the public but also in the view of Fenno. In 1793, as he prepared to submit two essays (signed by "Helvidius") for possible publication in the *Gazette of the United States* that contradicted Hamilton's pronouncements on foreign policy, for example, he informed Jefferson that he hoped to arrange to have them "copied into another hand." In addition to confessing his intention of disguising, by means of a calligrapher, his penmanship, Madison offered implicit evidence that Hamilton, who would try but fail to document his belief that the congressman cooperated with Jefferson in the directing of Freneau's *National Gazette,* was essentially correct.

Such concealing measures, Madison implied, were extraordinary and would not be necessary for the submission of one of his pieces to another paper. The only other journal, of course, from which he solicited attention was the one edited by Freneau, who apparently possessed a level of familiarity with his handwriting that did not cause Madison to hesitate. See Madison to Jefferson, 3 Aug. 1793, in Boyd, ed., *Papers of Jefferson*, 26: 623, 623–24n.

22. Henry Lee to Madison, 10 Sept. 1792, in Hutchinson et al., eds., *Papers of Madison*, 14: 363. See also E. Randolph to Madison, 12 Aug. 1792, ibid., 14: 349; Hamilton to Jonathan Dayton, 13 Aug. 1792, in Syrett, ed., *Papers of Hamilton*, 12: 196; Dayton to Hamilton, 26 Aug. 1792, ibid., 12: 275.

23. [Hamilton], "An American," *Gazette of the United States* (hereafter *Gazette*), 11 Aug. 1792; [Hamilton], "An American," Gazette, 4 Aug. 1792; John Quincy Adams to Thomas Adams, 2 Sept. 1792, Adams Papers, Massachusetts Historical Society, microfilm reel 375. See also [Hamilton], "Catullus," *Gazette*, 15 Sept. 1792; [Hamilton], "T.L.," *Gazette*, 25 July 1792; [Hamilton?], "Detector," *Gazette*, 28 July 1792; [Hamilton], "T.L.," *Gazette*, 28 July 1792; [Hamilton], "T.L.," *Gazette*, 11 Aug. 1792. While Jefferson put Freneau on the federal payroll, the placement of public notices by Hamilton and Secretary of War Henry Knox on the pages of the *Gazette* resulted in considerable profit for Fenno, as Freneau emphatically pointed out. See the *National Gazette*, 28 July 1792; *National Gazette*, 15 Aug. 1792.

24. [Hamilton], "An American," *Gazette*, 11 Aug. 1792; [Hamilton], "Catullus," *Gazette*, 15 Sept. 1792; [Hamilton], "Catullus," *Gazette*, 19 Sept. 1792; [Smith], *The Politicks and Views of a Certain Party, Displayed*, 22. On the public's adoration of Washington during his presidency, see Barry Schwartz, *George Washington: The Making of An American Symbol* (New York, 1987), esp. 58–69, 74–80. On Smith's relationship with Hamilton, see George C. Rogers, Jr., *Evolution of a Federalist: William Loughton Smith of Charleston (1758–1812)* (Columbia, S.C., 1962), 194, 197, 219, 237–39, 241.

25. [Hamilton], "An American," *Gazette*, 22 Sept. 1792. Richard Buel astutely observes that the Federalists' use of religion as a political issue would constitute one of their few successful tactics in battles for common people's support; see Buel, *Securing the Revolution: Ideology in American Politics* (Ithaca, N.Y., 1972), 138, 169–75, 231–34.

26. [Hamilton], "An American," *Gazette*, 15 Sept. 1792; [Hamilton], "An American," *Gazette*, 22 Dec. 1792; [Hamilton], "An American," *Gazette*, 13 June 1792. Of the "affected appeals" that Hamilton had in mind, an essay by "Kibrothnataavah," in the *National Gazette*, 12 Sept. 1792, likely stood among them. "Tom Jefferson," this writer contended, "is a particular friend of the President." He was unlike the Federalists, "who say the people are not . . . fit to be trusted."

27. Hamilton's authorship as "T.L.," "Catullus," "An American," and "Metellus," is confirmed by the *Papers of Hamilton*, where the essays are conveniently printed. According to Philip Marsh ("Hamilton's Neglected Essays, 1791–1793," *New-York*

Historical Society Quarterly 32 [Oct. 1948]: 291–93), Hamilton also authored the attacks on Jefferson signed "Detector." Harold C. Syrett, however, casts doubt on this attribution; see Syrett, ed., *Papers of Hamilton*, 12: 123, 266. The Treasury Secretary's involvement in the production of the "Scourge" essay is suggested by the fact that a draft of the polemic, in the handwriting of W. L. Smith, has been found in Hamilton's papers at the Library of Congress; see Syrett, ed., *Papers of Hamilton*, 12: 411–12.

28. Jefferson to Thomas Pinckney, 3 Dec. 1793, in Boyd, ed., *Papers of Jefferson*, 24: 696. See also Cunningham, *The Jeffersonian Republicans*, 29–32, 49–50.

29. Malone, *Jefferson and His Time*, 2: 463, 469–70; Jefferson to Edmund Randolph, 17 Sept. 1792, in Boyd, ed., *Papers of Jefferson*, 24: 387. See also editorial note, ibid., 16: 247.

30. On Jefferson's provision of information to Madison and Monroe regarding his 26 Sept. 1786 letter to Jay, see "Enclosure: Observations on the French Debt" [ca. 17 Oct. 1792], in Boyd, ed., *Papers of Jefferson*, 24: 496–97. For the essays that employed information contained in the letter, see [Madison and Monroe], *Dunlap's American Daily Advertiser*, 11 Nov. 1792; ibid., 3 Dec. 1792, 31 Dec. 1792.

31. Ibid., 22 Sept. 1792; Jefferson to Washington, 17 Oct. 1792, in Boyd, ed., *Papers of Jefferson*, 24: 494. With Washington, Jefferson made a practice of understating the level of his political involvement. Several months later, he told the president that he kept himself "aloof from all cabal and correspondence on the subject of the government." See "Notes of a Conversation with George Washington," 7 Feb. 1793; ibid., 25: 154.

32. Monroe to Madison, 9 Oct. 1792, in Hutchinson et al., eds., *Papers of Madison*, 14: 379. On the Secretary of State's knowledge of Madison and Monroe's essays, see "Jefferson, Freneau, and the Founding of the National Gazette" [editorial note], in Boyd, ed., *Papers of Jefferson*, 20: 725. Excerpts from Jefferson's letters to Madison (20 Dec. 1787, 3 May 1788, 31 July 1788, 18 Nov. 1788, 15 Aug. 1788, and 28 Aug. 1789), appeared after brief, unsigned essays by Madison and Monroe in *Dunlap's American Daily Advertiser*; see ibid., 22 Sept. 1792, 10 Oct. 1792, 20 Oct. 1792, 30 Oct. 1792, 8 Nov. 1792, 3 Dec. 1792, 31 Dec. 1792.

33. Jefferson to Madison, 7 July 1793, in Hutchinson et al., eds., *Papers of Madison*, 15: 43; Madison to Jefferson, 11 Aug. 1793, in Boyd, ed., *Papers of Jefferson*, 26: 655; Madison to Jefferson, 30 Aug. 1793, ibid., 26: 729; Jefferson to Madison, 13 Mar. 1791, in Hutchinson et al., eds., *Papers of Madison*, 13: 405. See also Jefferson to Madison, 21 Sept. 1795, ibid., 16: 88–89. Hamilton's friend Smith, in fact, suspected that Jefferson had been instrumental in the productions of Republicans' essays. "Most of them," he said, were "written either by our Hero [Jefferson] or under his influence." See [Smith], *The Politicks and Views of a Certain Party, Displayed*, 31.

34. Jefferson to Bache, 22 Apr. 1791, in Boyd, ed., *Papers of Jefferson*, 20: 246; Jefferson, "Notes of a Conversation with George Washington," 23 May 1793, ibid., 26: 102. Jefferson's also testified to his faith in the veracity of the *National Gazette*

when he wrote to a friend that "I need not write you news, since you receive Freneau's paper." See Jefferson to Dr. George Gilmer, 11 May 1792, ibid., 23: 492.

35. Writing as "Scourge," W. L. Smith informed newspaper readers that, while Jefferson seemed "cautious and shy, wrapped up in impenetrable silence and mystery, . . . he reserves his abhorrence [of Federalists] for the arcana of a certain snug sanctuary, where seated on his pivot-chair, [he is] . . . involved in all the obscurity of political mystery and deception." See [Smith] "Scourge," *Gazette of the United States*, 22 Sept. 1792. See also [Smith], *The Politicks and Views of a Certain Party, Displayed*, 32–33.

36. See Glenn A. Phelps, *George Washington and American Constitutionalism* (Lawrence, Kans., 1993), 12–14, 60–62, 74–75, 90, 94–95, 102, 110, 116–17, 123, 144, 148, 180, 191–92; Schwartz, *George Washington*, 119–48, 202–03; Garry Wills, *Cincinnatus: George Washington and the Enlightenment* (Garden City, N.Y., 1984), 4–5, 87–89, 151–53, 228; and Gordon S. Wood, "Interests and Disinterestedness in the Making of the Constitution," in Richard Beeman, Stephen Botein, and Edward C. Carter II, eds., *Beyond Confederation: Origins of the Constitution and American National Identity* (Chapel Hill, N.C., 1987), 90–91.

37. For a more elaborate elucidation of the rules of political combat, see Joanne B. Freeman, "Slander, Poison, Whispers, and Fame: Jefferson's 'Anas' and Political Gossip in the Early Republic," *Journal of the Early Republic* 15 (Spring 1995): 25–57, esp. 37.

38. Elkins and McKitrick, *The Age of Federalism*, esp. 360–61. For Jefferson's doubts about Washington's capacity as a leader, see Jefferson to Madison, [13 May 1793], in Boyd, ed., *Papers of Jefferson*, 26: 26.

39. The Secretary of State and his allies, according to John Beckley, understood "the attack on Mr. Jefferson . . . as the weak, insidious & contemptible efforts of Mr. Hamilton himself." See Beckley to Madison, 10 Sept. 1792, in Hutchinson et al., eds., *Papers of Madison*, 14: 361.

40. Robert R. Livingston to Jefferson [Feb.–Mar. 1793], in Boyd, ed., *Papers of Jefferson*, 25: 304.

41. Unsigned essay, *National Gazette* (Philadelphia), 8 Sept. 1792; "A Republican," *National Gazette*, 19 Sept. 1792. See also [Edmund Randolph] "Aristides," *National Gazette*, 26 Sept. 1792.

42. Unsigned essay, *National Gazette*, 8 Sept. 1792; "Columbus," from the *New York Journal*, in *National Gazette*, 10 Oct. 1792; [Madison and Monroe], from *Daily Advertiser*, in *National Gazette*, 13 Oct. 1792; "Justice," ibid., 24 Oct. 1792.

43. Unsigned essay, from *Dunlap's American Daily Advertiser*, in *National Gazette*, 26 Sept. 1792; ibid., 8 Sept. 1792.

44. Unsigned essay, *National Gazette*, 26 Sept. 1792; "Z.," *National Gazette*, 3 Oct. 1792; "Camillus," *National Gazette*, 24 Oct. 1792. See also [E. Randolph], "Aristides," *National Gazette*, 26 Sept. 1792.

45. [Madison and Monroe], *Dunlap's American Daily Advertiser*, 22 Sept. 1792.

46. Beckley to Madison, 2 Sept. 1792, in Hutchinson et al., eds., *Papers of Madison,* 14: 355; Fisher Ames to John Lowell, 6 Dec. 1792, in W. B. Allen, ed., *Works of Fisher Ames, as Published by Seth Ames* (2 vols.; Indianapolis, 1983), 2: 955; Ames to Aristides, [probably 1793], ibid., 2: 967, 973. Although Jefferson is not positively identified in the etching, which is dated 16 Aug. 1793 and sold for fifty cents, John Catanzariti notes that the "figure . . . dominating the group bears a strong resemblance to Jefferson, whom the artist could have met or seen when the Republican leader was serving as Secretary of State in New York City in 1790." Noble Cunningham, however, leaves open the possibility that the artist meant to portray Aaron Burr as the "Antifederal Club" leader. See "A Peep into the Antifederal Club," in Boyd, ed., *Papers of Jefferson,* 26: xliii; James C. Kelly and B. S. Lovell, comps., "Thomas Jefferson: His Friends and Foes," *Virginia Magazine of History and Biography* 101 (Jan. 1993): 144–45. (The etching is in the possession of the Historical Society of Pennsylvania.)

47. Jefferson to Martha Jefferson Randolph, 26 Jan. 1793, in Boyd, ed., *Papers of Jefferson,* 25: 97–98; Jefferson, "Notes of a Conversation with George Washington," 6 Aug. 1793; ibid., 26: 628. For earlier affirmations of his plan to retire, see Jefferson to Thomas Pinckney, 8 Nov. 1792, ibid., 24: 596; Jefferson to John Syme, 17 Sept. 1792, ibid., 24: 398; Jefferson to David Rittenhouse, 7 Jan. 1793, ibid., 25: 31. For a call for Jefferson's resignation, see [Hamilton], "Metellus," *Gazette,* 24 Oct. 1792. Although concern for his reputation was motivation enough for Jefferson to delay his retirement, the opportunity to quietly agitate for congressional censure of Hamilton provided him with an added incentive. See Eugene R. Sheridan, "Thomas Jefferson and the Giles Resolutions," *William and Mary Quarterly* 49 (Oct. 1992): 589–608. So may have Jefferson's realization that, as a member of the cabinet, as Livingston implored, no one else could provide a "better check . . . on the encroachments of administration." See Livingston to Jefferson [Feb.–Mar. 1793], in Boyd, ed., *Papers of Jefferson,* 25: 304.

48. Fewer than three years later, a pamphleteer noted that "Mr. Jefferson cannot be denominated an ambitious character; he retired from public grandeur into the vale of obscurity, with that tranquility and complacence of mind which ever characterizes true greatness. Like our beloved President or the renowned Cincinnatus, he knows how to support the burden of high office with dignity, or to resign it without a sign." See *President II, Being Observations on the Late Official Address of George Washington: Designed to Promote the Interest of a Certain Candidate for the Executive, and to Explode the Pretensions of Others* ([Newark], 1796), 15–16. Jefferson understood that his plan for retirement immunized him to charges for interestedness. Informing Washington that he would soon step down, Jefferson sought to convince the president that the post office, rich in its potential for corrupt patronage, should be transferred from the administration of the Treasury to the Department of State. Hamilton's retirement was nowhere in sight, he averred, because his finance program "embraced years in its view." See Forrest

McDonald, *Alexander Hamilton: A Biography* (New York, 1979), 242; Jefferson, "Memoranda of Conversations with the President," 1 Mar. 1792, in Boyd, ed., *Papers of Jefferson,* 23: 184. On first hearing of the Secretary of State's plans to step down, Oliver Wolcott reacted with skepticism: "Time will show whether this is a trick to gain a few compliments." See Wolcott Jr. to Wolcott Sr., 27 Jan. 1792, in Gibbs., ed., *Memoirs of the Administrations of Washington and John Adams,* 1: 86. Even after Jefferson's departure from Philadelphia, John Adams viewed Jefferson's resignation as evidence for—and not cause for absolution from—accusations of high ambition. It probably constituted a stunt, he told his son. "Jefferson thinks he shall by this step get a Reputation of a humble, modest, meek Man, wholly without ambition or Vanity," Adams averred. "But if a Prospect opens, The World will see and he will feel, that he is as ambitious as Oliver Cromwell. . . . And if Jefferson after the Death or Resignation of the President should be summoned," he would certainly serve as chief executive. See Adams to John Quincy Adams, 3 Jan. [1794], Adams Papers, Massachusetts Historical Society, microfilm reel 377.

49. North Carolina congressman William Barry Grove, for example, whose political sentiments would soon gravitate toward those of the Federalists, called Jefferson's retirement a "Melancholy thing" because few men could match his "Virtue, Knowledge,—Republicanism, or Rational Liberty & Equality." See Grove to James Hogg, 3 Apr. 1794, William Barry Grove Papers, Southern Historical Collection, University of North Carolina Library. See also Stewart, *The Opposition Press of the Federalist Period,* 45.

50. Jefferson to Horatio Gates, 3 Feb. 1794, in Malone, *Jefferson and His Time,* 3: 168 (quotation); Stephen Cathalan Jr., to Jefferson, 27 Feb. 1793, in Boyd, ed., *Papers of Jefferson,* 25: 278.

51. Jefferson, who possessed a similar view of himself, later recalled that as Secretary of State he "descend[ed] daily into the arena like a gladiator to suffer martyrdom in every conflict." See Jefferson to Madison, 22 Jan. 1797, in Hutchinson et al., eds., *Papers of Madison,* 16: 473.

52. Madison to Monroe, 26 Feb. 1796, ibid., 16: 232.

CHAPTER 4

Alexander Hamilton's View of Thomas Jefferson's Ideology and Character

JAMES H. READ

> Among the letters I receive . . . preferring Burr to Jefferson I observe no small exaggeration to the prejudice of the latter. . . . To my mind a true estimate of Mr. J's character warrants the expectation of a temporizing rather than a violent system. That Jefferson has manifested a culpable predilection for France is certainly true; but I think it a question whether it did not proceed quite as much from her *popularity* among us, as from sentiment, and in proportion as that popularity is diminished his zeal will cool. Add to this that there is no fair reason to suppose him capable of being corrupted, which is a security that he will not go beyond certain limits.
>
> —Alexander Hamilton to James A. Bayard,
> January 16, 1801

> Hamilton was not only a monarchist, but for a monarchy bottomed on corruption.
>
> —Thomas Jefferson, from the *Anas* (1818)

*T*HIS chapter seeks to describe the relation between Alexander Hamilton and Thomas Jefferson from Hamilton's point of view; and to contrast Hamilton's with Jefferson's perceptions of what was at stake in the long-running political and personal conflict between the two men (which

began sometime in 1791 and lasted at least until Hamilton's death in 1804).
For Jefferson, Hamilton was not so much an individual as an archetype of
monarchism and corruption; and what was at stake in the conflict with
Hamilton was nothing less than the survival of republicanism. For Hamilton, Jefferson always remained recognizably an individual, with his own
peculiar blend of virtues and flaws. Moreover, Hamilton's view of Jefferson's
politics was never as extreme as Jefferson's view of Hamilton's politics. Jefferson accused Hamilton of deliberately aiming to subvert the Constitution
in the interests of a foreign power (England). Hamilton—while he disagreed with Jefferson's constitutional ideas—did not question Jefferson's
basic loyalty to the Constitution and recognized that Jefferson's enthusiasm
for revolutionary France was limited by his commitment to upholding
American sovereignty.

What infuriated Hamilton about Jefferson was not his political principles but the real or perceived *personal* injuries Jefferson had inflicted on
Hamilton's career and reputation; and his judgment that Jefferson was a
"contemptible hypocrite"[1] who disguised his own great, though legitimate,
political ambitions. Furthermore, the rhythm and timing of the conflicts
between the two men was not synchronized. For Jefferson, the greater the
issue at stake, the more he feared and suspected Hamilton; Hamilton's
central public policies (funding, assumption, the Bank) were, from Jefferson's perspective, the proof of his subversive intent. In contrast, Hamilton's view of Jefferson was most balanced and detached when great public
issues were at stake, such as policy toward France in 1793 and the 1801 crisis over the Jefferson-Burr election standoff; it was most jaundiced and
vitriolic when there was least at stake publicly (e.g., Jefferson's employment of Philip Freneau as a translator for the State Department). Hamilton had strong principled disagreements with Jefferson — over
constitutional interpretation, international law and treaty obligations, the
proper role of government, to name a few.[2] But at least from Hamilton's
side, it was not these marked differences of political outlook that drove the
battle with Jefferson. It was rather Hamilton's perception of Jefferson's
devious and mischievous character, and what he had done to harm
Hamilton personally, that got Hamilton's blood boiling. But because Jefferson's chief offenses (in Hamilton's view) were personal, Hamilton could
play the part of the man who magnanimously puts aside personal considerations in the interest of the public, as in the 1801 election crisis.

In short, the struggle between Alexander Hamilton and Thomas Jefferson was neither parallel nor symmetrical. It was an argument in which the

participants could not agree on what the argument was about. While the contest between Jefferson and Hamilton may indeed have become a "Plutarchian struggle"[3] in American historical memory, the original protagonists do not seem to have agreed on the story line.

The argument of this essay does not necessarily contradict the thesis of Robert McDonald's essay "The Hamiltonian Invention of Thomas Jefferson" elsewhere in this volume. McDonald argues that Hamilton's public attacks on Jefferson as "the head of a party" helped raise Jefferson's stature as a national leader and unintentionally stimulated the development of a Republican press ready to defend Jefferson. The *tone* of Hamilton's public attacks on Jefferson was quite extreme, even when the actual accusations (presidential ambition, leading an opposition party) were less serious than Jefferson's accusations against Hamilton. Hamilton's public jabs at Jefferson may very well have backfired in the way McDonald describes. Moreover, Hamilton's attacks may have encouraged in other Federalists a view of Jefferson more extreme than Hamilton's own view. Thus Hamilton may have borne some responsibility for the demonized view of Jefferson that he sought to moderate during the crisis over the 1800 Electoral College tie.

There are excellent studies of Jefferson's opposition to Hamilton and Hamilton's system.[4] There are (to my knowledge) no comparable studies of Hamilton's opposition to Jefferson. It is perhaps natural that this should be the case. One cannot begin to understand Jefferson's politics of the 1790s, and the ideology of the Jeffersonian Republican opposition, without taking into account Jefferson's fears of the corrupting influence of Hamilton's financial system and his sincere belief that Hamilton sought to overthrow republicanism. Most of Hamilton's conflicts with Jefferson, in contrast, are not central to an understanding of Hamilton, in part because Hamilton's financial system—the "Hamiltonian Persuasion," so to speak —was largely complete before the battle with Jefferson began. Their exchange over the constitutionality of the Bank of the United States, which is indeed central to understanding Hamilton's thought, came early in the Hamilton-Jefferson antagonism, before it became heated and personal. Much of what comes later in the Hamilton-Jefferson conflict does not show Hamilton at his best.[5] Yet a full survey of the relationship, from Hamilton's perspective, reveals fascinating and unexpected insights into Hamilton himself and the political alignments of the period. It also provides a useful, if slanted, perspective on Jefferson.

The method employed in this reappraisal of the Hamilton-Jefferson relation is rather simple. It consisted of looking up every indexed reference to Jefferson in the *Papers of Alexander Hamilton.* In addition, I consulted some key writings of Jefferson on Hamilton, though I made no attempt here to be exhaustive. While the indexed references to Jefferson in the Hamilton papers probably miss many instances where Hamilton had Jefferson in mind without naming him, the picture that emerges from the indexed references is very rich and diverse. It also yields some surprising results. For example, one might have expected to find that divisions over the French Revolution and over U.S. relations with France had significantly inflamed the antagonism between Hamilton and Jefferson. In fact the opposite seems to have been the case: the 1793 crisis over how to deal with the French minister Edmund Genet actually seems to have improved Hamilton-Jefferson relations, at least from Hamilton's side.

Another interesting fact revealed by the documents examined here is that the contrast Hamilton draws between Jefferson and Aaron Burr during the 1800–1801 election crisis was already explicitly developed in his mind as early as 1792, at the height of his conflict with Jefferson. In 1792 the contrast between Jefferson and Burr arises in Hamilton's mind as part of his response to the accusation of monarchism. Hamilton replies that, in effect, Burr *truly* is the kind of danger to republicanism that Jefferson *falsely* accuses Hamilton of being.

Ultimately, in relatively detached moments, Hamilton judges that Jefferson is the kind of leader one must expect in a popular government, one who responds to popularity and political interest in a manner that, if not exactly admirable, is at least functional and even valuable in certain respects. The irony is that Hamilton's penchant for premising political behavior on the pushes and pulls of interest, a perspective that shocked and offended Jefferson, is exactly what enables Hamilton to come to terms with Jefferson—who, Hamilton says, "is not zealot enough to do anything in pursuance of his principles which will contravene his popularity, or his interest."[6]

The essay begins with a chronological overview of the Hamilton-Jefferson relation from Hamilton's perspective. One of the purposes of the overview is to demonstrate that Hamilton's animosity toward Jefferson was greatest when there was most at stake personally and least at stake publicly; and that Hamilton's view of Jefferson became more balanced when urgent public issues were at hand. The remainder of the essay consists of an exploration of themes and problems arising from a comparison of the two periods of time when Hamilton was most preoccupied with Jefferson: 1792 to early 1793, when he responded privately and publicly to

Jefferson's attacks on his policy and integrity; and late 1800 to early 1801, when Hamilton took up a personal crusade to convince Federalists to support Jefferson over Aaron Burr in resolving the Electoral College tie. The comparison takes as its starting point Hamilton's famous January 16, 1801, letter to James A. Bayard of Delaware. Themes to be discussed include Hamilton's view of Jefferson's constitutional thought, his view of Jefferson's "temporizing" political character, Jefferson's personal character, and the personal harm Jefferson (in Hamilton's view) had done to Hamilton over the years. The comparison will show that almost everything Hamilton says about Jefferson—and also about Burr—in 1801 had its roots in the fierce 1792 battle between Hamilton and Jefferson. The essay concludes by demonstrating the degree to which the long-running conflict between Hamilton and Jefferson was asymmetrical and nonparallel: they did not agree on what their disagreements were about.

Overview 1790–1804

References to Jefferson are extremely sparse in the first five volumes of the *Papers of Alexander Hamilton,* which cover the years up to 1789. Hamilton, as Washington's aide-de-camp, drafted wartime correspondence to Jefferson when the latter was governor of Virginia;[7] if Hamilton formed any opinion of Jefferson in the process, we cannot know what it was. (An interesting detail: Jefferson's copy of the *Federalist Papers* reached him in Europe via Angelica Church, Hamilton's sister-in-law, who received it from Elizabeth Hamilton.)[8] Hamilton later shows close acquaintance with Jefferson's *Notes on the State of Virginia* and with some key letters Jefferson wrote from France, but whether he began reading Jefferson's writings before or after they joined Washington's cabinet is not clear.

Quantitatively, the highest concentration of references to Jefferson in Hamilton's Papers fall, unsurprisingly, between March 1790, when Jefferson began his duties as Washington's Secretary of State, and December 1793, when Jefferson resigned from that office. But the nature of the references varies widely across that period. Simplifying somewhat, we could speak first of a period of polite if distant cooperation, which, from Hamilton's side, seems to have lasted until sometime in late spring 1791. While much of their correspondence and meetings during this period involve routine or unavoidable cabinet business, there are some substantive and apparently spontaneous exchanges of ideas and views. They worked together on plans for establishing a mint and exchanged ideas—though they ultimately disagreed—on whether to fix monetary units to precise units of weight.[9] They exchanged documents and occasionally commented upon one another's drafts.[10] Hamilton, for example, closely read Jefferson's "Report on Fisheries" and later drew from it in his own "Report on Manufactures."[11] Frank discussions of views at social occasions, about which we know principally through Jefferson's record, demonstrate great differences of political views between Hamilton and Jefferson, but also indicate—at least from Hamilton's side—a level of trust incompatible with any outright political or personal warfare.[12] It was during this period (June 1790) that Hamilton and Jefferson reached an agreement to trade assumption of state debts for locating the Capitol on the Potomac, though Jefferson later bitterly regretted that he had unwittingly lent support to Hamilton's program.[13] Most likely, Hamilton was aware from the beginning that Jefferson's political and constitutional views differed widely from his own, but for this very reason Hamilton could not feel surprised or betrayed by Jefferson's opposition. (Hamilton was surprised by Madison's opposition to his policies.) Even Hamilton's and Jefferson's famously opposed opinions on the constitutionality of a national bank[14] (February 1791) do not yet constitute a personal or political battle: cooperation on the mint and a substantive exchange of views on the status of the debt to France continues at least through April 1791.[15] Their differences over the constitutionality of a bank appear, in retrospect, to be the first shot of a long war. But the differences between Jefferson's strict and Hamilton's expansive construction of the Constitution do not by themselves account for the political and personal antagonisms that follow.

The second phase of the cabinet years can only be described as a phase of bitter political and personal battle between Jefferson and Hamilton. It commences, on Hamilton's side, sometime in mid-to-late 1791[16] (probably beginning earlier on Jefferson's side) and is at fever pitch throughout 1792 and into the early part of 1793. At the center of the storm was Jefferson's contention, which he communicated directly to Washington, that Hamilton was the leader of a "corrupt squadron, deciding the voice of the legislature" whose "ultimate object . . . is to prepare the way for a change, from the present republican form of government, to that of a monarch, of which the English constitution is to be the model."[17] Hamilton responded directly to Washington, defending his policies and denying the monarchism charge, and he began a public counterattack on Jefferson under a series of pseudonyms ("An American," "Metellus," "Catullus"). Hamilton's counterattack focuses on Jefferson's sponsorship of Philip Freneau, editor of the oppositionist *National Gazette,* whom Jefferson employed as a translator for the State Department; Jefferson's original reservations about the Constitution; and Jefferson's supposed willingness to violate the rights of public creditors. (Hamilton's "Metellus" and "Catullus" essays are discussed below.)

The conflict of 1791–93 in some sense endures to the end of both Hamilton's and Jefferson's lives—it is always under the surface, whatever the immediate issue. However, at least for Hamilton, a new and more moderate disposition toward Jefferson begins, ironically, with the partisan divisions over the French Revolution, the status of the treaty with France, and the conduct of French minister Edmund Genet, who arrived in April 1793. The immediate consequence of Washington's need to clarify the treaty obligations of the United States toward France was to force Hamilton and Jefferson back into principled debate and exchange of letters, drafts, and documents.[18] Jefferson and Hamilton differed over the obligations of the United States toward France under the 1778 Treaty of Amity and Commerce: Jefferson maintained that the treaty was with the French people, for whom Louis XVI was merely the agent, and thus still in force under the Revolutionary regime; Hamilton argued that the treaty's obligations were unclear with the change of regime, and that it should be "temporarily and provisionally suspended" to avoid war with England.[19] Hamilton replies at length—including in his "Pacificus" essays—to Jefferson's interpretation of the treaty, but his response treats Jefferson's position seriously and (at least compared with 1792's "Catullus" and "Metellus") is free from personal attacks.[20] Even more significant is Hamilton's disposition toward Jefferson during the Genet episode and its aftermath. Genet began fitting out privateers in American ports to attack British shipping, which Jefferson and Hamilton agreed was a violation of U.S. sovereignty; confronted with Washington's opposition to his conduct, he told Jefferson—from whom he apparently expected a sympathetic response—that he would go over Washington's head and appeal directly to the American people.[21] Given Washington's popularity and Jefferson's initial complicity in encouraging Genet, or at least not sufficiently restraining him, Hamilton could conceivably have exploited the situation and renewed the battle with Jefferson when Jefferson was most vulnerable. Instead, Hamilton—at least publicly—gave Jefferson credit for acting correctly, if belatedly, in the Genet episode.[22] It was Jefferson who wrote the August 16, 1793, letter to Gouverneur Morris, minister to France (a draft of which Hamilton reviewed) insisting upon Genet's recall.[23] In his subsequent "No Jacobin" public essays, which attack Genet, Hamilton specifically enlisted Jefferson against Genet: "What answer does the Secretary of State on behalf of the President give to [Genet's] inquiry? One certainly the reverse of confirming what Mr. Genet endeavors to have believed."[24] By implication, at least, Jefferson was likewise "No Jacobin" when, to have charged him with being one might have done most damage. Hamilton's correspondent Robert Troup, who had warned him in mid-1791 to watch out for Jefferson and Madison, wrote that "Jefferson's letter to Gouverneur Morris has blotted all the sins of the former out of the book of our remembrance."[25]

After mid-1794 Hamilton's references to Jefferson became far less frequent and remained at a fairly low level until 1800. While Hamilton probably thought and spoke privately, about Jefferson, on the available evidence he seems not to have been preoccupied with Jefferson through most of the 1790s.

Jefferson turned up as a kind of ironic authority in 1795 in Hamilton's public defense of the Jay Treaty. Jefferson, as an opponent of the Jay Treaty, may have been one of Hamilton's implicit targets. Yet Hamilton used Jefferson's interpretation of the Law of Nations, as expressed in his July 24, 1793, letter to Genet, as a legitimizing precedent for Jay's diplomacy.[26] The previous year, Hamilton had already suggested Jefferson as a possible minister to France to succeed Gouverneur Morris—a recommendation he was to renew in 1797.[27] (By way of comparison, Jefferson reacted with alarm to the rumor that Hamilton might be considered as special envoy to England: "A more degrading measure could not have been proposed" with the object of "placing the aristocracy of this country under the patronage of that government.")[28]

There is an expected increase in references during the 1796 election season, but most of these concern Federalist election strategy. Though Hamilton maintained that "every thing must give way to the great object of excluding Jefferson" from the Presidency, he actually said very little about Jefferson directly.[29]

One of the most peculiar of Hamilton's references to Jefferson occurs in the 1797 pamphlet describing the true nature of his connection with Maria Reynolds, and refuting charges of public corruption. The Reynolds pamphlet opens with what is probably Hamilton's most extreme denunciation of "Jacobinism." "The spirit of jacobinism," Hamilton wrote, "has been cloathed with a more gigantic body and armed with more powerful weapons than it ever before possessed. . . . Its progress may be marked with calamities of which the dreadful incidents of the French Revolution afford a very faint image. . . . It seems to threaten the political and moral world with a complete overthrow. A principal engine, by which this spirit endeavors to accomplish its purposes is that of calumny."[30] These "dreadful incidents," beside which the terror in revolutionary France pales in comparison, are of course the slanders directed against Hamilton himself, in misrepresenting as public misconduct what was in fact a sordid sexual affair. Jefferson, whom Hamilton did not accuse of Jacobinism during the Genet crisis, is here, by implication, included in the vast Jacobin horde. Jefferson's crime in the Reynolds affair seems to have been that he sent "friendly letters" to Andrew Fraunces, a former Treasury Department clerk who had passed information to Hamilton's enemies. Hamilton included two letters from Jefferson to Fraunces as appendices to the Reynolds pamphlet—letters that seem no more than polite refusals of assistance.[31]

The extreme denunciation of "Jacobinism" and the gratuitous slap at Jefferson in the Reynolds pamphlet are even more puzzling given that at roughly the same time Hamilton was recommending that Jefferson be one of the special commissioners to France; and that later, during the Jefferson-Burr standoff, Hamilton would argue at length against the predominant Federalist image of Jefferson as a dangerous Jacobin. The Reynolds pamphlet, like the Metellus and Catullus pamphlets of 1792, indicated that it was real or perceived private injuries that, from Hamilton's side, drove the battle with Jefferson; and that significant public issues had the effect of moderating his animosity toward Jefferson.

Hamilton was extremely alarmed by the Virginia and Kentucky Resolutions of 1798, fearing that they signify "a regular conspiracy to overturn the government," "to destroy the Constitution of the Ustates," and to "disunite the people of America." However, it is not clear what he knew or believed about Jefferson's role in the Virginia and Kentucky proceedings. Hamilton was convinced that "the people of Virginia" and even "the greater part of those who may have concurred in the legislature" remained loyal to the Constitution and the union, as opposed to a handful of "Chiefs" who directly intended to destroy the Constitution and dissolve the union.[32] He did not name Jefferson as one of these "chiefs," and it is impossible to tell whether he considered Jefferson a dangerous subversive at this moment in time. If he did (which is unlikely, given his subsequent support of Jefferson over Burr), he would only have held this view of Jefferson for a short time, during the height of the crisis.

There is an expected increase in references to Jefferson during the 1800 campaign, but again, as in 1796, most of these concern Federalist election strategy, especially Hamilton's insistence that Charles Cotesworth Pinckney, not John Adams, be the Federalist candidate to oppose Jefferson.[33] Hamilton spent far more time and political influence during the 1800 campaign exposing the shortcomings of John Adams than in denouncing Jefferson.[34] Indeed, despite one spirited denunciation of Jefferson as "an *Atheist* in Religion and a *Fanatic* in politics,"[35] it is difficult to avoid concluding, along with several Federalists of the time, that Hamilton considered reelection of Adams a greater misfortune than electing Jefferson.[36]

Hamilton's fullest and most balanced assessment of Jefferson came during the crisis in early 1801 over the Jefferson-Burr tie (which will be taken up in detail later in the essay). Once Jefferson took office, Hamilton seems to have resolved to lead an "honorable opposition"—"to support the chief magistrate, if he went right, and . . . to deter him if he appeared disposed to go wrong."[37] During the first several years of Jefferson's presidency, Hamilton published a series of essays called *The Examination* intended as a comprehensive review of Jefferson's policies. The topics in the series range widely, including the Louisiana Purchase, the Barbary pirates, Jefferson's First Inaugural Address and first Annual Message to Congress, as does Hamilton's evaluation of Jefferson. He appears to be unable finally to make up his mind about Jefferson and instead swings from cautious optimism to deep pessimism. He praises Jefferson's commitment to "freedom from alliances" and to "the preservation of credit."[38] He calls attention to an inconsistency between means and ends: Jefferson seeks to eliminate the public debt, yet reduces the revenues necessary to that end.[39] He returns occasionally to the principled debate over energetic versus strictly limited government that characterized the 1791 exchange over the constitutionality of the Bank: the "adepts of the new school" that "promises man, ere long, an emancipation from the burdens and restraints of government" maintain that "*Industry will succeed and prosper in proportion as it is left to the exertions of individual enterprise.* This favorite dogma, when taken as a general rule, is true; but as an exclusive one, it is false, and leads to error in the administration of public affairs."[40] Here Hamilton genuinely attempts to offer constructive opposition. The same was true of his response to the Louisiana Purchase, which, unlike most Federalists, he supported.[41] Sometimes his criticisms of Jefferson are not so much attacks on policy but complaints about Jefferson's taking undeserved credit for the Federalists'—and Hamilton's—accomplishments.[42]

1792 and 1801: *Continuities and Contrasts*

During two periods, Hamilton was overwhelmingly concerned with understanding and describing Jefferson's political principles and character. The first period began around May 1792, when Hamilton wrote a long letter to Edward Carrington of Virginia complaining of Jefferson's and Madison's opposition; it lasted until at least December 1792, when Hamilton's last "Catullus" essay appeared. The second period in which Jefferson was at the center of Hamilton's thoughts began in December 1800, when Hamilton wrote the first of a large number of letters advising Federalists to support Jefferson over Aaron Burr in resolving the Electoral College tie between the two, and lasted until the election was finally resolved in February 1801.

What strikes one most immediately in counterposing 1792 to 1801 is the contrast: in 1792, Jefferson seems to Hamilton a great evil, whereas in 1801 he is clearly the lesser of two evils. The question naturally arises whether Hamilton moderated his view of Jefferson between 1792 and 1801 on the basis of new evidence or under the influence of cooled political passion. Alternatively, one might hypothesize that Hamilton's view of Jefferson remained essentially unchanged between 1792 and 1801, but that the unexpected entry of a greater evil—the prospect of a Burr presidency— changed Hamilton's political calculations.

However, in comparing what Hamilton says about Jefferson in 1792 with what he says in 1801, one is struck at least as much by the continuities as by the differences. All of the central themes and categories with which Hamilton sought to describe Jefferson (positively, relative to Burr) in 1801 are already present, negatively and scornfully, in 1792. Where there is change—and Hamilton did modify his view of Jefferson in some important respects between 1792 and 1801—it occurs within channels already established in 1792.

What is especially interesting is that the contrast between Jefferson and Burr was already in his mind in 1792, at the height of his attack on Jefferson. The contrast Hamilton drew in 1792 between Jefferson and Burr occurred in the course of Hamilton's defense of himself against the charge of monarchism and the intent to subvert the Constitution. Hamilton was in effect saying that Burr was in fact the kind of subversive that Jefferson falsely accused Hamilton of being. So the comparisons Hamilton drew between Jefferson and Burr were, from the beginning, part of a three-way comparison: Jefferson, Burr, Hamilton.

It would be helpful first to lay out the full range of what Hamilton said about Jefferson in 1801 in order to identify themes and problems. In his famous letter to James A. Bayard, Federalist congressman from Delaware (as Delaware's only House member, Bayard singlehandedly decided the state's vote in resolving the tie), Hamilton wrote:

Among the letters I receive assigning the reasons pro & con for prefering Burr to J. I observe no small exaggeration to the prejudice of the latter & some things taken for granted as to the former which are at least questionable. Perhaps myself the first, at some expence of popularity, to unfold the true character of Jefferson, it is too late for me to become his apologist. Nor can I have any disposition to do it. I admit that his politics are tinctured with fanaticism, that he is too much in earnest in his democracy, that he has been a mischevous enemy to the principle measures of our past administration, that he is crafty & persevering in his objects, that he is not scrupulous about the means of success, not very mindful of truth, and that he is a contemptible hypocrite. But it is not true as is alleged that he is an enemy to the power of the Executive, or that he is for confounding all the powers in the House of R.'s. It is a fact which I have frequently mentioned that while we were in the administration together he was generally for a large construction of the Executive authority, & not backward to act upon it in cases which coincided with his views. Let it be added, that in his theoretic Ideas he has considered as improper the participations of the Senate in the Executive Authority. I have more than once made the reflection that viewing himself as the reversioner, he was solicitous to come into possession of a Good Estate. Nor is it true that Jefferson is zealot enough to do anything in pursuance of his principles which will contravene his popularity, or his interest. He is as likely as any man I know to temporize—to calculate what will be likely to promote his own reputation and advantage; and the probably result of such a temper is the preservation of systems, though originally opposed, which being once established, could not be overturned without danger to the person who did it. To my mind a true estimate of Mr J.'s character warrants the expectation of a temporizing rather than a violent system. That Jefferson has manifested a culpable predilection for France is certainly true; but I think it a question whether it is not proceed quite as much from her popularity among us, as from sentiment, and in proportion as that popularity is diminished his zeal will cool. Add to this that there is no fair reason to suppose him capable of being corrupted, which is a security that he will not go beyond certain limits. It is not at all improbable that under the change of circumstances Jefferson's Gallicism has considerably abated.[43]

Hamilton then went on to describe Aaron Burr as "a man of extreme & irregular ambition" who holds no "general principles" whatsoever. He then suggested that Burr would indeed subvert the Constitution if the opportunity presented itself.

It is past all doubt that he has blamed me for not having improved the situation I once was in to change the Government. That when answered that this could not have been done without guilt—he replied—"Les grands ames se soucient peu des petits morceaux"—that when told the thing was never practicable from the genious [*sic*] and situation of the country, he answered, "that depends on the estimate we form of the human passions and of the means of influencing them." Does this prove that Mr Burr would consider a scheme of usurpation as visionary [?][44]

From the letter to Bayard, the following themes and issues merit further exploration:

1. Hamilton's understanding of Jefferson's constitutional thought (not an enemy to "the power of the Executive," not for "confounding all the powers" in the House of Representatives).
2. Hamilton's understanding of Jefferson's political character more broadly ("too much in earnest in his democracy," "temporizing" rather than "violent," "tinctured with fanaticism," but not to the point of threatening his "popularity, or his interest").
3. Hamilton's view of Jefferson's personal character (seeker of "popularity," "hypocrite," "not scrupulous," but not "capable of being corrupted").
4. The personal harm Jefferson has done to Hamilton over the years ("it is too late for me to become his apologist").

Vehement Denunciation of Modest Offenses

Hamilton's understanding of Jefferson's constitutional thought was based on a close reading of Jefferson's writings on the subject, including the *Notes on the State of Virginia*, the letters Jefferson sent from France when the Constitution was being considered for ratification, and Jefferson's "Opinion on the Constitutionality of a National Bank." As a close reader of the *Notes on the State of Virginia,* Hamilton was in a position to know that Jefferson's "theoretic ideas" were opposed to "confounding all powers in the House of Representatives" as other Federalists feared Jefferson would favor—presumably on the model of Jacobin France. (It is likely, though it cannot be demonstrated here, that Hamilton read Jefferson's writings much more thoroughly than Jefferson read Hamilton's.) Hamilton's own "Opinion on the Constitutionality of an Act to Establish a Bank" is in large part a forceful and creative response to Jefferson's own strict constructionist argument, which he directly quotes and analyzes at length. During Jefferson's presidency, when in Hamilton's view Jefferson's policies threatened the independence of the federal judiciary, Hamilton quotes at length from Jefferson's "Query VIII" in *Notes on the State of Virginia* on the danger of legislative assumption of judicial powers. He praises Jefferson ironically for those "sentiments . . . delivered at a period when he can be supposed to have been under no improper bias."[45] In this instance, it would seem, Jefferson's "theoretic" principles are fine, but they are compromised by Jefferson's "temporizing" character as president.

To insist that Jefferson hold to his own constitutional principles is fair enough. However, in some other instances the use Hamilton made of Jefferson's constitutional ideas was extremely tendentious. This is especially true in the Catullus and Metellus essays of 1792, where he commented at length on Jefferson's original reservations about the Constitution. There is nothing inaccurate in Hamilton's characterization of Jefferson's reservations; the peculiar thing is what all this is supposed to prove.

In "Catullus No. II" (September 19, 1792) Hamilton opens by speaking of "the official connection between the Secretary of State and the Editor of the National Gazette" (Philip Freneau, whom Jefferson employed part-time as a translator for the State Department) and of the "conformity of the political principles and views of that officer, with those which are sedulously inculcated in the Gazette."[46] It is this attempt to demonstrate that Jefferson is behind the *National Gazette* that leads to a long discussion of Jefferson's constitutional views, which is continued in later Catullus essays. Hamilton proceeds to comment, accurately enough, on Jefferson's original reservations of the Constitution and on his proposal that nine conventions should ratify, but that four should hold out for amendments. He acknowledges that Jefferson then changed his mind and recommended adoption of the Constitution "on the ground of expediency."[47] In "Catullus No. IV," Hamilton speaks of Jefferson's insistence on a Bill of Rights and on his recommendation of the "principle of *rotation* in office and *most particularly* in the case of the President," which he describes as "a specimen of the visionary system of politics of its Author." Just for good measure he dissects some of the logical fallacies in Jefferson's statement, that "one Rebellion in thirteen states, in the course of eleven years is but one for each state in a Century and a half."[48]

The problem is that these are not exactly damning charges. They do not prove, and do not even attempt to prove, that there is anything dangerous or radical about Jefferson's constitutional ideas, or that Jefferson's original reservations meant that he was working to overthrow the Constitution. They actually amounted to a convoluted way of arguing that Jefferson was the real sponsor of Philip Freneau's *National Gazette.* Hamilton admits that Jefferson's original "dislike of the Constitution" was not "intended as the imputation of a positive crime" but was merely "one link in a chain of evidence tending to prove that the National Gazette was conducted under his auspices, and in conformity to his views."[49] While this was arguably true, its truth is certainly not demonstrated by an exegesis of Jefferson's constitutional views. At best, Hamilton demonstrates that Jefferson was closer in spirit to the Antifederalists than to the Federalists during the ratification contest. This may be true, but it hardly rises to the level of the charges that Jefferson made against Hamilton: that he is a secret monarchist, that he is working actively to subvert the Constitution through corruptions, that he is for reversing the results of the American Revolution. If Hamilton's purpose here was to retaliate against Jefferson for unfair charges against him (and that is clearly a strong motive), there was a very great disproportion in the gravity of the charges the two exchanged.

There is also a great deal in Catullus and Metellus about Jefferson's opposition to Hamilton's fiscal policies, which Hamilton identifies with the policies of the administration. Here too, the verbal heat of Hamilton's denunciation of Jefferson belies the comparatively modest character of the charge. Hamilton cannot claim and does not pretend to claim that there is anything subversive or criminal in Jefferson's opposition to Hamilton's fiscal policies. At best, Hamilton's arguments amount to a case against Jefferson's remaining a member of Washington's cabinet when he disagrees so strongly with the direction of its policies. In "Metellus No. XII," Hamilton argues that in Jefferson's situation "a just and necessary sense of decorum" would lead him to resign from the cabinet: "Let him renounce a situation which is a clog upon his patriotism; tell the people that he could no longer continue in it without forfeiting his duty to them, and that he had quitted [the office of Secretary of State] to be more at liberty to afford them his best services."[50] Hamilton here admits that Jefferson's opposition may be well intended, even patriotic, but argues that it should be pursued outside the administration, not from within. In other words, Hamilton's argument leads to a conclusion that Jefferson himself soon reached for his own reasons.

Given the mismatch between the tone of scorching anger toward Jefferson in these essays and the less than damning conclusions to which they lead, it is hard to avoid the impression that Hamilton's real motivation in the 1792 pamphlet assault was to retaliate for real or perceived offenses Jefferson had committed against him. Jefferson's claim that Hamilton was a monarchist seeking to overthrow the Constitution must have seemed especially galling to Hamilton because it stuck enough that he had to counter it repeatedly. Hamilton seemed intent on finding some equally serious charge to level against Jefferson in return, but there was nothing in Jefferson's political principles that allowed a proportionate response, and Hamilton was too careful a reader of Jefferson's writings to invent anything really serious. If there is any redeeming element to the Catullus and Metellus pieces, it is that they forced Hamilton into a close study of Jefferson's constitutional ideas—even if the immediate purpose of this research project was dubious.

Hamilton, Jefferson, and Burr: 1792 and 1801

The contrast Hamilton drew between Jefferson and Burr during the 1801 election standoff had been in Hamilton's mind at least since 1792, at the height of his battle with Jefferson. It was occasioned by Hamilton's response to Jefferson's charge that Hamilton was a monarchist who sought to subvert the Constitution.

On July 29, 1792, Washington sent a long letter to Hamilton, summarizing the objections that had been leveled against Hamilton and his policies. One of the accusations Washington reports is that Hamilton's funding system has created a "corrupt squadron, deciding the voice of the legislature" which has "manifested their disposition to get rid of the limitations imposed by the Constitution on the general legislature. . . . That the ultimate object of all this is to prepare the way for a change, from the present republican form of Government, to that of a monarchy; of which the

British Constitution is to be the model. . . . That this was contemplated in the Convention, they say is no secret."[51] The letter does not mention Jefferson as the source of the objections, but the list of objections closely parallels those set forth in Jefferson's May 23 letter to Washington, almost word for word in the case of the monarchism charge.[52] (The phrase "contemplated in the convention"—verbatim from Jefferson's letter—refers to the plan of government Hamilton proposed in his June 18, 1787, federal convention speech.) One can suppose that Hamilton knew these charges came from Jefferson.

Hamilton replied in detail in an August 18, 1792, to Washington. In countering the monarchism charge, Hamilton wrote:

> This is a palpable misrepresentation. No man, that I know of, contemplated the introducing into this country of a monarchy. A very small number (not more than three or four) manifested theoretical opinions favourable in the abstract to a constitution like that of Great Britain, but every one agreed that such a constitution except as to the general distribution of departments and powers was out of the Question in reference to this Country. The Member who was most explicit on this point (a Member from New York [Hamilton]) declared in strong terms that the republican theory ought to be adhered to in this Country as long as there was any chance of its success—that the idea of a perfect equality of political rights among the citizens, exclusive of all permanent or hereditary distinctions, was of a nature to engage the good wishes of every good man, whatever might be his theoretic doubts—that it merited his best efforts to give success to it in practice—that hitherto from an incompetent structure of the Government it had not had a fair trial, and that the endeavor ought then to be to secure to it a better chance of success by a government more capable of energy and order.[53]

Hamilton would make the same reply to the monarchism charge repeatedly over the years, publicly and privately.[54] The previous year, on August 13, 1791, he had given essentially the same description of his commitment to the success of the republican experiment directly to Jefferson, in a private conversation Jefferson recorded in his diary. Hamilton's actual words as recorded by Jefferson are broadly consistent with what Hamilton says elsewhere on this subject. Jefferson's own follow-up comments, however, indicate that he believed Hamilton was attempting to cover up his real views.[55]

In his reply to Washington, Hamilton seeks to turn the monarchism charge around, but not exactly at Jefferson.

> The truth unquestionably is, that the only path to a subversion of the republican system of the country is, by flattering the prejudices of the people, and exciting their jealousies and apprehensions, to throw affairs into confusion, and bring on civil commotion. Tired at length of anarchy, or want of government, they may take shelter in the arms of monarchy for repose and security.
>
> Those then, who resist a confirmation of public order, are the true Artificers of monarchy—not that this is the intention of the generality of them. Yet it would not be difficult to lay the finger upon some of their party who may justly be suspected. When a man unprincipled in private life desperate in his fortune, bold in his temper, possessed of considerable talents, having the advantage of military habits—despotic in his ordinary demeanour—known to have scoffed in private at the principles of liberty—when such a man is seen to mount the hobby horse of popularity—to join in the cry of danger to liberty—to take every opportunity of embarrassing the General Government & bringing it under suspicion—to flatter and fall in with all the non sense of the zealots of the day—It may justly be suspected that his object is to throw things into confusion that he may "ride the storm and direct the whirlwind."[56]

That Hamilton does not have Jefferson in mind in this passage is proved by the "advantage of military habits" line. Jefferson would instead fall into the category of the "generality of them" who, by resisting the necessary authority of government, unintentionally lend support to "some of their party" who would subvert republicanism.

That Hamilton is explicitly thinking of Burr is indicated in two letters from October 1792. In an October 10 letter to Charles Cotesworth Pinckney, Hamilton first speaks with alarm of the prospect of Jefferson's becoming vice-president: "That Gentlemen whom I once very much esteemed, but who does not permit me to retain that sentiment for him, is certainly a man of sublimated and paradoxical imagination—entertaining & propagating notions inconsistent with dignified and orderly Government." But of Burr, whose name had also been mentioned for vice-president, Hamilton says that he "has no other principle than *to mount at all events* to the first honors of the State & to as much more as circumstances will permit —a man in private life not unblemished."[57] He says the same thing of Burr in an October 15 letter to John Steele: Burr's "only political principle is, to *mount at all events* to the highest legal honours of the Nation and as much further as circumstances will carry him."[58]

There is additional evidence that Hamilton was specifically thinking of Aaron Burr: (1) In his letter to Washington, Hamilton, when he speaks of someone who has "scoffed in private at the principles of liberty," is clearly speaking of a *particular* individual known to him personally, not just a general type; this fits perfectly with the piece of private conversation Hamilton reports about Burr in his January 16, 1801, letter to Bayard ("he has blamed me for not having improved the situation I once was in to change the Government"). (2) The phrase "having the advantage of military habits," which could not be applied to Jefferson, fits Burr who had a distinguished military record in the Revolution. (3) The phrases "unprincipled in his private life" and "desperate in his fortune" echo the characterization of Burr as "a man in private life not unblemished" in the October 10, 1792, letter to Pinckney, and foreshadows Hamilton's characterization of Burr in a January 1801 letter: "The fair emoluments of any station, under our government, will not equal his expences in that station; still less will they suffice to extricate him from his embarassments & he must therefore from the necessity of his situation have recourse to unworthy expedients."[59]

This contrast between Jefferson and Burr that Hamilton draws in 1792 is interesting for a number of reasons. Most obviously, it demonstrates that the essentials of the Burr-Jefferson comparison of 1801 were in Hamilton's mind for a long time. It also shows the way in which Hamilton's thinking about Jefferson and Burr is not easy to disentangle from Hamilton's reactions to Jefferson's attacks on himself. Jefferson accuses Hamilton of conspiring to overthrow the republic. Hamilton does not return the accusation in kind. Instead he replies, in effect, that Burr is in fact the kind of man you falsely accuse me of being, and he is in your political camp, not mine.

Both Jefferson and Burr, in Hamilton's view, are demagogues of a sort, but there are many different varieties of demagogue. Jefferson plays with fire, but he does not really intend to burn down the house. On the contrary, he hopes to possess the house itself—to attain the highest elective office; for Burr, in contrast, even the presidency would not be enough.

Hamilton makes this point in a different way in his May 26, 1792, letter to Edward Carrington. After describing Jefferson's and Madison's "systematic opposition" to his policies, he remarks that "tis evident beyond a question, from every movement, that Mr. Jefferson aims with ardent desire at the Presidential Chair." Of course, this in itself is hardly a crime, but Jefferson's method of furthering his political ambitions threaten to damage the prize itself. Once you risk "rendering the Government itself odious," it will not be easy to "recover the lost affections & confidence of the people." Even here, Hamilton seems resigned to the prospect that Jefferson might actually succeed in becoming president; he implies that he is less worried about Jefferson's becoming president than about the unwitting damage to the authority of government Jefferson will have committed in the political fight to get there. Jefferson and Madison ought to appreciate "the natural resistance to Government which in every community results from the human passions, the degree to which this is strengthened by the organised rivalry of State Governments, & the infinite danger that the National Government once rendered odious will be kept so by these powerful & indefatigable enemies. They forget an old but a very just, though a course saying—That it is much easier to raise the Devil than to lay him."[60] Hamilton is in effect warning Jefferson—to borrow language from his 1801 letter to Bayard—that if you want to "come into possession of a Good Estate" you should cease your efforts to undermine my funding system.

In the same letter (which predates by several months Hamilton's response to Washington's list of objections) Hamilton once again suggests that there are men out there much more dangerous than Jefferson; and here too the subject arises in the course of Hamilton's defense of himself against the monarchism charge:

> If I were disposed to promote Monarchy & overthrow State Governments, I would mount the hobby horse of popularity—I would endeavour to prostrate the National Government—raise a ferment—and then 'ride in the Whirlwind and direct the Storm.' [Note the similarity of language here to a passage in the letter to Washington that almost certainly refers to Burr.] That there are men acting with Jefferson & Madison who have this in view I verily believe. I could lay my finger on some of them. That Madison does *not* mean it I also verily believe, and I rather believe the same of Jefferson; but I read him upon the whole thus—"A man of profound ambition & violent passions."[61]

The last line here shows Hamilton's unwillingness to come away without a parting shot at Jefferson, even at the end of a passage indicating that Jefferson is not the worst of evils.

Jefferson as Ordinary Democratic Politician

Thus it is evident that Hamilton's support for Jefferson over Burr in the 1801 electoral standoff did not by itself signify a major improvement in Hamilton's view of Jefferson. Even in 1792, at the height of his personal battle with Jefferson, he would have preferred Jefferson to Burr if forced to choose. (This does not mean that Hamilton's view of Jefferson had not improved at all—I argue below that some important modifications occurred between 1792 and 1801—but only that one cannot establish this simply on the basis of his 1801 preference for Jefferson over Burr for president.) Nor can Hamilton's support of Jefferson in 1801 be explained as resulting from an unexpected turn of events, raising the sudden prospect of a much greater evil. Though the details of the electoral tie could not have been foreseen, when it occurred it must have seemed to Hamilton a prophetic realization of a vision that had distressed his imagination for more than eight years. He responded passionately and thoughtfully as though he had been expecting something like this all along.

The most obvious difference between 1792 and 1801 is that in 1801 a great public decision was at stake that required Hamilton to suppress his personal animosity toward Jefferson. In 1792 there was no great public decision at issue: the essentials of Hamilton's financial system had already been accomplished, and the crisis over policy toward France was yet to come; thus Hamilton's disposition toward Jefferson that year was determined by comparatively trivial public issues (e.g., Freneau) and by Hamilton's response to what he regarded as unfair accusations against himself, proceeding from Jefferson. Once a major public issue came along, as it did in 1793 over Genet's conduct, Hamilton suppressed his personal dislike and gave Jefferson due credit for authoring the letter demanding Genet's recall.

If there was a modification of Hamilton's view of Jefferson between 1792 and 1801, it probably resulted in part from Hamilton's observations of Jefferson's course of action during the Genet crisis. At least one passage from Hamilton's January 1801 letter to Bayard seems a close match to the Genet episode: "That Jefferson has manifested a culpable predilection for France is certainly true; but I think it a question whether it did not proceed quite as much from her *popularity* among us, as from sentiment, and in proportion as that popularity is diminished his zeal will cool."[62] Jefferson was at first an enthusiastic supporter of Genet, but when Genet's conduct compromised American sovereignty, and especially when Genet foolishly went after an immensely popular president, Jefferson abandoned him and fell into line with cabinet policy. If Hamilton had additional incidents in mind in this passage, they would be repetitions of a pattern established during the Genet episode.

The passage quoted above is immediately preceded by Hamilton's observation that "Jefferson . . . is as likely as any man I know to temporize —to calculate what will be likely to promote his own reputation and advantage." A few lines later he counterposed Jefferson's "temporizing" to (presumably Burr's) "violent system." It is worth asking whether Hamilton employs the term "temporizing" merely to designate a lesser evil (bad, but not as bad as "violent"), or if there was some positive dimension to Jefferson's disposition to "temporize."

That there may be a positive dimension is suggested first by the shift in emphasis evident in the flurry of letters Hamilton wrote between December 16, 1800, and January 16, 1801. The earliest letters dwell more on the dangers of Burr than on the character of Jefferson. Hamilton's December 16 letter to Oliver Wolcott concentrates on the evils of Burr, and merely states that Jefferson "is by far not so dangerous a man and he has pretensions to character."[63] A December 22 letter to Theodore Sedgwick is entirely about the dangers of Burr. A December 27 letter to James Bayard is entirely about the dangers of Burr; Hamilton mentions Jefferson only to indicate his willingness to put personal considerations aside: "To contribute to the disappointment and mortification of Mr. J. would be on my part, only to retaliate for unequivocal proofs of enmity; but in a case like this it would be base to listen to personal considerations."[64] In comparing the December 27 letter to Bayard with the classic January 16 letter, which discusses Jefferson's political character at length, one suspects that Hamilton realized it was not enough just to insist on the dangers of Burr. He had to say something positive about Jefferson to challenge the much more negative view of Jefferson held by most Federalists. Otherwise they would have little reason to prefer Jefferson, a known evil, to Burr, a mere question mark.

Whether Hamilton only belatedly realized that he had to present a qualified positive characterization of Jefferson, or realized it all along but took a month to grit his teeth and do it, is an open question. In any case, he did seem to intend much of what he said in the January 16 letter to Bayard as positive in a limited degree. Jefferson was not merely less able to do mischief than Burr; he was more able to accomplish good: "In my opinion [Burr] is inferior in real ability to Jefferson."[65] In this spirit, let us return to Jefferson's "temporizing" and ask if there may be something positive in this epithet.

By Jefferson's "temporizing" Hamilton meant his disinclination "to do anything in pursuance of his principles which will contravene his popularity, or his interest," and his tendency "to calculate what will be likely to promote his own reputation and advantage . . . the probable result of such a temper is the preservation of systems, though originally opposed, which being once established, could not be overturned without danger to the person who did it."[66] If one were to disattach Jefferson's name from this description of a "temporizing" character, it would look very much like the description of a typical elected leader in a popular government—if not an exemplary leader, at least a functional one. Certainly Hamilton, of all people, would not have been shocked at the prospect of a leader responding to the pushes and pulls of reputation and interest. The importance of interest (which includes political interest, not just economic interest) was a central theme of Hamilton's contributions to the *Federalist*. It was also a presupposition of his policies as Treasury Secretary (how to enlist the political and economic interests of Americans on the side of national government as opposed to state sovereignty); it underlay his admiration for the "corrupt" English system. The political and economic interests to which Jefferson responded may have been different than the ones upon which Hamilton's system was premised, but the general principle was the same. If Jefferson was indeed "too much in earnest in his democracy," it is an excess of a tendency that in its ordinary degree—at least in the political circumstances of the United States—was normal and expected. Hamilton may not have admired it, but it would have been foolish to declare war upon it. Both Burr and Jefferson courted popular opinion, but Burr did it cynically and instrumentally, keeping an eye on "the human passions and of the means of influencing them,"[67] courting popularity in order to overthrow popular government. Jefferson traded in popular opinion as an honest broker.

What did seem to infuriate Hamilton was not Jefferson's political ambitions, but his unwillingness to admit to his ambition. In 1792 Hamilton had complained about Jefferson's image as "the quiet modest, retiring philosopher—as the plain simple unambitious republican" when he was in truth "the aspiring turbulent competitor."[68] This is probably part of Hamilton's meaning in the Bayard letter, where he describes Jefferson as "a contemptible hypocrite."[69] If Jefferson would admit to his own great but

entirely legitimate political ambitions and shed the mask of disinterestedness, there would be less to complain of in his public character.

The irony here is that it was precisely Hamilton's disposition to treat
pursuit of interest as normal and functional that so shocked Jefferson,
who saw Hamilton's reliance on governing through interest as the opening
wedge to British-style corruption.[70] (Jefferson seems to have believed that
Hamilton based everything on narrowly economic interests, but Hamilton's understanding of interest included the political interest in reputation
and continuance in office.) Jefferson's democratic methods were functional in America just as patronage was functional in the English system.
The same Hamiltonian principle that led Jefferson to suspect Hamilton of
designing to overthrow republicanism led Hamilton himself to reluctant
appreciation of Jefferson's political character.

An Asymmetrical Contest

We are now in a better position to understand some of the peculiar asymmetries in the Jefferson-Hamilton contest. They had fierce conflict as well
as occasional truces, but they did not agree on what the conflict was
about.

For Jefferson, what was at stake was nothing less than preserving republicanism from the deliberate efforts of Hamilton and his corrupted political instruments to overthrow popular government and replace it with an
English-style monarchy "bottomed on corruption." Hamilton, on the
other hand, while he disagreed with Jefferson's constitutional ideas and his
peculiarly narrow way of reading the document, never accused Jefferson of
intending to subvert the Constitution. He complained of Jefferson's excessive attachment to France but never questioned his fundamental loyalty to
the United States. At worst, Hamilton believed that Jefferson's intemperate
opposition could unintentionally encourage other, worse men (like Burr)
whose motives were very different from Jefferson's.

Jefferson's charge that Hamilton was a monarchist was central to the
conflict between the two men, but central for different reasons. For Jefferson it is an urgent public matter to expose the real import of Hamilton's
policies. For Hamilton, it was important mostly as a slander against himself that left him itching to retaliate, but having nothing equally damning
to charge in return. So he blasted away at Jefferson for inappropriately

supporting Freneau and for remaining in the cabinet when he could not support its policies.

For Jefferson, it was Hamilton's policies themselves that excited alarm: the assumption of state debts, the Bank of the United States, the Anglophile foreign policy. Though Jefferson tried to support his charges of Hamilton's corrupt monarchism by hearsay evidence and reported bits of social conversation,[71] it is clear that all this is secondary. The main evidence of Hamilton's monarchism was the tendency of the policies themselves, interpreted of course through Jefferson's own ideological lenses. For this reason, there was really nothing Hamilton could have done to persuade Jefferson that the monarchism charge was false. It is not surprising, then, that Jefferson never retreated an inch from this charge; what he says in 1818 in the *Anas*, long after Hamilton's death, is essentially the same as what he had said during the impassioned battles of the 1790s.[72]

Hamilton's view of Jefferson, on the other hand, had a basic core but shifted in its particulars depending on the magnitude of the public issue at stake and on what Jefferson was actually up to at the moment. The consequence of this was that Hamilton was more open to new evidence and to revision of his view of Jefferson than Jefferson was to changing his view of Hamilton. The greater the public issue, the more willing Hamilton was to moderate his animosity toward Jefferson—which is the reverse of the effect great public issues had on Jefferson's view of Hamilton.

One can better appreciate the asymmetries and nonparallels by asking what a symmetrical and parallel Hamilton-Jefferson battle might have looked like. Since Jefferson charged Hamilton with aiming to subvert the Constitution in favor of monarchism, Hamilton would have to charge Jefferson with something equally serious—with, for instance, intending to import Jacobinism and the guillotine to America. He would have made the most of Jefferson's flirtation of Genet rather than publicly, and repeatedly, citing Jefferson's letter demanding Genet's recall. Moreover, to answer Jefferson in kind, Hamilton would have had to make Jefferson himself into the central political evil in the same way that Jefferson made all political evil follow from Hamilton. That would rule out any possibility of supporting Jefferson over Burr, because Jefferson made a far more convenient ideological target than Burr, who unlike Jefferson held no "pernicious theories."[73] It is true that in moments of anger (especially in the Reynolds pamphlet) Hamilton sometimes fell into talking about Jefferson and the Jacobin menace in a way that was typical among Federalist partisans. But he didn't stick with it for very long, probably because he did not really believe it and in crucial moments was much readier to explain why Jefferson is not a Jacobin.

Conclusion

Given that Hamilton's opposition to Jefferson was never as extreme as Jefferson's opposition to Hamilton, it is worth asking what wider conclusions one might draw from this examination of the Hamilton-Jefferson conflict from Hamilton's point of view. It certainly makes a fascinating human story—which perhaps is justification enough—but what else can be learned?

First, a reexamination from Hamilton's point of view may help loosen the continued predominance, certainly in historical folklore and probably also among historians, of Jefferson's own view of what the conflicts of the 1790s were about. The only full-length book on the Jefferson-Hamilton contest, Claude Bowers's *Jefferson and Hamilton* (1925), presents the contest entirely in Jefferson's terms, as a "clear-cut fight between democracy and aristocracy."[74] The book is less about Hamilton than about what Hamilton's contemporaries were saying and thinking and the rumors that circulated about him. Bowers, for instance, matter-of-factly assumes that Hamilton was a monarchist; Hamilton's persistent denials are not even mentioned.[75] Stanley Elkins and Eric McKitrick's *The Age of Federalism* (1993) offers a much more balanced account of the Hamilton-Jefferson conflict (based, unlike Bowers's book, on what Hamilton actually said and did). Yet *The Age of Federalism,* while much fairer to Hamilton, still treats the Hamilton-Jefferson contest as parallel and symmetrical, as though the stakes were the same for both sides. The authors write that "the shadow of conspiracy and subversion that so obsessed Jefferson had its exact counterpart in Hamilton."[76] My own reading of the evidence indicates few exact counterparts in the Hamilton-Jefferson contest. Hamilton's conspiracy scenarios, moreover, are pale compared to Jefferson's: Hamilton's conspiracies are sporadic, undeveloped, unconvincing, usually occasioned by a real or perceived personal injury, and forgotten as soon as critical public issues are at stake.

Second, reconstructing the Hamilton-Jefferson contest from Hamilton's perspective raises some questions about the origins of American political parties and of the key ideological divisions in American politics. While

Jefferson constructed a coherent and powerful political ideology out of his opposition to Hamilton, Hamilton—despite occasional emphatic denunciations of "Jacobinism"—made no serious effort to build a party or an ideology on the basis of a demonized archetypical image of Jefferson.[77] In this case, what did not happen is as important as what did. Certainly there was a political market among Federalists for a demonized image of Jefferson. Hamilton fails to satisfy the customer. One wonders whether Hamilton, or someone in his place, *could* have created a "Hamiltonian persuasion" centered on opposition to Jeffersonian democracy; and if so, what the consequences would have been for the political stability of the early republic.

NOTES

1. Hamilton to James A. Bayard, January 16, 1801, *Papers of Alexander Hamilton* (hereafter *PAH*), ed. Harold C. Syrett et al., 27 vols. (New York: Columbia University Press, 1961–87), 25: 319.

2. Hamilton's and Jefferson's theoretical views on energetic versus strictly limited government are described in James H. Read, *Power versus Liberty: Madison, Hamilton, Wilson, and Jefferson* (Charlottesville: University Press of Virginia, 2000). That work does not, however, attempt to describe the personal dimension of the conflict between Hamilton and Jefferson, which is the aim of the present essay.

3. Claude G. Bowers, *Jefferson and Hamilton: The Struggle for Democracy in America* (Boston: Houghton Mifflin, 1966), v.

4. For example, Lance Banning, *The Jeffersonian Persuasion: Evolution of a Party Ideology* (Ithaca, NY: Cornell University Press, 1978); Herbert E. Sloan, *Principle and Interest: Thomas Jefferson and the Problem of Debt* (New York: Oxford University Press, 1995).

5. Stanley Elkins and Eric McKitrick in *The Age of Federalism: The Early American Republic, 1788–1800* (New York: Oxford University Press, 1993) write that Hamilton "was very good at defending himself but exceptionally bad at attacking others" (285). I tend to agree, but Hamilton's attacks on Jefferson are interesting and revealing nonetheless.

6. Hamilton to James A. Bayard, January 16, 1801, PAH, 25: 320.

7. PAH, 2: 225, 553.

8. *PAH*, 4: 293–94n.

9. *PAH*, 6: 389–90, 451, 465; *PAH*, 7: 512, 568, 605.

10. *PAH*, 6: 22–23, 423, 425–26; *PAH*, 8: 258, 284–85, 450, 503; *PAH*, 9: 111–12, 129.

11. *PAH,* 10: 40, 58.

12. See, for example, Jefferson's diary entry on a conversation with Hamilton for August 13, 1791, *PAH,* 9: 33–34 (editor's note); and recollection of a dinner conversation between Hamilton, Jefferson, and John Adams, in *Thomas Jefferson: Writings,* ed. Merrill Peterson (New York: Viking, 1984), 670–71.

13. Jefferson, *Anas,* from Peterson, *Writings,* 668–69.

14. Hamilton, "An Opinion on the Constitutionality of an Act to Establish a Bank," *PAH,* 8: 97–134; Jefferson, "Opinion on the Constitutionality of a National Bank," in Peterson, *Writings,* 416–421.

15. On the Mint, see Hamilton to Jefferson, April 14, 1791, *PAH,* 8: 284–85. On the French loan, see Hamilton to Jefferson, April 12, 1791 (*PAH,* 8: 278–79), and Hamilton to Jefferson, April 15, 1791 (*PAH,* 8: 289–90).

16. A June 15, 1791, letter from Robert Troup to Hamilton already assumes that Jefferson and Madison are Hamilton's "foes" and warns of worse ahead; *PAH,* 8: 478–79. But whether Hamilton perceived an outright battle by that date is unclear. Jefferson records a long conversation with Hamilton of August 13, 1791, in which Hamilton describes his commitment to giving a "fair course" to the republican experiment. Hamilton seems at this date to trust Jefferson more than Jefferson trusts him; *PAH,* 9: 33–34.

17. Jefferson to Washington, May 23, 1792, Peterson, *Writings,* 985–90.

18. See, for example, Hamilton and Edmund Randolph to Jefferson (commenting on draft of Jefferson letter), May 13–15, 1793, *PAH,* 16: 439–40; Jefferson to Hamilton, June 1, 1793, *PAH,* 14: 508–9, regarding Jefferson's draft of a letter to Genet "to order away the privateers fitted out in our ports"; Hamilton to Jefferson, June 3, 1793, responding to Jefferson's draft, *PAH,* 14: 513–14; Jefferson to Hamilton and Henry Knox, June 19, 1793, enclosing draft of letters to France and England, *PAH,* 15: 5; Jefferson to Hamilton and Knox, June 25, 1793, *PAH,* 15: 24–25, enclosing draft of letter to Genet; Hamilton to Jefferson, June 25, 1793, *PAH,* 15: 25–26, commenting on Jefferson's draft letter to Genet; Jefferson's minutes of cabinet meetings, August 1–2, 1793, where it was "unanimously agreed that a letter should be written . . . desiring the recall" of Genet, *PAH,* 15: 157.

19. Hamilton and Knox to Washington, May 2, 1793, *PAH,* 14: 367–96.

20. For "Pacificus" see *PAH,* 15: 33–34, 55–63, 65–69, 82–86, 90–95, 100–106, 130–35.

21. This episode is described in Elkins and McKitrick, *The Age of Federalism,* 341–54.

22. Privately, Hamilton worried whether Jefferson, a key witness to Genet's threat to "go over Washington's head," would go on the record with what he knew. See John Jay to Hamilton, Nov. 26, 1793, *PAH,* 15: 412–13.

23. *PAH,* 15: 158 (editor's note). See also Elkins and McKitrick, *The Age of Federalism,* 347–54.

24. "No Jacobin No. IX," *PAH,* 15: 304–6. See also Hamilton to Washington,

January 4, 1794, which describes Genet's action in violation of Jefferson's instructions; *PAH*, 15: 614.

25. Robert Troup to Hamilton, December 25, 1793, *PAH*, 15: 588.

26. "The Defence No. XXXI" (December 1795), *PAH*, 19: 475–79. See also *PAH*, 18: 438 (commentary on Jay Treaty prepared for Washington).

27. For 1794, see Hamilton's recommendations for Washington, *PAH*, 16: 422. For the 1797 suggestion that Jefferson be selected as a member of a three-man commission to France, see Hamilton to Timothy Pickering, March 22, 1797, *PAH*, 20: 545; and Hamilton to James McHenry, March 1797, *PAH*, 20: 574–75.

28. Jefferson to James Monroe, April 24, 1794, *PAH*, 26: 264 (editor's note).

29. Letter to unknown recipient, Nov. 8, 1796, *PAH*, 20: 377. See also *PAH*, 20: 418.

30. *PAH*, 21: 238.

31. *PAH*, 21: 242, 284–85.

32. Hamilton to Theodore Sedgwick, February 2, 1799, *PAH*, 22: 452–53.

33. See, for example, Hamilton to Theodore Sedgwick, May 10, 1800, *PAH*, 24: 474–75.

34. For Hamilton's lengthy indictment of Adams, see *PAH*, 25: 169–234.

35. Hamilton to John Jay, May 7, 1800, *PAH*, 24: 465. One might notice the contrast between Hamilton's here calling Jefferson a "fanatic," whereas in the January 16, 1801, letter to James A. Bayard (quoted at length below) recommending Jefferson over Burr, Hamilton says only that Jefferson's politics are "tinctured with fanaticism." This May 7 letter to Jay is also the only place I have found where Hamilton makes an issue of Jefferson's supposed atheism.

36. See, for example, Robert Troup to Rufus King, December 4, 1800: "General Hamilton makes no secret of his opinion that Jefferson should be preferred to Adams"; *PAH*, 25: 173 (editor's note).

37. April 10, 1801 speech, *PAH*, 25: 376–77.

38. *PAH*, 25: 377. Jefferson's supposed willingness to defraud public creditors was the theme of some of Hamilton's most tendentious arguments in the 1792 "Catullus" essays..

39. "The Examination Number II" (December 21, 1801), *PAH*, 25: 463.

40. Ibid., 467; emphasis in original.

41. Essay for *New York Evening Post*, July 5, 1803, *PAH*, 26: 129–36. Hamilton considered New Orleans the only important item and the trans-Mississippi territory a waste of money.

42. See, for example, "The Examination Number XVIII" (April 8, 1802), *PAH*, 25: 591–92.

43. Hamilton to James A. Bayard, January 16, 1801, *PAH*, 25: 319–20.

44. Hamilton to Bayard, January 16, 1801, *PAH*, 25: 321–23.

45. "The Examination Number XVI" (March 19, 1802), *PAH*, 25: 565–66.

46. *PAH*, 12: 393.

47. *PAH*, 12: 394–97.

48. *PAH*, 12: 580–82.

49. *PAH*, 12: 583.

50. *PAH*, 12: 616.

51. Washington to Hamilton, July 29, 1792, *PAH*, 12: 129–34.

52. Jefferson to Washington, May 23, 1792, Peterson, *Writings*, 985–90.

53. *PAH*, 12: 253.

54. See, for example, Hamilton to Timothy Pickering, September 16, 1803, *PAH*, 26: 147–49.

55. *PAH*, 9: 33–34.

56. *PAH*, 12: 252.

57. *PAH*, 12: 544.

58. *PAH*, 12: 568.

59. Hamilton to John Rutledge, Jr., January 4, 1801, *PAH*, 25: 296.

60. *PAH*, 11: 441–42.

61. *PAH*, 11: 444.

62. *PAH*, 25: 320.

63. *PAH*, 25: 257.

64. *PAH*, 25: 277.

65. *PAH*, 25:323.

66. *PAH*, 25: 320.

67. Hamilton to Bayard, January 16, 1801, *PAH*, 25: 323.

68. Catullus No. III, *PAH*, 12: 504.

69. *PAH*, 25: 319.

70. Jefferson, *Anas*, in Peterson, *Writings*, 666.

71. In the *Anas*, Jefferson claims, for instance, that when he arrived at the capitol in early 1790 "a preference for kingly, over republican, government, was evidently the favorite sentiment" at "table conversations"; Peterson, *Writings*, 665–66. But Jefferson's view of what constituted monarchism was so expansive that little weight can be given to this kind of evidence.

72. For commentary on this, see Lance Banning, *The Jeffersonian Persuasion*, 13–14.

73. Hamilton to Bayard, January 16, 1801, *PAH*, 25: 320.

74. Bowers, *Jefferson and Hamilton*, vii.

75. Bowers, *Jefferson and Hamilton*, 32.

76. Elkins and McKitrick, *The Age of Federalism*, 360.

77. It is not clear what to make of Hamilton's proposal in 1802 to create a "Christian Constitutional Society" that would seem to function like a political party with a popular base. See Hamilton to James A. Bayard, April, 1802, *PAH*, 25: 605–10. It is not clear how serious Hamilton is about building a popular party, nor is it clear what direction its ideology would have taken.

PART II

Hamilton's Republicanism

CHAPTER 5

Reforming Republicanism

Alexander Hamilton's Theory of Republican Citizenship and Press Liberty

ROBERT W. T. MARTIN

*I*N the very last letter he wrote, Alexander Hamilton famously called "democracy" a "disease" and a "poison." Myriad comments like this one have led many scholars since his death—and many of his contemporaries before it—to see Hamilton as an opponent of republicanism, even a closet monarchist. Happily, some recent scholarship has disabused us of this notion, making the nature of Hamilton's republicanism an interesting and important question. But as so often happens, the pendulum has swung too far. At the extreme, the political journalist Michael Lind has praised Hamilton as the founder of the "democratic nationalist" tradition in America, insisting that "Hamiltonians have been as committed to liberal democracy and social equality as Jeffersonians."[1]

Lind's democratic rendering of Hamilton is exaggerated; Hamilton was no more a democrat in our terms than in his own. But if he was neither a democrat nor a monarchist, the precise nature of his personal political beliefs has been notoriously difficult to plumb. Rather than dive into these murky depths directly, I seek here to analyze Hamilton's reconceptualization of republicanism in the face of withering criticism during the political battles of the late 1780s and the 1790s. Whatever his most intimate views were, Hamilton's performance as a defender of a particular theory of republicanism required him to develop a nuanced conception of citizenship that was precisely calibrated for the vigorous, elitist republic he envisioned. To gain an appreciation of this theory's advantages and limitations, we will need to examine it in contrast to the relatively more egalitarian and participatory rhetoric of his opponents, Anti-Federalists[2] and, later, Republicans. This examination will involve analyzing competing notions of representation and press liberty.

Criticism from those who labeled themselves "Republicans" forced Hamilton to reconceive republicanism so that it provided the strong government he sought but still included some meaningful role for the *demos.* This was no simple business, as Hamilton generally distrusted the common people with political power and sought a theory that would give the people a very limited role in government, chiefly as the electors of the "better sort" (wise, ambitious, and public-spirited men like himself). Similarly, his theory placed little faith in the power of public reason. Nevertheless, Hamilton's approach was not contemptuous of the people; he did not, as some have claimed, consider public opinion as generally worthless.[3] Rather, his notion of engendering public confidence was logical and built on a particular Federalist amalgam of new and conventional ideas of republican citizenship. Such a view was fitting for one of Hamilton's great genius and his consuming sense of public honor.

My analysis of Hamilton extends a new and heretofore unobserved development in the scholarly literature. A few recent studies have focused on the centrality of a particular conceptual divide in early American political thought: "responsibility" (or, relatedly, "confidence") versus "vigilance." Karl-Friedrich Walling, for example, recently explored this theme in Hamilton's thought, marking out, as the standard of Hamilton's politics, the statesman's responsibility to the public good and for the powers granted to him. This notion of responsibility allowed Hamilton to envision a federal government both more powerful *and* more accountable—to posterity and, indirectly, to the people. This view was opposed to the early American republican virtue of vigilance, the ever-suspicious eye that eighteenth-century Whigs such as Thomas Jefferson or Patrick Henry always turned toward governmental power.[4]

In Hamilton's theory of republicanism, ambitious men could be trusted with quantities of power extraordinary for republics because their historical reputations would so clearly depend on truly serving the public good. But if Walling's interpretation tells us a lot about what Hamilton expected of public officials, it does little to spell out the related expectations for citizens. Vigilance, after all, had always been expected of republican citizens; it was only with the emergence of the American republic that thinkers like Jefferson and Madison began to see it as the public virtue of political leaders as well. What then was the virtue of good citizens implicit in Hamilton's novel defense of a republican empire?

Confidence was the answer—confidence in the chosen and empowered leaders. As James H. Read has revealed, Hamilton expected public-minded statesmen like himself to act boldly, using the full measure of power necessary to serve the public good—whether that power had been formally granted or not. This required acting with confidence in themselves, but also with the confidence of the people. Often this public confidence had to be manufactured. Yet with this confidence, the public official could serve the public good, thus being a responsible statesman and earning the people's (post facto) consent once they understood how well they had been served.[5]

In this essay I will develop these emerging themes into a more expansive view of Hamilton's performance as a defender of a new theory of republican citizenship. To simplify greatly, the divisions between most Federalists—especially Hamilton—and their political adversaries can best be understood as competing visions of the proper virtue of republican citizens: confidence or vigilance.[6] These opposing views provide the context in which Hamilton's own ideas were formulated. After briefly sketching out these broader arguments, we will attend directly to Hamilton's theory of citizenship as he developed it in the 1780s and early 1790s. But the polarizing atmosphere of the 1790s provided a challenge to every manner of political thinking. Once the new currents of thought are briefly outlined in a debate over the nature of representation and press liberty, we will examine how Hamilton developed his theory of republican citizenship in a series of legal issues involving press liberty. Here we will find him incorporating the virtue of vigilance—reluctantly, narrowly, belatedly, and in a way that suggests the limits of his theory of republican citizenship.

The Federalist Papers

Federalism as a political persuasion emerged during the debate over the ratification of the Constitution and bloomed during the 1790s. As the prime contributor to *The Federalist Papers* and as President George Washington's most powerful and trusted aide (not to mention a prolific author), Hamilton was a leader—arguably, *the* leader—of this political mindset. But he was not alone, and the theory of republicanism he would defend drew on the broader Federalist current. That current stressed the need for a capable, energetic government, led by wise guides chosen by the people. Republican citizenship, then, was chiefly exercised in elections. Indeed, some Federalists were apprehensive of even that role for the common people. Roger Sherman, in opposing the direct election of the lower house by the people, maintained that "the people should have as little to do as may be about the government. They want [lack] information and are constantly liable to be deceived." Jefferson would have similar concerns, but for him, this was reason to see that the people were better informed. This distinction seemed slight at first, but grew during the 1790s as the rhetoric of those who fashioned the "Republican" persuasion— including Hamilton's erstwhile *Federalist* co-author James Madison— would envision a wider role for the (white, male) citizenry in the public sphere, if not necessarily in public office. Increasingly, most Federalists saw the virtue of these citizens as a matter not of conventional Whig "vigilance" (a suspicious jealousy of governmental power), but rather in a traditional deference to their public officers once chosen.[7]

Though they had little faith in the Federalists' energetic national government, those who contested the ratification of the unamended Constitution saw the need for a citizenry that was actively involved, informed, and vigilant. "To many Anti-Federalists," Lance Banning observes, "genuine democracy was more than just a matter of popular elections." Virginia Anti-Federalists, for example, included in a list of proposed amendments a clause that would protect the people's right to instruct their representatives. When a similar amendment was proposed in the First Congress, many Federalists feared that legislators would be bound by such instructions. The Anti-Federalists, on the contrary, were fearful of the end of meaningful political citizenship, especially for members of the "midling" class such as themselves. This early disagreement is telling because instructions undermined the notion of a deferential public, one that had enough confidence in elected officials to let them govern unquestioned; in turn, instructions also implied a watchful and engaged public that might be continually debating what their "public servants" ought to be instructed to do. Anti-Federalists, according to Saul Cornell, were rejecting "the deferential political message implicit in Federalist ideology" and instead defending an ideal "in which republican liberty and popular participation were the defining characteristics of political life."[8]

The theory of republicanism that Hamilton publicly developed during the late 1780s and the 1790s drew on this broad Federalist persuasion, and its visions of republican citizenship and press liberty fit well within the Federalist current. But his theory was much more nuanced, including the people in a much larger and more complex picture of political dynamics. His thinking, as we shall now see, also went much deeper than most men's, starting with an explicit picture of human nature and pursuing its various implications up through the levels of government, from the impassioned and easily deluded public to the ambitious but responsible elite.

Hamilton, even more than Madison in the *Federalist Papers,* presented humans as driven by passion rather than guided by reason. We are, of course, apt to recall Madison's famous aphorism, "If men were angels, no government would be necessary." Yet we easily forget that Hamilton had by then already asked, "Why has government been instituted at all? Because the passions of men will not conform to the dictates of reason and justice without constraint." Before Madison had even joined the project, Hamilton declared that "momentary passions, and immediate interests, have a more active and imperious control over human conduct than general or remote considerations of policy, utility, or justice." Indeed, where Madison saw a man's reason and self-love having a "reciprocal influence" on each other, Hamilton declared men's passions in "imperious control."[9]

"Of all the founders," his most recent biographer concedes, "Hamilton probably had the gravest doubts about the wisdom of the masses and wanted elected leaders who would guide them." This is not to say that Hamilton's theory envisioned no limits to human weakness. For example, he also cautioned Publius's readers that "the supposition of universal venality in human nature is little less an error in political reasoning than the supposition of universal rectitude."[10] It is worth noting, however, that this rare sanguine comment was made with regard to the president's character, not the people's. And as we shall see, Hamilton's theory placed great stress on the ability of the "better sort" to direct their passion (ambition) toward the public good.

If the people were driven by their (low) passions, they could be easily manipulated by clever demagogues who preyed upon those passions. Democratic despotism was a recurring and significant fear for Hamilton. In arguing for the electoral college, he praised the fact that an indirect national vote for president would avoid those unqualified characters who might be able to win the top job in any one state due to "talents for low intrigue, and the little arts of popularity." In fact, the people are frequently portrayed in Hamilton's *Federalist Papers* as very malleable, easily deluded for partisan purposes; rarely, if ever, are they depicted as capable of seeing through demagogic attempts, especially those of state officials.[11]

A populace driven more by their emotions than their reason could be dangerous. This was especially so in Hamilton's view because he saw opinions as influenced by appearances as much as by reality. Yet Hamilton knew this appreciation of human nature could cut both ways. If a properly run government could gain the confidence of the people, this confidence could give the government power and energy. And if people base their opinions on appearances, the government must appear confident in itself. Already in 1780, at the age of 25, Hamilton warned a friend that the Continental Congress needed more power—and also that it had to use what powers it had in the proper manner:

> The manner in which a thing is done has more influence than is commonly imagined. Men are governed by opinion; this opinion is as much influenced by appearances as by realities; if a Government appears to be confident of its own powers, it is the surest way to inspire the same confidence in others; if it is diffident, it may be certain, they will not only be distrusted, controverted, but contemned.[12]

Such efforts to appear confident would be of little use, however, if the people had little or no contact with the federal government that Hamilton's theory was meant to empower. Frequent interaction, on the other hand, would give the federal government a habitual "empire" over the minds of men. For it was not passion alone that guided men, but also habit: "Man is very much a creature of habit." Thus, while a few Federalists at least spoke feelingly about popular sovereignty (most notably James Wilson), Hamilton's argument tied the recommendation that the federal government reach the people directly to the need to gain their habitual attachment. The more the national government "is familiarized to their sight and to their feelings, the further it enters into those objects which touch the most sensible chords and put in motion the most active springs of the human heart, the greater will be the probability that it will conciliate the respect and attachment of the community."[13]

The power of this habitual attachment not only explains the need for the federal government to operate on the people directly, it also explains why Anti-Federalist fears of federal dominance over the state governments were overblown. The states, Hamilton argued, have "one transcendent advantage" that gives them a "decided . . . empire" over their citizens: "the ordinary administration of criminal and civil justice. This, of all others, is the most powerful, most universal, and most attractive source of popular obedience and attachment."[14]

Similarly, Hamilton argued for a legislature with a number of representatives (as compared to a unitary executive) not only as a protector of individual rights and interests, but also as a source of obedience to government. A republican legislature "is best adapted to deliberation and wisdom, and best calculated to conciliate the confidence of the people and to secure their privileges and interests."[15]

The theory Hamilton propounded in his *Federalist* essays, then, depicted a government that was well contrived to secure an "empire" over the people's minds by appeasing them and gaining their confidence (either through appearance or reality); but what was expected of the people? It was to have confidence in their chosen leaders. As Walling concedes, Hamilton "had little but contempt for idealized images of the people as repositories of unlimited public-spiritedness." Rather, he wanted to use the people's confidence in their government to create a powerful republican empire. In this, Hamilton drew on one of his great influences, the Swiss-born French financial minister Jacques Necker. Necker sought to mold public opinion to create enough confidence in government to make great deeds possible.[16]

But this theory gives rise to a limited conception of popular sovereignty, one that sees the people as best able to exercise self-government at a certain remove. To be sure, Hamilton's definition of the republican principle required that the "deliberate sense of the community should govern," but this did not mean "an unqualified complaisance to every sudden breeze of passion or to every transient impulse which the people may receive from the arts of men, who flatter their prejudices to betray their interests." Rather than pretend that the people are never mistaken, Hamilton's defense of an elite-driven republicanism praised the people as intending the public good even when they err. More importantly, his theory maintained that the people were aware of their weaknesses and had the good sense to hate the flatterer who tells them they are flawless. They know they have erred,

and the wonder is that they so seldom err as they do, beset as they continually are by the wiles of parasites and sycophants, by the snares of the ambitious, the avaricious, the desperate, by the artifices of men who possess their confidence more than they deserve it, and of those who seek to possess rather than to deserve it.[17]

Hamilton's clever rhetorical move here praises the people for being able to see through those who would obsequiously flatter them. Significantly, the passage demonstrates how in his approach the people's confidence in government is grounded on a proper understanding of their capacities and nature. More telling still is the response he envisions to the threat of an overpowering government in those few instances in the *Federalist Papers* where he concedes such a risk. For example, at one point Hamilton addresses the common Anti-Federalist fear that the new Constitution gives too much power to a distant federal government, one too remote for citizens to have "proper knowledge" of its public activities. To this, Hamilton replies that the situation is no worse than it is in distant parts of his state, New York, where the people must rely on the information of "intelligent men, in whom they confide." Any additional obstacles of distance are overcome, in Hamilton's view, by the "vigilance of the State governments," which are rival "sentinels" over the federal government and "can readily communicate [their] knowledge to the people." Moreover, these sentinels will "stand ready to sound the alarm when necessary." Elsewhere, Hamilton again tries to allay these fears by insisting that the state legislature will be ready enough "to sound the alarm to the people, and not only to be the VOICE, but, if necessary, the ARM of their discontent."[18]

These responses are sufficient, in Hamilton's argument, for a number of reasons that tell us a good deal about public confidence and public citizenship. Whereas Anti-Federalists were developing a vision of citizenship in which the people themselves continually supervised their public servants, Hamilton presents the people as following the local elite's view, having confidence in their chosen leaders, and reaffirming those chosen leaders at elections. Such citizens would really only need to intervene in the public sphere at times of crisis, such crises being declared to them by their betters. Thus, when Hamilton's theory discusses sovereignty, it is generally a question of state or federal—but not popular—power. Similarly, it is almost always governmental entities, not the people, that must be vigilant. On the sole occasion when it *is* the people who are to be vigilant, they are to be "vigilant" in giving the federal government sufficient *power*.[19]

A central aspect of Hamilton's innovation of republican theory is to stress the capacity of consent to legitimize governmental energy. Yet in the context of defending the federal against the state governments, that consent is not meant so much as a reflection of the popular will as it is meant to ensure that the federal government can survive without the use of military force. Hamilton maintains that government implies the power of making and enforcing laws, and thus must apply to citizens, "the only proper objects of government." But the critical question is the source of that authority. "For the sake of legitimacy," Walling rightly notes, "authority would arise from the people, collectively, as citizens," and then for effective rule, laws would apply to individuals.[20] For Hamilton's theory, and for most Federalists, the people's virtue lay not in vigilance, but confidence. Accordingly, a leader's responsibility was less a matter of direct accountability—as the Anti-Federalists expected of the "public servants" they hoped to "instruct"—than of fame and honor. To be sure, that honor could only be attained in a republic by serving the public good, but honor was the driving force.

When Hamilton discusses accountability in the *Federalist Papers,* it is generally a matter of executive accountability to other elites (e.g., the Senate). In those rare instances when Hamilton does speak of accountability to the people, it is an argument for a greater consolidation of power away from the people. He argues for a powerful unitary executive on the grounds that then everyone will know whom to blame (or credit) for the effects of a particular policy. Hamilton thus stresses that the possibility of "passing the buck" is always a serious complication for any representative government. Yet in his view this justifies moving governmental power farther from the people. The solution to classic problems of republicanism was not a closer connection to the *demos,* but a greater reliance on the ambitions of the elite. And for Hamilton, as for most Federalists, that elite was still generally thought of in terms of hereditary social and economic status, even if it now also incorporated an aristocracy of merit (including people like Hamilton). In concluding his argument in the *Federalist Papers,* Hamilton criticized his Anti-Federalist opponents for their relentless charges against "the wealthy, the well-born, and the great." Given his increasingly patrician stance and his considered skepticism for democracy, Hamilton sought to exclude rather than include the people in political power, preferring instead to risk, as Walling puts it, an "enlightened despotism of an ambitious few over a lethargic many."[21] Aside from actually electing their "wise guides" and then having complete, almost perfunctory, confidence in them, what did this vision expect from citizens?—To participate, perhaps, in the debates that preceded elections? To answer these questions and appreciate Hamilton's vision of the limited role of the republican press, we must first understand the new context in which he theorized and the competing conceptions it occasioned.

The Sedition Act

With the ratification of the Constitution, debates over its meaning were no longer rhetorical exchanges about possible interpretations and potential measures; they became real struggles over how the new government would actually work. A central question here was the role of the people, who had always been seen in republican theory as the watchful sentinels guarding against governmental tyranny. Though the Anti-Federalists had not won recognition for a right to instruct representatives, they had (thanks chiefly to Madison, who would soon break with Hamilton) secured a constitutional amendment declaring that "Congress shall make no law . . . abridging the freedom of speech, or of the press; or the right of the people peaceably to assemble, and to petition the government for a redress of grievances." Press liberty was an especially important barometer of the people's role, as a free press was the traditional bulwark of the people's other liberties; it would be even more important in the new government, as it was the chief medium of political information for the electorate.

As Hamilton continued to expound his novel theory of energetic, elitist republicanism in the years after ratification, this debate over the role of the people and the liberty of the press ultimately divided Federalists and Republicans. As the current authorities on the 1790s conclude, the Republicans, heirs to the Anti-Federalists, devised a "politics of inclusion" while "Federalism ended up as little more than a kind of strident exclusivism." Vigilance and confidence continued as the competing views of civic virtue. To be sure, leading Republicans like Jefferson and now Madison were gentlemanly in their manners, despite their increasingly democratic ideology. Still, as Richard Buel notes, for all Republicans, it "remained axiomatic" that government, even republican government, "had a tendency to trespass on popular liberties." Accordingly, Hamilton's theory of habitual confidence and retroactive consent was opposed by Republicans. "Implicit confidence is the parent of tyranny," insisted John Thomson. "Vigilance [is] the first duty of every republican." Similarly, Thomas Cooper cautioned that any confidence placed in government "ought not to be unlimited, and need not be paid up in advance; let it be earned before it be reposed." Madison preferred to place "confidence in the good sense and patriotism of the people."[22]

Federalists, however, resolutely maintained that confidence was properly placed in the government. The problem with the publication of falsehoods, Hamilton's philosophy made clear, was that they "destroy the confidence of the people" in government officials and supporters. The Republican insistence on vigilance and jealousy of governmental power was appropriate for a revolutionary period, he asserted, but the Constitution had necessarily provided for "strength and stability" in the new government. Similarly, one Federalist declared that

> nothing can be more mischievous . . . than the raising and harboring of idle fears and jealousies. The government stands on higher ground than we do, and of course sees to a greater distance, and are enabled to form a better judgment of what is necessary for the public welfare; and they are entitled to a generous and manly, not a blind confidence.

Other Federalists agreed and were much less equivocal. Verbal abuse of government officials elected by the people "was in direct opposition to the duties of a good citizen." By late 1799, Hamilton and Hamiltonian Federalists were privately discussing a proposed law, in addition to the Sedition Act, to punish a wider variety of "seditious practices" and thereby "preserve confidence in the officers of the general government."[23]

For Hamilton and many of his fellow Federalists, the people's principal political role was to choose wisely. Elections, not a free press, were seen as "a security paramount to all others," one anonymous Federalist maintained. Opposition should be confined to elections, after which confidence in, and obedience to, the chosen rulers should be the norm. Indeed, as Forrest McDonald pointed out, Federalists like Hamilton and Washington remained "quite unable to imagine that opposition could be loyal opposition." In Hamilton's model, the act of election "committed the administration of our public affairs" to government officials. Opposition to public men and measures between elections was antirepublican precisely because voting was the act of relegating the public business to the elected officials. "Those, who choose their civil magistrates, do voluntarily pledge their obedience," Rev. Nathanael Emmons preached in a fast-day sermon. "By putting power into the hands of their rulers, they put it out of their own; by choosing and authorizing them to govern, they practically declare . . .

their intention and willingness to obey." Ultimately, regulating the press was especially necessary in a republic because, as James Bayard explained on the House floor, "that falsehood which deprives men of the means of forming a true judgement of public affairs, in this country, where the Government is elective, is a crime of the first magnitude."[24]

Republicans, for their part, were busy shaping a concept of press liberty that exalted the people as active members of the republic's politics. As the philosophical descendants of the Anti-Federalists, the Republicans of the 1790s held that the people were the continual masters of their political servants and the more radical among them took to extending this notion. The people were the masters, and "the *President*—even the great Washington—the first *servant*." More importantly, Republicans began to argue that scrutinizing the conduct of annually elected assemblymen, no less than executive officers and indirectly elected senators, was central to the nature of a *republican* press liberty.[25]

What kind of press liberty was required for a genuinely republican government, according to Hamilton's Republican opponents? Most fundamentally, it demanded a concept of press liberty that was sufficiently broad to make room for unrestrained exchange of political information and opinion; otherwise the power of elections would be chimerical. Yet Republicans went further still. Having established the need for continual citizen vigilance, even in a republic, nascent Jeffersonians built on the Anti-Federalist notion of ongoing, active participation. Not surprisingly, it is Madison who most eloquently combines the negative and positive features of a Republican press freedom. Concerning any faulty governmental proceedings, "it is the duty as well as right of intelligent and faithful citizens, to discuss and promulge them freely, as well to control them by the censorship of the public opinion, as to promote a remedy according to the rules of the Constitution." For Madison, Jefferson, and other partisans to the Republican cause, political expression—not mere elections—was the sine qua non of popular government.[26]

Hamilton and Press Liberty

Given these Federalist and Republican approaches to press liberty, where precisely can we place Alexander Hamilton? What exactly was his view of the Sedition Act, and how did it advance the theory of energetic republicanism he had been developing and defending since the *Federalist*? Here we enter some contested academic terrain. Reacting to early, hagiographical treatments of Hamilton's views of the Alien and Sedition Acts, James Morton Smith—still the reigning authority on these acts—provides an unsympathetic account, bringing out a great many of the omissions of earlier historians and thus showing Hamilton to have been a "leading advocate of [the acts'] enforcement." More recently, scholars such as Read and Walling have sought to be more sympathetic, viewing Hamilton as a "libertarian," someone who exercised "moderation . . . in opposing the Alien and Sedition Acts."[27] But these views are exaggerated, largely because they obscure the important connections between Hamilton's position on press liberty and his larger vision of republican citizenship. His stress on confidence rather than vigilance led to a doctrine of seditious libel that protected the gentleman's reputation as a means of garnering the confidence the people ought properly to have in their wise rulers. To do anything else would be to undermine the people's chosen leaders, thus threatening the republican principle. However, if one could *prove* that a public official had truly violated the public trust, the public had a right to know this. Accordingly, Hamilton's concept of republicanism eventually permitted one to publish true facts of this nature, presuming one did so out of public virtue rather than mere private animus or partisan pique. And since such issues of motive were complicated admixtures of factual and legal questions of criminal intent—not to mention their tempting malleability in the hands of a politically biased judge—he broke with the traditional view that a libel jury should give a "special" verdict on the facts of publication only, leaving the legal work of defining "libel" to the judge. Instead, Hamilton insisted that the jury be accorded the "general" verdict powers of finding the defendant guilty or not. These are all important mitigations; but as we shall see, they were not as liberal as Hamilton's recent defenders suggest.

Hamilton's theory is evinced in his actions and comments during and after the Sedition Act crisis (1798—1800). When he saw the Senate's first and most draconian version of a sedition law, he jotted down a quick note to Treasury Secretary Oliver Wolcott. Given the different interpretations one might put on it, perhaps it should be presented at length:

> There are provisions in this Bill which according to a cursory view appear to me highly exceptionable & such as more than any thing else may endanger civil War. I have not time to point out my objections by this post but I will do it tomorrow. I hope sincerely the thing may not be hurried through. Let

us not establish a tyranny. Energy is a very different thing from violence. If
we make no false step we shall be essentially united; but if we push things to
an extreme we shall then give to faction *body* & solidarity.[28]

This brief, hasty, undeveloped response mixes elements of political
principle and partisan strategy. One can stress the principles seemingly at
play here by focusing on Hamilton's aversion to tyranny and violence. He
was probably at least in part voicing opposition to the bill's provisions that
named France an enemy and made anyone who aided or abetted that
country subject to punishment by death. Implicit here also might be an
early example of Hamilton's occasional opposition—later made explicit—
to seditious libel law that did not include provisions allowing truth as a
defense and granting broad jury powers. Nevertheless, to see this cursory
passage as powerful evidence of Hamilton's "moderation" is to ignore that
the statements of principle here are literally surrounded by concerns for
strategic imperatives.[29]

Hamilton never wrote again stipulating his precise "objections" to the
first draft, nor did he criticize later drafts or the final version of the Sedition Law. He scarcely had time, as the Senate was already redrafting the
first version—unbeknownst to Hamilton—even before he jotted down his
quick note to Wolcott. Writing at some length in late 1799, however,
Hamilton made it clear he did not think enough was being done to
counter the dangerous attacks that were robbing the government of the
people's confidence. Though about a dozen indictments had already been
returned, including some against the most prominent Republican printers
in the country, nearly all had yet to go to trial. To Senator Jonathan Dayton, who had only recently moved over from the House speakership,
Hamilton observed that "public opinion has not been ameliorated—sentiments dangerous to social happiness have not been diminished." Much of
the problem stemmed from the "opposition to the government," which
had "acquired more system than formerly," was "bolder" and "more enterprising." The result was "a gangrene begun and progressive." Among the
solutions were "laws for restraining and punishing incendiary and seditious practices." "It will be useful," Hamilton explained, "to declare that all
such writings &c which at common law are libels if levelled against any
Officer whatsoever of the UStates shall be cognizable in the Courts of
UStates."[30]

This passage is important because it is one of the few texts in which
Hamilton discussed the Sedition Act at any length during the controversy

it caused. The passage has also been the source of some dispute. What is clear is that Hamilton is arguing for an extension of the Sedition Act (1798), which made punishable "any false, scandalous and malicious writing or writings against the government . . . or either house of the Congress . . . or the President." Had Dayton and Congress followed Hamilton's advice, a new law would have been established that at least extended coverage to all governmental officers, himself included (as inspector general of the provisional army). What is not clear is whether Hamilton is here suggesting that the allowance for truth as a defense be removed from the Sedition Act. James Morton Smith sees this as at least one possible reading, due to the reference to the common law—which was still often seen as prohibiting the introduction of evidence as to truth. Walling objects to this reading, however, based on a passage two years later in an electioneering pamphlet where Hamilton seems to have conflated his own proposal here with the Sedition Act, claiming that the act *did* protect "the principal officers and departments of the federal Government." It did not extend to those officers or departments, but on this later occasion Hamilton explicitly (and accurately) defends the act for its "liberal and important mitigation of allowing the truth of an accusation to be given in evidence in exoneration of the accuser."[31]

Given Hamilton's praise of truth as a defense in this subsequent discussion and his extended elaboration of this view in the Croswell case a few years later (discussed below), it may seem that Hamilton was proposing to Dayton nothing more than a Sedition Act that extended further, including slanders against any federal official, not just the president. However, we should be careful not to use a clearly confused statement from two years later to explicate the Dayton letter, which shows no confusion, only ambiguity.

In fact, we need not leave our interpretation of the Dayton letter up to guesswork: There is important evidence that is contemporaneous with Hamilton's proposal to Dayton for an expanded law of seditious libel. Although Forrest McDonald's biography relegates it to a footnote and Walling ignores the issue entirely, the Frothingham case places Hamilton's views and principles in clearer perspective. A piece in the *Argus, or Greenleaf's New Daily Advertiser* charged Hamilton with trying to buy out the Philadelphia *Aurora* in an effort to silence its staunchly Republican voice, and Hamilton responded by asking the New York attorney general, his friend Josiah Ogden Hoffman, to prosecute those responsible. When David Frothingham, a journeyman printer, took responsibility for the article, he sought to shield the widowed proprietor, Ann Greenleaf, from the law. He may also have been confident that no journeyman had ever been held responsible for what came from the press, or he may have relied on the fact that he had merely reprinted the piece from the (Boston) *Constitutional Telegraph*. In the end, none of these facts saved him from a large fine and months in prison.[32]

Though Hamilton did not prosecute the case himself, it is illuminating for a number of reasons. First, it demonstrates that he was willing to turn to the common law of seditious libel to pursue those whom the Sedition Act failed to reach. It shows not only that he tolerated—even effectively validated—laws against seditious libel that failed to offer the "liberal and important mitigation" of admitting evidence of truth, but also that he was willing actually to use them, publicly, in a real case, with real consequences for the defendant. In fact, the state court held to the traditional common law interpretation, which asserted that truth was immaterial or, if anything, made the potential threat to public peace even greater. Accordingly, no one was sworn in as a witness on the question of the truth of the accusation. Nevertheless, once Hamilton was permitted to sit as a witness to explain the innuendoes in the article, the very first thing he did was declare the falsity of the accusation.[33]

Presumably, it was false. But Frothingham never got the chance to counter Hamilton's claim and mount a defense on the question of truth. Nor was the jury allowed to find a general verdict of "guilty" or "not guilty." Instead, in keeping with the traditional reading of the common law, they were restricted to a "special verdict"—that is, ruling on the facts of publication and the innuendoes only. So the two principal mitigating features of the Sedition Act—the very protections Hamilton would espouse a few years later in *Croswell* (see below), and which might be implicit in his earlier letters—were denied to Frothingham. Again, Hamilton was neither judge nor prosecutor in this case. But he was the prime mover behind it, calling for the case and then serving as an eager witness. And as an experienced New York lawyer, he could hardly have been surprised by the court's rulings: he knew full well that seditious libel law traditionally limited the jury to a special verdict and excluded truth as a defense. Thus, while Hamilton's recommendation to Dayton may have been ambiguous, his concurrent public actions—actions he knew would be publicized[34]—could not have been clearer. In the absence of the extended Sedition Act he sought, Hamilton's theory of republicanism supported protecting the character of a public official from scandalous comments with the most restrictive understanding of seditious libel law circulating in late eighteenth-century America. This contemporaneous public action suggests that the more convincing interpretation of his recommendation to Dayton is that he was requesting a broadened *and significantly more restrictive* Sedition Act.

A second aspect of this case is also critical to understanding Hamilton's view of the Sedition Act and of citizenship more broadly: the purposes he had in mind in seeking the prosecution of Frothingham. Here again we see Hamilton's vigorous efforts to secure public confidence in governmental officials. Typically, a gentleman refused to take notice of such scandalous accusations, but Hamilton feared that the Republicans were becoming more successful in their efforts to "overturn our government." Their scheme? "By audacious falsehoods to destroy the confidence of the people in all those who are in any degree conspicuous among the supporters of Government."[35] While many Americans might have lamented that misinformed public "masters" could well be led mistakenly to censure or remove worthy public servants, it was not so much a better informed people that Hamilton's theory sought as their confidence, to which federal officials were entitled.

Croswell

Hamilton's principles and actions with regard to the Sedition Act and the Frothingham case provide an interesting contrast to his role in the Croswell case only a few years later. But with the Jeffersonian "Revolution of 1800" placing Republicans in power, the political landscape was rife with irony. Republicans, who had spent the Sedition Act crisis loudly and creatively defending freedom of the press, prosecuted Harry Croswell, printer of the Federalist *Wasp*, for scandalous accusations against President Jefferson. More importantly, New York's chief justice Morgan Lewis, a Republican, used the same traditional interpretation of the common law of seditious libel that had been used against Frothingham, resulting in Croswell being found guilty. Hamilton, defending Croswell on appeal, was likewise given to an ironic about-face. Though the theory of energetic, elitist republicanism he had long publicly developed and defended stressed the need for public confidence in elected officials, he now noted the importance of public vigilance: "To watch the progress of . . . endeavours [to enslave the people] is the office of a free press."[36]

What Hamilton meant by the term "free press" may give us a good indication of how far he expected that public vigilance to go. Recognizing that republicanism required that the people have access to valid public information (as his theory always had), he defined press liberty as publishing with impunity "the truth, from good motives and for justifiable ends, though it reflect on government, on magistrates, or individuals." Though decidedly less restrictive than the antiquated common-law interpretation that Republicans were hypocritically using against Croswell (and had been used against Frothingham), Hamilton's approach to the common law of seditious libel was actually more restrictive than the Sedition Act, which he predicted "will one day be pronounced a valuable feature in our national character." While the act, at least in theory, required the prosecution to prove malicious intent, the doctrine Hamilton announced in *Croswell* shifted the burden of proof, requiring the defense counsel not only to prove the truth of the accusation, but also the defendant's good motives and justifiable ends.[37]

Truth was important to Hamilton because he, like so many Federalists and even increasingly a few Republicans, contradicted the traditional Whig view that the truth will prevail in an open contest with falsehood. Even the great General Washington's name would have been harmed by "falsehood eternally repeated," Hamilton maintained. "Drops of water, in long and continued succession, will wear out adamant." But even a proven truth was not enough to exonerate a defendant, since one can use "the weapon of truth wantonly," to disturb the peace or to reveal some "private Defects" unconnected to official conduct (which would undermine the public confidence his theory required).[38] Intent was thus critical, and Hamilton accordingly argued for a new interpretation of the common law that would grant juries the power to hear evidence of truth and intent, and to find a general verdict of guilty or not guilty.

But even as Hamilton sought to ensure that the broader jury powers recognized in the Sedition Act were brought into the common law, his defense of the republican role of the jury is presented in terms drawn from his argument's opposition between wise guides who deserve public confidence and demagogues who play on the people's passions. The broad use (and abuse) of jury powers had long been seen as a central pillar in the advancement of public liberty, necessary to check untrustworthy or biased judges. For Hamilton, however, such unscrupulous judges should not be seen as members of the better sort abusing their power. Rather, they were part of the wider problem of the people's fondness for demagogues: "The most zealous reverers of the people's rights, have, when placed on the highest seat of power, become their most deadly oppressors."[39]

What, ultimately, are we to make of Hamilton's approach—or, rather, approaches—to press liberty? He was hardly alone in bending principles for political advantage—then as now such principles were occasionally honored in the breach. And theories of press liberty were fluid in the extreme during the heightened political stakes of the early republic. But we can get some bearings by looking to Hamilton's context and the views espoused by others. One easily missed and often overlooked feature of this context concerns the use of "truth" as a defense against charges of seditious libel. Certainly, requiring people to refrain from publishing lies seems reasonable enough. And some scholars have indeed read Hamilton's support for an expanded Sedition Act and a truth defense as criminalizing public lying. This is to mistake the issue, however. One need not have *lied* to be found guilty of violating the Sedition Act or Hamilton's definition of seditious libel; rather, one need only publish an opinion one could not *prove* to be true in a court of law. And opinions cannot be true, only correct—or so Republicans claimed. Repeatedly during the late 1790s, Republicans asserted that political discussion concerned opinion far more than fact and that opinions could not be true or false. To many Federalists, even the distinction between fact and opinion was a "departure from common sense." Hamilton seems at one point to concede the distinction, but rather than recognize the complications such a distinction presented for his theory, he instead leaves the jury to judge the defendant's intent (and leaves the defense counsel to *prove* "good motives and justifiable ends").[40] In effect, Hamilton's definition of seditious libel was vastly more restrictive than simply a prohibition on lying.

Was Hamilton's theory of seditious libel more restrictive than most in the context of the time? Certainly the remaining history of the Croswell case suggests he was not far from the center of public, or at least elite, opinion. Hamilton's argument did not win Croswell a new trial, but it seems to have ensured that he did not need one. In a series of events that suggests a likely gentlemen's compromise—one aimed at quietly saving face for all involved—the deadlocked court failed to grant Croswell a new trial, but the prosecution simply neglected to move for judgment against him. This left Croswell free while the New York legislature unanimously passed a law enacting Hamilton's definition of seditious libel (in light of which a later court unanimously awarded Croswell a new trial, which was never pursued).[41]

Given this history, one can certainly conclude with James Read that Hamilton was "well within—even somewhat in advance of—mainstream republican thought at the time."[42] But in proposing a more restrictive interpretation of the common law than even the Sedition Act endorsed, it is clear he was far more repressive than the Republicans of the 1790s who fought the act and brought about the Jeffersonian "Revolution of 1800." Hamilton could easily have espoused much more broad-minded principles, since they were certainly circulating at the time. That he did not owes to his adherence to his principles and to his theory of energetic, elitist republicanism.

Conclusion

The complex thought and fluid context of our most prolific founder has left scholars with a wealth of source material on which to assess him as either a closet monarchist, an early democrat, a libertarian, or a moderate liberal. Whatever his private beliefs, Hamilton's bravura public performance as the Federalists' chief advocate of a new ideology is best understood as a reformulation of republicanism, elaborating and defending a novel approach that saw the need for public confidence to legitimate a responsible, vigorous government. His models of representation and press liberty are corollaries to this theory. We can see these connections all the more clearly, in all their complexity, if we look to the logic of his claims. Hamilton's reliance on the law of seditious libel was not a matter of lashing out at commoners he held in contempt, but thinking anew with his own good motives and justifiable ends. He was envisioning a new Federalist amalgam of received wisdom adapted to novel circumstances, in which the first modern, popularly elected government had good reason to expect the confidence of its electors, and was—due to its very nature—vulnerable to demagoguery to an unprecedented degree. As long as these threats to democracy continue, Hamilton's theory of an energetic, elitist republicanism will be worth our careful and measured attention.

NOTES

1. Alexander Hamilton [hereafter AH] to Theodore Sedgwick, July 10, 1804, *Papers of Alexander Hamilton* (hereafter *PAH*), ed. Harold C. Syrett and Jacob E.

Cooke, 27 vols. (New York: Columbia University Press, 1961–1987), 26: 309; Michael Lind, ed., *Hamilton's Republic: Readings in the American Democratic Nationalist Tradition* (New York: Free Press, 1997), xiv. Hamilton, like his contemporaries, often blurred the terms "republic" and "democracy" and occasionally used the terms interchangeably; see, e.g., *PAH*, 5: 150–51, and *Record of the Federal Convention of 1787,* ed. Max Farrand, 3 vols. (New Haven: Yale University Press, 1911), 1: 308–10.

2. Following Saul Cornell, I use the term "Anti-Federalist" (and its cognates) rather than "Antifederalist" or "anti-Federalist" to indicate a diversity of views within the general concord of Anti-Federalism; see Cornell, *The Other Founders: Anti-Federalism and the Dissenting Tradition in America, 1788–1828* (Chapel Hill: University of North Carolina Press, 1999), and Cornell, "Aristocracy Assailed: The Ideology of Backcountry Anti-Federalism," *Journal of American History,* 76 (Mar. 1990), 1148n1.

3. See, e.g., Philip S. Foner, ed., *The Democratic-Republican Societies, 1790–1800: A Documentary Sourcebook of Constitutions, Declarations, Addresses, Resolutions and Toasts* (Westport, CT: Greenwood Press, 1976), 29.

4. Karl-Friedrich Walling, *Republican Empire: Alexander Hamilton on War and Free Government* (Lawrence: University Press of Kansas, 1999). For an earlier, somewhat similar interpretation, see Gerald Stourzh, *Alexander Hamilton and the Idea of Republican Government* (Stanford, CA: Stanford University Press, 1970), 180–86.

5. James H. Read, *Power versus Liberty: Madison, Hamilton, Wilson, and Jefferson* (Charlottesville: University Press of Virginia, 2000), 55–87.

6. Robert W. T. Martin, *The Free and Open Press: The Founding of American Democratic Press Liberty, 1640–1800* (New York: New York University Press, 2001), 139–44.

7. *Roger Sherman in Records,* ed. Farrand, 1: 48; Jefferson to Edward Carrington, Jan. 16, 1787, *The Papers of Thomas Jefferson,* ed. Julian P. Boyd, 26 vols. (Princeton, NJ: Princeton University Press, 1950–), 12: 48. Stanley Elkins and Eric McKitrick, *The Age of Federalism* (New York: Oxford University Press, 1993), especially 21–29, 727–32.

8. Lance Banning, *The Sacred Fire of Liberty: James Madison and the Founding of the Federal Republic* (Ithaca, NY: Cornell University Press, 1995), 243, see also 181; Cornell, "Aristocracy Assailed," 1153. For the Virginia Anti-Federalists' list of amendments, see George Mason to John Lamb, June 9, 1788, reprinted in *The Documentary History of the Ratification of the Constitution,* ed. Merrill Jensen, 17 vols. (Madison: State Historical Society of Wisconsin, 1976–), 9: 821; *Creating the Bill of Rights: The Documentary Record from the First Federal Congress,* ed. Helen E. Veit et al. (Baltimore: Johns Hopkins University Press, 1991), 150–53.

9. Alexander Hamilton, James Madison, and John Jay, *The Federalist Papers* (hereafter *FP*), ed. Clinton Rossiter (New York: New American Library, 1961), 322 (#51), 110 (#15), 56 (#6), 78 (#10).

10. Ron Chernow, *Alexander Hamilton* (New York: Penguin Press, 2004), 232; *FP*, 458 (#77).

11. *FP*, 414 (#68). For AH's fears of democratic despotism, see Chernow, *Alexander Hamilton*, 220–21; Walling, *Republican Empire*, 71; and *FP*, 366 (#59).

12. AH to James Duane, [Sept. 3, 1780], *PAH*, 2: 417.

13. *FP*, 176 (#27).

14. *FP*, 120 (#17); see also AH, "New York Assembly. Remarks on an Act Granting to Congress Certain Imposts and Duties," *PAH*, 4: 82.

15. *FP*, 424 (#70).

16. Walling, *Republican Empire*, 70. On Necker's influence, see Colleen A. Sheehan, "Madison and the French Enlightenment: The Authority of Public Opinion," *William and Mary Quarterly*, 3rd series, 59 (Oct. 2002), 938.

17. *FP*, 432 (#71); see also 214–15 (#35), and "New York Ratifying Convention Remarks" (June 24, 1788), *PAH*, 5: 68.

18. *FP*, 517 (#84), 172 (#26); see also AH, "New York Assembly."

19. See *FP*, 156 (#24), and cf., e.g., 94 (#12), 366 (#59), 172 (#26), 516 (#84). Also cf. Madison's use of "vigilance," *FP*, 353 (#57).

20. *FP*, 109 (#15); Walling, *Republican Empire*, 113; see also *FP*, 100, 106–107.

21. *FP*, 522 (#85); Walling, *Republican Empire*, 169, citing Paul Rahe's use of the term "enlightened despotism" (see, e.g., Rahe, *Republics Ancient and Modern: Classical Republicanism and the American Revolution* [Chapel Hill: University of North Carolina Press, 1992], 585–86).

22. Elkins and McKitrick, *The Age of Federalism*, 28, 27; Richard Buel, Jr., *Securing the Revolution: Ideology in American Politics, 1789–1815* (Ithaca, NY: Cornell University Press, 1972), 258; John Thomson, *An Enquiry Concerning the Liberty and Licentiousness of the Press, and the Uncontroulable Nature of the Human Mind* (New York: Johnson and Stryker, 1801), 49; Thomas Cooper in *State Trials of the United States during the Administrations of Washington and Adams*, ed. Francis Wharton (Philadelphia: Carey and Hart, 1849), 665; Madison, *Annals of Congress*, 3rd Congress, 934. See also St. George Tucker, *Letter to a Member of Congress* ([1799]), 36, 37; *Argus*, Apr. 6, 1798; *Independent Chronicle*, Jan. 8, 1798; and Madison's "Virginia Report" in *The Virginia Report of 1799–1800* (Richmond: J. W. Randolph, 1850), 166.

23. AH to Josiah Ogden Hoffman, Nov. 6, 1799, *PAH*, 24: 5–6; AH, "New York Ratifying Convention Remarks" (June 24, 1788), *PAH*, 5: 68; *Observations on the Alien and Sedition Laws* (Washington, PA: John Colerick, 1799), 42–43; *State Trials*, 663; Hamilton to Jonathan Dayton, [Oct.–Nov. 1799], quoted in James Roger Sharp, *American Politics in the Early Republic: The New Nation in Crisis* (New Haven: Yale University Press, 1993), 216, 324n29; for more on this letter, see below. For similar Federalist views, see also, e.g., *New-York Gazette*, Nov. 8, 1799; Nathaniel Chipman to AH, [June] 9, 1794, *PAH*, 16: 465–70; *State Trials*, 670; and

Alexander Addison, *Liberty of Speech and of the Press: A Charge to the Grand Juries* . . . (Washington, PA: John Colerick, 1798), 23–24.

24. *Columbian Centinel* (Boston, MA), Sept. 21, 1791; Forrest McDonald, *The Presidency of George Washington* (Lawrence: University of Kansas Press, 1974), 93–94; "T.L." [Hamilton], *Gazette of the United States* (Philadelphia, PA), July 25, 1792; Nathanael Emmons, *A Discourse Delivered on the National Fast* [1799], reprinted in *American Political Writing during the Founding Era, 1760–1805,* ed. Charles S. Hyneman and Donald S. Lutz, 2 vols. (Indianapolis: Liberty Fund, 1983), 2: 1027; *Annals of Congress,* 5th Congress, 2961.

25. *Independent Chronicle* (Boston, MA), Dec. 9, 1793. On republican scrutiny and press liberty, see *Argus* (New York), Mar. 15, 1796; *National Gazette* (Philadelphia, PA), May 3, 1792; *Independent Chronicle* (Boston, MA), July 5, 1798, May 9, 1799; *Argus* (New York), Mar. 15, 1796; Thomson, *Enquiry,* 21; *Virginia Report,* 220; and *Blackstone's Commentaries with Notes of Reference* . . . , ed. St. George Tucker, 5 vols. (Philadelphia: William Young Birch and Abraham Small, 1803), 2: Appendix G, 3–30.

26. *Virginia Report,* 225; see also *Virginia Report,* 221; John Park, "Boston, January 23, 1804. Repertory: To the Publick . . ." ([Boston, 1804]), Broadsides Collection, American Antiquarian Society, Worcester, MA; and *Independent Chronicle,* Mar. 4, 1799. For the essential nature of free political expression, see, e.g., Tucker, *Letter to a Member of Congress,* 45; Tucker, *Blackstone's Commentaries,* 2: Appendix G, 16; Thomas Cooper to William Duane, Mar. 25, 1800, reprinted in *Aurora* (Philadelphia, PA), Mar. 27, 1800, quoted in James Morton Smith, *Freedom's Fetters: The Alien and Sedition Laws and American Civil Liberties* (Ithaca, NY: Cornell University Press, 1956), 316.

27. James Morton Smith, "Alexander Hamilton, the Alien Law, and Seditious Libels," *Review of Politics,* 16 (July 1954), 309; Read, *Power versus Liberty,* 55; Walling, *Republican Empire,* 272. Read, however, wisely disavows any intention of presenting Hamilton as a "towering champion of press freedom" (*Power versus Liberty,* 68).

28. AH to Oliver Wolcott, [June 29, 1798], *PAH,* 21: 522.

29. Walling, *Republican Empire,* 272; see also 249–50 and epigraph [vii].

30. AH to Jonathan Dayton, [Oct.–Nov. 1799], *PAH,* 23: 604.

31. *Statutes at Large,* I: 596–97, quoted in Smith, *Freedom's Fetters,* 442; AH, "An Address to the Electors of the State of New-York," *PAH,* 25: 364. For the competing interpretations, see Smith, "Alexander Hamilton," 310–11; and Walling, *Republican Empire,* 262.

32. Though an exact date for the letter to Dayton cannot be ascertained, the editors of Hamilton's papers place the letter in "October–November 1799" (see *PAH,* 23: 599), making it more or less contemporaneous with Hamilton's November 6 request for the seditious libel prosecution of the editor of the *Argus* (see

immediately below). Working from an earlier collection of Hamilton's papers, which misplaces the Dayton letter, Smith draws on the letter but was unable to make this connection between the letter and the case in his discussion of *Frothingham*; see Smith, "Alexander Hamilton," 309–10, 309n15 (the Dayton letter); 313–33 (the Frothingham case). It is still not clear why Smith explicitly claims that the *Argus* article makes Hamilton out to be no "Republican," when in fact the article uses the term "republican." The capitalization of the letter "R" was critical in the case because claiming Hamilton was no "Republican" (i.e., a member of the nascent political party lead by Jefferson and Madison) arguably could not be scandalous, since he was known as a Federalist. See Smith, "Alexander Hamilton," 325n55, and accompanying text, and Smith, *Freedom's Fetters*, 410n72, and cf. the *Argus*, Nov. 6 and Dec. 9, 1799, Newspaper Collection, New-York Historical Society. For much of this history, see *Argus, or Greenleaf's New Daily Advertiser* (New York), Nov. 6 and Dec. 4, 9, 1799, Newspaper Collection, New-York Historical Society. See also Forrest McDonald, *Alexander Hamilton: A Biography* (New York, 1979), 448n10; Chernow, *Alexander Hamilton*, 575–77; and John C. Miller, *Alexander Hamilton: Portrait in Paradox* (New York: Harper, 1959), 486–88; but cf. Smith, "Alexander Hamilton," 313–33, and Smith, *Freedom's Fetters*, 400–417.

33. *Argus*, Dec. 9, 1799, Newspaper Collection, New-York Historical Society.

34. Indeed, his letter requesting prosecution appeared—immediately and predictably—in New York newspapers; see, e.g., *New-York Gazette*, Nov. 8, 1799, (New York) *Commercial Advertiser*, Nov. 8, 1799; and *Greenleaf's New-York Journal and Patriotic Register*, Nov. 13, 1799, Newspaper Collection, New-York Historical Society.

35. AH to Josiah Ogden Hoffman [Nov. 6, 1799], *PAH*, 24: 6. Note too that Hamilton's letter pointed to the accusation's "dangerous tendency" to weaken public confidence in government, a phrase common in traditional attacks on press liberty going back to the seventeenth-century English Court of Star Chamber and essential to the most influential defense of the traditional common law interpretation of seditious libel law; see William Blackstone, *Commentaries on the Laws of England*, 4 vols. (Oxford: Clarendon Press, 1765–1769), 4: 150–52.

36. *The Law Practice of Alexander Hamilton: Documents and Commentary* (hereafter *LPAH*), ed. Julius Goebel, Jr., 5 vols. (New York: Columbia University Press, 1964), 1: 831.

37. *LPAH*, 1: 809; *LPAH*, 1: 829. The day of appreciation for the Sedition Act has not yet arrived; rather, "the attack upon [the act's] validity has carried the day in the court of history" (New York Times v Sullivan [1964], 376 U.S. 276). In practice, under the Sedition Act, biased judges led packed juries to presume the defendant's malicious intent.

38. *LPAH*, 1: 810; *LPAH*, 1: 820; *LPAH*, 836; see also AH, "Reynolds Pamphlet," [25 August 1797], *PAH*, 21: 242. For similar Federalist views, see *Annals of Congress*, 6th Congress, 87 (Uriah Tracy), 409 (James Bayard).

39. *LPAH*, 1: 811–12.

40. *State Trials,* 695; *LPAH,* 1: 813. On criminalizing lying, see Walling, *Republican Empire,* 263. For Republicans on opinion, see *Aurora* (Philadelphia, PA), Jan. 30, 1799; *Independent Chronicle* (Boston, MA), May 9, 1799; *The Bee* (New London, CT), Mar. 26, 1800; *Annals of Congress,* 5th Congress, 2162, 2167, 2169; Thomson, *Enquiry,* 68; and Read, *Power versus Liberty,* 70. For another Federalist critique on the fact/opinion distinction, see Addison, *Liberty of Speech,* 23.

41. *LPAH,* 1: 843, 846. Hamilton's definition of seditious libel would be widely adopted in nineteenth-century America.

42. Read, *Power versus Liberty,* 70. However, Read goes too far in placing Hamilton "toward the liberal end of the spectrum of the age" (184n35). This assessment may make sense based on an understanding of "the spectrum of the age" drawn from Leonard Levy's *Legacy of Suppression* (Cambridge, MA: Harvard University Press, 1960), which Read cites, but this understanding must be thoroughly modified in light of Levy's own revision of *Legacy* and subsequent studies that show Levy continuing to ignore evidence that demonstrates libertarian rather than suppressive arguments. See Leonard W. Levy, *Emergence of a Free Press* (New York: Oxford University Press, 1985), and cf., e.g., Jeffery A. Smith, *Printers and Press Freedom: The Ideology of Early American Journalism* (New York: Oxford University Press, 1988). Or, for my disagreements with each of them, see Martin, *The Free and Open Press.*

CHAPTER 6

Understanding the Confusing Role of Virtue in *The Federalist*

The Rhetorical Demands of Two Audiences

BARRY ALAN SHAIN

𝑀UCH work has been done during the past fifty years on Alexander Hamilton's and James Madison's principal authorship, under the pseudonym of Publius, of *The Federalist*;[1] indeed, one might argue that more than enough has been written to last another fifty years. There are, however, three reasons for renewed attention. First, in contrast to the received wisdom of an earlier generation of scholars, today among influential political theorists (and at least one prominent historian, Lance Banning) there are those who argue that *The Federalist* defends the necessity of virtue in popular government. Second, Publius often writes in an apparently contradictory fashion.[2] This allows for parallel readings of *The Federalist*. Those defending the view that Publius is a modern political theorist who has little interest in political virtue can cite passages congenial to their perspective, as can those defending the opposite view. Third, Publius's innovative combination of republican and monarchical elements in a liberal political theory has not been sufficiently explored nor appreciated. Thus, the role of virtue in *The Federalist*, central to a proper understanding of its political theory, demands examination.

Neither side, though, considers the evidence that stands in opposition to its point of view, nor has it offered an explanatory scheme with which to interpret contradictory claims. What is absent from these opposed accounts is an understanding that explains Publius's diverse stances on virtue and their rhetorical utility when addressing a divided nation. As G. Wood has observed, Publius was following the contours of his "liberal education in rhetoric" and adopting his argument "to the nature and need of . . . [his] audience." Language "was to be deliberately and adroitly used for effect," and this "depended on the intellectual leader's conception of his audience."[3] For Publius, this demanded writing for at least two audiences.[4] One, mostly elite and Federalist, had rejected the Revolutionary-era view that popular government must rest on a foundation of political virtue.[5] This population had embraced an identifiably modern stance that held that through the careful manipulation of selfish passions an enduring popular government might be constructed. Moreover, for them, a selfless love of the polity, that is, political virtue, could not be relied on.[6] As Hamilton argued, "We must take man as we find him, and if we expect him to serve the public [we] must interest his passions in doing so. A reliance on pure patriotism had been the source of many of our errors."[7] Publius's other audience, often popular and Antifederalist, believed that political virtue was essential for successful popular government.[8]

To understand accurately *The Federalist*, therefore, an interpretative strategy is needed that can rank-order Publius's virtue claims and determine which of his rhetorical voices best represents his authentic political theory.[9] Put differently, the central problem facing careful readers of *The Federalist* is deciding how to discriminate between virtue claims essential to understanding his political theory, and those that are peripheral to it but necessitated by rhetorical demands.[10] Publius provided guidance by declaring that two questions lay at the heart of *The Federalist*'s political theory.

He declares that "in framing a government which is to be administered by men over men, the great difficulty lies in this: [1] you must first enable the government to control the governed; and [2] in the next place oblige it to control itself."[11] But it is not only here that Publius tells us that these are the two central problems that he believes the Constitution must solve. In number 10, he emphasizes the centrality of the first problem, writing that "to secure the public good and private rights against the danger of such a faction, and at the same time to preserve the spirit and the form of popular government, is then the great object to which our inquiries are directed."[12] And in number 48, highlighting the second problem, he writes that "the next and most difficult task is to provide some practical security of each [branch of government], against the invasion of the others. What this security ought to be, is the great problem to be solved."[13] The government must prevent the governing majority from infringing on the liberties of minorities and, next, it must insure that no part of the government usurps the prerogatives and powers of any other part.[14]

In stating this, Publius guides us to the essence of his political theory, a system that channels men's selfish natures rather than encouraging self-limiting virtue.[15] This is as it should be because for Publius men are selfishly passionate and, with a few exceptions, rarely led by reason or by the selfless demands of Christianity or Americans' Christianized understanding of classical republican virtue. For Publius, human nature is consistently "ambitious, vindictive, and rapacious . . . [man is a lover] of power . . . preeminence and dominion," and this is known empirically from the "accumulated experience of ages." Has it not "been found that momentary passions, and immediate interests, have a more active and imperious control over human conduct than general or remote considerations of policy, utility, or justice."[16] "How often," he continues, is it that "the great interests of society are sacrificed to the vanity, to the conceit, and to the obstinacy of individuals."[17] Those qualities of men that are not self-directed are most rare and cannot be relied upon to solve the problems of government that most concerned Publius.

With such a pessimistic view of human nature,[18] Publius insists in Machiavellian language that it is "time to awake from the deceitful dream of a golden age, and to adopt as a practical maxim for the direction of our political conduct that we, as well as the other inhabitants of the globe, are yet remote from the happy empire of perfect wisdom and perfect virtue."[19] "In a nation of philosophers," the manipulation of selfish passions would not be necessary, for "a reverence for the laws would be sufficiently inculcated by the voice of an enlightened reason. But a nation of philosophers is as little to be expected as the philosophical race of kings wished for by Plato. And in every other nation, *the most rational government will not find it a superfluous advantage to have the prejudices of the community on its side.*"[20] Publius rejects utopian rationalism and instead relies on rationally channeling self-directed passions.[21]

The government, something like a well-designed planetary system, must be constructed so that "its several constituent parts may, by their mutual relations, be the means of keeping each other in their proper places."[22] His Newtonian solution of men moving like planets, driven by blind internal drives,[23] rests on "supplying, by opposite and rival interests, *the defect of better motives,* [that] might be traced through the whole system of human affairs, private as well as public."[24] Through opposing forces, without virtuous or reasoned intention, a properly designed government will keep all parts moving in their proper orbit. For Publius, the "aim of political organization was not to educate men, but to deploy them; not to alter their moral character, but to arrange institutions in such a manner that human drives would cancel each other or, without conscious intent, be deflected towards the common good."[25] A rationally engineered system must balance opposing irrational forces, ambition against ambition, avarice against avarice,[26] in solving the central dilemmas of popular government.

Publius's understanding of the limited role of virtue in the proposed government with its Machiavellian and Newtonian overtones is seemingly straightforward. As M. Smith wrote in 1960, "Everyone knows that *The Federalist* openly disparaged of reason as well as rectitude, and that it proposed to substitute for these qualities institutions so designed that the clash of selfish and passionately-conceived interests would redound to the public good."[27] Although this was the accepted understanding of virtue's limited role by an earlier generation of scholars,[28] today this understanding is contested.[29] Prominent theorists read Publius as defending virtue as essential to the maintenance of popular government.[30] Some even suggest that it is a mistake to associate Publius with modern political theory in which passions are accommodated rather than overcome; instead, they find his theory of government closely linked to key elements of the virtue-centered teachings of earlier political theorists, most importantly, according to them, Aristotle and Locke.[31] The role of virtue in *The Federalist* and its foundational political theory is no longer a settled matter and, given the centrality of these essays to the nation's self-understanding, such disagreements invite renewed exploration.

Publius's Two Audiences and His Rhetorical Strategy

To comprehend why Publius found it valuable to write in two voices, one must take note of the historical environment in which he wrote and the rhetorical strategy it invited. It was one in which most Americans supportive of the War for Independence had believed that republican government depended on the inculcation of morality in the citizenry, and had been confident in their possessing the requisite political virtue.[32] This is the thinking that undergirded America's separation from Britain for "the sacrifice of individual interests to the greater good of the whole formed the essence of republicanism and comprehended for Americans the idealistic goal of their Revolution." J. Greene finds that "insofar as they thus saw egocentric and factional behavior as corruption, colonial British Americans were, in effect, using the term . . . to mean any form of self- or group-centered behavior that favored personal or group concerns over the larger weal of the public."[33] But, as powerful as this Revolutionary-era consensus might have been, its life proved rather short.

This was particularly true among the elite as a sense of deep disappointment took hold. "What was apparent to the few during the war became visible to many after the war—Americans seemed to be, in fact, greedy, self-interested, and ambitious individuals. . . . [As Jay observed to Jefferson] 'there is reason to fear that too much has been expected *from the Virtue and good Sense of the People.*'"[34] Author after author, mostly in the private correspondence of someone of sufficient prominence to have his correspondence saved, found most Americans bereft of the virtue believed necessary for popular government. "Insofar as American republicanism was based both in theory and practice on the expectation of civic virtue, the knowledge that Americans, by and large, had no civic virtue was a deadly realization."[35] Many socially elevated Americans were desirous of a new way to envision popular government. They needed a way to understand popular government that rested on a foundation appropriate for a people who were a "Luxurious, Voluptuous, indolent expensive people without Oeconomy or Industry."[36] "By the mid-1780s gentlemen up and down the continent were shaking their heads in disbelief and anger at the 'private views and selfish principles' of the men they saw in the state assemblies, 'men of narrow souls and no natural interest in the society.'"[37] What these gentlemen, who "regarded themselves as a group of men who, by character, learning, circumstances, and opportunities were exempt from the corruption of their contemporaries and progeny,"[38] sought was a new foundational ethic for popular government and it is this that Publius provided in his defense of a modern political theory of accommodating rather than transforming passions.

Even if Publius is today among the most widely recognized of those defending this elite understanding of the limits of popular government, he was not alone in publicly addressing this audience. Noah Webster, writing two weeks before Publius, held that "the system of the great Montesquieu will ever be erroneous, till the words *property or lands in fee simple* are substituted for *virtue,* throughout his *Spirit of Laws. Virtue,* patriotism, or love of country, never was and never will be, till men's natures are changed, a fixed, permanent principle and support of government."[39] Similarly, consider John Adams who, having during the Revolution defended Americans' unequaled popular virtue,[40] ten years later argued for the necessity of republics to rest on a foundation "based not on self-sacrifice but rather on the check of competing private interests . . . [and] existing selfish interests."[41] In resting his defense of the proposed constitution on a new understanding of popular politics, one that abandoned the linkage between popular government and popular virtue, Publius was writing in a manner that spoke to the most progressive of his readers and offered them renewed confidence in the likely success of America's experiment in popular government.

These different understandings of the grounds of popular government suggest that there was a class division in eighteenth-century America, as C. Beard so famously argued,[42] but its contours were more nuanced and less starkly economic than he believed. Instead, it appears to have followed different class-based understandings of localism versus nationalism, piety versus rationality, and the true bearer of political virtue.[43] (How little, in certain respects, has America changed.) The well-born believed in their own virtue while doubting in that of the people. The people believed the opposite.[44] Ironically, the people had learned their suspicion of governmental virtue from their "betters" during a century of British imperial tension.[45] Speaking for many Antifederalists, the prominent Luther Martin condemned elite pretensions and warned that

> we have no right to expect that our rulers will be more wise, more virtuous, or more perfect than those of other nations have been, or that they will not be equally under the influence of ambition, avarice and all that train of baleful passions, which have so generally proved the curse of our unhappy race. We must consider mankind such as they really are . . . and not suffer ourselves to be misled by interested deceivers or enthusiastick visionaries; and therefore in forming a system of government, to delegate no greater power than is clearly and certainly necessary.[46]

Patrick Henry similarly claimed that "the Constitution reflects in the most degrading and mortifying manner on the virtue, integrity, and wisdom of the state legislatures; it presupposes that the chosen few who go to Congress will have more upright hearts, and more enlightened minds."[47] Of course, Martin and Henry were not alone in their doubts concerning national governmental virtue.

Whatever doubts Antifederalists may have had regarding elite virtue, most continued to insist that a virtuous citizenry was necessary for successful popular government. This was especially true in New York, where the Antifederalists were a large majority,[48] and the debate over ratification critically turned on contrasting understandings of political virtue. In New York, "the Antifederalists were keenly aware of what was at stake in the transformation from a confederacy to the compound or extended republic of Madison. For them, the federalism of the extended republic might be able to provide for the common defense, but whether it could retain the civic virtue of good republican citizenship was questionable."[49] Some Antifederalists went farther and claimed that the Federalists were contemptuous of those who believed that popular government necessitated a virtuous citizenry. Following Montesquieu, to whom most Antifederalists slavishly wedded themselves,[50] "Cato" held that "the same observations of a great man [Montesquieu, III, ch. 5] will apply to the court of a president possessing the powers of a monarch, that is observed of that of a monarch —*ambition with idleness—baseness with pride—the thirst of riches without labour . . . but above all, the perpetual ridicule of virtue.*"[51]

Antifederalists like Cato concurred with their leading spokesman, Melancton Smith, in his charge that "in all parts of the country, gentlemen [were] ridiculing that spirit of patriotism and love of liberty, which carried us through all our difficulties in times of danger . . . [now] patriotism was already nearly hooted out of society."[52] Smith continued claiming that

> a recollection of the change that has taken place in the minds of many in this country in the course of a few years, ought to put us upon our guard. Many who are ardent advocates of the new system, reprobate republican principles as chimerical and such as ought to be expelled from society. Who would have thought ten years ago, that the very men who risked their lives and fortunes in support of republican principles, would now treat them as the fictions of fancy?[53]

In New York, both sides understood that at the core of their differences were disparate evaluations of the necessity of political virtue and who need possess it. For Publius, who knew how to deploy "political theories to extract their rhetorical usefulness,"[54] this demanded that, if he wished to appeal to both sides, he would have to defend two understandings of virtue's role and its importance.

These Antifederalist authors adhered to the principles that had led to America's revolutionary separation from Britain and to their belief that popular government was impossible without a virtuous citizenry.[55] They rested their case on Montesquieu's authoritative characterization of the essences of republican and monarchical government: virtue in the first instance and honor in the next. He had claimed to a receptive European and North American audience that "virtue is not the spring of this government [monarchical] . . . if one spring is missing, monarchy has another, HONOR, that is, the prejudice of each person and each condition, takes the place of political virtue."[56] Many Antifederalists understood that the vision of government defended by Publius was one that had taken Montesquieu's essence of monarchical government, a striving for honor and recognition, and had transformed it into a foundation for a new kind of popular system with republican form and monarchical essence. This was necessary for "only one rhetorical strategy was open to the Federalists: to show that the *form* of the proposed government was 'republican'" and that meant dependent on popular virtue.[57] In offering solutions to the central problems of popular government, Publius held to a strategy of filling republican forms with what must have appeared to Antifederalists as a monarchical essence that made clever use of the selfish desires for wealth and fame.

One such author, "A Republican Federalist" who rejected Publius's novel hybrid, noted that in Montesquieu "'as *virtue* is necessary in a *republic,* and *honour* in a *monarchy,* so *fear* is necessary in a *despotick* government: With regard to *virtue* [in a despotism], there is no occasion for it, and *honour* would be extremely dangerous.' Thus has a declaration been made in Pennsylvania [by the Constitutional Convention], in favour of a government which substitutes *fear* for *virtue,* and reduces men *from rational beings* to the *level of brutes.*"[58] Although he exaggerated by comparing the Federalist project to despotism rather than, more accurately, to monarchy, sympathetic readers were sure to forgive his hyperbole. More accurate, though, was the incisive Elbridge Gerry who understood perfectly well Publius's combining of disparate elements and complains in one of the most frequently reprinted essays of the period, again in the hotly contested state of New York, that the proposed federalist government rested "on a Republican *form* of government, founded on the principles of monarchy."[59] The new plan of government, as defended by its boldest and most progressive apologist, had rejected the wisdom of Montesquieu and the ideological grounds of the American Revolution[60] and sought to defend a hybrid governmental system with a monarchical essence and a republican form that borrowed heavily from Hume and Smith, if not Mandeville.

Publius and many of his supporters had lost confidence in the political virtues of their fellow citizens and had found in classically liberal thinkers a new approach to popular government that rejected a traditional republican reliance on virtue and instead rested it on the monarchical-inspired channeling of selfish passions.[61] Again, with New York in mind, C. Eubanks describes how in this deeply divided world "two distinct and essentially class-based views of republican government [emerged in which] . . . one can witness the transformation of the language of republican virtue into a language of self-interest and, thus, the transformation of a political vision dominated by concerns about virtue to one concerned with commerce and empire," if you will, no longer the language of republics.[62] But in the messy world of early national American politics, both groups demanded their due: the larger one adhered to the truths of the Revolution and the republican politics of virtue, while a smaller one, though influential, looked forward, as had most Loyalists a decade earlier, to a new politics of interest that made political virtue unnecessary. Attempting to persuade both audiences, these distinct visions of virtue and popular government defined the contours of Publius's rhetorical world.

Virtue Here, Virtue There: A Carney's Shell Game

With credible allegations of aristocratic, monarchical, and even Mandevillean pretensions swirling around the warmest supporters of the proposed plan of government,[63] Publius hoped to defend "the conformity of the proposed Constitution to the true principles of republican government."[64] He promised to "'give a satisfactory answer to all objections' that were worth noticing. From paper No. 39 onward he could turn this promise to advantage . . . [and] the edge of the argument in these later papers thus arose from the Antifederalists, to be smoothed by an expert Publius."[65] In the second half of The Federalist, aptly titled "The Conformity of the Proposed Constitution to the True Principles of Republican Government," Publius made sure that one could find evidence that the new government would depend on a virtuous citizenry of one sort or another.

In these essays, Publius defends the republicanism of the proposed government and describes the separation of powers and the working of the House, Senate, presidency, and judiciary. At times, he argues that those in government will possess a certain level of virtue. Two related features of his position, though, demand notice. First, he suggests that future governmental officeholders will not possess the kind of virtue that he and fellow gentlemen do, that is, they will lack the requisite quality of regularly choosing the good of the whole over private good.[66] In other words, Publius claims for himself and other Federalist elite, political or civic virtue traditionally understood, while admitting that this quality will be uncharacteristic of governmental officeholders to follow.[67] As Diamond argues, "the Founding Fathers' belief that they had created a system of institutions and an arrangement of the passions and interests, that would be durable and self-perpetuating, helps explain their failure to make provisions for men of their own kind to come after them. Apparently, it was thought that such men would not be needed."[68] Second, when discussing the virtue of future leaders, it is difficult to know what Publius actually has in mind. He seems to hold them to a lower standard and expects them only to be able to resist personal malfeasance,[69] more particularly the taking of bribes while in office.[70] This is difficult to know with any certainty because Publius avoids clearly defining critical concepts like virtue, federalism, and republicanism, whose meanings he is subtly but pointedly changing.[71]

Importantly adding to this lack of clarity, Publius claims for the new plan of government a high level of built-in redundancy, as one would expect in a well-designed machine. He demonstrates that when a particular government institution is apt to fail, then another governmental branch, operating as a fail-safe, would be available to step into the breach. In making this argument, Publius regularly claims that the branch of government serving as a back-up will contain the needed virtue, however understood, with which to resist corruption. Pages or even paragraphs earlier, however, the same branch or its members were described as lacking such virtue and in need of support from the branch now characterized as lacking the requisite virtue. This clever sleight-of-hand is in keeping with the frequently shifting line of argument advanced by Hamilton and Madison at the Philadelphia Convention that led George Mason to observe that "it is curious to remark the different language held at different times. At one moment we are told that the Legislature is entitled to thorough confidence, to indefinite power. At another, that it will be governed by intrigue & corruption, and cannot be trusted at all." He chose, however, "not to dwell on this inconsistency."[72] A similar pattern is followed by Hamilton and Madison in their defense of the new government as they strategically moved the locus of confidence and the site of needed virtue to whatever institution was under Antifederalist challenge. When read collectively rather than piecemeal, and against the background of contemporary private statements, each claim of institutional virtue can be seen to rest on

the disparagement of a previous one, and the entire plan seems comparable to a carney's shell game.

Beginning with the virtue of the people, while arguing in defense of the
proposed size of the House of Representatives, Publius finds that some
level of optimism is necessary in "the genius of the whole system . . . and
above all, the vigilant and manly spirit which actuates the people of America."[73] A few essays earlier, Publius offered, possibly, his most ringing
endorsement of popular (and legislative) virtue when he wrote that

> there is a degree of depravity in mankind which requires a certain degree of
> circumspection and distrust, so there are other qualities in human nature
> which justify a certain portion of esteem and confidence. Republican gov-
> ernment presupposes the existence of these qualities in a higher degree than
> any other form. Were the pictures which have been drawn by the political
> jealousy of some among us faithful likenesses of the human character, the
> inference would be, that there is not sufficient virtue among men for self-
> government; and that nothing less than the chains of despotism can restrain
> them from destroying and devouring one another.[74]

But, in attacking the likeness of the people advanced by others, is Publius
being fully ingenuous? Wasn't it Hamilton who had written months earlier
that "the voice of the people has been said to be the voice of God; and
however generally this maxim has been quoted and believed, it is not true
in fact. The people are turbulent and changing; they seldom judge or
determine right."[75] Indeed, writing as Publius, Hamilton found that government had been instituted "because the passions of men will not conform to the dictates of reason and justice, without constraint."[76]

Possibly still more telling, though, was Madison's obstinate insistence
on renewing the national veto over state legislation previously exercised by
the British monarch. This was absolutely necessary, he insisted, so that the
rights of individuals and minorities could be protected from the will of
popular majorities. As he had outlined in number 55 above, some feared
that only elite constraint could keep the people "from destroying and
devouring one another." Madison was one of them. Thus, he bitterly
explained at the close of the Philadelphia Convention that other delegates
had failed to comprehend that "a constitutional negative on the laws of the
States seems equally necessary to secure individuals against encroachments on their rights."[77] Apparently, then, at least in private and at the
time that they were writing their essays as Publius,[78] both of the principle

authors of *The Federalist,* like much of their elite audience, had little confidence in the people's virtue and sought to retain certain elements of monarchical government.[79]

We must not be surprised, then, that when outlining how the new plan of government will control the threat of majoritarian faction, Publius refuses to trust that the people will follow reason, act virtuously, or freely serve the public good. Rather, he anticipates that they will follow their selfish passions in behest of factional and individual interests. As Publius explained, as long as "the connection subsists [in man] between his reason and his self-love, his opinions and his passions will have a reciprocal influence on each other; and the former will be objects to which the latter will attach themselves." Among the people, remote considerations will "rarely prevail over the immediate interest which one party may find in disregarding the rights of another or the good of the whole."[80] As in less public essays and private correspondence, Publius makes no mention of the people's virtues when describing the mechanisms offered by the Constitution to control the people's propensity to invade the rights of minorities and individuals.

Even if Publius placed little confidence in popular virtue, he makes more frequent references to the virtues of future officeholders. Take Publius's assertion that the representatives' "enlightened views and virtuous sentiments [will] render them superior to local prejudices."[81] Responding to Antifederalists who feared that the members of the House would not be drawn from the people and that, accordingly, it would fail to represent their interests,[82] Publius attempted to assuage their fears.[83] He argued that "the aim of every political constitution is, or ought to be, first to obtain for rulers men who possess most wisdom to discern, and most virtue to pursue, the common good of the society; and in the next place, to take the most effectual precautions for keeping them virtuous while they continue to hold their public trust."[84]

But when defending the Senate, Publius teaches that the otherwise public-spirited members of the House are prone to betray "the people [who in contrast with the logic of number 10] can never willfully betray their own interests."[85] In addition, "in all very numerous assemblies [such as the House would soon become], of whatever character composed, passion never fails to wrest this scepter from reason. Had every Athenian citizen been a Socrates, every Athenian assembly would still have been a mob."[86] Why is this the case? Because, according to Madison, "in all cases where a majority are united by a common interest or passion, the rights of the minority are in danger. What motives are to restrain them? A prudent regard to the maxim that honesty is the best policy is found by experience to be as little regarded by bodies of men as by individuals."[87] Continuing elsewhere, Publius warns that one must be wary of the House for "the danger from legislative usurpations . . . must lead to the same tyranny as is threatened by executive usurpations."[88] The virtue of the House is lauded when compared to that of the people whose parochial views it is to "refine and enlarge," yet at other times, the virtue of House members is questioned, most particularly when compared to that of the members of the Senate or the president.

Publius's endorsement of senatorial virtue, though, is far from unqualified. When endorsing a limited presidential veto he warns his readers not to view it as an assertion of the "superior wisdom or virtue in the Executive," but rather as confirmation "that the legislature will not be infallible; that the love of power may sometimes betray it into the disposition to encroach upon the rights of other members of the government; that a spirit of faction may sometimes pervert its deliberations."[89] Going still further, Publius claims that in the Senate, "we must expect to see a full display of all the private and party likings and dislikes, partialities and antipathies, attachments and animosities, which are felt by those who compose the [state] assembly." In the Senate, "it will rarely happen that the advancement of the public service will be the primary object either of party victories or of party negotiations."[90] Claims of robust political virtue last, apparently, only as long as needed.

The rhetoric of virtue increases as one moves toward the likeness of a king. While defending the electoral college system, Publius writes that "the process of election affords a moral certainty, that the office of President will never fall to the lot of any man who is not in an eminent degree endowed with the requisite qualifications. . . . It will not be too strong to say, that there will be a constant probability of seeing the station filled by characters preeminent for ability and virtue."[91] This is bold language. Later, in defending the president's proposed appointment power, Publius is more measured and finds that "the institution of delegated power implies, that there is a portion of virtue and honor among mankind, which may be a reasonable foundation of confidence; and experience justifies the theory." He concludes that "a man disposed to view human nature as it is, without either flattering its virtues or exaggerating its vices, will see sufficient ground of confidence . . . to rest satisfied."[92] But knowing Publius's view of human nature, expressed by Hamilton and Madison in

Philadelphia and under the cover of their joint persona, one must question the sincerity of this endorsement.

And in defending the mode of compensating the president, Publius responds by confirming that "there are men who could neither be distressed nor won into a sacrifice of their duty," before lamenting that "this stern virtue is the growth of few soils; and in the main it will be found that a power over a man's support is a power over his will." It is important, therefore, that the legislature be able to "neither weaken his fortitude by operating on his necessities, nor corrupt his integrity by appealing to his avarice."[93] Not even pecuniary rectitude, apparently, could be assumed for those in the highest offices. Publius emphasizes that even those possessing such an elevated office will often be unwilling to support legislation, no matter how salutary, for which they are unlikely to receive public credit. As Publius notes, this likelihood affords "melancholy proofs of the effects of this despicable frailty, or rather detestable vice, in the human character."[94] Still more emphatically, Publius remarks that in the presidency, "an avaricious man might be tempted to betray the interests of the state to the acquisition of wealth [and] an ambitious man might make his own aggrandizement, by the aid of a foreign power, the price of his treachery to his constituents." A president will regularly "be under temptations to sacrifice his duty to his interest, which it would require superlative virtue to withstand," but this is not to be expected for "the history of human conduct does not warrant that exalted opinion of human virtue."[95] Even concerning the president's virtue, Publius recognizes that political virtue cannot be trusted.

Concerning the federal judiciary, however, such fears were rarely raised.[96] Still, Publius is unwilling to leave federal justices free of scrutiny. He offers a few suggestions that indicate that the natural proclivities toward ambition and avarice found in the members of the two other branches of the national government will also be present in the members of the federal bench, and that again appropriate institutional safeguards must be put in place. "It is impossible to keep the judges too distinct from [e]very other avocation than that of expounding the laws. It is peculiarly dangerous to place them in a situation to be either corrupted or influenced by the Executive." He goes on to note that "the temptations to prostitution which the judges might have to surmount, must certainly be much fewer, while the cooperation of a jury is necessary, than they might be, if they had themselves the exclusive determination of all causes."[97] Of course, institutional safeguards were necessary; they were only men. With the possible exception of federal judges, neither the people nor the occupant of a government office would act free from ambition for fame or greed for wealth as "the love of wealth [is] as domineering and enterprising a passion as that of power or glory."[98] And this is surely Publius's most consistent teaching on matters political.

Popular Government without Political Virtue

With Publius advancing evasive understandings of elite virtue and two different stances concerning the need for popular virtue, it would seem impossible to assess which understanding of virtue is essential to his political theory. Yet, the status of virtue is central to understanding whether his theory is principally a modern one that accommodates and channels selfish passions, or a more traditional one that attempts to elevate men above self-centered passions. No matter how difficult this question is, it is the one that must be answered. Without some overarching way of assimilating the essays into a unified whole, it cannot be adequately answered. But such a metric for rank-ordering virtue claims in these essays was provided by Publius when he claimed that it is solving the two most intractable problems of popular government—preventing popular and governmental tyranny—that frames his core political teachings in *The Federalist*. When this is done, we will find that Publius's essential view was that good government was possible without a politically virtuous people or a truly virtuous government; in short, political virtue was unnecessary.

Publius hints at this when explaining that "neither moral nor religious motives can be relied on as an adequate control" over self-serving passions, and that "pure democracy . . . can admit no cure for the mischiefs of faction . . . [where] there is nothing to check the inducements to sacrifice the weaker party or an obnoxious individual."[99] If the traditional republican remedy, the inculcation of virtue, could not be trusted to control the effects of democratic factions, a new method was needed. Thus, in outlining how the new government will remedy the first problem of popular government, majoritarian faction, Publius turns to mechanistic solutions. The new government would control faction by expanding the size of the society to be governed so that it would contain groups with diverse economic interests.

Similarly, the traditional monarchical solution to factions, to which Publius could not openly appeal,[100] would have demanded "introducing into the government a will not dependent on the" majority of the people, that is, a king.[101] In a certain sense, Publius's alternative was also concerned with controlling the will of the majority, but now through a new mechanical means, "the ENLARGEMENTH of the ORBIT with which such systems are to revolve."[102] With this mechanism, a factious majority's will would be blunted by taking "in a greater variety of parties and interests . . . [and making] it less probable that a majority of the whole will have a common motive to invade the rights of other citizens."[103] In other words, "society itself will be broken into so many parts . . . [that there] will be little danger from interested combinations of the majority."[104] With an end in common with that putatively animating monarchical government, control over a majority in service of its own "true" good, Publius even suggests that it is likely that a small group of the people's natural superiors would better understand their needs than a majority of citizens for "it may well happen that the public voice, pronounced by the representatives of the people, will be more consonant to the public good than if pronounced by the people themselves."[105] Nowhere, though, in his explication of this essential feature of the proposed new system and its means to control factions is there any mention of the people's putative virtue, the traditional republican grounding of popular government. Rather, Publius offered a new solution with a republican form and a monarchical-like aspiration to control the majority's will.

In lamenting that the "*causes* of factions cannot be removed, and that relief is only to be sought in the means of controlling its *effects*,"[106] Publius distances himself still further from traditional republican aspirations. He continues this line of argument and holds that even if virtuous statesmen were elected, they would be unable to guide the populace in embracing needed policies because this would demand that the people be moved by "indirect and remote considerations," and these, he contends, will "rarely prevail over the immediate interest which one party may find in disregarding the rights of another or the good of the whole."[107] Something other than the nostrums of republican virtue was needed to control factions.

Similarly, in objecting to frequent constitutional conventions, Publius writes that "there appear to be insuperable objections against the proposed recurrence to the people," most particularly because "frequent appeals would in great measure, deprive the government of that veneration which time bestows on every thing, and without which perhaps the wisest and freest government would not possess the requisite stability."[108] The people can't be trusted with direct political control because "the *pas-

sions . . . not the *reason,* of the public . . . sit in judgment. But it is the reason, alone, of the public, that ought to control and regulate the government. The passions ought to be controlled and regulated by the
government."[109] Although Publius believes that reason and virtue ought to
control the people's actions, he is emphatic in acknowledging that it is
their selfish passions that will dominate and that the new government
must utilize them along with blind veneration in governing. Hume had
explained some decades before that correctly designed political institutions demand that "every man ought to be supposed a *knave,* and to have
no other end, in all his actions, but private interest. By this interest we
must govern him, and, by means of it, make him cooperate to public
good."[110] Publius's Humean pragmatism, almost Mandevillean at times,
demands that the new plan of government rest on what will be, not what
ought to be.[111]

This meant that, among the people, self-interested motivations were to
be supported, in particular, for the majority, a dominating desire for
wealth. This might be described as a kind of bourgeois virtue involving
"moderation, frugality, and industry,"[112] that in the emerging commercial
world was to become "the first object of government."[113] Publius accepts
that society is divided "into different interests and parties"[114] and that "the
regulation of these various interests forms the principal task of modern
legislation."[115] Publius does not mean by this that it is the government's
legitimate role to diminish, as it had been for most earlier Western theorists, the selfish motivations that lead to such divisions. In fact, to the contrary, he finds that an enlarged republic "promises the cure for which we
are seeking" by incorporating not fewer but more economic and other
interests, so that "you make it less probable that a majority of the whole
will have a common motive to invade the rights of other citizens."[116] In
short, the first of the essential problems of popular government, majority
faction, could be controlled (at least in theory) without depending on
republican inculcation of virtue or monarchical oversight. By employing a
republican form that rested on the channeling of a universally available
popular passion, Publius had provided his most skeptical readers new
hope for the success of America's experiment in popular government.

In addition to controlling the effects of popular faction through proper
institutional design, Publius promised that the new government would be
equally adept at controlling the other central pathology of government, a
factious (or tyrannous) loss of a balance of powers.[117] Given that he dis-
misses simple constitutional pronouncements as useless "parchment bar-

riers" or "a mere parchment delineation" of powers,[118] Publius had to seek other remedies. Again, as with factions, two traditional solutions were available: one republican and the other most readily associated with monarchy. The traditional republican solution relied on a virtuous and selfless leadership or on frequent electoral recurrence to the people. The monarchical remedy linked different governmental functions with formal organic estates built into society—the one, the few, and the many—and their disparate and contentious interests. In America, however, after the Revolution there was no hereditary monarch nor an organic nobility. If the traditional monarchical approach lacked the requisite materials and, for his most progressive readers, the republican one was deemed unrealistically utopian, Publius would have to offer these readers an alternative mechanism to explain how the new plan of government could remain popular and yet prevent governmental tyranny. Again, he would make use of republican forms and a certain monarchical spirit. For his Antifederalist readers, alternatively, he would have to defend his plan by appealing to some combination of governmental virtue or frequent recurrence to a virtuous people.

After laying out the nation's dilemma in *Federalist* number 47, and then rejecting both traditional republican and monarchical solutions, Publius answers at the culmination of this theoretically rich series of essays (47–51) that the essential solution utilized in the new government would rest on a new foundation—the desire for fame and honor of each individual officeholder. He sought to convince his readers that salutary outcomes need not depend, as monarchies had, on appealing to the corporate interests of distinct estates,[119] the officeholder's political virtue as traditional republics had emphasized, nor the short electoral cycles favored by American republicans; rather, the public good could be advanced through an appeal to individual ambition. Publius's modern solution makes use of individual desire, balanced and carefully engineered, for enhanced personal reputation. In a fashion that creatively followed, yet altered, Hume's understanding of the British Walpolean monarchy,[120] Publius describes a system that would strive to excite individual interests and tie them to public institutional needs.[121]

As Publius memorably describes this new system, it would work "by so contriving the interior structure of the government as that its several constituent parts may, by their mutual relations, be the means of keeping each other in their proper place."[122] More exactly, how was this to be done? By, Publius tells us, insuring that "ambition must be made to counteract

ambition. The interest of the man must be connected with the constitutional rights of the place." He reiterates that the key to this magnificent
intellectual edifice for maintaining internal balance within the government is that "the private interest of every individual [in government] may
be a sentinel over the public rights." "That such devices should be necessary to control the abuses of government," Publius admits, is "a reflection
on human nature." But "what is government itself, but the greatest of all
reflections on human nature?"[123]

This critical explanation of how the new government was to work,
developed so powerfully in number 51, is found intermixed as well in Publius's subsequent discussion of the two branches of the national legislature
and the executive. With the House in mind, Publius suggests that one of
the forces that will bind the representative most closely to his constituents
will be "motives of a more selfish nature. His pride and vanity attach him
to a form of government which favors his pretensions and gives him a
share in its honors and distinctions."[124] In defending the length of the senatorial term against Antifederalist challenge, Publius argues that this small
group of men is to be trusted because "it can only be found in a number
so small that a sensible degree of the praise and blame of public measures
may be the portion of each individual."[125] In regard to both houses of
Congress, it is upon their members' desire for fame, and their mutually
restrictive ambitions, that for his most skeptical audience Publius principally rests the new government's ability to maintain a balance of power.

Possibly, however, it is in defending the new national executive that
Publius most fully gives substance to the logic of using the selfish desires
of the officeholder to serve public ones.[126] In defending the Constitution's
original lack of presidential term limits, we can see how the right institutional design (no term limits) leads to the encouragement of the right passion (desire for honor), and how the wrong design (term limits) would
have led to the elevation of the less desirable passion (desire for wealth).
For Publius, there are only two choices—encourage ambition and a desire
for fame, or encourage venality and a desire for wealth—and which of
these is dominant will be decided not by moral appeals nor pious
upbringing, but by the correct design of political institutions. In the new
government, with the president's term in office not artificially limited, "his
[long-term] avarice might be a guard upon his [short-term] avarice. Add
to this that the same man might be vain or ambitious, as well as avaricious. Add to this that the same man might be vain or ambitious. . . . And
if he could expect to prolong his honors by his good conduct, he might

hesitate to sacrifice his appetite for them [vanity and ambition] to his appetite for gain."[127] Even concerning the president, Publius's understanding of the proposed government was that it would depend on a correct management of passions, not republican political virtue.

Not only does Publius's understanding of the proposed system not necessitate virtue; one might reasonably conclude that virtue would undermine it. Consider that, at the level of both the people and the government, for Publius's system of interest checking interest to work, a particular interest must be opposed by others. To the degree, then, that a particular group of individuals might be willing to act in a selfless manner and unwilling to defend their economic interest against others, the system of an extended sphere taking in diverse interests so that none would dominate would fail. Similarly, in the system outlined by Publius to protect against usurpation by one branch of the national government from another, his vision depends on each officeholder being motivated by a selfish desire for honor, not an overly rare desire to sacrifice himself in service of the common good. Again, if a number of officeholders, in deference to their understanding of the common good, were self-deprecating and unwilling to defend their prerogatives against usurpation by others, the system of checks based on tying personal interest to government function would fail.

The desire for fame among those who would govern, however, was essential. Adair recognized that for Publius, "the love of fame is a noble passion because it can transform ambition and self-interest into dedicated effort for the community, because it can spur individuals to spend themselves to provide for the common defense, or to promote the general welfare."[128] Yet, no matter how attractive this passion might be in comparison to avarice, it is a self-interested motivation in which political leaders' "minds are however still on themselves,"[129] thus not in a traditionally accepted sense, one embraced by most Americans in the 1780s, political virtue. As Montesquieu had observed, "in well-regulated monarchies everyone will be almost a good citizen, and one will rarely find someone who is a good man; for, in order to be a good man, one must have the intention of being one and love the state less for oneself than of itself."[130] It was this republican goal of political virtue that Publius had abandoned, and in its place had offered a planned dependence on a selfish quest for fame in those who would govern.

We should not, then, confuse the relatively desirable selfish passions for wealth and fame—if you will, bourgeois virtues—with the higher standards set by Roman republicanism, much of pagan philosophy, or Christianity and their common insistence that one of the most, if not the most, important functions of government was the inculcation of a higher order of virtue.[131] Again, it is Diamond who reminds us that "the ends of political life were reduced [by Publius] to a commensurability with the human means readily and universally available." He captures the essence of Publius's new science of politics that simultaneously looks backward toward Montesquieu's spirit of monarchy and forward toward a contemporary form of democratic government that emphasizes the acquisition of wealth rather than the development of the virtues.[132] Diamond observes that

> character formation was no longer the direct end of politics, the new science of politics . . . for the achievement of its lowered ends, could rely largely instead upon shrewd institutional arrangements of the powerful human passions and interests. Not to instruct and to transcend these passions and interests, but rather to channel and to use them became the hallmark of modern politics.[133]

For Publius, a leading figure in the defense of modern liberal politics,[134] government should not be in the business of soul crafting, but instead should encourage the right development of normally occurring passions that, when properly channeled, can be directed to serve important public ends. If Americans were to embrace his understanding of the new plan of government, they would have the freedom to acquire wealth, political liberty, more extensive personal liberty, but the Revolutionary promise of a republic of virtue was not to be theirs.

Publius confronted two audiences divided by class: one suspicious of elite virtue, and the other even more suspicious of popular virtue. The former, however, believed in virtue's necessity, while the latter was prepared to accept that it was unnecessary. Publius, in his solutions to the two most intractable problems of popular government, aligned himself with progressive liberal thought in arguing that each could be solved without recourse to traditional republican remedies. Instead, he offered institutional solutions that sought to channel individual passions: avarice in the people, and ambition in those to govern. Although each passion might be made to serve the public good and might even, in a certain light, be viewed as a quasi-virtue, neither met the then accepted standard of political virtue. At times, though, Publius did insist on the value of an undefined virtue either in the people or the government. But given the vague nature of such claims, their frequently being in response to Antifederalist challenges, and the shifting placement of virtue in one governmental institution while withdrawing it from another suggests that such claims were more rhetorical than essential in Publius's political theory.

His political theory innovatively adapted republican and monarchical elements in the creation of something we today describe as liberal. In confronting each of the central pathologies of popular government, Publius offered solutions that made use of republican forms animated by what at the time was understood to be a monarchical spirit that sought to channel selfish passions rather than transform them. Publius's creative relationship to early classical liberal theory is more readily demonstrated than his putative embrace of some kind of traditional defense of virtue. In sum, those contemporary theorists in search of a politics of virtue would be better served by looking elsewhere and returning Publius to his proper place in the pantheon of creative liberal theorists.

NOTES

1. George W. Carey, *The Federalist: Design for a Constitutional Republic* (Urbana: University of Illinois Press, 1989); Robert Dahl, *Preface to Democratic Theory* (Chicago: University of Chicago Press, 1956); Gottfried Dietze, *The Federalist: A Classic of Federalism and Free Government* (Baltimore: Johns Hopkins University Press, 1960); David F. Epstein, *The Political Theory of The Federalist* (Chicago: University of Chicago Press, 1984); Albert Furtwangler, *The Authority of Publius: A Reading of The Federalist Papers* (Ithaca, NY: Cornell University Press, 1984); Charles Kesler, ed., *Saving the Revolution: The Federalist Papers and the American Founding* (New York: Free Press, 1987); Garry Wills, *Explaining America: The Federalist* (New York: Penguin Books, 1981); and Morton White, *Philosophy, The Federalist, and the Constitution* (New York: Oxford University Press, 1987).

2. On the frequently contradictory nature, if "not outright inconsistency" of *The Federalist,* see Jack Rakove, "Early Uses of *The Federalist,*" in *Saving The Revolution,* ed. Kesler, 238.

3. Gordon Wood, "The Democratization of Mind in the American Revolution," in *The Moral Foundations of the American Republic,* ed. Robert H. Horowitz, 3rd ed. (Charlottesville: University Press of Virginia, 1986), 123, 117.

4. See Daniel Walker Howe, "Language of Faculty Psychology in *The Federalist Papers,*" in *Conceptual Change and the Constitution,* ed. Terence Ball and J. G. A. Pocock (Lawrence: University Press of Kansas, 1988), 118.

5. See Howe, "Language of Faculty Psychology," 127, and Bernard Bailyn, *To Begin the World Anew* (New York: Alfred A. Knopf, 2003), 108–9.

6. See Martin Diamond, "Democracy and *The Federalist*: A Reconsideration of the Framers' Intent," *American Political Science Review* 53 (Mar. 1959): 64, and George F. Will, *Statecraft as Soulcraft: What Government Does* (New York: Simon and Schuster, 1983), 43, who writes that with Publius "the task of restraining and transforming the appetites is replaced by the task of directing them into useful, or at least not harmful, channels."

7. Hamilton, "Speech [22 June 1787]," in Max Farrand, ed., *The Records of the Federal Convention of 1787*, 4 vols., rev. ed. (New Haven: Yale University Press, 1937), 1: 376.

8. See Terence Ball, "A Republic—If You Can Keep It," in *Conceptual Change and the Constitution*, ed. Terence Ball and J. G. A. Pocock (Lawrence: University Press of Kansas, 1988), 151–52; John T. Agresto, "Liberty, Virtue, and Republicanism: 1776–1787," *Review of Politics* 39 (Oct. 1977): 473–504; David E. Narrett, "A Zeal for Liberty: The Anti-Federalist Case against the Constitution in New York," in *Essays on Liberty and Federalism: The Shaping of the U.S. Constitution*, ed. David E. Narrett and Joyce S. Goldberg (College Station: University of Texas Press, 1988), 73; and Saul Cornell, *The Other Founders: Anti-Federalism and the Dissenting Tradition in America, 1788–1828* (Chapel Hill: University of North Carolina Press, 1999).

9. I treat Hamilton and Madison as a collective author, Publius. In support, see George W. Carey, "Publius—A Split Personality?" *Review of Politics* 46 (Jan. 1984): 18–19; Martin Diamond, "The Federalist's View of Federalism," in *Essays in Federalism*, ed. George C. S. Benson (Claremont, CA: Institute for the Study of Federalism, 1961), 34; and Thomas S. Engeman, Edward J. Erler, and Thomas B. Hofeller, eds., *The Federalist Concordance* (Chicago: University of Chicago Press, 1988), xii. In opposition, see Alpheus Thomas Mason, "The Federalist—A Split Personality," *American Historical Review* 57 (Apr. 1952): 62; Lance Banning, *The Sacred Fire of Liberty: James Madison and the Founding of the Federal Republic* (Ithaca, NY: Cornell University Press, 1995), 199; and Douglass Adair, "The Authorship of the Disputed Federalist Papers [1944]," in *Fame and the Founding Fathers: Essays by Douglass Adair*, ed. Trevor Colbourn (New York: W. W. Norton, 1974), 55.

10. See Wood, "Democratization of Mind," 123.

11. Alexander Hamilton, John Jay, and James Madison, *The Federalist Papers* (hereafter *FP*), intro. Edward Mead Earle (New York: Modern Library College Edition, [1941]), 337 (#51).

12. *FP*, 57–58 (#10).

13. *FP*, 321.

14. For a similar emphasis, see Gary L. McDowell, "The Complex Balance of *The Federalist*," review of *The Political Theory of The Federalist*, by David L. Epstein, *Public Interest* 83 (Spring 1986): 137–39; and Ralph A. Rossum, *Federalism, the Supreme Court, and the Seventeenth Amendment: The Irony of Constitutional Democracy* (Lanham, MD: Lexington Books, 2000), 170; and Paul A. Rahe, *Inven-*

tions of Prudence: Constituting the American Regime, vol. 3 of *Republics Ancient and Modern* (Chapel Hill: University of North Carolina Press, 1994), 45–46.

15. See Mason, *"The Federalist,"* 632–33, and Benjamin Fletcher Wright, Jr., *"The Federalist* on the Nature of Political Man," *Ethics* 59 (Jan. 1949): 3–4.

16. *FP*, 27, 30 (#6).

17. *FP*, 458 (#70).

18. See Barry Alan Shain, *The Myth of American Individualism: The Protestant Origins of American Political Thought*, reprint ed. (Princeton, NJ: Princeton University Press, 1996), 226; Howe, "Political Psychology of *The Federalist*," 502; J. P. Diggins, *The Lost Soul of American Politics: Virtue, Self-Interest, and the Foundations of Liberalism* (New York: Basic Books, 1984), 7, 67, 83.

19. *FP*, 33 (#6). See Niccolo Machiavelli, *The Prince*, ed. David Wootton (Indianapolis: Hackett, 1995), 48, who wishes to focus on "how things are in real life and not waste time with a discussion of an imaginary world . . . [for] the gap between how people actually behave and how they ought to behave is so great that anyone who ignores everyday reality in order to live up to an ideal will soon discover he has been taught how to destroy himself."

20. *FP*, 329 (#49) (emphasis added).

21. See J. Peter Euben, "Corruption," in *Political Innovation and Conceptual Change*, ed. Terrence Ball, James Farr, and Russell L. Hanson (Cambridge, UK: Cambridge University Press, 1989), 239.

22. *FP*, 336 (#51).

23. See Farrand, ed., *Records*, 1: 165, where Madison describes the power of the proposed national government as "the great pervading principle that must controul the centrifugal tendency of the States; which, without it, will continually fly out of their proper orbits."

24. *FP*, 337 (#51) (emphasis added).

25. Sheldon S. Wolin, *Politics and Vision: Continuity and Innovation in Western Political Thought* (Boston: Little, Brown, 1960), 389, and cf. Joseph F. Kobylka and Bradley Kent Carter, "Madison, *The Federalist*, and the Constitutional Order: Human Nature and Institutional Structure," *Polity* 20 (Winter 1987): 206.

26. See Otto Mayr, *Authority, Liberty and Automatic Machinery in Early Modern Europe* (Baltimore: Johns Hopkins University Press, 1986), 155, for his account of how new theories were gaining popularity that taught that equilibrium could be maintained through a proper understanding of Newtonian forces; and 148, where he cites Woodrow Wilson describing the American system of government as "an unconscious copy of the Newtonian theory of the universe."

27. See Maynard Smith, "Reason, Passion and Political Freedom in *The Federalist*," *Journal of Politics* 22 (Aug. 1960): 526.

28. See Dahl, *Preface to Democratic Theory*, 19; Diamond, "Democracy and *The Federalist*," 62–64; Richard Hofstadter, *The American Political Tradition and the Men Who Made It* (New York: Vintage Books, 1948), 8–12; James P. Scanlon, *"The*

Federalist and Human Nature," *Review of Politics* 21 (Oct. 1959): 668–69; Herbert J. Storing, "The 'Other' *Federalist Papers*: A Preliminary Sketch," *Political Science Reviewer* 6 (Fall 1976): 239–40; Wolin, *Politics and Vision*, 389; and Wright, "*The Federalist* on the Nature of Political Man," 11.

29. Most historians and some contemporary theorists, though, continue to defend the traditional understanding: see Terence Ball and J. G. A. Pocock, "Introduction," in *Conceptual Change and the Constitution*, ed. Terence Ball and J. G. A. Pocock (Lawrence: University Press of Kansas, 1988); James Conniff, "The Enlightenment and American Political Thought: A Study of the Origins of Madison's *Federalist* Number 10," *Political Theory* 8 (Aug. 1980): 395–96; Theodore Draper, "Hume and Madison: The Secrets of *Federalist Paper* No. 10," *Encounter* 58 (Feb. 1982): 46; Rossum, *Federalism*, 68; and Will, *Statecraft as Soulcraft*, 37–38. Thomas L. Pangle, *The Spirit of Modern Republicanism: The Moral Vision of the American Founders and the Philosophy of Locke* (Chicago: University of Chicago Press, 1988), takes an intermediate position.

30. See Harvey Mansfield, Jr., "Constitutional Government: The Soul of Modern Democracy," *Public Interest* 86 (Winter 1987): 59–60, and Mansfield, *America's Constitutional Soul* (Baltimore: Johns Hopkins University Press, 1991), 212; Jean Yarbrough, "Republicanism Reconsidered: Some Thoughts on the Foundation and Preservation of the American Republic," *Review of Politics* 41 (Jan. 1979): 63; Colleen A. Sheehan, "Madison and the French Enlightenment: The Authority of Public Opinion," *William and Mary Quarterly* 59 (Oct. 2002): 955; Richard C. Sinopoli, *The Foundations of American Citizenship: Liberalism, the Constitution, and Civic Virtue* (New York: Oxford University Press, 1992), 103; William Kristol, "The Problem of the Separation of Powers," in *Saving the Revolution: The Federalist Papers and the American Founding*, ed. Charles R. Kesler (New York: Free Press, 1987), 117; and Thomas G. West, "The Rule of Law in *The Federalist*," in *Saving the Revolution*, 153.

31. See Paul Eidelberg, *The Philosophy of the American Constitution: A Reinterpretation of the Intentions of the Founding Fathers* (New York: Free Press, 1968), 18–28, and Eidelberg, *A Discourse on Statesmanship: The Design and Transformation of the American Polity* (Urbana: University of Illinois Press, 1974), 101–31, 214–15; and most recently, Harvey Mansfield, *Taming the Prince: The Ambivalence of Modern Executive Power* (New York: Free Press, 1989), 294.

32. The evidence of this being the American norm in the mid-1770s is voluminous. The most celebrated remark is Washington's in his "Farewell Address [19 Sept. 1796]," in *George Washington: A Collection*, ed. W. B. Allen (Indianapolis: Liberty Fund, 1988), 521, in which he holds that "religion and morality are indispensable supports . . . virtue or morality is a necessary spring of popular government." See, as well, dozens of essays and sermons in Charles S. Hyneman and Donald S. Lutz, eds., *American Political Writing during the Founding Era, 1760–1805*, 2 vols. (Indianapolis: Liberty Press, 1983), and Ellis Sandoz, ed., *Political Sermons of the American Founding Era, 1730–1805* (Indianapolis: Liberty Press, 1991).

33. Gordon S. Wood, *The Creation of the American Republic, 1776–1787* (New York: W. W. Norton, 1972), 53; Jack P. Greene, *Imperatives, Behaviors, and Identities: Essays in Early American Cultural History* (Charlottesville: University Press of Virginia, 1992), 227; and see Agresto, "Liberty, Virtue, and Republicanism," 475–76; and Shain, *Myth of American Individualism*, 21–47. Cf. Lance Banning, "Some Second Thoughts on Virtue and the Course of Revolutionary Thought," in *Conceptual Change and the Constitution*, ed. Terence Ball and J. G. A. Pocock (Lawrence: University Press of Kansas, 1988), 207, and Yarbrough, "Republicanism Reconsidered," 63.

34. Agresto, "Liberty, Virtue, and Republicanism," 486, citing Jay to Jefferson, [9 February 1787], emphasis added.

35. Agresto, "Liberty, Virtue, and Republicanism," 483, and see 494–99.

36. James Currie to Thomas Jefferson, 2 May 1787, cited by Agresto, "Liberty, Virtue, and Republicanism," 483.

37. Gordon Wood, "Interests and Disinterestedness in the Making of the Constitution," in *Beyond Confederation: Origins of the Constitution and American National Identity*, ed. Richard Beeman, Stephen Botein, and Edward C. Carter II (Chapel Hill: University of North Carolina Press, 1987), 75–76, and see the latter pages of volume 2 of Hyneman and Lutz, eds., *American Political Writing*, for an extensive inventory of such sentiments.

38. Euben, "Corruption," 239.

39. [Webster, Noah], "Examination," in *Pamphlets on the Constitution of the United States*, ed. Paul Leicester Ford, reprint ed. (New York: Burt Franklin, 1971), 59.

40. Cited in Shain, *Myth of American Individualism*, 47.

41. Agresto, "Liberty, Virtue, and Republicanism," 491–92. As well, Agresto finds in "Liberty, Virtue, and Republicanism," 490–91, that for Adams, "the democracy of Montesquieu, and its principles of virtue, equality, frugality, etc. . . . , according to his definitions of them, are all mere figments of the brain, and delusive imaginations."

42. See Charles A. Beard, *An Economic Interpretation of the Constitution of the United States*, reprint ed. (New York: Free Press, 1941), 17–18, ff.

43. See Agresto, "Liberty, Virtue, and Republicanism," 480–81, 483, 485–86, 488, 489, 490–92, 494–95, and 496–98; Wood, "Interests and Disinterestedness," 75–76, and 82; and Cornell, *Other Founders*, for his sensitive depiction of class distinctions.

44. See Michael Lienesch, "In Defence of the Antifederalists," *History of Political Thought* 4 (Feb. 1983): 83; John Zvesper, "The Madisonian Systems," *Western Political Quarterly* 37 (June 1984): 250–51; and Cornell, *Other Founders*, 86.

45. See Richard L. Bushman, *King and People in Provincial Massachusetts* (Chapel Hill: University of North Carolina Press, 1985), 123–24, 128, and 178; Bernard Bailyn, *The Ideological Origins of the American Revolution* (Cambridge, MA: Harvard University Press, 1967), 33–54; and Jack P. Greene, *Peripheries and*

Center: Constitutional Development in the Extended Polities of the British Empire and the United States, 1607–1788 (New York: W. W. Norton, 1990), 191.

46. Luther Martin, "Letter VI," in *Essays on the Constitution of the United States*, ed. Paul Leicester Ford, reprint ed. (New York: Burt Franklin, 1970), 378–79.

47. Patrick Henry, "Speech [6 September 1788]," in *The Debates in the Several State Conventions on the Adoption of the Federal Constitution*, ed. Jonathan Elliot, 5 vols. (Philadelphia: J. B. Lippincott, 1876), 3: 167.

48. See Jackson Turner Main, *The Antifederalists: Critics of the Constitution, 1781–1788*, reprint ed. (New York: W. W. Norton, 1974), 249, 256, who writes that because nationwide "the Federalists were a minority in at least six and probably seven states, they ought surely to have been defeated . . . all told, at least sixty delegates, perhaps as many as seventy-five, who were chosen as Antifederalists, ended by voting for ratification . . . the converts came from the regions near the coast and from the upper socio-economic stratum of society"; and Cecil L. Eubanks, "New York: Federalism and the Political Economy of Union," in *Ratifying the Constitution*, ed. Michael Allen Gillespie and Michael Lienesch (Lawrence: University Press of Kansas, 1989), 314, who finds that of the 65 delegates chosen in New York, 46 were Antifederalists.

49. Eubanks, "New York," 331–32.

50. See Russell L. Hanson, "'Commons' and 'Commonwealth' at the American Founding: Democratic Republicanism as the New American Hybrid," in *Conceptual Change and the Constitution*, ed. Terence Ball and J. G. A. Pocock (Lawrence: University Press of Kansas, 1988), 183, and unpersuasively claiming the contrary, Banning, "Some Second Thoughts on Virtue," 207.

51. "Letters of Cato," *The Complete Anti-Federalist*, ed. Herbert J. Storing (Chicago: University of Chicago Press, 1981), 2.6.27, emphasis added.

52. Melancton Smith, in *The Anti-Federalist*, ed. Herbert J. Storing, abridged by Murray Dry (Chicago: University of Chicago Press, 1985), 337.

53. Smith, in *Anti-Federalist*, 344.

54. Zvesper, "Madisonian Systems," 236–37.

55. See Bushman, *King and People*, 207; John Murrin, "1787: The Invention of American Federalism," in *Essays on Liberty and Federalism: The Shaping of the U.S. Constitution*, ed. David E. Narrett and Joyce S. Goldberg (College Station: University of Texas Press, 1988), 21; and Dahl, *Preface to Democratic Theory*, 19, who writes that "pre-revolutionary writers had insisted upon moral virtue among citizens as a necessary condition for republican virtue."

56. Baron de Montesquieu, *The Spirit of the Laws*, trans. Anne Cohler, Basia Miller, and Harold Stone (Cambridge, UK: Cambridge University Press, 1989), 26, and see Pangle, *Spirit of Modern Republicanism*, 67.

57. Hanson, "'Commons' and 'Commonwealth,'" 180.

58. "Letters of a Republican Federalist," in *Complete Anti-Federalist*, ed. Storing, 4:13:21.

59. "Observations," in *Pamphlets*, ed. Ford, 7. Ford comments in the introduction that "the [Anti] Federal Committee" in New York reprinted and "distributed sixteen hundred and thirty copies to the local county committees of that State."

60. See Greene, *Peripheries and Center*, 182–86.

61. See Pangle, *Spirit of Modern Republicanism*, 124.

62. Eubanks, "New York: Federalism," 300–301.

63. See Wood, "Democratization of Mind," 122, and Cornell, *Other Founders*, 30.

64. *FP*, 6 (#1). See Herbert J. Storing, *What the Anti-Federalists Were FOR* (Chicago: University of Chicago Press, 1981), 15–23; Ball, "'A Republic—If You Can Keep It,'" 157; Donald Rolland Wagner, "'The Extended Republic' of *The Federalist*: An Examination of Publius' Rhetoric," Ph.D. diss., University of Georgia, 1979, 21; and Banning, *Sacred Fire*, 220, who also finds that much of Madison's commentary in *The Federalist* was guided by his need to respond to Antifederalist concerns.

65. Furtwangler, *Authority of Publius*, 74–75.

66. See Ball, "'A Republic—If You Can Keep It,'" 150–51.

67. See Thomas L. Pangle, "The Federalist Papers' Vision of Civic Health and the Tradition Out of Which That Vision Emerges," *Western Political Quarterly* 39 (1986): 591–92.

68. Diamond, "Democracy and *The Federalist*," 68, and see Lienesch, "In Defence of the Antifederalists," 80.

69. See Euben, "Corruption," 222–23, for his thoughtful discussion of corruption, both personal and political, that forms a mirror image to this discussion of virtue.

70. I thank David Wootton for this insight.

71. See Ball and Pocock, "Introduction," 1–3; Ball, "'A Republic—If You Can Keep It,'" 157–60; and J. G. A. Pocock, "States, Republics, and Empires: The American Founding in Early Modern Perspective," in *Conceptual Change and the Constitution*, ed. Ball and Pocock, 71–72.

72. Farrand, ed., *Records*, 2: 31.

73. *FP*, 373–74 (#57).

74. *FP*, 365 (#55).

75. Farrand, ed., *Records*, 1: 299.

76. *FP*, 92 (#15).

77. Madison, "To Thomas Jefferson [24 October 1787]," in James Madison, *The Papers of James Madison*, ed. Robert A. Rutland (Chicago: University of Chicago Press, 1962), 10: 212; and see Charles F. Hobson, "The Negative on State Laws: James Madison, the Constitution, and the Crisis of Republican Government," *William and Mary Quarterly* 36 (Apr. 1979): 231, and Larry D. Kramer, "Madison's Audience," *Harvard Law Review* 112 (Jan. 1999): 634. Madison's first contribution

to *The Federalist,* number 10, was published 24 November 1787, a mere month after this letter to Jefferson.

78. Cf. Sheehan, "Madison and the French Enlightenment," 955–56. Without entering into the debated question of Madison's inconsistency, it is surely errant to conflate the thought of an earlier period with that which would follow (which also would be reversed). See Marvin Meyers, *The Mind of the Founder: Sources of the Political Thought of James Madison* (Indianapolis: Bobbs-Merrill, 1973), xlii–xlv, and Zvesper, "Madisonian Systems," 236, 250–52.

79. See Hamilton in Farrand, ed., *Records,* 1: 288, who writes that "he was sensible . . . that it would be unwise to propose one [form of government] of any other form [than republican]. In his private opinion he had no scruple in declaring, supported as he was by the opinions of so many of the wise & good, that the British Govt. was the best in the world: and that he doubted much whether any thing short of it would do in America."

80. *FP,* 55, 57 (#10).

81. *FP,* 61 (#10).

82. See Cornell, *Other Founders,* 81–120.

83. Yet, in an earlier essay, number 35, Publius had argued that "the idea of an actual representation of all classes of the people, by persons of each class, is altogether visionary" (213). Thus, mechanics and manufacturers are to give their votes to a merchant who is their "natural patron and friend," for he can more effectively advance their interests because of his greater education and superior abilities (213).

84. *FP,* 370 (#57).

85. *FP,* 411 (#63).

86. *FP,* 361 (#55).

87. Farrand, ed. *Records,* 1: 135.

88. *FP,* 322 (#48).

89. *FP,* 477 (#73).

90. *FP,* 493 (#76).

91. *FP,* 444 (#68).

92. *FP,* 495, 496 (#76).

93. *FP,* 475 (#73).

94. *FP,* 458 (#70).

95. *FP,* 487 (#75).

96. See Benjamin Fletcher Wright, Jr., "Introduction," in *The Federalist by Alexander Hamilton, James Madison, and John Jay* (Cambridge, MA: Harvard University Press, 1961), 74–76.

97. *FP,* 481 (#73), 545 (#83).

98. *FP,* 30 (#6).

99. *FP,* 58, 58 (#10).

100. See Publius (*FP* , 243, [#39]), who writes that the Constitution had to appear republican because "it is evident that no other form would be reconcilable

with the genius of the people of America"; and see Ball, "'A Republic—If You Can Keep It,'" 157, 160; Hanson, "'Commons' and 'Commonwealth,'" 180; and Wood, "Democratization of Mind," 123.

101. *FP,* 341 (#51).

102. *FP,* 49 (#9).

103. *FP,* 61 (#10).

104. *FP,* 339 (#51).

105. *FP,* 59 (#10) and see 213 (#35).

106. *FP,* 57 (#10).

107. *FP,* 57 (#10).

108. *FP,* 328–29 (#49).

109. *FP,* 331 (#49).

110. Hume, "Of the Independency of Parliament," in *Political Essays,* ed. Knud Haakonssen (Cambridge, UK: Cambridge University Press, 1994), 24, and see Hamilton's embrace of this theory, "The Farmer Refuted," in Alexander Hamilton, *The Papers of Alexander Hamilton,* ed. Harold C. Syrett et al., 26 vols. (New York: Columbia University Press, 1961–1979), 1: 95.

111. See Douglass Adair, "That Politics May Be Reduced to a Science: David Hume, James Madison, and the Tenth Federalist [1957]," in *Fame and the Founding Fathers* (New York: W. W. Norton, 1974), 97–98, 100, and 103; but Ralph L. Ketcham, with far less notice, published "Notes on James Madison's Sources for the Tenth Federalist Paper," *Midwest Journal of Political Science* 1 (May 1957): 20–35, in the same year and observed that "David Hume outlined practical theories of government . . . that were very similar to the ideas of Madison held on these subjects," 23. See Dennis F. Thompson, "Bibliography: The Education of a Founding Father: The Reading List for John Witherspoon's Course in Political Theory, as Taken by James Madison," *Political Theory* 4 (Nov. 1976): 523–29.

112. Pangle, *Spirit of Modern Republicanism,* 94; and see Wood, "The Fundamentalists and the Constitution," *New York Review of Books,* February 18, 1988, 35, and Howe, "Language of Faculty Psychology," 111.

113. *FP,* 55 (#10).

114. *FP,* 55, and see 56 (#10).

115. *FP,* 56 (#10).

116. *FP,* 59, 61 (#10).

117. See Publius (47, 313), who writes that "the accumulation of all powers, legislative, executive, and judiciary, in the same hands, whether of one, a few, or many, and whether hereditary, self-appointed, or elective, may justly be pronounced the definition of tyranny."

118. *FP,* 321–26 (#48), 476 (#73).

119. His solution deviated from the monarchical tradition by openly tying the selfish interests of individuals, rather than organic estates, to governmental functions.

120. See Edmund S. Morgan, "Safety in Numbers: Madison, Hume, and the Tenth Federalist," *Huntington Library Quarterly* 49 (Spring 1986): 110.

121. See Maynard Smith, "Reason, Passion and Political Freedom," 531.

122. *FP*, 336 (#51).

123. *FP*, 337 (#51).

124. *FP*, 372 (#57).

125. *FP*, 408 (#63).

126. Cf. Mansfield, *Taming the Prince*, 263–64. It is here that Mansfield seems most confident that he has discovered the reservoir of virtue built into Publius's system. He writes that "when Publius comes to describe the particular powers, especially the executive, we shall see that the mechanism of separated powers gives opportunity to virtue as much as it supplies the lack of virtue."

127. *FP*, 471 (#72).

128. Adair, "Fame and the Founding Fathers," 11–12. In addition, see Daniel Walker Howe, "The Political Psychology of *The Federalist*," *William and Mary Quarterly* 44 (July 1987): 485–509. There are numerous references in *The Federalist* to the love of fame; see #17, 101–2, and quite possibly the most famous, #72, 470.

129. Epstein, *Political Theory of The Federalist*, 185; and see Smith, "Reason, Passion and Political Freedom," 537; and Adair, "Fame and the Founding Fathers," 7–8.

130. Montesquieu, *Spirit of the Laws*, 26.

131. See Pangle, *Spirit of Modern Republicanism*, 35 and 48–49.

132. See Wood, "Interests and Disinterestedness," 92, who notes that, in a certain regard, Publius's insistence on ambition rather than avarice being the dominant passion of those in politics was looking backward rather than forward to the future of American politics.

133. Martin Diamond, "Ethics and Politics: The American Way," in *The Moral Foundations of the American Republic*, ed. Robert H. Horowitz, 3rd ed. (Charlottesville: University Press of Virginia, 1986), 83, and see 94–95, 97–98, 100–101, and 106; and "The Federalist," in *History of Political Philosophy*, ed. Leo Strauss and Joseph Cropsey, 3rd ed. (Chicago: University of Chicago Press, 1987), 678.

134. See Meyers, *Mind of the Founder*, xix, xxxvii; Pangle, *Spirit of Modern Republicanism*, 21; Jack Rakove, *James Madison and the Creation of the American Republic*, 2nd. ed. (New York: Longman, 2002), 54–55; and cf. Alan Gibson, "The Commercial Republic and the Pluralist Critique of Marxism: An Analysis of Martin Diamond's Interpretation of *Federalist 10*," *Polity* 25 (Summer 1993): 524–25, and Banning, *Sacred Fire*, 209, 215, who questions that Madison "moved America decisively toward modern, liberal assumptions."

CHAPTER 7

Madison versus Hamilton

The Battle over Republicanism and the Role of Public Opinion

COLLEEN A. SHEEHAN

*T*HE feud between James Madison and Alexander Hamilton that began early in the Washington administration left a lasting impression on the American political landscape. It led to the formation of the first political parties in the United States, to the decisive victory of the Republicans over the Federalists in the election of 1800, and to the establishment of participatory politics in the American republic.[1] Although it is one of the most noted political battles of American history, the cause of the dispute remains to this day a source of controversy among scholars. In 1792 Hamilton himself was unclear about the reasons for the quarrel, expressing surprise at Madison's systematic opposition to his fiscal program. After all, they had not only worked in tandem to produce *The Federalist Papers,* they had also spent considerable time at the outset of the new government exchanging ideas and friendly advice. They must have appeared to those around them, and to themselves as well, as political allies. What, then, occasioned the divergence between them? Was the quarrel grounded in a difference of principle, or was it merely personal or political in the ordinary sense of the term?

In 1791–92 Madison took the lead in providing a philosophical defense of the republican opposition to Hamilton's policies.[2] Although Hamilton initially speculated that Madison's opposition was motivated by personal ambition or partisan rivalry, possibly resulting from Jefferson's influence over him,[3] he later acknowledged what Madison had long claimed—that the war between Republicans and Federalists stemmed from a difference

166 COLLEEN A. SHEEHAN

of principle. "[I]n reality the foundations of society, the essential interests of our nation, the dearest concerns of individuals are staked upon the eventful contest," Hamilton wrote in 1801. "[T]he contest between us is indeed a war of principles," though not a war "between monarchy and republicanism," but "between tyranny and liberty."[4] Hamilton's modification of his earlier perspective is often overlooked by scholars, perhaps because it is easy to see it as just another partisan shot at his political opponents. Yet this is precisely what Hamilton warns his contemporaries against: those who persist in seeing the conflict as nothing more than zealous partisanship and a struggle for power are deceived.

Hamilton's more mature and, I would argue, more trenchant assessment of the party contest provides a valuable insight into the democratic implications of Madison's and the Republicans' agenda.[5] By 1801, and probably earlier, Hamilton recognized that Madison's opposition to him and the Federalists was propelled by a fundamental philosophic disagreement over the nature and role of public opinion in a republic. Tied to Madison's and Hamilton's differing perspectives on public opinion were conflicting interpretations of the Constitution and divergent visions of America's economic future. These disagreements between the two leading Publii shattered their Roman alliance of 1787–88.

Madison's opposition to the perpetuation of the debt, to the national bank, and to governmental support of manufactures were tied together by a single philosophic principle: the sovereignty of the people. In Madison's mind, the principle of popular sovereignty meant the recognition of the supremacy of the Constitution, understood and administered in a manner consistent with the sense of the people who ratified and adopted it. It also meant the *ongoing sovereignty of public opinion,* which requires the active participation of the citizenry in the affairs of the political community. Madison did not believe that participatory politics ends with the constitutional ratification process, the amendment process, or even with elections. Rejecting Hamilton's and the Federalists' narrow dependence on the wealthy few to produce political stability and strength, Madison advocated the politics of public opinion, through which he intended to foster and form an enlightened public voice that would control and direct the measures of government. Hamilton feared that the Republican agenda embraced the naïve democratic optimism of his age, that in fact it had close connections across the seas to the "vain reveries of a false and new fangled philosophy" of the French Enlightenment. Madison did not dispute the claim of French Enlightenment influence. Since the latter part of the 1780s Jefferson had been sending Madison crates of books on the subject, and Madison had been avidly reading French thought on public opinion.

Both Madison and Hamilton considered the contest between Republicans and Federalists to be one that would essentially determine the character and fate of republicanism in America. The ultimate victory of the Republicans meant the triumph of the Madisonian commitment to the sovereignty of public opinion and participatory republicanism in the United States. In contrast, Hamilton advocated a less active, more submissive role for the citizenry and a more energetic and independent status for the administration and political elite. For him, public opinion was the reflection of the citizens' "confidence" in government. While Madison did not deny to political leaders and enlightened men a critical place in the formation of public opinion, he fought against Hamilton's thin version of the politics of public opinion. In opposition to the Hamiltonian view of an economically distracted and politically subservient people, Madison advanced the image of an active and responsible citizenry with a substantial role in republican government.

The outcome of the battles of the 1790s had far-ranging implications for the future of democracy in America and the West, as Tocqueville recognized and astutely analyzed a generation later.[6] Although Madison's particular conception of participatory politics was intended to circumvent the problem of the tyranny of the majority, it nonetheless encouraged the communication of the citizens' views and the formation of a united public voice, thereby widening the path of opportunity for the power of public opinion. In Hamilton's view, this threatened the checks on majoritarian politics contrived by the framers; it asked more of the people than they could realistically contribute to political life. Madison too was well aware of the potential dangers associated with majority opinion—surely none of the founders was more mindful of such dangers. Nevertheless, he consciously took upon himself the role of chief philosophic architect and political co-leader of the republican effort to institute the politics of public opinion in America.

The following pages will examine the philosophic disagreement between Madison and Hamilton in the first Washington administration over the proper role of public opinion in republican government. Their insights and analyses concerning public opinion are no less relevant to contemporary American citizens than they were to citizens of the early republic. In fact, with extraordinary advances in communications technology over the past few decades, the potential power of public opinion in the United States is today at its historic height. Yet, as Daniel Yankelovich has perceptively noted, in our age little attention is given to how we might identify and enhance the *quality* of public opinion. There is a critical difference between "mass opinion" and "public judgment," Yankelovich argues, and while we "have learned a great deal about how to measure public opinion (and how to manipulate it) [we] . . . have almost nothing to say about how to improve it."[7] In contrast, both Madison and Hamilton consciously sought to cultivate and form public opinion, albeit with competing visions about the mode of its formation, the character of its composition, and the extent of its influence on government.

Madison's Offense

Beginning in October 1791 and continuing through December of the following year, Madison published a series of nineteen articles in Freneau's newly established *National Gazette*.[8] In these *Party Press Essays,* Madison attacked certain policies of the administration as "antirepublican" and presented his alternative "republican" conception of government. Although Hamilton is never mentioned by name, his role in initiating measures such as the funding system, the national bank, and governmental support of manufactures is clearly implicated in the alleged trend toward monarchy or aristocracy in America. Only a few years earlier at the Constitutional Convention, Hamilton had remarked that in his "private opinion" he considered the British government to be the best in the world and doubted whether anything short of it would secure good government in America.[9] Madison had listened to and recorded this day-long, rather brazen speech favoring a high-toned government for America, just as he noted Hamilton's endorsement of the British practice of "influence" and "corruption" in government.[10] Perhaps all this would have been forgotten or chalked up to savvy political maneuvering had not Hamilton's public deeds and unguarded words later revealed otherwise. At the legendary dinner party hosted by Jefferson and attended by John Adams and Alexander Hamilton in April 1791, Hamilton once again demonstrated how audacious he could be. In response to Adams's pedantic remarks on the near perfection of the British constitution, which, he said, needed only to be purged of its corruption and equality of representation established in its popular branch, Hamilton's riposte must have tested the bounds of his host's civility: "Purge it of its corruption, and give to its popular branch equality of representation," Hamilton purportedly said, "and it would become an *impracticable* government: as it stands at present, with all its supposed defects, it is the most perfect government which ever existed."[11] Almost certainly Jefferson's good Madeira was flowing at table that spring evening, loosening Hamilton's already sassy tongue, and just as surely Jefferson repeated Hamilton's provocative remarks to his friend Madison the next time they talked.

Whether Hamilton actually sought to establish hereditary distinctions in America was not the central issue—though some Federalists probably did, and Hamilton's financial program played into their schemes. Regardless, Hamilton's program provided the chief impetus toward new-modeling the American government on the British system. Hamilton's measures were "more accommodated to the depraved examples" of monarchy and aristocracy than to the genius of republicanism, and, whether intended or not, might well "smooth the way to hereditary government" in America.[12] In contrast to Jefferson's accusations of monarchism leveled against Hamilton, Madison's implicit attacks on the Treasury Secretary in the *Party Press Essays* are more circumspect; they are couched in terms of the *impetus* or *tendency* of Hamilton's measures toward the establishment of a British style system in the United States. By early 1791 Madison saw a pattern emerging in the administrative measures Hamilton avidly advocated, and by the end of that year, with an advance copy of Hamilton's "Report on Manufactures" in hand, Madison's worst fears had been realized. Hamilton meant, by administrative fiat, to undermine the Constitution as ratified and adopted by the American people, and to alter the substance, and perhaps the form, of American republicanism. In Madison's perspective, Hamilton's funding system, the national bank, and governmental support of manufacturing were linked together in a clever scheme that mimicked the British financial system and, if successful, would increase the powers of the national government and establish a powerful and influential monied class in America. The pages of the "Report on Manufactures" revealed to Madison that Hamilton intended nothing less than the transformation of the economic and political life of America.

Madison believed that the foundation of Hamilton's plan rested in measures that invested the national government with "influence," thereby enabling it to dispense money and emoluments.[13] This was accomplished by the institution of a funding system, which would continue to provide the source for political influence as long as the debt was perpetuated. Madison suspected that Hamilton intended to fund the debt in perpetuity.[14] Madison regarded the establishment of a national bank as an unconstitutional usurpation of power by the national government, believing it neither *necessary* nor *proper* according to the Constitution, though he fully recognized that it was a necessary element of Hamilton's scheme to establish a class of wealthy industrialists who would wield political power in America. Taken together, the national bank and funded public debt encouraged a "spirit of speculation" within and without government.[15] Hamilton's system of public finance appealed to the avidity of public officials, tempting them to substitute the motive of private interest in the place of public duty.[16] It directed governmental measures to the interest of the few, providing the "monied men" with irresistible opportunities for further enrichment.[17] The wealth accumulated by the frenzy of speculative activity was to be channeled into the manufacturing industry, again by an unconstitutional exercise of power. Governmental manipulation of the choice of occupations via the artificial encouragement of manufactures would promote the interest of this class at the expense of other interests in the society, particularly the agricultural interest. Landholders would be burdened with arbitrary taxes while rich merchants were granted new and "*unnecessary* opportunities" to capitalize on their wealth.[18] This show of partiality to the wealthy few, though touted as advancing the prosperity and happiness of the nation as a whole, would in time, Madison argued, actually give "such a turn to the administration, [that] the government itself may by degree be narrowed into fewer hands, and approximated to an hereditary form."[19] Designed to simulate the practices of the British system, it would introduce corruption and venality into government and encouraged self-interest as its driving force. Madison contemptuously described this governmental model in "Spirit of Governments":

> A government operating by corrupt influence; substituting the motive of private interest in place of public duty; converting its pecuniary dispensations into bounties for favorites, or bribes to opponents; accommodating its measures to the avidity of a part of the nation instead of the benefit of the whole: in a word, enlisting an army of interested partizans, whose tongues, whose pens, whose intrigues, and whose active combinations, by supplying the terror of the sword, may support a real domination of the few, under an apparent liberty of the many.[20]

Despite Montesquieu's categorization of this type of government as a republic, Madison argued, it is in reality "an imposter." Such a government is not yet "on the west side of the Atlantic," and "it will be both happy and honorable for the United States, if they never descend to mimic the costly pageantry of its form, nor betray themselves into the venal spirit of its administration."[21]

Madison believed that Hamilton's measures were intended to reproduce the equilibrium of the British model, if not by the creation of hereditary class distinctions, then by a mimetic equivalent that provided additional checks on the *demos* and presumably enhanced the stability of the political order.[22] This is a perverse understanding of the republican solution to the problem of parties, he argued in the *Party Press Essay* "Parties." Since parties exist naturally in all political societies, legislators and statesmen must find ways to alleviate their baneful effects. The art lies in preventing or accommodating parties, to the extent possible, and when not possible, making them mutual checks upon one another. By contrast, the notion of promoting the creation of new parties or strengthening existing ones, in order to achieve additional mutual checks in society, to add "more scales and . . . more weights to perfect and maintain the equilibrium," Madison declared, is "absurd." Though this is the theory that undergirds the use of artificial distinctions such as king, nobles, and plebians to attain a balanced government, it is not the republican way. Such a political model is analogous to promoting vices in ethics so that they may be used to counteract other vices, and it "is as little the voice of reason, as it is that of republicanism."[23]

Madison further pursued the faulty analysis that he believed underlay Hamilton's (and Adams's) praise of the British model with his direct critique of it in the essay "British Government." The "boasted equilibrium" of the British government, so far as it is even true, is not primarily due to "the form in which its powers are distributed and balanced."[24] Stability and liberty are not secured by limiting the share of the people to a third of government and counteracting their influence by two grand hereditary orders with conflicting and hostile feelings, habits, and interests, nor by any simulation of the British model of class warfare or party contestation.[25] The stability of the British government "is maintained less by the distribution of its powers, than by the force of public opinion."[26] The Federalists, he believed, failed to recognize the dominant role played by public opinion in the British system and, moreover, denied public opinion its rightful place as sovereign in a free polity. Instead of heeding the authoritative voice of the public, the antirepublicans demanded that the people simply have confidence in their government and submit to its acts.[27] By promoting a political design that would make the government independent of the will of the public, they were denying the right of a republican people to govern themselves.

Hamilton's Defense

Hamilton's financial system consisted of three essential elements. First and foremost was the need to establish public credit in the United States. The initial step in accomplishing this was the establishment of an adequate system of funding the national debt. Whereas an unfunded debt is the object of excessive speculation, drains the nation of capital, and diverts funds from useful and productive industry, a properly instituted funding system supplies active capital in a country deficient in capital. Once public securities have acquired an adequate and stable value and the confidence of the community is established, the debt may serve as an engine of credit by promoting the transfer and exchange of funds. With additional capital in circulation, interest rates decrease; the stabilization of public stock moderates the spirit of speculation and directs capital to more useful channels. In Hamilton's view, the depreciated condition of landed property in America resulted from the scarcity of money. The increased quantity and circulation of capital would contribute to improve the state of agriculture. Further, it would unclog the wheels of commerce, thereby promoting commerce and manufacturing as well.[28] While Hamilton conceded that his program benefited the monied men of America, he denied that it created a special monied interest adverse to other citizens. Rather, he argued, investment in public stock promotes the economic growth of the nation, including all the useful industries in which the citizens are engaged. Productivity is increased and employment rises, further increasing the active and actual capital of a nation. Industry in general flourishes, "and herein," Hamilton declared, "consist[s] the true wealth of a nation."[29]

The second prong of Hamilton's financial program involved the establishment of a national system of banking that would fortify the establishment of public credit. The institution of a national bank was in his opinion more than an optional supplement to the funding system. Whereas banks are "*useful* in Countries greatly advanced in wealth," he argued, they are absolutely "*necessary* in Countries little advanced in wealth."[30] The advantages derived from a national bank include (1) the augmentation of the active and productive capital of the nation; (2) a greater facility by the government to obtain financial support, especially in times of emergency; and (3) the assistance in the payment of taxes. A national bank increases the supply of active capital by its ability to lend and circulate greater amounts of capital than the actual sum of its stock in coin. For all practical purposes, then, industry and trade would receive an absolute increase of capital infusion, and economic enterprise would be enlarged. In this way, banks are "the nurseries of national wealth."[31] Hamilton defended the constitutional authority of the national govern-ment to establish a national bank on the grounds that the right to erect corporations is inherent in the very definition of government. In defend-ing the bank in a private letter to Washington, Hamilton couched his case in more practical terms: "[T]he most incorrigible theorist among [the bank's] opponents would in one month[']s experience as head of the Department of the Treasury be compelled to acknowle[d]ge that it is an absolutely indispensable engine in the management of the Finances, and would quickly become a convert to its perfect constitutionality."[32]

It was in response to the third prong of Hamilton's financial scheme that Madison mounted a full-scale opposition against his "antirepublican" program and, with his political allies, adopted the appellation, the "repub-lican party." Hamilton's "Report on Manufactures" was premised on the idea that the accelerated growth of manufacturing in the United States was essential to the national interest.[33] The manufacturing industry, Hamilton argued, enhances the produce and revenue of the community, contributes to the diversification and division of labor, increases employment and productivity by engaging persons not ordinarily working, promotes for-eign emigration, furnishes a broader scope for the differing talents and dispositions of persons, increases the demand for agricultural produce, and makes the United States less dependent on foreign markets. Despite the clear and certain economic benefits that the growth of manufactures would produce in the nation, this does not guarantee that it will naturally occur, or occur as quickly as the country requires. Human beings are crea-tures of habit and tend to adopt untried industries reluctantly and slowly. "To produce the desirable changes, as early as may be expedient," he wrote, "may therefore require the incitement and patronage of government."[34] The supply of active capital needed to encourage manufacturing in the new republic was already in place via the funded debt and the national bank. Speculation in public stocks could thus be directed to useful purposes and away from its sometimes pernicious effects. Although the encouragement of manufactures in America would be disadvantageous to the other classes of society and to consumers in the short term, Hamilton argued that the long-term, permanent effect would be to the benefit of all classes of society and the nation as a whole.

Hamilton's economic program was designed to stabilize the fiscal situation of the country, stimulate productivity, and set America on the course of prodigious material prosperity. His intent was to establish the economic foundation on which political stability and greatness depended. He had no wish, he repeatedly claimed, to establish monarchy or aristocracy in America or to introduce hereditary distinctions of any kind. That he was bent on corrupting a portion of the legislature he pronounced false and malignant. He rebuffed the charge that he was attempting to overturn the state governments or pervert limited government; there is a good deal of ambiguous ground concerning the demarcation between the general and the state governments over which honest men might disagree, he asserted. Finally, he flatly denied that he and the Federalists were conspiring to overthrow republican government in the United States, or even that their measures would *tend* to subvert the republican form or *prepare the way for* monarchy.[35] In exasperation, Hamilton could only ask in regard to his opponents' accusations: When ever were "men more ingenious to torment themselves with phantoms?"[36]

Hamilton's economic blueprint for America was designed to achieve both individual security and national strength. His conception of the connection between political stability and economic prosperity was presented most explicitly in his day-long speech of June 18 at the Constitutional Convention. In societies where industry is encouraged, Hamilton argued, individual security is often threatened by the clash of the distinct and rival interests between the few and the many, that is, between the wealthy, well-born, educated citizens and the mass of the people. If either group has all the power, it will oppress the other. "Both therefore ought to have power that each may defend itself agst. the other."[37] Moreover, given the "violence & turbulence" of the democratic spirit, it is particularly crucial to establish a separate and permanent body to check the unsteadiness and imprudence of the mass of the people.[38] The principle of representation is not sufficient to resist "the popular current," for the most popular branch of the legislature will predominate, and within it a few individuals tend to prevail.[39] Dependent on the favor of the people for the continuation of their position and power, these leaders often sacrifice the permanent interest of the nation to the passionate and partial interests of the many.

The problem of the force of majority faction is therefore not solved by the representative principle. Neither is the difficulty overcome by the establishment of a government over a large extent of territory. Although representatives chosen from larger districts may be of some benefit, frequently a small portion of a large district carries an election.[40] The representatives of an extensive nation still meet in one room and are liable to the same influences of those in a small country, including the charm of a powerful demagogue. The determinant influence of the size of a nation to deter the formation of a majority faction is, Hamilton claimed, of doubtful veracity. Combinations on the basis of interest will not be as difficult or unlikely as some may suppose. Geographical and economic factors can and will influence the people and their representatives, and "it is easy to conceive a popular sentiment pervading" one portion, even a major portion, of the legislature.[41] In essence, Madison's analysis of the problem of majority faction and his proffered solution of the extended republic and representation, which he presented on June 6 on the Convention floor and later summarized in the tenth *Federalist,* was inadequate to the task of remedying the defects of popular government. In Hamilton's view, Madison's proffered solution was not a well-thought-through solution to the problem at all.

Hamilton contended that the problem of majority tyranny necessitates the establishment of a "permanent barrier" in government that would counteract the passionate demands of the many, particularly their covetousness toward the property of others.[42] The British provided for this barrier in their House of Lords. Hamilton believed that an equally effectual check on the turbulent and changing multitude was needed in America. Accordingly, he proposed that senators serve for life or during good behavior, arguing that the seven-year Senate term supported by some delegates, including James Madison, was not sufficient to answer the purpose sought.[43] But just as there ought not be too much dependence on the popular sentiments, neither ought there be too little.[44] Hamilton recommended a House of Representatives of enlarged numbers, elected directly by the people every three years. The two branches of the legislature would balance each other in terms of the many versus the few, turbulence versus inertia, and protection of equal rights versus security for property rights. One chamber manifests the "sensibility" of the populace, the other "knowledge and firmness" in public affairs.[45] It is a kind of balance and "happiest mode of conciliating" contraries, anticipating Jane Austen's felicitous equipoise in *Sense and Sensibility*.

The two-weighted scale protects the few and the many from oppression by each other, thereby contributing to the security of individual rights. Hamilton advocated adding a third weight to the scale in the form of a single elected executive serving for life or for good behavior. The executive would possess an absolute negative on legislation and, in turn, would himself be subject to counterbalancing checks by the legislature. Accordingly, the executive would provide an additional check against the passage of laws based on partial interest. In positive terms, Hamilton's executive was to serve as the dominant active agency in government. Characterized by unity, duration, and energy, his ambitions would be virtually one with the interests of the nation. He would move government to act with vigor, dispatch, and regularity, providing a sense of national character, strength, and permanency of will. An independent judiciary supplements the checks against the legislature and its natural tendency to dominate in popular governments. This check on legislative power would further increase the proportionate authority of the republican executive.

Hamilton's central objective in his June 18 speech was to demonstrate the need for a "permanent *will*" in the government.[46] His plan was partly modeled on the British constitution, particularly in regard to the separation of powers based on two distinct interests in society and an energetic executive who embodies the interest of the nation as a whole. However, unlike the British model, Hamilton claimed that his plan was fully consistent with the principles of republicanism. In it, "the Executive and Legislative organs are appointed by a popular Election, and hold their offices upon a responsible and defeasible tenure."[47] Granted, subsequent to (indirect) election by the people, the Senate and executive would be as far removed from popular will as republican principles would allow. A democratic assembly simply cannot be properly checked by a democratic senate, and both of these by a democratic executive, Hamilton argued.[48] Gouverneur Morris described the problem in earthier tones: "[T]he members of both Houses are creatures which, though differently born, are begotten in the same way and by the same sire. . . . The President can . . . do what he pleases, provided it shall always please him to place those who lead a majority of the Representatives."[49] Hamilton urged his colleagues to see that the only effectual method to secure the ends of republican government was to overcome the contest between the few and the many. Like a host of renowned thinkers before him, Hamilton saw in the British constitution a model that effectually neutralized this struggle at the governmental level. He borrowed from the vaunted British model the idea of achieving an equilibrium of the predominant and rival passions and interests within the legislature, albeit without deriving the competing humors from a hereditary ranking.

The key to the success of the British political system was the creation of institutions and practices that neutralized the destabilizing effects of the rival passions in society and at the same time utilized those passions to energize and bolster the government. Hamilton believed that if the American republic was to succeed, it too must incorporate a political scheme that channels men's selfish passions and interests and utilizes them to support the government.[50] Besides force, Hamilton listed four other factors that prompt men to the support of government, *viz.*, interest, opinion, habit, and influence.[51] Of these, self-interest is "the most powerful incentive of human action," he argued, explicitly following Hume in his assessment of human nature.[52] No regime derives benefit from neglecting to utilize this dominant force in man, Hamilton declared in 1775. He restated this idea at the Constitutional Convention: the key to constructing a stable and good government is to interest the passions of men and make them serve the public.[53]

The conjunction between Hamilton's economic and political philosophy occurs at two principal axes. First, Hamilton believed that economic diversification is necessary to the security of individual rights. Second, he held that economic prosperity leads to an opinion of confidence in government, thereby providing the foundation for public strength. The diversification of occupations throughout the union, he predicted, would contribute significantly to overcoming the rivalry between northern and southern interests, that is, between industry and agriculture, between free and slave-holding states.[54] Economic diversification would help to control the problem of majority faction by diminishing the most powerful engine of faction in America—interests grounded in geographic/occupational distinctions. Moreover, increased diversification would lead to a preponderance of members of the learned professions—especially the legal profession—in Congress. Unlike men of industry and agriculture, men of the professional ranks "form no distinct interest in society" and are likely to be impartial arbiters between the others.[55] Economic diversification also fuels prosperity—and vice versa. Economic prosperity instills in the people an opinion of the benefit of government to their own well-being and inspires in them a confidence in its measures. Public confidence in government stabilizes the regime and endows it with public strength. This is particularly true in republican government which, even more than other political forms, depends on opinion.[56]

In 1787 the United States was predominantly an agricultural nation. To achieve Hamilton's goals of economic diversification and prosperity meant that America must become a commercial republic. This transformation depended on the institution of his three-pronged fiscal program, beginning with the establishment of public credit and a national bank and culminating in governmental support of manufactures. Accordingly, Hamilton sought to connect the interests of the monied men to the interests of the nation—an idea he never dispensed with.[57] The first wave of his economic program depended on this connection. It would stabilize public credit, wean men from state attachments to support of the national government, and provide the avenue for economic prosperity and a train of events that would usher in a new economic and political era in America. Like Montesquieu, Hamilton believed that in a republic, where all the passions are free and unmodified, it is natural that the passion for material aggrandizement dominates men's souls. A commercial republic allows the passionate pursuit of economic gain and rewards it with success. Commercial prosperity multiplies "the means of gratification," promotes the circulation of charming, shiny metals—"those darling objects of human avarice and enterprise"—and increases prosperity throughout the society.[58] The multiplication of the means of gratifying the acquisitive desire is much more the result of commercial prosperity than the mere size of the territory. By getting the monied men interested in the prosperity of the nation, Hamilton sought to start a chain reaction that would promote the commercialization of the entire country. The consequences of this economic metastasis were far reaching on the political front. By multiplying and diversifying occupations and interests in America, the age-old battle between the haves and have-nots would be replaced by a new and much less dangerous rivalry in society. The likelihood of a majority faction forming would be greatly reduced and the stability of the political order would be significantly enhanced. Moreover, the commercial republic possesses the advantage over other forms of government because it tends "to interest the passions of the community in its favor [and] beget[s] public spirit and public confidence."[59]

Hamilton viewed human nature as consisting of two very different types of men: the mass of men who are motivated largely by self-interest, and an exclusive class of men whose souls are dominated by the desire for distinction. Hamilton accepted the generality of human nature as it was and did not attempt to transform it into something it could not become. He relied on the average republican citizen to pursue his own economic advantage, neither expecting nor encouraging him to develop a public spiritedness unconnected with his perception of self-interest. The vast majority of citizens were not called to participate actively in the affairs of government, the extent of their peacetime responsibilities essentially limited to electing the better sort of men to political office, and supporting the government they had chosen.[60] Their attachment to the new American republic, Hamilton believed, would result largely from their opinion of its necessity and utility.

A train of prosperous events, brought about by a wise and energetic administration, would result in an attachment of the people to their government and instill in them a confidence in its measures.[61] Indeed, "the confidence of the people will be easily gained by a good administration," Hamilton contended.[62] "Confidence" results largely from the gratification of men's acquisitive desires, producing habits of obligation and obedience to government. Since all governments, and particularly free republics, are dependent on public opinion, the wise republican statesman will cultivate an opinion of confidence by promoting measures that gratify the average citizens' passion for material gain, thereby increasing the stability and strength of the nation. In turn, the statesman himself is rewarded by the favor of public opinion, that is, by the confidence and esteem of his fellow citizens, thereby gratifying his distinctive desire for fame. In this way the most powerful passions of the many and the ruling passion of the noblest minds are directed toward the support of government.

Hamilton learned from Jacques Necker the importance of directing public opinion to the support of government by means of publicity, particularly publicity in the area of national finance. Necker's theory emphasized the influence of public ministers on public opinion to produce unity, confidence, and obedience to the government. "A skilful administration," he wrote, "has the effect of putting in action those it persuades, of strengthening the moral ideas, of rousing the imagination and of joining together the opinions and sentiments of men by the confidence it inspires."[63] "Confidence" is "that precious sentiment which unites the future to the present" and "lays the surest foundation of the happiness of the people."[64] Hamilton took Necker's advice and wrote prolifically for the public press in an effort to influence public opinion and inspire a spirit of confidence in the government and obedience to its measures. Although Hamilton believed that the citizens generally possess the ability to perceive their interests with sufficient clarity, he also recognized that they are sometimes misled by opinions built on false appearances of the advantageous.[65] During the 1790s his earlier sanguinity about the effects easily gained by a good administration was dashed by the successes of opponents who, in his view, misjudged or misled the common man.

Hamilton's Offense

Hamilton believed that systematic opposition to his economic measures was instigated by naive projectors and ambitious demagogues. Aaron Burr was clearly of the latter description.[66] Jefferson, Hamilton thought, had some of the demagogue in him, but was fundamentally a man whom nature had ill-endowed with a "sublimated paradoxical imagination."[67] Having drunk too much of French philosophy, his "mind [was] prone to projects . . . incompatible with the principles of stable and systematic government."[68] Madison's character was more subtle, complex, and difficult to discern. In 1792 Hamilton accused him of changing his mind concerning the public debt. He was not entirely sure, however, about Madison's motivations for the switch. Were personal animosity and the desire for political advantage the cause of Madison's newfound opposition? Or had Madison fallen under the influence of Jefferson and undergone a sincere change of mind?

In later years, Hamilton undoubtedly concluded that Madison was sincere in his attachment to the principles he espoused in the 1790s. He saw that Jefferson was not alone in his "vain reveries of a false and new fangled philosophy" and attachment to a "wild and fatal" political scheme that would destroy sound government in America.[69] Like the French writers from whose well of speculative philosophy they were imbibing, the Republicans were bent on a fanaticism in political science that miscalculated the force of the human passions and was "unsuited to the nature of man."[70] They were simply "too much in earnest" about "democracy."[71] Prostrating themselves before the opinion of the majority, as if *vox populi* were *vox dei*, they encouraged a spirit of anarchy and flirted with tyranny, its natural ally. They stimulated the restless passions of the people and excited a reckless censure, destroying public confidence in the government and its leaders.[72] Following in the path of their Jacobin cohorts, the

Republicans worshiped at the altar of the "Goddess of Reason," rejecting the "mild reign of rational liberty, which rests on the basis of an efficient and well-balanced government."[73]

Men are for the most part ruled by their passions, Hamilton believed, and rather more "reasoning tha[n] reasonable animals." Yet his opponents were intent on molding "a wise, reflecting and dispassionate people."[74] They eulogized reason, but in reality they courted men's vanities and cheated the people out of their confidence. Left unchecked, the Republican brand of politics would succeed in "corrupting public opinion till it becomes fit for nothing but mischief."[75] Moreover, they claimed for public opinion a moral status in free government and invoked its authority to circumvent the prescribed constitutional amendment process—the only legitimate channel of appeal to the people in their collective capacity.[76] The Republican politics of public opinion threatened to undermine all the hard work done by the men at Philadelphia in 1787, and the source of their new creed was none other than the fanatics of the French Enlightenment. Hamilton named names: "In vain was the collected wisdom of America convened at Philadelphia. In vain were the anxious labours of a Washington bestowed. Their works are regarded as nothing better than empty bubbles destined to be blown away by the mere breath of a disciple of *Turgot*; a pupil of *Condorcet*."[77] Whatever diminution of respect Hamilton had felt in the early 1790s for the force of Madison's mind and soundness of his judgment, a decade later his opinion of the Virginian's political sagacity sunk lower still. From Hamilton's perspective the loss of Madison as a political and philosophic ally must have been a genuine disappointment. This was the mind that had conspired with him at the convention, penned with him *The Federalist,* and seemed to understand, if not fully, at least better than most of his colleagues, the age-old dilemma of the few versus the many and the republican road that could overcome it.

Madison's Defense

Madison believed that, if successful, Hamilton's plan to perpetuate the national debt, establish a national bank, and enact a policy of governmental favors for select interests would subvert republican government in America. Madison's assaults on Hamilton's program were not merely measures of resistance to the Federalist agenda, however; his aim was also to pave an alternate economic and political route that accorded with the principles of republicanism, as he understood them. He attempted to prevent measures he believed were contrary to the sovereign authority of public opinion as expressed in the Constitution *and* to establish and secure a political system conducive to the ongoing formation of public opinion, on which government remains dependent in its ordinary operations.[78] If Hamilton believed the attainment of American glory to be contingent on increasing the power of the national government and tying the interests of the monied class to it, thereby achieving economic prosperity and political stability and strength in one fell swoop, Madison believed the glory of America to consist in her discovery of the way to educate public opinion in a republic so that power and right would be on the same side. This fundamental challenge was one Madison wrestled with in the 1780s and continued to think through in the 1790s. He was convinced that the solution depended on modifying the sovereignty in popular government.[79]

Madison's opposition to Hamilton's proposals to establish a national bank and provide governmental support for manufactures stemmed from his understanding of enumerated constitutional powers, his laissez faire economic theory, and his commitment to participatory politics. As is well known, Madison viewed the institution of a national bank as contrary to the Constitution, as understood by the people who ratified and adopted it.[80] Hamilton's proposal called for the national government to use unconstitutional means to accomplish legitimate ends; his "Report on Manufactures" went even farther: it proposed the national exercise of power to achieve *ends* not mandated by the Constitution.[81] Madison viewed the Constitution of the United States as the embodiment of the highest expression of the opinion of the public. No opinion in the regime, however widespread and popular, is superior to the voice of the people expressed in its most sovereign capacity in this document.[82] Only the extraconstitutional invocation of the right of revolution can *claim* moral superiority. The idea of constitutionalism is derivative of the principle of popular sovereignty, which forms the democratic basis for the doctrine of originalism. No one took this doctrine more seriously than Madison. He viewed Hamilton's broad construction of the Constitution as more than a point of legal debate—it struck at the very philosophical basis of republican government.[83] The idea of consent of the governed means that something was consented to—understood and agreed to—by the people in their most sovereign capacity. The people are "the only earthly source of authority," Madison wrote. The charters authenticated by their seal in the solemn act of founding constitute the most sacred of trusts. Constitutions are, in essence, the holy writs of this world, the "political scriptures" of faithful citizens. "They are bound on the conscience by the religious sanction of an oath . . . , [transcending] all other land-marks, because every public usurpation is an encroachment on the private right, not of one, but of all."[84] The American founding represents a charter of power granted to the government by a free people. It was a revolution in the annals of human history without parallel, as momentous a part of the American Revolution as the shots fired at Lexington and Concord, and probably even more so. Hamilton's interpretation of the Constitution effectively removed the limitations on the power of government placed there by the sovereign authority of the people, undermining the core principles of republican government.

Given Madison's commitment to the doctrine of constitutionalism, public officials, including the representatives of the people, are bound by oath and sacred trust to abide by the provisions and principles of the Constitution, even when a majority of citizens demand measures to the contrary. Nonetheless, Madison's theory of republicanism was no more an elite theory of statesmanship devised to circumvent majoritarian politics than it was a theory constructed to stymie democracy or substitute pluralism in place of justice as the end of government.[85] He had as little confidence that enlightened statesmen would always be at the political helm as he had that a simple or aggregate majority of the community would always and only demand those things consistent with natural and political right. In the 1780s he focused his mental energies more on solving the problem of majority faction than minority faction because he was committed to the principle of majority rule and intended that the majority would ultimately determine the law. Majority faction is the greatest threat and requires the most intense theoretical scrutiny in all polities in which majority opinion actually does reign supreme.[86] Madison did not change his mind about this in the 1790s. In the battle with Hamilton and the Federalists he fought *against* schemes that would undermine the formation and force of the public and substitute an independent governmental will. And he fought *to establish* in practice what he had conceived at his writing desk. I doubt that he was as surprised about the political realities of the new administration with men such as Hamilton and Adams in power as is often thought. He knew a fair amount about their views, though he did not know for certain how they would pursue their ideas given the decisions that had been made at Philadelphia and endorsed by the people. He soon saw, however, that their attachment to the antirepublican British model remained strong and that the policies they advocated threatened to sever the American government from the people and public opinion. Madison remained committed to majority rule and to solving the problem of majority faction in a way consistent with democratic principles. Throughout his life his practical efforts were based on two equally important theoretical maxims: the majority must ultimately rule, and it must have right on its side.[87]

I believe that it is a serious misreading of Madison to see his rejection of a certain kind of majoritarianism as a rejection of majority rule. He opposed simple democratic majoritarianism in order to prevent the ascendancy of a factious majority. If Madison had meant to render the majority impotent, that is, either to deadlock democracy or create a vacuum that could be filled by the political elite, there would have been no reason for him to have limited the size of a republican territory to a "practicable sphere."[88] No nation can be too large if the object is to thwart majority rule. Nor can it be oversized if the aim is merely pluralism. The setting for a conflict of multiple, diverse interests out of which can emerge an aggregate interest does not require any limitation on territorial extent. Madison's repeated insistence on limiting the size of the territory to a practicable sphere in the 1780s and 1790s is logical only if he intended a positive political role for a majority united by common opinion. When the various components of Madison's thought are viewed as part of a single design informed by an overarching, positive theory of participatory politics and constitutional majoritarianism, his arguments fit together to form a coherent philosophical vision. Madison encapsulated this constructive vision in his theory of the sovereignty of public opinion.

In republican government, Madison wrote in preparatory study for the Constitutional Convention, "the majority however composed, ultimately give the law."[89] The problem of course is that the majority may have power but not right on its side. Madison insisted on both. Majority rule is a necessary but not sufficient condition of free government. Its legitimacy depends on the respect and protection the majority accords to the rights of the minority. In the manifestation of their freedom, the citizens have a moral obligation to extend "that debt of protection" they mutually owe each other in the exercise of natural and positive rights, and for which they as a "public" pledged their "faith . . . by the very nature and original conditions of the social pact."[90] A government independent of the will of the society is unrepublican and illegitimate, but so too is a government that has force, but not right, on its side.[91]

Accordingly, Madison did not equate public opinion with the mere will of the majority. He rejected the Rousseauian notion that public will alone constitutes a legitimate standard for public decisions. According to the eighteenth-century conception, public opinion is not constituted by a mere aggregate of the sentiments of the populace, nor is it synonymous with "popular opinion(s)."[92] This view stands in sharp contrast to the current one, which equates public opinion with the results of daily polling aggregates. For Madison, public opinion was not the sum of fleeting and uneducated views. Neither was it a disembodied theoretical construct— reflecting a "ghostly body politic"[93]—disassociated from the actual minds and hearts of the people. The people are not a mythical entity and public opinion is not a fiction. Rather, Madison's conception of public opinion embraces a continuous, dynamic process of refinement and enlargement of the actual views, sentiments, and interests of the citizens.[94] The opinion of the constitutional majority is a modification of the views of a latent majority. This is achieved through established constitutional processes in an extensive, federal republic, which provides an arena in which to collect, temper, and refine the public views into an opinion that accords with the rights of others and the good of the whole.

The will of the society is manifested in government through the constitutionally prescribed processes that give to the legislature preeminence in public policy making. A frequently elected legislature is more closely aligned with the will of the people than are the other branches of government. In a large republic it is less likely to be the pawn of majority faction than in a small one. Nevertheless, Madison recognized the problem that worried Hamilton: whatever the size of the nation, assemblies are to some degree susceptible to the influence of demagoguery and the heat of capital politics.[95] Madison did think that the clash of arguments in public bodies can contribute substantially to the deliberative process, but he also acknowledged that the advantages are often outweighed by false reasoning and the easy contagion of opinion and passion in a body that meets under one roof in a politically charged city. The problem of securing "the benefits of free consultation and discussion" is especially great in numerous assemblies, where proceedings are often marked by the confusion and immoderation that generally accompanies mass gatherings.[96] To counteract these dangers Madison endorsed the auxiliary precaution of separation of powers, including the division of the legislature into two houses and the attendant devices of checks and balances. However, the "primary control" on the government, he declared in *Federalist 51*, is "a dependence on the people."[97]

Publius's explicit declaration of a reliance on the people as the chief control on government deserves greater attention by scholars. As Madison would later argue in the *Party Press Essay* "British Government," separation of powers and checks and balances are important prudential devices to control the will of the government and protect liberty, but they are auxiliary to a primary dependence on public opinion.[98] This is true both empirically and normatively. Public opinion is more powerful than parchment barriers and institutional arrangements. Madison believed that public opinion is also the fundamental authority in republican government. In the conclusion of the 51st *Federalist* he restates his case for a dependence on the people in even broader terms than he initially had in the essay: the will of the government must be dependent on the will of the society. Accordingly, the public is not only the primary guardian whose watchfulness keeps government within its prescribed boundaries, it is also the active agency upon which the movement of government depends. When the assertions in *Federalist 51* are attended to in the context of the two preceding *Federalist Papers,* a nascent idea beats in the ear of Publius's audience. It is reason, not passion, which ought to prevail over legislative decisions. Specifically, it is the reason *of the public* that ought to control the government.[99] In the *Party Press Essay* "Spirit of Governments," Madison pounded the republican drum to a rolling cadence. Contrasted with the imposter republican government advanced by some, which is actuated by private interest and avidity and pretends to operate by the liberty of the many, but in fact is supported by the domination of the few, Madison set forth the true republican model:

> A government, deriving its energy from the will of the society, and operating by the reason of its measures, on the understanding and interest of the society. Such is the government for which philosophy has been searching, and humanity sighing, from the most remote ages. Such are the republican governments which it is the glory of America to have invented, and her unrivalled happiness to possess.[100]

In the same vein of thought that runs through *Federalist* 49, 50, and 51, "Spirit of Governments" reinforces and intensifies the claims of Publius.

The spirit of republicanism, Madison emphatically pronounced in the *Party Press Essays*, requires that the will of the government be dependent on, "or rather the same with," the will of the society, and the will of the society be subject to "the reason of the society."[101] The process of subjecting the public will to the precepts of reason directs popular government toward the ends of justice and the general good. In turn, the resulting laws inform the citizens' understanding and influence their perception of the public interest. This has been the ambitious quest of philosophy and the ardent longing of humanity for time immemorial, Madison declared. America has answered humanity's call, and upon her soil the greatest of political aspirations are to be realized.

In *The Federalist* Madison argued for a political system that regulates the interests and passions within society, and which itself is dependent on the will and reason of the public. As he continued to think through and hone his theory of public reason in the ensuing years, he gave it added emphasis and clarity. In the 1780s and into the '90s Madison avidly read French texts on the subject of public opinion. French interest in the subject had emerged about 1770 and captured the minds of the French intelligentsia in the 1780s.[102] Due in large measure to Jefferson's generous shipment of crates of books from Paris to Montpelier during his tenure as ambassador to the French court, Madison studied a host of French authors on the subject of *l'opinion publique* and agreed with them about the undesirability of the British model of corporate political conflict so admired by Montesquieu (and Hamilton and Adams). Though, unlike most of them, he did not reject the doctrine of separation of powers and checks and balances, he did agree that the key to achieving political stability and individual liberty is not by a system that pits the interests of the few against those of the many, but by the force of an enlightened public opinion that results from a continuing process of communication among men in society.

Madison was in general agreement with the French writers who moved substantially beyond Necker's conception of public opinion as confidence in government and envisioned a more energetic role for the public in the political life of a nation. Theorists such as Turgot, Condorcet, and Peuchet emphasized both the influence of the enlightened men on public opinion *and* the directive influence of public opinion on government, conceiving of public opinion as both acted upon as well as itself an active agent. In a complex and layered process of civic participation and communication, the diverse views of citizens are modified to form a united public reason.[103] The enlightened members of society bear an important responsibility to shape the public views, but it is equally important that the public be enlightened, active, and united. When their opinion is fixed and their voice united, it directs the decisions of government. Madison subscribed to this idea of an activated public whose opinion carries political force. Contrary to those who would devise schemes that detach the government from the people, warn it to be vigilant against the centrifugal tendency of the people, and ask of the people only that they obey their wise and enlightened rulers, Madison argued that the goal is to awaken and *enlighten the people,* warn *them* to be united and vigilant, and to obey the government that is of their own making.[104]

Hamilton's allegations of ties between American Republican theory and French Enlightenment thought were not unfounded. Though no mere follower or devotee of French theory, Madison was influenced by the works he read and even adopted key language from them. For example, Condorcet argued that over time public opinion derives force from the effect of "fixed principles" and unites society under "an empire of reason."[105] Peuchet said that in the modern world Christian morality has united men as brothers; scientific discoveries have led to an increase in communication and the circulation of knowledge among men and "extended the sovereign empire of reason."[106] The optimism of the French and their wont for the felicitous expression captured Madison's ear and imagination. "Let it be the patriotic study of all," he declared, "to erect over the whole [society], one paramount *Empire of reason,* benevolence and brotherly affection."[107]

"Public Opinion," Madison wrote in the *Party Press Essay* of that title, "sets bounds to every government, and is the real sovereign in every free one."[108] In all governments public opinion operates as a force that limits the power of government. In all free governments public opinion is the ground of all legitimate authority; it functions as both a defensive agency that controls government and an active agency that directs the will of the government. As the embodiment of the highest expression of public opinion, the Constitution may provide a source to which officials and citizens can appeal to limit the power of governmental agencies, as well as a source of instruction concerning individual rights and responsibilities and the boundaries of limited government. The latter is what Madison meant by the beneficial effects of a bill of rights over time, as it is sanctified and incorporated into the public opinion.[109] In addition to its manifestation in the Constitution, public opinion has three other modes of expression: as the censor of governmental acts, as the constitutional majority, and as the general spirit that permeates the nation (and perhaps beyond). The censorship of governmental measures by public opinion finds expression via state political organs and by educated men via the media.[110] These are essentially defensive measures against political usurpation. The appeal may be to the people of the states or even directly to the people as a collectivity. However, public opinion in these cases does not carry the force of law, though it may well "lead to a change in the legislative expression" of the public will or even to a change in judicial opinion.[111] The directive agency of public opinion manifests itself through the constitutional mechanisms of free elections and representation, by which "the will of the largest political body may be concentered and its force directed to any object which the public good requires."[112] In this expression of public opinion by the constitutional majority the people's agency is not direct, but it is nonetheless their will, and not a government insulated from the actual views of the people, which directs public measures. Finally, public opinion in its broadest sense consists of the settled views and general convictions of the people. Its potential power is prodigious: it can preserve or alter public morality, it can support or scorn the laws. The formation of constitutional majorities occurs within a sphere permeated by a ubiquitous public opinion. When settled, the opinion of the constitutional majority is absorbed by public opinion, contributing to the ongoing modification and construction of public opinion in a republic.[113]

When public opinion is fixed, Madison taught, it must be obeyed by the government. When not settled, it may be influenced by those in government. Madison's advocacy of a large but practicable extent of territory should be understood within this context. A nation should be large enough to include a multiplicity of interests and sects, in order to neutralize the effects of interest and passion by denying any one of them majority status. His purpose in placing limitations on the size of a republican territory was to ensure that all representatives could feasibly travel the distance and to allow for the communication of ideas and formation of public opinion. The extensive size of the territory makes it difficult for a faction to "counterfeit" the opinion of the public; the limitation on size to a practicable sphere enables the "real" opinion of the public to form and carry effect.[114]

Madison argued in both *The Federalist* and the *Party Press Essays* that the practicable boundaries of a republic can be stretched without sacrificing the formation of the public voice if conditions that ease intercommunication among the citizens are present. These conditions include good transportation routes, improvements in interior navigation, the free circulation of newspapers, and representatives traveling to and from the capital city, all of which act as equivalents to a contraction of the territorial size.[115] In contrast to a nation which is too small and where a majority faction easily arises, or to one that is too large and the public voice cannot be collected, a territory of practicable extent provides the conditions for the communication of ideas, the proper formation of public opinion, and its appropriate degree of influence on the representatives. Under these circumstances the representatives are effectively distanced from the influence of the ephemeral passions and partial interests of the diverse factions within their districts, while simultaneously kept dependent on the will of the society.[116]

Lance Banning argues that the representatives must reflect the diverse interests within society in order for Madison's remedy of the extended republic/multiplicity of interests to work.[117] Alan Gibson interprets Madison's remedy of an impartial arbiter to consist in the formation of just majorities in Congress.[118] I take Madison's republican remedy to be something more than this. Madison did think that generally the representatives should represent the views and interests of their constituents, and that this rivalry at *the level of government* would help to prevent rule by a majority faction. But Madison goes substantially beyond this and applies the theory of the extended republic to *the level of society.* His goal was not merely the distillation of the people's will *by representatives in Congress,* but even more importantly, the establishment of "an equilibrium in the interests & passions of the Society itself" in order to create the conditions necessary to refine and enlarge the opinion *of the society.*[119] Madison's insight into how territorial size contributes to the positive achievement of the just majority consists of more than a technical dependence on the people via their representatives in Congress. It also entails, to the extent possible, the tempering of factious impulses and the elevation of opinion within the society by means of a dynamic process of communication throughout the land. Madison's "modification of the sovereignty" is not merely the alteration of the people's views by the legislature. It is also the modification of public opinion itself.

Madison believed that the sovereign authority of public opinion is limited *by* the act of constitutional ratification. But he rejected the idea that it is limited *to* the act of constitutional consent or is merely an intermittent expression of authority at times of elections.[120] The doctrine that has "so ardently been propagated by many, that in a republic the people ought to consider the whole of their political duty as discharged when they have chosen their representatives," and "that the people ought at all times to place an unlimited confidence in rulers" they have chosen is false, he protested. "In no case ought the eyes of the people to be shut . . . nor their tongues tied." If left uncontrolled by the people, government "ever will be administered by passions more than by reason."[121] Just as he had indicated in *The Federalist* a decade earlier, in "Political Reflections" Madison insisted that the people are the primary control on the government, that they have a real and ongoing role in the political life of their country, and that the manifestation of the reason of the public results from their active political participation and the communication of ideas.

In the contest with Hamilton, Madison routinely applied his theory of the ongoing authority of public opinion to the practical issues of the day. In respect to the issue of the public debt, Hamilton was correct to think that he had Madison's general support for funding, and indeed Madison argued on the floor of the House of Representatives in early 1790 that the debt incurred in the war for independence must be funded. However, Madison's general view was that although funding was at times necessary in the life of a nation, it was nonetheless an evil.[122] While he assented to those measures necessary to reestablish public credit and retire the debt, he was adamantly opposed to a perpetuation of it, and in fact had been so for many years.[123] The unnecessary protraction of public debt might accomplish the aim some envisioned, that is, of cementing together the interests of the wealthy with those of the nation. But this was not Madison's goal. The extension of the debt would only further the distance between the national government and the interests of the people. Public debt generally results from the costs of running war and fitting an army, all of which tends toward the increase of the discretionary power of the executive branch, of corruption in government, and of the independence of government from the popular will.[124] Such has been the ploy used by governments to extend and perpetuate arbitrary power throughout human history. The cure for this, Madison declared, is to make the will of the government "subordinate to, or rather the same with, the will of the community."[125] Furthermore, to the extent possible, each generation should bear the financial burdens of debt it has taken on, thereby prompting "avarice . . . to calculate the expences of ambition" and "in the equipoise of these passions, [leaving] reason . . . free to decide for the public good." By "permanent and constitutional maxims of conduct" the executive temptation for war must be moderated by the legislative representatives' willingness for war, contingent on the opinion of their constituents. The people's temptation to war is controlled by "subjecting the will of the society to the reason of the society."[126]

Hamilton's proposed show of political favoritism to manufacturing was contrary to the idea of the free market, an economic doctrine Madison had earlier and publicly endorsed.[127] Moreover, Madison believed that privileging one industry over another violates both the rights of property and the rights of persons.[128] Property is not secure, he asserted, when unequal taxes burden one kind of property and reward another; nor is it protected when a part of the citizenry is denied the free exercise of their faculties and the free choice of their occupations. Building on *Federalist* 10's claim that the rights of property originate in men's free exercise of their diverse faculties, he claimed that the individual's free use of his faculties and choice of occupation not only constitute his property, but are also the "means of acquiring property."[129] Viewed in this context, Madison's alarm at Hamilton's "Report on Manufactures" seems understandable. The protection of these different faculties, Madison had written in *The Federalist*, "is the first object of government."[130]

Stemming from the free exercise of his faculties, man has a property "in his opinions and in the free communication of them."[131] When the power of government is excessive and unjustly interventionist, no man is secure in his opinions or in the effective communication of them. This is a particular danger in a large republic, since the size of a nation has the effect of making intercommunication and the discovery of a united purpose more difficult. If public opinion is to exert adequate and proper control on the government, it must, Madison contended, have sufficient channels through which it can be expressed, formed, and enlightened. The process of collecting, coalescing, and shaping public opinion is accomplished by a variety of conditions and processes, including state and local governmental bodies, educational institutions and the learned professions, the circulation of newspapers throughout the nation, and the interplay between representatives and their constituents.

Madison was always committed to preserving the boundaries of governmental power delineated by the constitutions of the United States, as Lance Banning has so persuasively argued.[132] That the people had, by their sovereign authority, established a partition of government between the union and the states was sufficient grounds to insist on respect for the constitutional limitations on power. But Madison had an additional reason to stress the importance of the federal character of the American republic: he considered the state and local governments essential to the collection and articulation of the public voice. Without a due degree of power at the state and local levels of governments, the extent of the territory would make it impossible for the people to communicate effectively and convey a united voice by which to control government.[133] Conversely, "the most arbitrary government is controuled where the public opinion is fixed."[134] Federalism is a critical element in maintaining governmental responsibility to the people; it lends significantly to shaping an environment conducive to the communication of ideas and the mobilization and expression of public opinion in a large republic. Madison would apply his long-held conception of the importance of the states in marshaling public opinion later in the 1790s, *viz.*, in the Virginia Resolutions and his battle to overturn the Alien and Seditions Acts.[135]

The advent of circulating newspapers significantly increased communications among men and contributed to the power of public opinion in the eighteenth century, a phenomenon clearly grasped by Madison and many of his contemporaries abroad. The rise of the mass media also made communication over a large territory possible for the first time in history. It was now possible to found a nation large enough to impede the formation of a majority faction and at the same time establish the circumstances that make possible a genuine "commerce of ideas" throughout an extensive territory. To my knowledge, this original, momentous insight belonged to James Madison. Madison envisioned newspapers serving as vehicles for the circulation of the ideas of the literati to the people of the extensive American republic, resulting in the refinement and enlargement of the public views and the emergence of an enlightened public opinion. The literati, in fact, occupy a central place in the process of civic education and public enlightenment that Madison hoped to see in America. They are "the cultivators of the human mind—the manufacturers of useful knowledge—the agents of the commerce of ideas—the censors of public manners—the teachers of the arts of life and the means of happiness."[136] In Madison's view, their role is absolutely indispensable to the proper formation of public opinion. Their influence on the ideas and manners of the people can serve to anchor a republican citizenry in the moral principles of free government. Madison's use of the language of agriculture and manufacturing in his description of the highest aims of the new republic was clearly no accident. He intentionally meant to contrast his vision of the American commercial republic and its hero, the merchant of ideas and mores, with the narrower Hamiltonian vision of commerce as material exchange and profit.

The energy Madison expended to stop Hamilton's measures to perpetuate the public debt, establish a national bank, and favor manufacturing was proportionate to the threat he perceived: Hamilton's program would destroy the limitations on government established by the Constitution and undermine the rightful authority of public opinion in the American republic. The thrust of Hamilton's financial package was the creation of a system that promoted inequality of property by governmental fiat and tied the interests of the favored opulent class to the national government. Madison believed that this clever scheme would have the effect of strengthening and consolidating the powers of the national government and undermining the constitutional and practical limitations placed on its authority. The concentration of power at the national level would diminish the power of the state governments. Since a single national legislature is not competent to regulate all the objects of government over so large a territory, the power of the national executive would unduly grow; this would open the way for legislative corruption and render less effectual the voice of the people and their control on the legislature.[137] Hamilton's plan would eventually transform the executive office into one of "unlimited discretion," in opposition "to the will and subversive of the authority of the people."[138] Ultimately, it might even produce a "universal silence," leaving the national government to act independent of the will of the society and free to pursue a "*self directed course.*"[139]

Madison's advocacy of the politics of public opinion was his sustained attempt to solve the problem of majority opinion in a manner fully consistent with the form and spirit of popular government. The *spirit* of free government cannot be attained by achieving the people's consent and then disassociating them from the acts of government. The spirit of republicanism is present only when it is embodied in the minds and mores of the citizens and sustained by the activity of political participation and the commerce of ideas throughout the land.[140] The construction of public opinion involves a process of instructive dialogue and deliberation that permeates the whole society, from the influence of the literati and statesmen on the mores and views of the citizens, to the communication of ideas throughout the great body of the people, to the influence of the settled opinion of the community on the representatives in government. The process of forming public opinion is a time-consuming and complex one, much like the process of establishing precedents in courts of law. Majority opinion in a republican polity is constantly in the process of constructing itself within an intellectual, moral, and psychological milieu larger than itself. This architectonic influence over the minds and morals of the public in turn influences the decisions of government and the laws of the land, which further operate on the understanding and interest of the public. This is Madison's solution to the difficult challenge he set himself when preparing for the Federal Convention: how to achieve a "modification of the Sovereignty."[141] Public opinion is the sovereign authority in a genuine republic whose mild voice of reason is capable of transforming the will of a nation. It is no surprise, then, how often Madison himself put pen to paper in the public press, or that he urged his fellow citizens, despite all artificial and circumstantial distinctions, to come together as one people under the mantle of the "Empire of reason."[142]

Conclusion

The disagreement between Madison and Hamilton that led to the formation of the first political parties in the United States cannot properly be understood as merely personal or partisan. It was a battle over the very character of republican government and the extent to which the people are capable of governing themselves. Hamilton did not think Madison's solution of the extended republic and representation went far enough to remedy the problem of majority tyranny. Madison thought Hamilton's measures substituted private interest for public good and undermined the sovereign authority of public opinion. Interestingly, scholars have generally attributed the vision of a modern commercial republic composed of diverse and rival economic interests actuated by the untutored passion of acquisitiveness to James Madison. But this was not, nor ever had been, Madison's vision of republicanism. It is closer to Hamilton's.[143] In fact, Hamilton fits better the description that has traditionally been reserved for Madison, while Madison was a more unhesitating democrat than is generally believed. Hamilton is the chief American theorist of the modern commercial republic, Madison the philosophic architect of the politics of public participation and republican self-government in America.

Madison and Hamilton did not differ about the need to filter the interests, passions, and opinions of the citizens or about the need to achieve a reasonable and durable will in government, but they did very much disagree about who or what legitimately gives voice to this will and whether the process involves modifying the actual views of the citizens. Hamilton attempted to solve the problem of the predominance of partial interests, the contagion of passion, and the danger of demagoguery in the legislature by establishing a system of institutional counterbalances within the government. He sought to achieve a reasonable and permanent will via an independent and energetic executive whose administration would advance the interest of the nation and inspire in the people an opinion of confidence and obedience. By contrast, Madison's solution was to call the representatives to stand before the bar of public opinion. He sought to establish an equilibrium of passions and interests in the society in order to reduce the likelihood of majority faction as well as to shape an environment conducive to the formation of a public will tempered and modified by the commerce of ideas.

Hamilton relied on the people to pursue their own material advantage and to support a government that benefits them economically. He did not see the wisdom in encouraging political hyperactivity among the citizenry, which only invites demagoguery and civil unrest—as the French example too perfectly illustrated. For Madison, the citizens' political duties were substantial and ongoing. They did not end at choosing the better sorts of men to represent them; their guardianship over public affairs was not an intermittent responsibility. Both Hamilton and Madison relied significantly on an educated elite to accomplish their ends. However, in the one case it was a type of statesmanship that sought to inspire respect and confidence more than to teach. In the other case it was a kind of civic leadership that aspired to cultivate civic understanding, refine mores and manners, and educate the people for their indispensable role in a self-governing republic.

At least by the time of the election of Jefferson to the presidency, Hamilton understood clearly that the attachment by leading Republicans to the theory of public opinion had had much to do with the rifts and party battles of the past decade. He also saw that their philosophy translated into a political strategy, and that that strategy was winning. The Federalists had lost political ground by relying too much on the good effects of their administration, all while the Republicans gained ground by appealing directly to the American people. Reluctantly, Hamilton reconciled himself to the fact that he and his fellow Federalists would also have to give much more attention to cultivating public opinion. However, he refused to do so in a way that he considered humiliating and unworthy of a republican statesman, though he did admit that it would be necessary to countenance some modes of action that "may be denominated irregular, such as in a sound & stable order of things ought not to exist."[144] Accordingly, he proposed the establishment of a Christian Society whose object was to support the Christian religion and the Constitution and to collect a public force that could significantly influence the outcome of elections.

Hamilton's political ally and correspondent, James Bayard, cautioned Hamilton against such a measure. The type of organization that can accomplish the goal Hamilton had in mind must be grounded upon a stronger motive in man than reason, or even common interest, he argued. Be patient, Bayard counseled, and the Republicans will in a short while demonstrate to all the country the soundness of Federalist doctrines and the imbecility of their own. In free governments such as the United States, he continued, there must always be a degree of "agitation and vibration of opinion," for it is "in the nature of things . . . impossible to fix public opinion."[145] Good men would do better to exert themselves against the evils of selfish and ambitious demagogues and otherwise wait patiently for the Republicans to self-destruct. Hamilton could only wish his friend were right, but he knew that he was not. The advent of the new politics of public opinion had forever changed the face and fabric of republican government. The unrivaled power of public opinion that Tocqueville would observe decades later was already fast becoming a political reality in America. Hamilton continued to resist the new politics, but knew that his brand of patriotism was of "the old school," and that the "disciples of the new creed" had won the battle to make public opinion queen of the world.[146]

NOTES

1. Stanley Elkins and Eric McKitrick claim that in the 1790s Madison intended to establish a two-party system in the United States (Elkins and McKitrick, *The Age of Federalism: The Early Republic, 1788–1800* [Oxford: Oxford University Press, 1993], 296. James Roger Sharp argues that the Federalists and Republicans were in fact "proto-parties," each of which aimed to vanquish the other (Sharp, *American Politics in the Early Republic: The New Nation in Crisis* [New Haven: Yale University Press, 1993], 7–9). Sharp's view more accurately describes the way in which Madison, Jefferson, and Hamilton conceived of their respective party's mission during this era. Nonetheless, during his vice presidency, Jefferson built a party apparatus and used it to win the election of 1800, setting the pattern for party politics in America from then on.

2. See Madison's "Party Press Essays," identified in *The Papers of James Madison* (hereafter *PJM*) as "Essays for the National Gazette," *PJM,* 17 vols., ed. William T. Hutchison, William M. E. Rachal, Robert A. Rutland, Charles F. Hobson, et al. (Chicago: University of Chicago Press [vols. 1–10] and Charlottesville: University Press of Virginia [vols. 11–17] [1962–1991], 14:117–22, 14:137–39, 17:559–60, 1.302–10, 14:170, 14:178–79, 14:191–92, 14:197–98, 14:201–2, 14:206–9, 217–19, 14:233–34, 14:244–46, 14:257–59, 14:266–68, 14:274–75, 14:370–72, 14:426–27.

3. The political battles of the 1790s between the primary co-authors of *The Federalist* have often been viewed by scholars within the context of the "Jefferson versus Hamilton" thesis regarding the origins of American political parties. This interpretation owes it origins to Hamilton's own initial assessment of the feud. At the commencement of the new government, Hamilton claimed, there existed a similarity of thinking between him and Madison. Despite their disagreement on debt discrimination and the assumption of state debts during the second session of the First Congress, Hamilton remained disposed to believe in Madison's honesty, fairness and goodwill. By the spring of 1792, however, he became convinced that Madison acted in cooperation with Jefferson, that Madison was actuated by "personal and political animosity" against him, and that his character was in fact subtle, complicated, and artificial in a way that the Treasury Secretary had not previously understood (Alexander Hamilton, *The Papers of Alexander Hamilton* [hereafter *PAH*], 27 vols., ed. Harold C. Syrett [New York: Columbia University Press, 1961–87], 11:432–34). Either Jefferson had so influenced Madison that the latter had undergone a material change of mind, or Madison was simply a common political calculator, pursuing measures to feed his own political popularity and/or the advantage of his particular state. See, for example, Forrest McDonald's endorsement of this thesis (McDonald, *Alexander Hamilton* [New York: W. W. Norton, 1979], 199–200, 175, 254; McDonald, *The Presidency of George Washington* [New York: W. W. Norton, 1974], 80–81). In contrast, the more recent scholarship of Elkins and McKitrick (*Age of Federalism*), Lance Banning (*The Sacred Fire of Liberty: James Madison and the Founding of the Federal Republic* [Ithaca, NY: Cornell University Press, 1995], and James H. Read (*Power Versus Liberty* [Charlottesville: University Press of Virginia, 2000]) view the battle as a real disagreement over constitutional and political ideas.

4. *PAH,* 25:352–53, 370.

5. No one has done more to correct the misinterpretations of Madison than Banning, *Sacred Fire.* Though from the contemporary perspective Madison would probably be seen as a conservative, by eighteenth-century standards he would have been considered "very much a democrat—and even by some tests that many of the most self-righteous modern democrats would fail" (*Sacred Fire,* 372). My argument in the following pages both builds upon and offers a further treatment of Banning's analysis of Madison's republican theory, particularly his conception of political participation and the active sovereignty of public opinion.

6. Alexis de Tocqueville, *Democracy in America*, ed. Harvey C. Mansfield and Delba Winthrop (Chicago: University of Chicago Press, 2000), 166–70.

7. Daniel Yankelovich, *Coming to Public Judgment: Making Democracy Work in a Complex World* (Syracuse, NY: Syracuse University Press, 1991), 15–23, 1, xi–xii.

8. Colleen A. Sheehan, "Madison's Party Press Essays," *Interpretation: A Journal of Political Philosophy* 17 (Spring 1990): 356, and passim.

9. *PAH*, 4:192; cf. *PAH*, 4:184, 200, 204, 207.

10. Adrienne Koch, ed., *James Madison's Notes of Debates in the Federal Convention of 1787* (Athens: Ohio University Press, 1966), 131–32, 175.

11. Adrienne Koch and William Peden, eds., *The Life and Selected Writings of Thomas Jefferson* (New York: Modern Library, 1972), 126.

12. *PJM*, 14:274.

13. *PJM*, 14:427, 371, 233.

14. *PJM*, 13:106, 317; cf. *PJM*, 15:474, 14:208, 274–75.

15. *PJM*, 14:274.

16. *PJM*, 14:233.

17. *PJM*, 14:371.

18. *PJM*, 14:197.

19. *PJM*, 14:371.

20. *PJM*, 14:233.

21. *PJM*, 14: 233–34.

22. *PJM*, 14:197–98.

23. *PJM*, 14:198.

24. *PJM*, 14:201–2, 202.

25. *PJM*, 14:427.

26. *PJM*, 14:202.

27. *PJM*, 14:426–27.

28. *PAH*, 6:70–72.

29. *PAH*, 2:618.

30. *PAH*, 8:220.

31. *PAH*, 7:306.

32. *PAH*, 12:251.

33. *PAH*, 230–340.

34. *PAH*, 10:267.

35. *PAH*, 12:248–53; cf. *PAH*, 12:131–33.

36. *PAH*, 12:209.

37. *PAH*, 4:192.

38. *PAH*, 4:185, 193, 200, 204.

39. *PAH*, 4:185.

40. *PAH*, 4:166.

41. *PAH*, 4:165.

42. *PAH*, 4:192.

43. See the discussion regarding the Senate of Maryland throughout the convention debates.

44. *PAH*, 4:214.

45. *PAH*, 5:81.

46. *PAH*, 4:186.

47. *PAH*, 25:537.

48. *PAH*, 25:537.

49. Harvey Flaumenhaft, *The Effective Republic: Administration and Constitution in the Thought of Alexander Hamilton* (Durham, NC: Duke University Press, 1992), 186.

50. *PAH*, 5:85.

51. *PAH*, 4:180.

52. *PAH*, 1:92.

53. *PAH*, 4:187, 217.

54. *PAH*, 10:293; see also Richard Brookhiser, *Alexander Hamilton: American* (New York: Free Press, 1999), 97.

55. Alexander Hamilton, James Madison, and John Jay, *The Federalist Papers,* ed. Clinton Rossiter, intro. by Charles R. Kesler (New York: Mentor Books, 1999) (hereafter *FP*), 183 (#35); see also William B. Allen, with Kevin A. Cloonan, *The Federalist: A Commentary* (New York: Peter Lang, 2000), 167–74.

56. *PAH*, 5:37.

57. Forrest McDonald (*Novis Ordo Seclorum* [Lawrence: University Press of Kansas, 1985], 137) claims that in his maturity, Hamilton rejected the idea of tying the interests of the wealthy to the interest of government, pointing particularly to his seemingly modified argument in 1795 in "The Defence of the Funding System" (see *PAH* , 19:40–41; cf. *PAH*, 2:248). Hamilton's argument in "The Defence," however, is more nuanced. Although Hamilton claims that the bonding of the interests of the monied men to the national interest was not his primary aim in his plan to fund the debt—indeed, that it was the consideration upon which he relied the least—it was nonetheless included in his calculation.

58. *FP*, 59 (#12).

59. *PAH*, 4:163.

60. *PAH*, 3:102–3, 544–45; cf. Flaumenhaft, *Effective Republic*, 15–16, 216.

61. *PAH*, 5:39–40.

62. *PAH*, 5:39.

63. Jacques Necker, *A Treatise on the Administration of the Finances of France,* vol. 1, trans. Thomas Mortimer (London: J. Walter, 1785), xii.

64. Necker, *Treatise,* x.

65. Gerald Stourzh, *Alexander Hamilton and the Idea of Republican Government* (Stanford, CA: Stanford University Press, 1970), 92–93.

66. *PAH*, 25:321.

67. *PAH*, 12:544.

68. *PAH*, 12:581, 11:439

69. *PAH*, 12:249, 26:740.

70. *PAH*, 26:739.

71. *PAH*, 25:319.

72. *PAH*, 13:394–95.

73. *PAH*, 25:353, 370.

74. *PAH*, 25:605.

75. *PAH*, 25:605–6.

76. *PAH*, 25:606.

77. *PAH*, 25:501.

78. Sheehan, "Madison's Party Press Essays," and Colleen A. Sheehan, "The Politics of Public Opinion: James Madison's 'Notes on Government,'" *William and Mary Quarterly* 49 (October 1992): 609–27.

79. *PJM*, 9:357, 10:214.

80. *PJM* , 13:372–87, 395–96; Max Farrand, ed., *The Records of the Federal Convention of 1787*, 3 vols. (New Haven : Yale University Press, 1966), 3:533–34.

81. *PJM*, 14:180, 193.

82. Marvin Meyers and Gary Rosen argue that Madison's changed position on the issue of the national bank reflected his view of the power of precedent (Meyers, ed., *The Mind of the Founder: Sources of the Political Thought of James Madison* [Hanover, NH: Brandeis University Press, 1981], 389–90; Rosen, *American Compact: James Madison and the Problem of Founding* [Lawrence: University Press of Kansas, 1999], 140). He allowed the force of ordinary public opinion and established precedent to trump the authority of the Constitution. I read Madison's explanation of his changed stance on the bank differently (see Meyers, *Mind of the Founder,* 389–93). He was not arguing that ordinary public opinion—even when settled over a course of many years and a precedent is established—is ever superior to the Constitution. His argument was that for over twenty years public opinion had acquiesced in the decision to establish a national bank, demonstrating that the generation that ratified the Constitution was in fact not adverse to it and did not understand it to be contrary to the Constitution—even if Madison, in "his solitary opinion" did. Therefore, according to the original intent of those who ratified and adopted the Constitution, the bank was not nor ever had been unconstitutional. As president, Madison could respect the legislative precedent because the institution of the bank was not an unconstitutional usurpation but only an ordinary legislative act. Essentially, Madison admits that he misread public opinion in the early 1790s. He did not make an exception to the sovereign authority of the Constitution, as understood by those who breathed life into it. Indeed, he remained absolutely committed to the doctrine of constitutionalism throughout his life. "A Constitution being derived from a superior authority," he said in 1831, "is to be expounded and obeyed, not controlled or varied, by the subordinate authority of a Legislature" (Meyers, *Mind of the Founder,* 391, emphasis added).

83. See Jack N. Rakove, *Original Meanings: Politics and Ideas in the Making of the Constitution* (New York: Alfred A. Knopf, 1996), 339–65.

84. *PJM*, 14:191.

85. Madison's solution of the extended republic has sometimes been presented as a theory devised to thwart the formation and influence of majorities and either deadlock the democratic process or establish the conditions for pluralism and interest-dominated politics. (See Robert Dahl, *A Preface to Democratic Theory* [Chicago: University of Chicago Press, 1956], 1–33; Martin Diamond, "Ethics and Politics: The American Way," in *The Moral Foundations of the American Republic*, ed. Robert H. Horwitz [Charlottesville: University Press of Virginia, 1977], 39–72.) Other scholars have contended that Madison's idea of the extensive territory is subordinate to the principle of representation, arguing that his primary aim was to establish the rule of elite, enlightened statesmen (See Garry Wills, *Explaining America: The Federalist* [Garden City, NY: Doubleday, 1981], 179–264; Gordon Wood, "Interests and Disinterestedness in the Making of the Constitution," in *Beyond Confederation: Origins of the Constitution and American National Identity*, ed. Richard Beeman, Stephen Botein, and Edward C. Carter [Chapel Hill: University of North Carolina Press, 1987], 91–93; Sharp, *Politics in the Early Republic*, 26). In the latter case, Madison's warning that we cannot depend on the presence of enlightened statesmen in office is downplayed or ignored, and in both cases his insistence on preserving the form and spirit of popular government has received inadequate attention (see *FP* #10).

86. Banning, in his path-breaking work on Madison, takes seriously Madison's claim that the will of the majority is actually the ruling authority in a republic. Banning writes: "Madison was adamant that once the proper checks had been imposed and passing passions had been cooled, the will of the majority must rule" (*Sacred Fire*, 372).

87. Madison does not completely lay out his solution to the problem of majority faction in the 1780s, but rather claims that it is still in need of a full discussion (*PJM*, 10:212). He repeats this claim in 1791, when he undertakes this fuller and more "thorough investigation" (*PJM*, 14:159). For a contrasting view, see Jack N. Rakove, *James Madison and the Creation of the American Republic* (Glenview, IL: Scott, Foresman/Little, Brown Higher Education, 1990), 100, who argues that in the 1780s Madison worried about the dangers of too much democracy and sought to insulate politics at the national level from public opinion, but then "changed his opinion towards public opinion" in the 1790s. See also Elkins and McKitrick, who claim that in the 1790s Madison developed a "new feeling for the legitimacy of majorities" and embarked on a "new course of theorizing" (*Age of Federalism*, 266).

88. *FP*, 68 (#14), 293 (#51); *PJM*, 14: 170.

89. *PJM*, 10:355.

90. *PJM*, 14:267.

91. *FP*, 292–93 (#51); cf. *PJM*, 9:350, 355. Madison's analogy of a majority based only on strength in the state of nature illustrates that in both instances the absence of justice is tantamount to the absence of legitimate government (*FP*, 292–93 [#51]).

92. Mona Ozouf, "Public Opinion at the End of the Old Regime," trans. Lydia C. Cochrane, *Journal of Modern History* 60 (Supplement: 1993): S8–9, n24; Jacques Peuchet, "Discours préliminaire," in *Police et municipalities,* vol. 9 of *Jurisprudence, Encyclopédie méthodique,* ed. Charles Panckoucke (Paris, 1789): ix–x.

93. Joshua Miller argues that the Federalists (including Madison) "ascribed all power to a mythical entity that could never meet, never deliberate, never take action. The body politic became a ghost." The government was intended to be "distant from the people and not participatory," Miller argues (Miller, "The Ghostly Body Politic: The Federalist Papers and Popular Sovereignty," *Political Theory* 16 [February 1988]: 99, 104, 114). Robert H. Wiebe also claims that for the founders "the people" were a mere abstraction. Madison's appeal to "the reason of the public" in the 49th *Federalist* was actually a way for the gentry to free themselves of their "sovereigns" (Wiebe, *The Opening of American Society: From the Adoption of the Constitution to the Eve of Disunion* [New York: Alfred A. Knopf, 1984], 38–39). Moreover, Wiebe argues, there is "no basic ideological conflict separating Hamilton and his Federalist associates from Jefferson and his Republican colleagues." They shared "a commitment to a common brand of gentry governance" and the party battles between them was hardly more than a disagreement over fashion décor: they merely struggled over "the interior design of the same ideological house" (Wiebe, *Opening of American Society,* xiii). Wiebe views Madison's idea of public opinion as the equivalent of "community values," and argues that it is not until the nineteenth century that public opinion became a political power (Wiebe, *Self-Rule: A Cultural History of American Democracy* [Chicago: University of Chicago Press, 1995], 38–40). For a detailed argument regarding Madison's conception of the political—and not merely social—power of public opinion, see Colleen A. Sheehan, "Madison and the French Enlightenment: The Authority of Public Opinion," *William and Mary Quarterly* 59 (October 2002): 925–56.

94. Read offers a brief but insightful account of Madison's theory of public opinion as the "enduring sense of the community" in his recent work (*Power versus Liberty,* 28). Read's stress on public opinion as constituted by the citizens' agreement on "clear boundaries to governmental power," above all the fundamental agreement as expressed in the Constitution, is certainly not inaccurate, but does perhaps have the tendency to diminish the ongoing, participatory nature and directive quality of public opinion that Madison conceptualized. Rosen identifies the social compact as central to Madison's political theory and the political disputes of the 1790s. Rosen is correct that for Madison the "sense" of the community is the true voice of popular sovereignty, and this "sense" is expressed in the ratified

Constitution (*American Compact*, 165). However, his insistence that "Madison's solution was a kind of constitutional passion, an unthinking attachment to the Constitution as an end in itself" is problematic (American Compact, 127). It neglects to address how the people are to understand the meaning of the Constitution they are to venerate, so that they might apply that meaning to the issue(s) at hand when there is disagreement on its meaning. Moreover, it presents an extremely limited role for the people, given that the majority of political issues in the United States are not constitutional issues. In essence, Rosen fails to take into account the formative processes and dynamic character of public opinion for Madison, its operation in the everyday life of the polity, and the way in which it reflects Madison's commitment to democratic politics. Sharp also imbues Madison's conception of public opinion with a static quality. He argues that although Madison called for a dependence on an enlightened and watchful public, in the early 1790s he did not suggest how public opinion would be collected and articulated, regarding it as "a fixed entity that was supportive of republicanism but essentially inert" (*Politics in the Early Republic*, 45). Sharp further contends that the importance Madison placed on the role of public opinion in the 1790s is a change from the stance he took in *The Federalist*. In *Federalist* 49 he had warned against frequent appeals to the people on constitutional matters because this would deprive the government of "veneration" and "stability." Although Madison's argument in this essay was about constitutional and not legislative issues, in the first administration legislative issues ultimately depended on how one interpreted the Constitution, Sharp states. I read Madison's argument in *Federalist* 49 in a different way. Madison is addressing constitutional issues in this essay, and the remedies he is discussing are specifically constitutional ones, i.e., constitutional conventions. Madison rejected frequent appeals of this sort to enforce constitutional boundaries of power (*FP*, 282). His argument here should be viewed together with that of *Federalist* 44, where he contended that unconstitutional usurpations by the central government can be remedied by a nonconstitutional road to the opinion of the people. In these cases, the state legislatures may "sound the alarm to the people, and . . . exert their local influence in effecting a change of federal representatives," thereby "annul[ing] the acts of the usurpers" (*FP*, 254; cf. *FP*, 266 [#46]).

95. *FP*, 328–29 (#58); *PJM*, 14:165–66, 13:93–94.

96. *FP*, 310 (#55).

97. *FP*, 290 (#51).

98. *PJM*, 14:202; cf. *PJM*, 14:218.

99. *FP*, 287 (#50), 285 (#49). Elkins and McKitrick claim that there is no place in Madison's argument in *The Federalist* "for a majority coalition through which to assert a legitimate majority will" (*Age of Federalism*, 265). This assertion seems to ignore Madison's arguments in *Federalists* 49 and 50 regarding "the reason of the public" that is to sit in judgment on public measures, and *Federalist* 51's argu-

ment that government actions are to be dependent on the will of a "coalition of a majority of the whole society" (*FP*, 293 [#51]). Miller goes farther, declaring that the Federalists "intended . . . [to] undermine the formation of a public that could direct the operation of [the] government" ("Ghostly Body Politic," 100).

100. *PJM*, 14:234.

101. *PJM*, 14:207.

102. These authors included Raynal, La Bruyère, Necker, Turgot, DuPont de Nemours, Le Trosne, Louis-Sébastien Mercier, Le Mercier de La Rivière, Comte de Mirabeau, Brissot de Warville, Condorcet, Barthelemy, and Peuchet. Madison had in his possession in the 1780s works by all of these writers, and in fact he packed and shipped works by most of these authors to his residence in the temporary capital city of Philadelphia in the summer of 1790 (*PJM*, 13:286–89). For a more extensive treatment of the French theories of public opinion, see Sheehan, "Madison and the French Enlightenment."

103. Madison believed that, when properly formed, public opinion is tantamount to the reason of the public, but he disagreed with some French authors about what constitutes public reason and how it is achieved, e.g., the physiocrats' and Condorcet's reliance on evidence and mathematical calculations to produce public reason. See Sheehan, "Madison and the French Enlightenment," 939–40, 954–55. In contrast, McLean and Schofield see Madison as accepting Condorcet's early form of rational choice theory (Iain McLean, "Before and after Publius: The Sources and Influence of Madison's Political Thought," in *James Madison: The Theory and Practice of Republican Government*, ed. Samuel Kernell [Stanford, CA: Stanford University Press, 2003], 14–40; Norman Schofield, "Madison and the Founding of the Two-Party System," in *James Madison: Theory and Practice*, ed. Kernell, 302–27).

104. *PJM*, 14:426–27.

105. Keith Michael Baker, ed., *Condorcet: Selected Writings* (Indianapolis: Bobbs-Merrill, 1976), 58.

106. Peuchet, "Discours préliminaire," viii.

107. *PJM*, 14:139, emphasis added.

108. *PJM*, 14:170; cf. 161–62.

109. *PJM*, 14:162–63, 170; Meyers, *Mind of the Founder*, 221.

110. See *PJM*, 10:214; *FP* #44 and #46; Meyers, *Mind of the Founder*, 262–64.

111. Meyers, *Mind of the Founder*, 270.

112. *FP*, 68–69 (#14).

113. *PJM*, 9:355.

114. *PJM*, 14:170.

115. *FP*, 70–71 (#14); *PJM* 14:170, 161.

116. In his most recent work on Madison, Garry Wills continues to discount the importance Madison places on the distinction between a small and large republic, arguing that majority tyranny is a problem only in direct democracy and

not in representative governments, however small or large the territory (Wills, *James Madison* [New York: Henry Holt, 2002], 31). Wills's interpretation is contrary to Madison's repeated claims about the effects of a larger, practicable sphere of territory on the formation of majority opinion.

117. Banning, *Sacred Fire*, 209.

118. Alan Gibson, "Impartial Representation and the Extended Republic: Towards a Comprehensive and Balanced Reading of the Tenth Federalist Paper," *History of Political Thought* 12 (1991): 263–304.

119. *PJM*, 14:158–59.

120. See *PJM*, 17:238. Richard K. Matthews claims that Madison wanted the people's involvement in politics limited to voting—"to kicking the bums out of office when they got out of line"—an interpretation which is clearly at odds with Madison's own explicit statement on the matter (Matthews, *If Men Were Angels: James Madison and the Heartless Empire of Reason* [Lawrence: University Press of Kansas, 1995], 159; cf. 162–63).

121. *PJM*, 17:238–39; cf. *PJM*, 14:426–27; *FP*, 285 (#49), 287 (#50).

122. *PJM*, 13:75.

123. *PJM*, 13:106, 317; cf. *PJM*, 13:37; 6:272, 298.

124. *PJM*, 14:206–8, 274–75; 15:474, 518. In the exchange with Pacificus (Hamilton), Madison as Helvidius insisted on the legislative nature of the power to declare war and make treaties, as intended in the Constitution. The Helvidius essays are in part a continuation of the argument he presented in his 1792 Party Press Essay, "Universal Peace" (*PJM*, 14:206–7). In this essay Madison emphatically declared that in order to prevent the movement toward unlimited executive discretion that so often results from war and public debt, the will of the government must be made to depend on the will of the society. Madison's opposition to Hamilton and the Neutrality Proclamation did concern separation of powers and institutional arrangements, but underlying this was his deeper concern that government must depend on the will of the public.

125. *PJM* , 14:207.

126. *PJM* , 14:208, 207.

127. Early in the first session of the first Congress, i.e., before Jefferson's return from France and before Hamilton had even been offered the position of Secretary of the Treasury, Madison declared himself "a friend to a very free system of commerce" and distinguished between the limited cases of existing manufactures that warrant government support and all other cases (*PJM*, 12:70–72).

128. *PJM*, 14:266–67.

129. *PJM*, 14:267.

130. *FP*, 46 (#10).

131. *PJM*, 14:166.

132. Banning has solidly demonstrated that Madison was never a nationalist of the Hamiltonian stripe, and that he was always a strict constructionist and deeply

committed to popular government and majority rule (*Sacred Fire*, 128). Let us hope that "the ghost of counterrevolutionary sentiments" has finally been laid to rest.

133. *PJM*, 14:138; see also *FP* #46 and #48.

134. *PJM*, 14:192.

135. See Madison's commentary on the Virginia Resolutions in his "Virginia Report" (Meyers, *Mind of the Founder*, 229–73). Madison argued that "it is the duty, as well as the right, of intelligent and faithful citizens to discuss and promulgate [the proceedings of government] freely—as well to control them by the censorship of public opinion, as to promote a remedy according to the rules of the Constitution." The Virginia Resolutions, he explained, utilized the states in order to excite public reflection and influence public opinion.

136. *PJM*, 14:168.

137. *PJM*, 14:138.

138. *PJM*, 14:274.

139. *PJM*, 14:138.

140. Alan Gibson attempts to bridge the gulf between scholars who claim that Madison advocated a scheme that relied on the heroic impartiality of representatives and those who believed Madison relied primarily on the structural solution of an extended territory with a multiplicity of interests and religious sects (Gibson, "Impartial Representation," 288). Gibson concludes that Madison combined both of these components to achieve his goal of impartial representation and reconcile this with popular sovereignty. On the one hand, Gibson argues that public opinion is constituted by "an underlying consensus [that] allows citizens to openly communicate and form coalitions that have the principles of right, of reason and of the Constitution on their side." On the other hand, Gibson argues that "in general, the 'public mind' as Madison referred to public opinion, was simply a public consciousness formed from the aggregate of individual sentiments" ("Impartial Representation," 285). Madison rejected the idea of reforming the citizens of an unjust majority and generally of educating and forming civic character (Gibson, "Ancients, Moderns and Americans: The Republicanism-Liberalism Debate Revisited," *History of Political Thought* 21 [2002]: 287, 282). Not only did he want to exclude the people in their collective capacity from governing, but he sought to minimize the influence of the majority in the formation of public policy ("Impartial Representation," 300–301). Madison's view of popular sovereignty is one that recognizes the fundamental authority of the people in the act of founding and amending the Constitution and is incongruent with participatory schemes of democracy ("Impartial Representation," 300). Gibson is correct that Madison's scheme does not make it easy for majorities to form, but I would take issue with the claim that he sought to minimize the influence of majorities in public decisions. According to Madison, the formation of the "will of the society" is critical to maintaining the true spirit of republican government (see *FP* #51; *PJM*, 14:138, 207,

234). If the will of the society is to be consistently nonfactious and reasonable, a process of educational refinement is necessary. This can only be accomplished by the kind of communicative activity that results from political participation. Gibson does not give sufficient attention to the importance Madison places on the communication of ideas and the process of enlightenment in *The Federalist* and the *Party Press Essays* (e.g., *FP*, 70–71 [#14]; *PJM*, 14:138–39, 170, 192, 207, 245, 266, 371, 426; see also *PJM*, 14:159, 161–63, 168; cf. Sheehan, "The Commerce of Ideas and Cultivation of Character in Madison's Republic," in Bradley Watson, ed., *Civic Education and Culture* [Wilmington, DE: Intercollegiate Studies Institute, 2005]).

141. *PJM*, 9:357.

142. *PJM*, 14:139.

143. For example, Martin Diamond ("Ethics and Politics," 54–55; Diamond, "The Federalist," in *History of Political Philosophy*, ed. Leo Strauss and Joseph Cropsey [Chicago: Rand McNally, 1972], 648) attributes to Madison the theory that a large republic supplies the remedy for faction only if it is also a commercial republic. However, I would argue that Diamond's presentation of the commercial republic theory is actually a much more apt interpretation of Hamilton's political and economic thought. According to Diamond's interpretation, the historical battle between the haves and have-nots was to be replaced with a new factional struggle based on the diversity of economic interests. This required magnifying the operation of interest (and taming or devitalizing passion and opinion), so that citizens would divide themselves on the basis of narrow and particularized economic interests, thereby allowing the society to evade the fatal kind of factionalism caused by opinion and class interest in the past. Diamond further argued that the proponents of this theory rejected any attempt to refine and improve the citizens' opinions of the advantageous and just. Instead, they accepted as "irredeemably dominant" the self-interested passions sown in human nature. In light of this, they sought to channel the powerful passions and interests of the society by way of shrewd institutional arrangements rather than engage in the futile attempt to form the character of the citizenry. While the commercial republic theory presented by Diamond captures much of Hamilton's thought, it does not correctly characterize Hamilton's vision in one important respect. Hamilton's theory of the commercial republic did not merely rest on a multiplicity of rival interests to effect the common good, nor did it advance the notion of a multiplicity of factions. (Nor did Madison's.) Like Necker, Hamilton sought to achieve an opinion of confidence and unity of national sentiment via the effects of a good administration. At the New York Ratifying Convention, Hamilton proclaimed that the objective was "to abolish factions, and to unite all parties for the general welfare" (*PAH*, 5:85).

144. *PAH*, 25:606.

145. *PAH*, 25:613.

146. *PAH*, 25:354.

PART III

Hamilton's Legacies

CHAPTER 8

Alexander Hamilton and the
1790s Economy
A Reappraisal

CAREY ROBERTS

*H*ISTORIANS and political scientists commonly credit Alexander Hamilton's economic plans for revitalizing the American economy and providing the impetus for extended economic progress. Such arguments usually take for granted many of the criticisms levied against the policies of the states and Confederation during the 1780s. They further assume that the weakness of the American economy stemmed from the decentralized nature of its financial institutions, lack of specie, and burdensome problems of the Revolutionary debt.

There is little doubt that economic problems prevailed under the Articles of Confederation; however, it remains unclear how much Hamilton's policies corrected those problems. Hamilton's program of assumption and funding resulted in an overall increase in the nation's monetary base. The Bank of the United States (BUS) furthered the monetary expansion by following a pattern of fractional-reserve lending up until 1795. As a result, inflation continued to affect the economy during the early 1790s. Burdensome taxes were levied to pay off government debts at face value rather than at prevailing market values. And significant opposition formed against Federalist officials due to the perceived joining of monied interests to the federal government.

Without understanding the short-term consequences, our praise for the long-term results seems strained at best. If what is called "Hamiltonian" finance resulted in short-term problems, or even disasters, long-term success would be less likely. If long-term success could actually be attributed to Jeffersonian policies carried forward by Jacksonian Democrats, the place of Hamiltonian finance in our history would change drastically. Furthermore, even if it is determined that the American economy surged after 1791, attributing the rise to beneficial market conditions totally independent from federal politics could jeopardize Hamilton's place as a financial genius. Such is not the scope of this essay, nor is it a challenge to the dominant interpretation of Hamilton's character and financial vision. However, puzzling discrepancies present themselves when one compares the effects of the Federalist financial plan and its short-term consequences in the 1790s. Limitation of space prevents a full treatment of the period, but it is hoped that the following might serve as a prolegomena for further study.

Economic Problems of the 1790s

The first decade under the new constitution was not a period of strong economic growth, nor was it free from periods of economic distress. Data are sketchy at best, and debate still rages as to whether the economy of antebellum America was rapidly expanding or mediocre. Likewise, we may never have a complete grasp on the economic condition for the period between 1789 and 1800, a problem further complicated by the loss of records, especially those of the BUS, during the War of 1812.[1]

While the fine details of economic growth remain elusive, much can still be said about economic conditions both before and after Hamilton and Congress implemented Hamilton's plan for the national economy. A speculative crash occurred in New York City in 1792 and spread sporadically across the eastern seaboard. Steep inflation rates existed between 1791 and 1796. And while infrastructure investments bustled throughout the East and the developing West, their creation coincided with a rapid increase in bankruptcy and insolvency. Even at this early date, the cyclical activity of the American economy appeared in short booms and busts.

Several explanations could be offered for the development of an early boom-bust cycle. One might suggest business cycles are a natural element of capitalism, and as the economy modernized, cyclical fluctuations would be expected. Sheer greed on the part of speculators could have produced more services than consumers demanded, thus causing overproduction. The financial infrastructure may have remained too immature to adequately finance the needs of investors despite Hamilton's attempt to strengthen it. State governments may have improperly managed their economic situation either by refusing to cooperate with other states or by failing to sufficiently support newly chartered companies. Investors and promoters may have been unsuccessful in getting farmers and minor merchants to see how they could benefit from a vigorous—and united—national economy.

Another explanation for a business cycle emerging early in the 1790s suggests that far from stabilizing the economy, Hamilton and the Federalist Congress destabilized financial markets causing entrepreneurs to misread the market and make incorrect business decisions.

Many important entrepreneurs in the early republic also held most of the domestic debt. As the country's public credit rose, debt holders profited from debt redemption. The Bank of the United States added to the potential for increased investment by pursuing a policy of easy money until 1796. By receiving higher profits and easier credit than market conditions allowed, entrepreneurs took much greater risks with their subsequent investments. They also mistook the dramatic deflation of the late 1780s and the inflation of the early 1790s as evidence of a strengthening economy. Prices surged after ratification of the Constitution due to perceived political actions of Congress, not due to Americans being in a position to demand more goods and services. The resulting malinvestments in transportation improvements, banking, and manufacturing far exceeded market demand and resulted in the Panic of 1792 and would add to the distress in 1796. To complicate matters further, the Treasury, following Hamilton's "Report on the Mint," fixed the exchange rate of specie so that gold slightly overvalued silver. The decision instigated a classic example of Gresham's Law, where "bad" money chases out "good" money, and in this case, the country's gold supply was steadily depleted in favor of silver.

Debt Funding, Conversion, and the Bank of the United States

There is no need to regurgitate the intricacies of the financial program proposed by Alexander Hamilton while Secretary of Treasury. Yet misunderstanding Hamilton's goals and the monetary effects of his plans creates a distorted view of Hamilton's role. Hamilton was neither a defender of an aristocracy of wealth nor was he the architect of America's economic "take-off."

Alexander Hamilton laid clear plans as to what he wished to do with the Revolutionary debt. Though not a dedicated bullionist, like most economic nationalists of his day Hamilton believed the country's economic problems grew from a lack of sufficient specie in circulation. The underlying goal required augmenting existing specie by converting federal and state government securities into a capital pool for financiers and entrepreneurs.[2] Financiers, traders, merchants, manufacturers, and all other businessmen would benefit by having access to cheap credit while consumers would have sufficient currency with which to purchase products. Hamilton never questioned the federal government's role in providing specie, albeit to him, that role was supervisory rather than regulatory.[3]

Hamilton publicly reasoned that the country's credit problems weakened the federal government's ability to get more specie. Low public credit also prevented private citizens from getting loans at reasonable interest rates. The economy needed a jump-start, but not by a direct infusion of specie. Entrepreneurs, who knew how to use capital to spur on economic growth, needed the specie before average citizens. Getting specie to entrepreneurs first (or at all) proved problematic given the immature state of the country's commercial credit system. Hamilton's solution involved bringing in enough specie and then using the federal government to provide a financial network to dispense capital where it was best used. The Revolutionary War debt offered the means of accomplishing both.

Influenced by the predominant view that the economy suffered from a shortage of specie, Hamilton assumed a new credit network needed something other than a finite amount of specie. To be feasible, it must grow with the needs of the people. A rigid specie standard and a credit market where all banknotes equaled specie reserves would be too tight.[4] The best strategy must include a combination of specie, redeemable bank notes, and government securities, where all forms of money and money substitutes traded as currency. Hamilton envisioned nothing less than a sophisticated credit market that could aid investors and supply the country with much needed currency, or as he called it, "the active capital of a country."[5]

Hamilton believed banks could issue more credit than they held in specie reserves as long as all notes were fully redeemable in specie on demand. Like many advocates of commercial banking, Hamilton understood that a bank's depositors rarely demanded all their specie at once. At any given time, banks easily lent out more credit than they held on deposit.[6] He did not understand, however, that the subsequent alteration in the overall purchasing power of money distorted rather than stabilized prices.

Three distinct but interrelated events came together between 1788 and 1791: funding the federal debt through the federal government, not the states; converting the old debt into new debt; and using the Bank of the United States to facilitate the acceptance of securities and bank notes as currency.[7] Only Hamilton advocated all three from a position of high political office. Some congressmen supported him on this. But like many of the great compromises in American history, a majority probably did not exist in support of all three segments combined, only on each segment individually.

As the Philadelphia convention met and produced a new constitution, the market value of debt securities rose based on the expectation of payment. Never did the securities become worthless, but never did they actually reach par with their face value before conversion in 1790.[8] Speculators stood to make impressive gains from buying the debt cheap in the early 1780s and selling high, as many did, in the late 1780s. Furthermore, those who kept their securities through the conversion process stood to gain even more. As late as 1789, confused debt holders did not know what to expect from Congress with regard to the debt. Their only anchor during the hectic first session of Congress was that most congressmen favored paying the debt in some manner.[9]

Congressmen differed on whom to pay and how much. Many opponents of funding, James Madison and Thomas Jefferson excepted, knew the problem was not forsaking the initial common people and soldiers who held the debt. Rather, they saw the issue as a battle between market value on the one hand and a sizable expansion of credit, high taxation, and enlargement of the federal debt's market value, on the other.[10] There were few if any true "repudiationists" in Congress at the time it debated funding.

Thanks to James Madison, the discrimination, or market value forces, lost. Madison, knowingly or not, sidetracked the opponents of face value funding on to questions of morality and social obligation as opposed to financial questions and taxation. By the end of the debate, discrimination meant giving original holders a portion of *face* value, illustrating how Hamilton's most vocal opponents moved toward the center.[11] To make the opposition's position on discrimination less tenable, the difference between market value and face value shrank as the debate dragged on.

Indeed, talk of funding during the ratification process had already increased the market value of the debt and caused a wave of deflation to sweep the economy. Between 1787 and 1789 prices fell between 4 and 7 percent across the country. In Philadelphia alone, extending the dates from 1784 to 1790 shows a 20 percent deflation rate overall.[12] By itself, deflation probably caused some market distortions, and regardless of which policy Congress followed, whether Hamilton's or an alternative, some malinvestments likely would have occurred.

Congress finally agreed to take specie from a new European loan and apply it to the national debt and the assumed value of state debts. Congress offered to exchange old securities for stock, substituting two-thirds of the principal for 6 percent stock and one-third for 6 percent deferred stock. It also paid all remaining interests and indents at 3 percent and old continental currency at 100: 1.[13] The process of conversion both raised the market value of the debt by fully backing it with specie and turned it into usable currency. But conversion also reduced the new currency's purchasing power by infusing the economy with new specie and new notes whose value must have been slightly higher than the highest market value of old notes in the summer of 1790.[14]

One would think conversion continued the process of deflation, but such was not the case since new notes were issued based on the face value of old notes. Because conversion exchanged notes rather than allowed the old ones to continue in circulation and because the federal government injected more notes than the total market value of the old notes, the overall supply of money increased. The resulting inflation appeared immediately as prices increased nationwide. Between 1791 and 1796, prices in Charleston increased 57 percent, Cincinnati grew by 38 percent, and Philadelphia prices rose an astonishing 98 percent.[15] Additional foreign loans (of specie) and creating the Bank of the United States compounded the situation by further increasing the supply of specie *and* redeemable notes. Had Congress followed a policy of paying the old debt at market value, even market value over a period of months, Congress might have continued the deflation.[16] Corresponding taxation may have softened the monetary expansion, but it was unlikely to significantly counteract its effects given the variety of products taxed and the variation of the tax burden.

It is important not to focus merely on general monetary phenomena, but to suggest monetary changes that affected individual entrepreneurs. One must be careful to keep in mind that holders of the debt purchased the bulk of it at prices far below what they were worth after 1790. Prices paid for the debt and the profits debt holders made did not reflect market demand for the debt so much as it reflected Congress's demand for its own debt. In other words, the American economy did not cause the price of securities to increase, Congress's decisions did. The subsequent rise in prices cannot be attributed to a rise in consumer spending, but to a drop in the purchasing power of government securities and BUS notes.

Far ahead of his time, Hamilton took possible inflation into account. In fact, he expected it and anticipated its effect on government securities in terms of bringing down the rate of interest. When Hamilton's proposal went to Congress, some congressmen wished to pay interest on the new stock at present rates of interest, or around 8 percent. But having more money and money substitutes available for banks to lend, the price of money dropped. Betting on interest rates to fall, Hamilton hoped to get debt holders to agree to 6 percent stock that would sell at a premium if interest rates dropped below 6 percent.[17]

Beyond conversion and assumption, other aspects of Hamilton's plan exercised significant influence over prices. Hamilton hoped the Bank of the United States would create a commercial credit network, pool capital for investors, and strengthen the country's merchant base. But like funding and conversion, the Bank exercised an inflationary effect. It certainly increased available commercial credit to individual entrepreneurs as well as to new commercial banks chartered by various states. The bank and its branches fully redeemed its notes upon demand, but the banknotes were not fully backed by specie reserves, and notes circulated in a high proportion to specie in the vaults especially before 1796.[18]

During the first years of the Bank's operation, it followed a course of fairly rapid credit expansion. The BUS played a substantial role in the Panic of 1792, and it may have accounted for some of the economic distress of the period up to 1796. Taking into account the Bank's proportion of notes to specie between 1792 and 1794, the Bank held about a 2:1 ratio. By January 1795, the ratio increased to 5:1 only to drop down slightly by the end of the year. The excess of fiduciary currency, or the notes issued in excess of specie reserves, likely contributed to the rise in prices from 1792 forward. New commercial banks, which pyramided their assets on top of BUS notes and stock, compounded the situation. Wisely, BUS officials changed course by late 1796, boosted their specie holdings, and the notes to specie ratio evened out to near equity by 1799–1800.[19] Not coincidentally, 1796 marked a turning point where the Bank began loaning more capital to private investors than it did to the federal government.[20]

Even assuming the BUS followed a conservative path, those banks whose capital came from BUS notes pursued a different course until competition from BUS branches intensified.[21] Hamilton's consternation with state banks rested on their willingness to expand credit through fiduciary offerings at a much faster rate than the BUS. While some Federalists supported the coexistence of state banks with the Bank and its branches, Hamilton worried the inflationary tendency of the combined circulation of BUS notes and notes of state banks would wreck the fledgling commercial credit system. State banks, Hamilton thought, could not be trusted to control their credit emissions. Should the notes of state banks begin to depreciate, BUS notes might slip as well, thus jeopardizing the whole system.[22] Hamilton must also have known other banks could curtail credit, making loans more expensive, thereby raising interest rates and detrimentally affecting the BUS.[23]

Hamilton mistakenly saw credit as a means of stimulating investment and failed to recognize that demand for credit does not correlate to demand for the investments created with it. If credit expansion prompted investors to place that credit in things for which the economy was not strong enough to endure, then consumer demand would not be strong enough to make investments pan out. At least publicly, Hamilton insisted the opposite would occur. Investors, he claimed, would place their money in ventures sure to make a profit instead of "permanent" improvements like canals and manufacturing.[24] Such was not the case.

A counterargument to the one given here might suggest that inflation is desirable and that deflation is to be avoided. Critics might also insist that the purpose of Hamiltonian finance, as he stated, was to raise the credit rating of the United States government and American businessmen seeking capital or credit from abroad, or to set better terms on foreign contracts. From this perspective, Hamilton was successful, thus contributing to the increase of foreign trade and the export-led expansion of the economy. If not this, then he helped lay the groundwork for institutions that used securities for a finance-led expansion of the economy.

Another way of examining Hamilton's contributions may be in order. Though many debt holders did quite well, many notable exceptions occurred that cannot be attributed to poor luck or lack of entrepreneurial wisdom. Instead, it seems that the inflationary tendencies of Hamiltonian finance produced faulty economic "signals" that misled entrepreneurs into thinking the economy was better than it actually was. Rather than analyzing what influence debt holders exerted over the formation of the new government and Hamilton's plan, a focus on how federal policies influenced their business practices reveals much about the effects of funding, conversion, and the First Bank. Such an approach would follow the one briefly outlined below concerning William Duer.

The Panic of the Early 1790s

The example of the much-maligned William Duer illustrates how economic repercussions from funding and assumption were far from positive. Duer was English by birth and, like Hamilton, spent time in the West Indies, though Duer did so only long enough to manage his father's plantation. Also like Hamilton, Duer settled in New York and married into a wealthy family. The wives of both men were even cousins. Duer briefly served in the Continental Congress but made a fortune fulfilling contracts with the Continental Army. Following the war, he speculated in real estate holdings and served on the Confederation's Treasury Board. He then became Assistant Secretary of Treasury under Hamilton in 1789 and assisted Hamilton in the creation of the Society of Useful Manufactures. Duer often used inside information to exploit the government securities market, but his misapplication—or corrupt application—of this information can account for most of his financial mistakes. [25]

Duer lost with deflation leading up to debt conversion and with the subsequent inflation. Scholars rightly distance Hamilton from Duer with regard to their personal relationship. And Hamilton had no control over Duer's speculations. However, lack of personal involvement does not mean that repercussions from Hamilton's financial plan failed to influence Duer's decisions.

No doubt Duer's life followed that of a frontier gambler more than it did a New York aristocrat. Yet the most incredible of his speculative endeavors depended on specific actions of the federal government, either under the Articles of Confederation or under the Constitution. Two examples merit mentioning: his role in the Scioto land company and his direct influence over the Panic of 1792.

Following the Revolution, Americans started pushing the bounds of the western territory. Given the perceived shortage of specie, prospective land customers petitioned Congress in the late 1780s to accept debt certificates in the place of hard currency. Two companies led the way: the Ohio Company of Association and the Scioto Company. Duer participated in the creation of both since they were part of the same deal, though he directly influenced the Scioto Company. Land developers wished to use the companies to purchase land cheaply and sell it to needy settlers. When Congress agreed to accept specie *and* debt certificates as payment, Duer and his clients stood to make a substantial profit if the market value of the debt certificates remained low.[26] In other words, they based their assessment of the situation on current prices in 1787 and did not expect the rapid rise in market value. In the end, the Scioto Company went broke due to mismanagement and the substantial increase of land costs as government debt values increased.[27]

The Scioto example should not be used to discount Hamiltonian finance, which began operation after the Scioto Company became insolvent. It does, however, indicate how entrepreneurs based their decisions on the value of government securities and how changes in their value harmed some investors. Regardless of what Congress did, debt certificates would have fluctuated in value to some extent. In hindsight, Scioto investors should have known better. But how could they? There was no certainty in 1787 that Congress would even pay the national debt, and less certainty existed over whether Congress would pay the debt at face value.

Integral to Duer's association with the Scioto Company was his use of it to manage his personal speculation in government securities. In fact, the same forces that injured the land company encouraged Duer to try his hand at another form of speculation. While assistant to Hamilton, Duer counted on uncertainty about a new congressional policy: full funding of state debts. He busily purchased as much outstanding debt as possible before Congress reached a final decision in August 1790.[28]

Afterwards, as interest rates dropped, new government debt traded at a premium. Additional stock and securities came onto the market as the Bank of the United States commenced business and supported the creation of new commercial banks. BUS shares, bank stocks, and new securities traded openly in major American cities, but no city contained as much speculative buying as New York. At the center of all this stood William Duer.

Duer participated in the selling of most forms of stocks and securities, and he worked both sides of the market. Able to control vast sums of capital, Duer bought and traded the same stock, virtually cornering the market and creating his own profits. Like other speculators in government securities, Duer commenced planning a number of important new companies ranging from banks and factories to bridges and canals. Thinking the market rise in securities knew no limit, Duer plunged everything he had into the market. He began buying on margin by taking out loans from all possible sources, including the fledgling Society for the Erection of Useful Manufacturers and wealthy New Yorkers. The activity of speculators, drawing on the extensive new credit system created by the Federalists under Alexander Hamilton, peaked in March 1792. When directors of the Bank of New York realized credit had been extended too much, their decision to stop all loans commenced a credit contraction spelling the end to William Duer's operation. By the end of March, the panic that began in New York became nationwide.[29]

Ultimately, the federal government and Hamilton bore the greatest economic cost of the Panic of 1792. By late 1792 Hamilton and members of Congress realized projected revenue would not meet the government's demands for expenses and interest payments on the debt. The situation forced Hamilton to take out another foreign loan. The combination of economic distress and the apparent inability of the funding system and BUS to "fund" the debt without more loans elicited stern attacks from Hamilton's opponents in Congress. William B. Giles of Virginia, with the assistance of William Findley of Pennsylvania and Nathaniel Macon of North Carolina, pushed through a series of resolutions questioning Hamilton's leadership of the Treasury and accusing him of misallocation of funds.

The economy momentarily improved, but inflation rates continued to climb until 1796. At that point, the economy slipped back into a panic, albeit less severe than the one in 1792.

The question must be asked: Was William Duer representative of American entrepreneurs during the 1780s and 1790s? Certainly not, especially when considering that all American entrepreneurs did not speculate in government securities and lose all their investments in the Panic of 1792. However, Duer illustrates how expansive credit systems, like that proposed by Hamilton, cannot be sustained indefinitely and how credit booms mislead entrepreneurs and thus lay the groundwork for credit bursts. More importantly, if an insider like William Duer could not make good decisions based on the information at his disposal, how could average entrepreneurs?

Duer shows how politically generated conditions encourage speculative behavior. He based his decisions in part on the signals he received from the securities market—prices boosted by funding and assumption. And if Winifred Rothenberg is correct, debt holders were not the only people basing their decisions on market prices. Though Rothenberg's coverage covers mainly New England, it is safe to say that by the 1780s and 1790s an increasing number of Americans relied exclusively on market prices for economic decisions, prices made possible by moving away from bartering.[30] A different policy, one that allowed for the gradual redemption of securities at market value, may have alleviated some of the extreme cases of speculation and price distortions.

Other speculators who benefited from funding and assumption followed a pattern similar to Duer's. Men like Robert Morris, Thomas Willing, James Greenleaf, Nathaniel Massie, and John Nicholson took profits made from government securities and invested them in projects the market could not sustain.[31]

Land prices rose faster than any other investment in the inflationary climate of the early 1790s, leading numerous speculators to place investments on western expansion (or even on undeveloped land in the East). The Ohio Company, the North American Land Company, the Connecticut Land Company, and the Yazoo land claims, to name a few, began after investors wildly exaggerated the gains to be made in land development. One of the best examples fueled by inflating land prices, Washington, D.C., included several prominent debt holders like Uriah Forrest and Robert Morris, who plunged into an uncertain market and were financially ruined.[32]

Investors thought higher land prices resulted from higher demand for property. When land prices began dropping, developers went to great lengths to get returns on their investments. William Blout, Nicholas Romayne, and John Chisholm went so far as inviting Great Britain to get Spanish holdings in North America.[33]

The credit boom of the early 1790s also coincided with the expansion of internal improvement companies and commercial banks, whose capital was often pyramided on BUS funds, state subsidies, or mutual credit extensions. To help prospective settlers move west, or to link local eastern markets together, transportation companies quickly emerged with the assistance of state legislatures. The number of banks grew from one in 1790 to twenty in 1795. Thirty-two new navigation companies, including canals and waterways, were charted between 1790 and 1795. States granted twelve new charters in 1796, alone. Charters for bridges increased from one per year in 1791 to as many as fourteen per year in 1795, totaling forty-four between 1791 and 1796. And by 1796, there were sixteen new turnpike charters.[34] Naturally, not all of these new companies relied on bank credit, nor did former debt holders promote them all by themselves. Some companies evolved from lucrative family holdings or from capital raised from investors. But even if some did not rely directly on credit expansion, their customers and investors often did.

New internal improvement companies faced obstacles similar to those encountered by land companies. Most investors wished to build improvements in order to expand their markets. They assumed that Federalist financial measures reinvigorated the economy and continued growth would offset the expense of linking markets together. In doing so, rural markets could be tapped to further commercial potential. Those relying exclusively on prices and available commercial credit, however, ignored the economy's weakness as well as latent hostility to their projects from farmers.[35]

State laws required companies to have charters, which carried certain advantages such as monopoly status, state grants, and the ability to exercise eminent domain.[36] However, charters also carried numerous restrictions that ultimately hindered profitability. And since companies often undermined the property rights of common people, rural farmers condemned the new companies for their special, political privileges.[37] Like the land schemes, most internal improvement projects faced substantial losses. Promoters repeatedly returned to state legislatures for additional support only to be turned away by politicians weary of mounting demands and disillusioned with development schemes. In the end, national fiscal measures encouraged investment, whereas state and local policies were ignored only to the detriment of uncanny or misled investors.

Great wealth was made, as such prominent examples of John J. Astor and Stephen Girard show. But the 1790s were far from the boom time many speculators imagined. In fact, business failures, missed opportunities, and collapsed fortunes may have been the norm. Even wealth made in the decade later diminished as competition intensified and the monetary shocks wore off.[38]

Detractors of this argument may be prepared to accept both the benefits and costs of this boom-bust cycle. The market would never have produced the transportation improvements so quickly. And in the long run, society still enjoys the fruits of the products such as better roads, canals, and a commercial banking network. All modernization efforts proceed along a bumpy path, but society ultimately benefits by laying the foundation for future stages of economic growth.

However, one must take into account that insolvent companies cannot maintain their investments. Bridges fell into disrepair, roads washed away, and canals remained unfinished. Above all, long-run benefits must take into account not only the material costs of malinvestments, but the social and political costs as well. The Federalist financial system did not solidify broad support for the federal government and Federalist Party. In fact, Hamilton's financial program failed to secure the continued support of the "monied" interests to which his opponents claimed he catered. No elite group of financiers found continued fortune at the hands of the Federalists.

Political Ramifications of Hamiltonian Finance and Federalist Policy

The political success of the Federalist Party depended upon the success of Alexander Hamilton and his financial policies. From the beginning, supporters of the Federalists counted on the new government to meet their financial interests. Three major political results proceeded from Federalist financial arrangements.

First, the economic malaise of the early 1790s undermined popular faith in the Federalist Party. As Albert Gallatin insisted in 1796, "Far from strengthening government," aspects of Hamiltonian finance "created more discontent and more uneasiness than any other measure."[39] It is inconceivable to assume political and cultural differences alone could have instigated the first party system. It is true that issues like Jay's Treaty, for example, aggravated party feelings, as did the economic conditions of the late 1790s, for which Hamilton was not directly responsible. It is also true that the self-appointed leaders of the opposition, Madison and Jefferson, worked with Hamilton to pass key aspects of the Federalist program, including the BUS and assumption. Nevertheless, partisan attacks against Hamilton and the Federalists carried great weight as inflation intensified during the mid-1790s.[40]

Second, confidence in the federal government shrank in light of the increasing tax burden to fund the full debt. Direct taxes, particularly that on liquor, provoked heated debate in Congress, which ultimately spilled over into the Whiskey Rebellion. However, direct taxes continued after

Hamilton's departure from Philadelphia. Whether Fries's Rebellion or the Virginian assault on the carriage tax, animosities toward Federalist finance served as a conduit for even greater animosity toward the federal government.

Third, in a few cases, Hamiltonian finance enabled some people to aggrandize their wealth through political influence. John Beckley, James Monroe, and John Taylor attacked the Federalists early on for creating a privileged elite. They pointed to the large number of debt holders in Congress who passed the major elements of Hamilton's program as evidence of corruption. Examples of privilege enabled the Jeffersonians to adopt portions of the antiwealth rhetorical tradition of eighteenth-century England and extend it well into the nineteenth century.

The link between Hamiltonian finance and the business problems of the 1790s is not tenuous. Many investors profited handsomely from debt conversion and found additional resources available from new commercial banks. They had to put their new money somewhere, and, though risky, land companies and internal improvements seemed to offer the best returns. Here was the problem. Because of the new credit and steep profits from conversion, investors could afford to take advantage of pioneering companies, whereas those with limited funds were more careful with their investments. Not everyone lost, but overall, new investments in the 1790s offered disappointing results and intensified political conflict. By the late 1790s, when the Federalist leadership under John Adams began questioning financial incentives for business, or when Federalists in Congress could not pass bankruptcy protection for suffering ventures, those entrepreneurs most dependent on state aid migrated to the Republican Party.

Alexander Hamilton cannot be blamed for all of this. But the bulk of his defense of the Constitution implied that it protects and promotes the various interests of the country. Far from classical republicanism, Hamilton recognized that a government cannot deny the existence of different interest groups, nor can it seek to destroy those interests most people consider legitimate. Hoping to promote as many economic interests as possible, Hamilton constructed a financial plan from which as many people as possible got something. Entrepreneurs gained easy credit, debt holders received payment, assumption restored stability for debtor states, moral nationalists got taxes on whiskey, and politicians at least paid lip service to manufacturers and then promised farmers that grain exports would lift them to prosperity.

Entrepreneurs received mixed signals as new government securities and credit spread through the economy. The increased value of debt certifi-cates, the lowering of interest rates, the ready availability of capital, and the expansion of banking reflected an artificial boom. The federal govern-ment was in no position to sustain the boom, and even if it were, the economy could not elevate consumer demand high enough to return investors' profits on their infrastructure improvements. At precisely the same time that Americans embraced a mature market system based on prices rather than barter, monetary shocks implemented by Alexander Hamilton and the Federalists rendered available prices insufficient to sup-port entrepreneurial decisions.

NOTES

1. Economic historians continue to disagree about the rate of economic growth between the Revolution and the Civil War. Most think the 1780s exhibited dismal economic performance and that a burst of economic activity occurred after 1840. At present, the best that can be said is that between 1789 and 1840 the economy grew between 0.5 and 1.5 percent per year on average with major inter-ruptions in 1808–9, 1812–15, and 1819–20. The debate can be followed in Douglass North, *The Economic Growth of the United States, 1790–1860* (Englewood Cliffs, NJ: Prentice Hall, 1961); Donald R. Adams, Jr., "American Neutrality and Prosper-ity, 1793–1808: A Reconsideration," *Journal of Economic History,* 90 (Dec. 1980): 313–337; and Claudia D. Golden and Frank D. Lewis, "The Role of Exports in American Economic Growth during the Napoleonic Wars, 1793 to 1807," *Explo-rations in Economic History,* 17 (1980): 6–25.

2. See his "Report on Public Credit," in Harold C. Syrett et al., eds., *The Papers of Alexander Hamilton* (hereafter *PAH*) (New York: Columbia University Press, 1963), 6: 65–168. Particularly useful in understanding the origin and extent of Hamilton's views are Syrett and Cooke, "Introductory Notes," *PAH,* 6: 51–65; For-rest McDonald, *Alexander Hamilton: A Biography* (New York: W. W. Norton, 1979), 165–171; and Swanson and Trout, "Alexander Hamilton's Report on the Public Credit (1790) in a European Perspective," *Journal of European Economic History,* 19 (1990): 623–633.

3. *PAH,* 6: 70–71 and 7: 306–309. Few people before Hamilton offered alterna-tives to increasing the country's specie holdings. The cry for more specie dated back to colonial times when British North Americans complained about the dearth of coinage. After several experiments with fiat currency and manipulation of coinage values by colonial governments, most Americans welcomed the stabil-ity offered by specie-backed currency. At the same time Hamilton and Federalist

Congressmen designed their economic plan, a rival vision was emerging. For example, Noah Webster, a leading Federalist in his own right, suggested any amount of specie on hand would suffice for economic exchange since prices automatically adapted. There was no need then to bring in more specie. Some Jeffersonians agreed. See John Taylor, *An Enquiry into the Principles and Tendency of Certain Public Measures* (Philadelphia: Thomas Dobson, 1974).

4. The most succinct statement of Hamilton's views on currency and banking can be found in his "Report on a National Bank," *PAH*, 7: 305–342, especially 320–323. See also *PAH*, 7: 251–253.

5. *PAH*, 7: 308.

6. *PAH*, 7: 306–310.

7. Several states made payment on the federal debt by the middle of the 1790s, thus jeopardizing the principal focus of Federalist finance: the national debt. See Edwin Perkins, *American Public Finance and Financial Service, 1700–1815* (Columbus: Ohio State University Press, 1994), 209–211.

8. See E. James Ferguson, *The Power of the Purse* (Chapel Hill: University of North Carolina Press for the Institute of Early American History and Culture, 1961), 251.

9. Ferguson, *Power of the Purse*, 285.

10. See James Jackson, 8 February 1790, *Annals of Congress*, 1st Cong., 2d Sess., 1141; Samuel Livermore, *Annals*, 1st Cong., 2d Sess., 1155–1156, and to a certain extent, Thomas T. Tucker, *Annals*, 1st Cong., 2d Sess., 1181.

11. James Madison, 11 February 1790, 1st Cong., 2d Sess., 1192.

12. U.S. Department of Commerce, *Historical Statistics of the United States, Colonial Times to 1970* (Washington, DC: Government Printing Office, 1976), 204–206.

13. Ferguson, *Power of the Purse*, 297.

14. The total federal debt in 1787 can be estimated at just over $27 million with a market value of $16.6 million. Adding the assumed state debts placed the total market value of federal debt at around $42 million. Counting interests, total national debt in 1790 was around $72 million. Funding and assumption appear to have acted as a credit infusion of around $25 million if considering principal alone. See Ferguson, *Power of the Purse*, 252; and Curtis P. Nettels, *The Emergence of a National Economy* (New York: Holt, Rinehart and Winston, 1962), 115–116.

15. These are cumulative, not yearly rates of inflation. *Historical Statistics*, 202, 204–206.

16. Hamilton appeased hard money advocates by establishing a sinking fund whereby a special commission would purchase as much outstanding debt as possible. Overall, the commission accomplished little except to alarm hard-money Jeffersonians already suspicious of Hamilton's activities.

17. Hamilton faced stiff opposition from his own potential supporters given that a 6 percent interest lowered the face value of government securities from an

average of 8 percent. See Donald F. Swanson and Andrew P. Trout, "Alexander Hamilton, Conversion, and Debt Reduction," *Explorations in Economic History,* 29 (October 1992): 417–429.

18. Hamilton, *PAH,* 7: 313–314. The purpose here is not to use "high" to denote a qualitative analysis. Quantitatively, specie reserves of the Bank of the United States before 1796 were far less than what it held by the end of the decade. See James O. Wettereau, *Statistical Records of the First Bank of the United States* (New York: Garland, 1985), passim.

19. These figures have been compiled using the bank statements found in Wettereau, *Statistical Records.* The exact cause of the Bank's change of course remains clouded. Bank officials must have responded to some of the inflationary tendency by raising specie reserves in proportion to notes in circulation. The decision by Federalists in Congress and in the Treasury to commence selling the government's shares in the Bank possibly prompted a more conservative stance. See Carl Lane, "For 'A Positive Profit': The Federal Investment in the First Bank of the United States, 1792–1802," *William and Mary Quarterly,* 3d series, 65 (July 1997): 609.

20. Perkins, *American Public Finance,* 256.

21. See Stuart Bruchey, "Alexander Hamilton and the State Banks, 1789–1795," *William and Mary Quarterly,* 27 (1970): 347–378.

22. Hamilton to William Seton, 18 January 1792, *PAH,* 10: 525. See Bruchey, "Alexander Hamilton," passim, and Perkins, *American Public Finance,* 243–245.

23. Bruchey, "Alexander Hamilton," 363.

24. Hamilton, *PAH,* 10: 295–296.

25. The best study of Duer's life can be found in Robert F. Jones, *"King of the Alley," William Duer: Politician, Entrepreneur, and Speculator* (Philadelphia: American Philosophical Society, 1992). See also Robert F. Jones, "William Duer and the Business of Government in the Era of the American Revolution," *William and Mary Quarterly,* 3d series, 32 (July 1975): 393–416; and David Sterling, "William Duer, John Pintard, and the Panic of 1792," in Joseph Frese and Jacob Judd, eds., *Business Enterprise in Early New York* (Tarrytown, NY: Sleepy Hollow Press, 1979), 99–132.

26. For a brief survey of land speculations as they relate to Hamiltonian finance, see McDonald, *Alexander Hamilton,* 152–157.

27. Jones, *William Duer,* 119–124 and 149–150. See also Timothy J. Shannon, "The Ohio Company and the Meaning of Opportunity in the American West, 1786–1795," *New England Quarterly,* 64 (1991): 393–413.

28. Jones, *William Duer,* 130–132. Jones estimates Duer's potential profits to be as much as $375,000.

29. Jones, *William Duer,* 172, 176–177; and Robert Sobel, "William Duer and the Origins of the New York Stock Exchange," *Mankind: The Magazine of Popular History,* 2 (February 1970): 81. For another popular yet very scholarly treatment of the

event, see John Steele Gordon, "The Great Crash (of 1792)," in *The Business of America* (New York: Walker Publishing, 2001), 169–173. A recent scholarly treatment is David Cowen, "The First Bank of the United States and the Securities Market Crash of 1792," *Journal of Economic History*, 60 (December 2000): 1041–1060. A full-length treatment can be found in David Cowen, *The Origins and Economic Impact of the First Bank of the United States, 1791–1797* (New York: Garland, 2000).

30. Winifred Rothenberg, chapter in Peter Temin, ed., *Engines of Enterprise: An Economic History of New England* (Cambridge, MA: Harvard University Press, 2000).

31. Robert E. Wright, "Thomas Willing: Philadelphia Financier and Forgotten Founding Father," *Pennsylvania History*, 63 (1996): 525–560; Jonathan J. Bean, "Marketing 'The Great American Commodity': Nathaniel Massie and Land Speculation on the Ohio Frontier, 1783–1813," *Ohio History*, 103 (1994): 152–169; and Barbara Chernow, "Robert Morris; Genesee Land Speculator," *New York History*, 58 (1977): 195–220. Of course, this picture refrains from showing those would-be speculators who sold their securities too early to take advantage of full conversion. See Christopher Collier, "Continental Bonds in Connecticut on the Eve of the Funding Measure," *William and Mary Quarterly*, 22 (1965): 646–651.

32. Bob Arnebeck, "Tracking the Speculators: Greenleaf and Nicholson in the Federal City," *Washington History*, 3 (1991): 112–125. See also George R. Lamplugh, "John Wereat and Yazoo, 1794–1799," *Georgia Historical Quarterly*, 72 (1988): 502–517; Dwight L. Smith, "John Cleves Symmes," *Timeline*, 5 (1988): 20–23; Ronald R. Van Stockum, "Nicholas Meriwether in Early Kentucky: Land Locator, Entrepreneur, Settler," *Filson Club History Quarterly*, 59 (1985): 223–250; and Robert Arbuckle, "John Nicholson and Land as a Lure in the Infant Nation, 1790–1800," *Pennsylvania Heritage*, 9 (1983): 8–11.

33. See William B. Eigelsbach, "The Blout Conspiracy: Notes of Samuel Sitgreaves on the Questioning of Dr. Nicholas Romayne on July 13 and 14, 1797, Before the House Impeachment Committee," *Journal of East Tennessee History*, 66 (1994): 81–96.

34. Joseph Stancliffe Davis, *Essays in the Earlier History of American Corporations* (Cambridge, MA: Harvard University Press, 1917), 37, 118, 188, and 216. See also J. Van Fenstermaker, *The Development of American Commercial Banking, 1782–1837* (Kent, OH: Kent State University Press, 1965): 111–183.

35. Daniel P. Jones, "Commercial Progress versus Local Rights: Turnpike Building in Northwestern Rhode Island in the 1790s," *Rhode Island History*, 48 (1990): 20–32, particularly 21–24. A survey of the literature relating to market development in the early republic can be found in Thomas C. Cochran, "The Business Revolution," *American Historical Review*, 79 (1974): 1449–1466.

36. Jones, "Commercial Progress," 23.

37. Jones, "Commercial Progress," 24.

38. See Brian Harte, "Land in the Old Northwest: A Study of Speculation, Sales, and Settlement on the Connecticut Western Reserve," *Ohio History,* 101 (1992): 114–139.

39. Albert Gallatin, *The Writings of Albert Gallatin,* ed. Henry Adams, vol. 1 (Philadelphia: J. B. Lippincott, 1879), 131.

40. See, for example, Fischer Ames's reply to accusations on 1 May 1794, *Annals,* 3d Cong., 1st Sess., 617; William B. Giles, 14 January 1794, *Annals,* 3d Cong., 1st Sess., 281–283; and William Findley, 14 January 1794, *Annals,* 3d Cong., 1st Sess., 233–234.

Hamilton and Haiti

DANIEL G. LANG

*H*AITI, the one-time French colony of Saint Domingue ("Santo Domingo" to the Americans), after a brief time off the front pages in the late 1990s, has resurfaced in the news again with another round of stories of political instability, economic distress, and ecological disaster. Jean-Paul Aristide, whose restoration to rule as a democratically elected president was an object of American foreign policy for Presidents George H. W. Bush and Bill Clinton, has once again been driven from office because of threatened violence. The first time, his ouster was led by officers in the Haitian military in alliance with political and economic elites who felt threatened by Aristide's leftist agenda and popular appeal; the second time, alleged abuses of power, continuing economic misery, and discontent from below fueled riots and demonstrations against him.[1] President George W. Bush's two predecessors had sided with Aristide in the name of democracy and human rights. Bush's administration felt itself constrained—for the same reasons —to persuade Aristide to leave. Human-rights groups had found much to criticize in Aristide's conduct as president: failure to enforce the rule of law, empowerment of armed gangs to intimidate and even kill political opponents, holding rigged elections, and nurturing a cult of personality around himself.[2] Previously, international aid donors had suspended aid, awaiting serious evidence that the Aristide government was prepared to fight the growing traffic in drugs, strengthen the police and the judiciary, carry out economic reforms, and include opposition members in the cabinet.[3] The economic, as well as the political, outlook for the country remains grim. Alexander Hamilton's assessment of the country's prospects offered to Secretary of State Thomas Pickering in 1799—that "no regular system of liberty" seemed suitable—still rings sadly true over two hundred years later.

Given the rather hopeless condition in which Haiti finds itself—easily the poorest country in the Western Hemisphere—it comes as something of a surprise to discover how important the island was in American foreign-policy thinking in the 1790s. Presidents Bush and Clinton justified American intervention in the 1990s largely on humanitarian and "human rights" grounds. Two hundred years ago, strategic considerations played a much larger role in American thinking about Haiti and about the West Indies generally; nevertheless, as we shall see, humanitarian and human rights concerns were prominent then as well. The questions I wish to address in this essay are: How did Hamilton approach these strategic and human rights issues involving Haiti in American foreign policy in the 1790s? Is there anything we can learn from him as we enter the twenty-first century?

On the eve of the French Revolution, Saint Domingue was arguably France's most important colony, contributing two-thirds of France's tropical produce and one-third of its foreign trade. Strategically, the colony's trade provided French sailors for the national navy and foreign exchange to purchase vital naval stores from countries in northern Europe. The colony also contained the most secure naval base in the West Indies, the Mole Saint Nicholas.[4] With 655 sugar plantations, 1,962 coffee plantations, and 398 cotton and indigo plantations, the colony also proved a tempting target for American traders in defiance of French navigation acts. The planters of Saint Domingue were glad to exchange large amounts of sugar, rum, and molasses for fish, salted meat, and other provisions, and the slaves that American traders brought them. In fact, the island was second only to Great Britain in the foreign commerce of the United States.[5]

Saint Domingue's economic success depended heavily on slave labor. In 1787 the colony had about 460,000 inhabitants, approximately 410,000 of whom were black slaves. The white population stood at 24,000, with the remainder consisting of mulattos and free blacks. United on the race issue, the whites were nevertheless profoundly divided among themselves according to economic interests: merchants against lawyers, sugar planters against coffee planters. The free "coloured" sector was exceptional in the West Indies for its size and wealth. Legally their color disqualified them from enjoying the rights of citizenship, subjecting them to humiliating restrictions in dress, transportation, and contact with whites. Not surprisingly, these *gens de couleur* chafed at such lack of recognition; the planter elite, in turn, resented the "despotism" of the French colonial system, which prevented them from trading freely with whomever they chose.[6] Thus, both the colony's whites and the mulattos were inclined to embrace the ideas of the French Revolution—until the French National Assembly sided with the mulattos and their claim of citizenship rights. Equality with the mulattos was something the whites refused to accept. The two parties were thus brought into collision: in their struggle with each other they "dropped a match into the immense powder-magazine upon which they lived," in Henry Adams's memorable phrase. As the two factions came to blows and social chaos set in, "the slave, completely astonished, searched to know the causes of this restlessness" and soon recognized that the "moment was favorable in order to throw off the chains of barbarity."[7] On August 22, 1791, the slaves rose up in revolt. Soon the whole northern province was ablaze in fire and drenched with blood, engulfing the colony in a horrific conflict that lasted more than a decade.

How should the American government, an avowed friend of liberty, respond to the situation? Clues to Treasury Secretary Hamilton's thinking could be found in *Federalist* 11. There, Hamilton discussed the strategic importance to the United States of the West Indies and touched on the scourge of race-based slavery as well. That paper revealed Hamilton's vision of national greatness, with the United States as a prospectively powerful player on the stage of world politics: if the United States established a strong central government, equipped it with powers to regulate foreign commerce, and built a respectable navy, it would be in a position to dictate "the terms of the connection between the old and the new world."[8] As Gerald Stourzh has pointed out, Hamilton clearly saw the balance of power as more than domestic structural arrangements to preserve liberty; for him, the United States was already part of a global balance-of-power system. In the near term, American weakness limited the role the Americans might play on the world stage; in the long term, he held out the prospect of "grandeur and glory."[9]

Where did he anticipate his country playing such a role? One obvious place was in the West Indies, where the French, the Spanish, and the British had a well-established rivalry. There, relatively close to the continental United States, "a few ships of the line, sent opportunely to the reinforcement of either side, would often be sufficient to decide the fate of a campaign on the event of which interests of the greatest magnitude were suspended."[10]

Recognition of the value of the islands, and the possible role the United States could play in the region, had already been anticipated in the Franco-American Treaty of 1778. There, the United States pledged itself to protect France's West Indian colonies in the event of their being attacked in return for French assistance in the American war of independence. How that commitment could be made consistent with the balancing role presented in the *Federalist*, Hamilton did not address. For the United States to be a "balancer," some way would perhaps have to be found for the nation to release itself of the French connection.

Hamilton's vision in *Federalist* 11 extended beyond such considerations of *realpolitik*, however. The grandeur he envisioned for his adopted country had world-historical dimensions: "to vindicate the honor of the human race, and to teach that assuming [European] brother moderation."[11] By adopting the Constitution and instituting the other measures Hamilton recommended, the United States could put itself in a position to check Europe's arrogant pretensions to rule the world on behalf of the rest of mankind—the American, Asian, and African portions that currently found themselves under European hegemony.

Unlike Thomas Jefferson, whose acceptance of natural history as a guide for political analysis led him to make race a basic unit of classification and distinction, Hamilton insisted on the unity of mankind.[12] The stress in *Federalist* 11 on a nature common to all human beings meant that Hamilton supported the idea that the people of any race or continent possessed the capacity to develop free, race-blind governments. Hamilton's opposition to slavery was unequivocal and long standing; his commitment to the eventual abolition of slavery was clear. During the Revolutionary War, he had advocated the use of black soldiers "to give them their freedom with their muskets" as a "dictate of humanity." In the 1780s, he helped establish the Society for the Manumission of Slaves and petitioned the New York State legislature to abolish the slave trade.[13] Now, in the *Federalist*, he attached American foreign policy to the antislavery cause.

The first opportunity for the United States to be a "balancer" and to "vindicate the honor of the human race" came sooner than Hamilton probably expected and too soon for the fledgling republic to make much of a difference. Indeed, because of its alliance commitments and its financial debt to France, the United States found itself relatively powerless to affect events. In important ways, the capacity of the country to survive as an independent nation remained an open question.

Within a month of the slave revolt in Haiti, a representative of the French government, Jean de Ternant, approached the American government asking for funds and supplies to help the French planters reestablish their plantations. Although Ternant did not have formal authorization from his government, the American government "on account of the debt owed to France" authorized several advances for the purchase of supplies in America.[14] This, in a way, implicated the Americans against the Haitian revolutionaries because the funds were going to the white counterrevolutionaries. The slave revolt horrified Americans with the tales of indiscriminate bloodletting and widespread destruction of property. Thousands of white refugees fled to the United States in 1792 and 1793; their plight led Congress to establish a fund for their relief.[15] News of events in Saint Domingue intensified fears in the South of a slave revolt spreading throughout the West Indies and into the United States as well. Some states expelled blacks that had come from Saint Domingue; Georgia and South Carolina temporarily suspended the slave trade itself. Southern legislatures also moved to curtail the few privileges enjoyed by blacks, whether free or slave.[16]

Against this backdrop, Ternant in March 1792 and again in November 1792 requested additional sums for the relief of the colony. Hamilton offered a more cautious response to the third request, citing the continued political instability in France. (The National Convention had abolished the monarchy in September.) He regarded it as entirely likely that future French governments might not regard any American payments on their debt to the current regime as legitimate. Therefore he recommended that "as little as possible ought to be done" pending a resolution of the political situation in France. Emergency aid to Saint Domingue should be provided, but principally on humanitarian grounds: "Whatever may be done should be cautiously restricted to the single idea of preserving the colony from destruction by famine."[17]

At this point and later, Secretary of State Jefferson urged more enthusiastic support for granting Ternant's, and then his successor Genet's, requests for aid, arguing for the legitimacy of the new French government. For Jefferson this was partly a question of the principle that one ought to acknowledge "any government to be rightful which if formed by the will of the nation substantially declared," but his view also reflected greater optimism than Hamilton's that the French National Convention would be able solidly to establish itself against its enemies internal and external.[18]

The situation became more complicated with news in April 1793 of the outbreak of war between France and Great Britain, Spain, and Holland. A general war in Europe would certainly test, among other things, the American treaty guarantees of the French West Indies. All of the members of Washington's cabinet agreed that the preservation of peace and pursuit of a policy of neutrality would be the best policy for the United States, but there were clear disagreements about particular policy actions. Hamilton argued that the treaties should be considered suspended, pending some clearer sense of the outcome of the political struggle within France. Moreover, he maintained that the treaties were "personal" in nature—made by the French king with the American government. Thus the obligation of the United States had expired with the execution of the king. Anticipating the possibility that the French might ask the Americans to fulfill their obligation to the French West Indies, Hamilton argued that it would be better to suspend the treaties than to admit the continued force of the obligation, but then make excuses for not living up to it.[19]

Jefferson, by contrast, maintained that the treaties were still in effect: the treaties were "real"—made between nations—and could only be suspended under conditions of real danger, conditions he did not think held in this case. He acknowledged the awkwardness of the guarantee of the French West Indies, but suggested that the French would not call on the United States to act on it, knowing that the Americans were not in a position to effect much of a difference. Citizen Genet said as much when he arrived in Washington in midyear. When the British in September 1793 launched an invasion of Saint Domingue, the French chose not to invoke the treaty.

In the event, President Washington sided with Jefferson and chose not to suspend the treaties, due in part to the quick recognition the United States had already extended the provisional government in France, but he did appear to accept Hamilton's views on the inapplicability of the guarantee. In his written opinions to the president and in the "Pacificus" and "Americanus" essays, Hamilton forcefully presented the case that the guarantee was inoperative because of the nature of the war. The French had begun the war, so it was offensive in nature: France's declaration of war and initiation of hostilities clearly made her the offensive part, whatever the merits of her cause. The 1778 treaty was clearly a defensive alliance, therefore the treaty obligations to the islands were nonoperational: "The express Denomination of this Treaty is 'Traite D'Alliance eventuelle et defensive.' . . . By this principle, every stipulation in it is to be judged."[20]

In his written opinion to Washington, Hamilton distinguished general from specific guarantees. Political connections may be altered in cases where fulfilling the obligation would needlessly expose the party expected to perform to great danger. The payment of financial debt, however, he considered a "perfect and strict obligation" that "must be done at all events." Questions of property differ from those of political alliance. Where changes in government may affect the latter, they cannot affect the former. New governments, whatever their character, assume the nation's property and debts. Based on the principle of reciprocity, "the Sovereign in possession is to receive the debts due to the Government of the nation." Whether or not the United States withdrew or suspended the treaties, it retained its strict obligation to repay the debt.[21] Though scornful of those who believed that "commercial republics" would be more peaceful than other regimes, Hamilton nevertheless credited the "modern law of nations" for having established the protection of property rights, thereby transforming international relations. Establishing a stable international financial system on the basis of "strict" obligation opens up a modern world in which traders and investors can move goods and money freely from one country to another, stimulating production and commerce and extending the blessings of liberty to more and more of mankind.[22]

Liberty, Hamilton suggested, was more likely to be secured through the application of the modern law of nations than by military intervention. He found the justice of France's war "not a little problematical" in spite of French claims that its cause was the cause of liberty. In the French Convention of 1792, Revolutionary France challenged all Europe in saying that she would grant fraternity and assistance to every people who should desire to recover its liberty. Hamilton considered himself a friend of liberty, but not when one nation sought to impose that liberty on another.

> For though it be lawful and meritorious to assist a people in a virtuous and rational struggle for liberty, when the particular case happens; yet it is not justifiable in any government or Nation to hold out to the world a general invitation and encouragement to revolution and insurrection, under a promise of paternity and assistance. Such a step is of a nature to disturb the repose of mankind, to excite fermentation in every country, to endanger government everywhere.[23]

The "pretext of propagating liberty" should not obscure the fundamental principle that "Every nation has a right to carve out its own happiness in its own way, and it is the height of presumption in another to attempt to fashion its political creed."[24] France's actions evoked troubling memories of a Europe torn by religious strife, where the principles of internal rule came under the scrutiny of other states. Better to accept the European balance of power system with its foundation principle of state sovereignty than to hazard the renewal of the imposition of "universal monarchy" where one nation gave the law to the rest.

We have no record of Hamilton's opinions about the course of the "cause of liberty" in Haiti. We know that he was horrified by the excesses of the French Revolution and could hardly have condoned the conduct of Haiti's revolutionaries. He could easily have applied his prediction that the eventual outcome of the revolution in France would be the emergence of a strong-armed dictator to Saint Domingue as well. Henry Adams was not the first to comment on the remarkable similarities between Napoleon Bonaparte and Toussaint Louverture.[25] Logically, of course, Hamilton's reasons not to aid France would have had to apply to Haiti as well. As sympathetic as he may have been to the antislavery cause, his principles would have had to preclude direct American support or intervention in the name of "human rights," politically impossible in any case. If we are to find evidence supporting American involvement vindicating human nature, we will have to look for indirect support.

As events transpired in Saint Domingue in the middle and late 1790s, the effect of American foreign policy decisions did make the reestablishment of slavery there less likely. After some initial successes, the British invasion of the island launched in 1793 to claim it from the French—and to re-impose slavery—bogged down. The British had the support of the planters and refugees who wanted a restoration of the old order. Yellow fever and other diseases, the climate, and the insurgents' resistance worked against them. The decision of the French National Convention in 1794, under the leadership of Robespierre, to abolish slavery throughout the French empire brought Toussaint Louverture, the former slave and emerging leader of the island's blacks, to the side of the French against the English and the Spanish in the struggle for control of the island.[26] The key to the island's fate lay increasingly with Louverture, not with the French, and the question of independence for Haiti began to surface. The main American preoccupation, however, was how to enforce the neutrality it had proclaimed for itself without tearing the country apart.

In conjunction with its invasion of Saint Domingue, the British government in late 1793 ordered the seizure of all French and neutral ships carrying produce to and from the French West Indies. The seizures resulted in the capture of over three hundred American vessels and their cargoes. War with the Americans seemed certain. Hamilton sent Washington a memorandum proposing a series of measures for national defense, including the establishment of a navy, the enactment of an embargo against Britain, and the dispatch of a special minister to London to see what could be negotiated. The British responded by relaxing their regulations and permitting the resumption of virtually unchecked American trade with the French West Indies.[27]

With the Senate's ratification of the unpopular Jay Treaty in 1795, the United States found itself increasingly at odds with the French. British acceptance of American trade meant that commerce between the United States and Saint Domingue prospered. Over six hundred American ships were engaged in that trade that year.[28] Now it was France's turn to attack American shipping. Between July 1796 and June 1797, French vessels seized over three hundred American ships, bringing those two countries to the brink of war. By then, John Adams had ascended to the presidency and Hamilton had returned to private life. However, because of his continuing close relationships with Secretary of State Thomas Pickering and Treasury Secretary Oliver Wolcott, Hamilton continued to exert considerable influence on the direction of foreign policy.

For Hamilton, the damage to American shipping paled in comparison to the threat that France might regain Louisiana and establish a stronghold on the North American continent. Hamilton's case for the possibility of a French invasion went as follows. France had real claims in North America, indigenous support in Louisiana, Canada, and the United States, and bases in the West Indies from which a military expedition could be launched. The British Navy presented the most substantial opposition to such a plan, but France under Napoleon could overcome it by forcing Britain to negotiate a peace treaty, leaving the French free to pursue their North American designs.[29]

Publication of the infamous "X, Y, Z" papers that revealed French efforts to bribe the special American envoys sent to negotiate with France temporarily united the country. Congress responded by funding a navy and raising an army with Washington and Hamilton at its head. It also abrogated the 1778 treaty, suspended commerce with France, and authorized American armed ships to protect American commerce and to capture French vessels. Alexander Hamilton, among others, raised the possibility of pursuing the "independence of the French colonies, under the Guarantee of the United States," and suggested that negotiations to that end be considered.[30]

What effect did these events have on Saint Domingue? By 1798 Toussaint Louverture had driven out the British from all but a few places on the island and basically dictated policy to the French colonial officials nominally in charge. Although the colony remained legally France's, Louverture turned to the United States, asking for aid and recognition, in defiance of French policy. In other words, the black leader recognized a coincidence of interests between his government and the United States, both economic and political. Both wanted to expand trade, both wanted to see a reduction in French (and British) influence in the Caribbean. Toussaint offered to help the Americans by suppressing French privateering out of Saint Domingue and by securing American trade. By then, the British invasion had fizzled and they were looking for a way out. British diplomacy might succeed where their armies had failed.

Preoccupied with other matters, the Adams administration finally took up Toussaint's offer in February 1799. Secretary of State Pickering wrote to Hamilton asking his advice about the situation and the appropriate American response. The Congress had authorized the president to reopen trade relations with Saint Domingue when he thought American shipping would be safe. According to Jacob Meyer, the American consul on the island, Toussaint was ready to declare the island independent "if certain of our commerce." Pickering added, "This act of independence I fully expect; and I persuade myself that Great Britain will consent to share in it." Should the United States recognize Toussaint as the ruler of the island French nation? To do so would encourage American trade with the island and hurt the French, who still claimed it.[31] Hamilton responded promptly, offering cautious support for Haitian independence, yet concerned not to provoke France too greatly. There should be "[n]o guaranty, no formal treaty—nothing that can rise up in judgment. It will be enough to let Toussaint be assured verbally, but explicitly, that upon his declaration of independence a commercial intercourse will be opened."[32]

President Adams decided to send Dr. Edward Stephens to Cap Français to meet with Toussaint and "conciliate the good opinion of that General and his people." Pickering's instructions to Stephens directed him to seek (a) to end privateering from the ports of Saint Domingue; (b) to help Toussaint consolidate control of the island; and (c) to encourage Haitian independence.[33] Stephens was a native of the West Indies who had emigrated to the United States and become a highly respected physician; he was also one of Hamilton's oldest friends, possibly even a half-brother. Stevens quickly won Toussaint's confidence; together they established an informal alliance. With Stevens's help, Toussaint concluded a treaty with the British that removed their forces from the island; American merchants and ships were given unrestricted access to Saint Domingue's ports. With American naval support, Toussaint was able to defeat the sizable mulatto force that threatened his control of the colony. The American experience with armed intervention in a foreign civil war started here.

Stevens's actions reflected the consistent direction of Federalist—Hamiltonian—foreign policy in the 1790s: redress the balance between France and Great Britain, preferably reducing the influence of both; promote American commerce; and erode the hold of slavery in the New World. Encouragement of Haitian independence served all three of these ends, and all three are necessary for explaining that policy.[34]

Pickering also invited Hamilton to comment on an appropriate government for Saint Domingue. Observing that "no regular system of liberty will at present suit," Hamilton proposed a military government with a single executive to hold office for life, with his successor chosen by the other military commanders. All males would be required to do military duty; laws and taxes were to be proposed by the executive to a military assembly composed of generals and commanders of the regiments for their acceptance or rejection. All of these recommendations "partake of the feudal system" that was the legacy of colonial rule in the West Indies."[35] The constitution of 1801 that the Toussaint-controlled General Assembly adopted included several features Hamilton had suggested: the lifelong executive, the enrollment of all males in the militia, and the protection of property. It also did not include a statement of independence from France; the island would remain nominally a French colony, though functionally be independent.[36]

Napoleon Bonaparte's decision to strengthen the French empire by regaining Louisiana from Spain meant also recovering Saint Domingue, destroying Toussaint, and restoring slavery. In the end, the French invasion of 1801–1802 failed, as had the British invasion before it. Again, yellow fever, the climate, and the resistance of the black population who fought a return to slavery thwarted Napoleon's plans. Meanwhile, the new Jefferson administration reversed Adams's approach and sought to distance the United States from the colony. Jefferson thought it more important to maintain good relations with France, building on the new Franco-American accord of the Treaty of Mortefontaine of 1800. His policy also sought to calm the fears of Southern slaveholders who feared the consequences of an independent black nation, even though it meant a significant reduction in the substantial American commerce. Not only did Jefferson's policy offer no help to Saint Domingue, it put the United States in a precarious position. As Thomas Ott points out, "by encouraging Bonaparte to conquer Saint-Domingue, Jefferson had unknowingly made a French occupation of Louisiana both more attractive and possible."[37] Once that threat became known, Jefferson opted to wait, hoping that time was on the American side. Hamilton characteristically argued for action: "Seize at once on the Floridas and New-Orleans, and then negociate [sic]."[38] In the end, Jefferson's luck held and Napoleon agreed to the sale of Louisiana.[39]

Hamilton's final reference to Saint Domingue credits the "courage and obstinate resistance of the black inhabitants" as the key factor, along with the climate, in Bonaparte's decision to sell Louisiana. Having wasted time, men, and resources in the fruitless effort to retake the island, Bonaparte's designs for Louisiana had to be abandoned to deal with the renewed outbreak of war with Great Britain.[40]

Conclusion

What conclusions may we draw about the place of strategic considerations and humanitarian and human rights in American foreign policy from this examination of Hamilton and Haiti? Let me suggest the following.

First, whatever force a nation's general obligations to humanity might have—and Hamilton asserted that nations do have such obligations—they are superseded by specific, contractual, obligations. The French loan had to be repaid, even though doing so might benefit white planters seeking to restore a slave-based plantation economy. As the political situation in France became more and more unstable, Hamilton did raise doubts about the legitimacy of the new French government to argue for the suspension of the debt repayment. Once a stable government emerged, however, the American financial obligation would be have to be fulfilled.

Second, the doctrine of state sovereignty stood as a counter to antislavery universalism. What sovereign states owed each other as states was to mind their own business: the internal arrangements of states are their own affair. Only when one state's actions threatened the security of another could intervention be justified. In the case of a revolution, Hamilton's rule seemed to be to wait until the revolution had gained some legitimacy and showed it had staying power: "To incite to revolution everywhere, by indiscriminate offers of assistance before hand, is to invade and endanger the foundations of social tranquility."[41] Hamilton argued that the French had violated this rule in their conduct, casting doubt on the justice of their cause; likewise, Hamilton neither embraced nor repudiated the cause of the Haitian revolutionaries. The moral foundation for the neutrality policy he advocated for the United States begins here.

Human rights—the antislavery cause, in this case—could, however, be promoted indirectly. American promotion of commerce in the West Indies, American efforts to reduce the influence of both Great Britain and of France in the Western Hemisphere, and the establishment of relations with Toussaint Louverture arguably made the hold of slavery on Saint Domingue more tenuous. Once the French National Assembly had abolished slavery in the colony, support for the status quo implied resistance toward turning back the clock. Likewise, American support for Haitian independence, de facto as well as de jure, demonstrated Hamilton's willingness to embrace a nation of free blacks in close proximity to the United States provides further evidence of the consistency of his antislavery views.

Third, Hamilton's political science makes clear that enthusiasm for republican government, the regime most consistent with human liberty, should be tempered by the knowledge that it may not be appropriate in all circumstances. Many of the favorable circumstances that made republican government possible in the United States were not necessarily present elsewhere. Hamilton was skeptical of the prospects for an American-style constitution for France, and thought that monarchy should continue to play a role in a properly constructed French constitution. In an exchange with Lafayette in 1798–99, Hamilton put his doubts this way: "I shall only say that I hold with Montesquieu that a Government must be fitted to a nation as much as a Coat to the Individual, and consequently that what may be good at Philadelphia may be bad at Paris and ridiculous at Petersburg."[42]

Hamilton's recommendation for the government of Haiti was not a republican one. This did not necessarily make him a partisan of monarchy; rather, it reflected his understanding of the social realities on the island and an awareness of the historical patterns in its experience.

America's experience with Haiti in the 1990s suggests the continuing validity of at least some of Hamilton's principles. The impulse to intervene on behalf of democratic "nation building" must be tempered by the recognition that governments must fit the culture and experience of the people in their care. Beyond this practical point lies a moral one: "Every nation has a right to carve out its own happiness in its own way, and it is the height of presumption in another to attempt to fashion its political creed."[43] Finally, democracies may or may not advance liberty. Just as Hamilton treated with skepticism claims by the supporters of the French Revolution that theirs was the cause of liberty, so we may wonder if the restoration of the form of democracy in Haiti necessarily and unequivocally means an advance for human rights there. More important than the establishment of democracy from a Hamiltonian perspective would be the establishment of the rule of law.

"Realists" in international relations theory and in American foreign policy have embraced Hamilton as one of their own.[44] Reviewing the record of Hamilton's thinking about Haiti, one can certainly see why. A sober view of human nature, an expectation of the persistence of conflict in the world, a focus on the national interest, the inclusion of the United States in the international balance of power system, and an aversion to the easy application of moral absolutes in the politics among nations all are clearly part of the intellectual framework that shaped Hamilton's responses to Haiti and to the world more broadly. Yet, as Walter Russell Mead has suggested, Hamiltonian realism differed from Continental realpolitik, especially in its recognition of the centrality of commerce in defining the American national interest. From this flowed Hamilton's interest in securing the public credit, establishing an American manufacturing center, promoting the navy, strengthening international legal and economic institutions, and opening markets overseas.[45] Reflecting on Hamilton and Haiti allows us to see Hamilton go beyond realism in another sense: namely in his concern for "fame," "glory," and "grandeur." Acutely aware of American weaknesses and often frustrated by his countrymen's short-sightedness, Hamilton nevertheless held fast in his counsels on Haiti to a long-term vision of American (and by reflection his own) greatness. For himself there was the fame that would come from being the founder of an empire, for his country the glory of vindicating the honor of the human race.

NOTES

1. For an extensive account of Aristide's rise, fall, and return see Alex Dupuy, *Haiti in the New World Order* (Boulder: Westview Press, 1997). Dupuy notes that

both the Bush and Clinton administrations pursued a dual policy of public support of returning Aristide to power and privately pressuring him to make concessions to his adversaries, see 139–146.

2. See *The Economist,* February 28, 2004, 35–36, and March 6, 2004, 38–39.

3. See *The Economist,* February 10, 2001, 1.

4. David Geggus, "The Haitian Revolution," in Franklin Knight and Colin Palmer, eds., *The Modern Caribbean* (Chapel Hill: University of North Carolina Press, 1989), 22.

5. Thomas Ott, *The Haitian Revolution, 1789–1804* (Knoxville: University of Tennessee Press, 1973), 6–8; Charles C. Tansill, *The United States and Santo Domingo, 1798–1873* (Baltimore: Johns Hopkins University Press, 1938), 1; Michael Zuckerman, *Almost Chosen People: Oblique Biographies in the American Grain* (Berkeley: University of California Press, 1993), 180.

6. Ott, *Haitian Revolution,* 9; see also Henry Adams, *History of the United States of America,* vol. I (New York: Antiquarian Press, 1962), 378–80.

7. Francois Lacroix, "Memoires pour servir à l'histoire de la révolution de Saint-Domingue," quoted in Ott, *Haitian Revolution,* 42.

8. Alexander Hamilton, James Madison, John Jay, *The Federalist Papers* (hereafter *FP*), ed. Clinton Rossiter (New York: New American Library, 1961), 91 (#11).

9. Gerald Stourzh, *Alexander Hamilton and the Idea of Republican Government* (Stanford, CA: Stanford University Press, 1970), 193–98; see also Karl-Friedrich Walling, *Republican Empire: Alexander Hamilton on War and Free Government* (Lawrence: University Press of Kansas, 1999).

10. *FP,* 87 (#11).

11. *FP,* 91 (#11); see discussion of *Federalist* 11 in James Ceaser, *Reconstructing America* (New York: Yale University Press, 1997), 53–61.

12. John Chester Miller, *The Wolf by the Ears: Thomas Jefferson and Slavery* (New York: Free Press, 1977), 46–59. Jefferson's belief that blacks were naturally inferior to whites did not mean that he thought they were intended by nature to be slaves; nevertheless, he thought race a valid category of analysis.

13. Robert Hendrickson, *The Rise and Fall of Alexander Hamilton* (New York: Van Nostrand, 1981), 190; see also Forrest McDonald, *Alexander Hamilton: A Biography* (New York: W. W. Norton, 1979), 34 and 373; Michael D. Chan, "Alexander Hamilton on Slavery," *Review of Politics,* 66 (Spring 2004): 207–31.

14. See Hamilton to Ternant, September 21, 1791, in *The Papers of Alexander Hamilton* (hereafter *PAH*), ed. Harold C. Syrett et al., 27 vols. (New York: Columbia University Press, 1961–87), 9: 219–20.

15. Washington to Hamilton, March 4, 1794, *PAH,* 16: 117.

16. Ott, *Haitian Revolution,* 54; McDonald, *Alexander Hamilton,* 279–80; Simon P. Newman, "American Political Culture and the French and Haitian Revolutions," in David Geggus, ed., *The Impact of the Haitian Revolution in the Atlantic World* (Columbia: University of South Carolina Press, 2001), 72–89.

17. Hamilton to Washington, November 19, 1792, *PAH,* 13: 169–73. See also the editorial note for the letter from George Latimer to Hamilton, January 2, 1793, *PAH,* 13: 443–47; Hendrickson, *Rise and Fall,* 504.

18. Dumas Malone, *Jefferson and the Ordeal of Liberty* (Boston: Little, Brown, 1962), 41–44.

19. Hamilton to Washington, May 2, 1793, *PAH,* 14: 367–96.

20. *PAH,* 14: 408.

21. *PAH,* 14: 395.

22. "The Defence, No. XXI," *PAH,* 19: 365–76; Walter Russell Mead, *Special Providence: American Foreign Policy and How It Changed the World* (New York: Alfred Knopf, 2001), 110–11.

23. *PAH,* 14: 403.

24. *PAH,* 14: 407.

25. Adams, *History,* 382–83.

26. Ott, *Haitian Revolution,* 82–83.

27. McDonald, *Alexander Hamilton,* 293.

28. Ralph Adams Brown, *The Presidency of John Adams* (Lawrence: University Press of Kansas, 1975), 156.

29. Robert Tucker and David Hendrickson, *Empire of Liberty: The Statecraft of Thomas Jefferson* (New York: Oxford University Press, 1990), 101–35.

30. Hamilton to Wolcott, June 5, 1798, *PAH,* 21: 486–87.

31. Pickering to Hamilton, February 9, 1799, *PAH,* 22: 473–75.

32. Hamilton to Pickering, February 9, 1799, *PAH,* 22: 475.

33. Brown, *Presidency of John Adams,* 158–59.

34. Zuckerman, *Almost Chosen People,* 185; Chan, "Hamilton on Slavery," 221.

35. Hamilton to Pickering, February 21, 1799, *PAH,* 22: 492–93; see also Tansill, *United States and Santo Domingo,* 13–18.

36. Ott, *Haitian Revolution,* 119.

37. Ott, *Haitian Revolution,* 142.

38. "To the Evening Post," February 8, 1803, *PAH,* 26: 83.

39. Tucker and Hendrickson, *Empire of Liberty,* 132–34. Tim Mathewson offers a more sympathetic account of Jefferson's actions, emphasizing more than I do here the constraints placed on Jefferson by public opinion, especially in his native South. See his "Jefferson and Haiti," *Journal of Southern History,* 61 (May 1995): 209–48.

40. "Purchase of Louisiana," *PAH,* 26: 130.

41. "The Stand, No. 2," *PAH,* 18: 394.

42. Hamilton to Lafayette, January 6, 1799, *PAH,* 22: 404.

43. *PAH,* 22: 407.

44. See, for example, Hans Morgenthau, *Scientific Man versus Power Politics* (Chicago: University of Chicago Press, 1965), and Kenneth Waltz, *Man, the State and War: A Theoretical Analysis* (New York: Columbia University Press, 1959).

45. Mead, *Special Providence,* 99–112.

CHAPTER 10

Hamilton, Croly, and
American Public Philosophy

PETER McNAMARA

$\mathcal{M}$Y exploration of Hamiltonianism as an American public philosophy consists of two parts.[1] First, I consider Herbert Croly's treatment of Alexander Hamilton, especially in his influential 1909 book, *The Promise of American Life.*[2] Croly's work has long been acknowledged as one of the critical sources of the progressive liberal public philosophy that dominated twentieth-century American politics.[3] The second part of my paper turns to Hamilton himself. I focus on what Croly took to be the key Hamiltonian insight: the use of "constructive" legislation and policy in pursuit of a *national* principle. The contrast between Croly's Hamilton and the actual Hamilton is illuminating and instructive with regard to current debates about public policy and public philosophy. The intellectual and political troubles that have in recent decades beset the progressive liberal attempt to use Hamiltonian means for Jeffersonian ends suggest the need to reconsider precisely the very idea of Hamiltonian "means" as well as the original ends to which they were directed. I am not suggesting that Hamiltonianism is an appropriate public philosophy for today, only that an inquiry into the precise nature of Hamiltonianism as a public philosophy is an important undertaking; it is necessary for understanding the course of progressive politics in the twentieth century. It would also be necessary either to write an adequate obituary for the progressive era or as a prelude to any future public philosophy.

Croly's Hamilton

Croly uses a critical survey of the tradition of American political thought to suggest a *new* public philosophy, partly based on elements of that tradition and partly based on an injection of new ways of thinking. While contemporary historians and political theorists have focused on the tension between the "liberal" and the "republican" elements in American political thought, Croly's survey identifies two main strands of American political thinking: a Hamiltonian "national idea" and a Jeffersonian "democratic idea," which engage in a constant, almost dialectical process of opposition and combination. Croly granted that the necessity of combining the two ideas had long been recognized, but he maintained that the two had never been mixed in "just the proper proportions."[4] The first to make such a combination, according to Croly, was Thomas Jefferson himself, who, on coming to power in 1800, did not dismantle the Federalist *constitutional* system. Croly believed that consistency with the democratic idea required such a step. He proposed blending the national idea and the democratic idea by using the power and expertise of the national government to create the conditions for a full flourishing of human individuality. This would require a thorough democratization of American government and the transcendence of local and particular interests in favor of a national community devoted to social and individual improvement. The project as a whole is captured nicely in the title of Croly's other great political work, *Progressive Democracy.*[5]

Croly may have admired Lincoln, Theodore Roosevelt , and, perhaps, Bismarck more than Hamilton, but one must say that he was fascinated with Hamilton, the man and his deeds. At the level of Hamilton the man, Croly was deeply impressed by Hamilton's "unpopular integrity," that is, his willingness to follow the right course in the face of intense popular opposition. Hamilton exhibited a rare kind of "moral and intellectual independence." Furthermore, at least in part, Hamilton's unpopularity was due to his "high conception of the duties of leadership." With respect to Hamilton the statesman, Croly had similarly high praise. Moreover, Croly saw the Hamiltonian phase of American political history as unique for reasons he found deeply interesting. Croly praised Hamilton and the Federalists for bringing to an end the "policy of drift" followed under the Articles of Confederation. At a "critical moment" the Federalists were able to secure the Constitution through "the conversion of public opinion by means of powerful and convincing argument." Yet for all the credit this step won the American people and their leaders, the resulting Constitution was still in many respects a "compromise." By contrast, the two administrations of Washington were a "tolerably pure example of Hamiltonian Federalism" in which the United States was "governed by [Hamilton's] ideas, if not by his will." Moreover, Hamilton's ideas reflected a "definite theory of governmental functions," a "political philosophy."[6] Thus the period in question was sharply distinct from the usual course of American politics in which bargaining and compromise prevail and where ideas and those who live by them often seem all but irrelevant.

To Croly's mind, Hamilton's economic program was admirably suited to accomplishing the important but limited goals he set out. First, Hamilton wanted to deal with the short- and long-term economic problems of the nation. This involved restoring the public finances and setting in motion the creation of a diverse and balanced economy. With regard to this latter goal, Croly praised the "wise and moderate national spirit" of Hamilton's suggested policies to encourage manufacturing. Second, Hamilton wished to establish the authority of the new government by demonstrating its effectiveness and by creating support for the new government, particularly among the financial and propertied classes. Both elements of Hamilton's program required a decidedly national approach to policy. Moreover, such "constructive legislation" required "selection" or "discrimination," to use Croly's terms, among the different segments of society in an effort to realize the long-term national interest.[7]

What was Hamilton's conception of the national interest? To answer this question, Croly, somewhat strangely, given the care of much of his analysis of Hamilton, resorts to a kind of national stereotype. Hamilton, he says, was "possessed by the English conception of a national state, based on the domination of special privileged orders and interests." Furthermore, Hamilton

wished . . . like the Englishman he was, to protect and encourage liberty, just as far as such encouragement was compatible with good order, because he realized that genuine liberty would inevitably issue in fruitful social and economic inequalities. But he realized that genuine liberty was not merely a matter of a constitutional declaration of rights. It could be protected by an energetic and clear-sighted central government, and it could be fertilized only by the efficient organization of national activities.

Hamilton was, then, an English constitutional liberal who believed that an energetic national government led by an "aristocracy of ability" drawn from those of "education and means" was necessary for the protection of liberty. Thus Hamilton "was no democrat," says Croly.[8] Hamilton, he argues, saw the Constitution as a bulwark against the disorderly forces of democracy. However much Hamilton's national approach may have unintentionally fostered democracy, which Croly suggests it did,[9] Croly argues that Hamilton's openly acknowledged fears of democracy and particularly his policies aimed at fostering the support of the monied interest provoked a lasting resentment that was harmful to the very national idea he sought to promote. By contrast, Hamilton's great rival Jefferson was "filled with a sincere indiscriminate and unlimited faith in the American people."[10]

As noted, what Croly thought was needed was a combination of Hamilton and Jefferson, a nationalization of America's democratic ideal that Croly defined as not just democratic political "machinery" but also a dedication to promoting "individual distinction and social improvement."[11] Croly saw elements of this kind of public philosophy in the presidencies of Woodrow Wilson and especially Theodore Roosevelt. Wilson, despite the Jeffersonian theories in his New Freedom program, had in practice passed much "constructive legislation," thereby making the New Freedom in practice an approximation of Roosevelt's New Nationalism.[12] Roosevelt, Croly believed, by reviving the "Hamiltonian ideal of constructive national legislation" had given "democratic meaning and purpose to the Hamiltonian tradition and method." Yet, for Croly, even Roosevelt had in theory at least not broken sufficiently with the Jeffersonian tradition. Roosevelt, despite his personal devotion to the "strenuous life," was more attached to the narrow Jeffersonian idea of individual rights than the higher individualism of a "democracy of individual and social improvement." Croly did believe that Roosevelt's policies did in practice *imply* such a break. He concludes his treatment of Roosevelt hoping that "the day may and should come when a national reformer will come more in the guise of St. Michael armed with a flaming sword and winged for flight."[13] Put more plainly, one might say that Croly hoped for strong and charismatic leadership unfettered by constitutional restraints.

What was Croly's ideal reform program?[14] Croly seems to have envisaged a two-stage reform process. The first stage would entail democratizing the Constitution, especially the executive branch, which would now assume the primary leadership role in American politics. It would also involve expanding the role of and increasing the social standing of policy experts, in the executive branch and outside it. These new political arrangements would be charged with the task of formulating a program of national constructive legislation to reduce economic inequality so as to create the social conditions necessary for the pursuit of a new, fuller kind of individualism—one that does not measure "its results in cash." Croly seems to have believed that in a second stage there would emerge a new kind of a national spirit that embraced the new individualism as a national goal. Critical to this development would be the new habits and outlooks inculcated by the very process of formulating and implementing national constructive legislation. The nation would go to "school" by engaging in "collective action" for a "collective purpose." Just what the nature and ends of this kind of new individualism will pursue are not dwelt on, perhaps appropriately—to specify them would be to curtail individuality. However, Croly is much more explicit about what will hold this new national community together: a "hard and inextinguishable faith" in the newly conceived democratic ideal. Indeed, such faith will become a new "religion."[15]

Just what to make of this fervent, theological language and this kind of thinking is hard to say.[16] At other times, however, Croly speaks a more political and familiar language, at least to political theorists and historians, when at the end of *The Promise of American Life* he proclaims that, explicitly invoking the authority of Montesquieu, the "principle of democracy *is* virtue."[17] This was not just a passing rhetorical flourish on Croly's part. Indeed, he returned to the theme in *Progressive Democracy* and not only reaffirmed the principle, but incorporated it in such a way as to revise his account of the founding period in a significant way.[18] In that later work, the road apparently pointed to by Montesquieu now appears as the road not taken. After discussing the basic question of how to make popular rule both just and effective, Croly writes:

> The real problem of rationalizing the exercise of popular political power was evaded rather than faced by the early American law-givers. The way to rationalize political power is not to confine its exercise within the limits defined by certain rules, but frankly to accept the danger of violence and reorganize the state so that popular reasonableness will be developed from within rather than imposed from without.[19]

Croly seems to mean that the framers' institutional focus distracted from the deeper political task of shaping the characters of citizens. Central to Croly's idea of the good citizen then would be a deep faith in the workings of the democratic process that is both manifested in and cultivated by participation in a national democratic political community. When viewed in this light, one might say that Croly's public philosophy proposes to revive the idea of cultivating civic virtue as the central goal of political life.[20] This particular civic virtue would be compatible with and indeed provide the support for that higher individualism Croly believed to be embodied in true democratic statesmanship.

Having given this sketch of Croly's public philosophy, we are now in a position to turn to Hamilton. Before doing so it is worthwhile to recapitulate that Croly's contention regarding Hamilton's great insight—his national principle—was that he saw the way in which an energetic national government could contribute to vital national interests. Hamilton's greatest failing was that his vision of the national interest was limited by his fear of democracy. Hamilton was an intellectual prisoner of an English heritage that distrusted democracy.

Hamiltonian Ends

What were Hamiltonian ends as understood by Hamilton himself? We might divide Hamiltonian ends into two categories: first, there is the transcendent end of all government, and, second, there are the secondary but critical practical and contingent ends necessary for the realization of that transcendent end. Hamilton believed that the ultimate end of government is liberty.[21] In the particular circumstances of the United States, however, he believed that the great and historic challenge was to combine liberty and republican government. Meeting this challenge might be said to be the fundamental Hamiltonian end, his essential definition of the national interest. In the past, Hamilton believed, republican government had been unable to secure liberty. In itself, this view was not unusual. What set Hamilton apart was that his concerns about the viability of republican government went considerably beyond that of many of his countrymen.

The best place to begin our consideration of Hamilton's national principle is to return to Croly's suggestive remarks about Montesquieu and democracy. This claim was the launching point for a favorite Antifederalist argument and it was one Hamilton was forced to respond to at length. The new Constitution, the Antifederalists argued, threatened republican government because of its novel attempt to establish republican government over a large area. In such circumstances they predicted the death of republican virtue. In its place all that a national government could rely on would be force of arms. Hamilton also wrote extensively on two other distinct but related issues. The first issue was the power of the states, in particular the large states, and the ongoing threat it posed to the very possibility of a viable national government. The second issue was the unprecedented size of the United States. With regard to this issue, it is often overlooked that Hamilton shared many of the reservations of the Antifederalists about the possibility of a large republic. Hamilton's thinking through of the problems of republican virtue, the power of the states, and the size of the nation began during the Revolutionary War and continued until his death in 1804.

In the *Spirit of the Laws,* Montesquieu classifies the three essential regime types as republics (democratic or aristocratic), monarchies, and despotisms.[22] Each regime has its own principle or spring of action. In despotisms it is fear. The principle of monarchy is honor. Moderation is the principle of an aristocratic republic. The principle of democratic republics is, as already noted, virtue. Montesquieu maintained that democratic republics require a rigorous and continual supervision of morals. Furthermore, he suggested that beyond a certain very limited size republics would become corrupt. In small republics the common good is "better felt, better known and lies nearer to each citizen." In large republics, by contrast, the "common good is sacrificed to a thousand considerations."[23] He depicts the successful democratic republics of antiquity as places where "political virtue"—understood as a competitive devotion to the common good—flourished but, with the possible exception of Athens, also as places governed by military discipline and where human aspirations were kept to a very narrow channel. The corruption of small republics followed from a widening of human aspirations beyond political virtue and a lessening of military discipline. Montesquieu contributed another closely connected element to the founding debate over the possibility of republicanism over a large area. His brief discussion of confederacies was a major source of the Antifederal emphasis on the need for an association of republics, a confederated republic, in order to combine the external security advantages of a monarchy with the internal advantages of republican government. But Montesquieu is extraordinarily vague about the precise terms upon which a confederation might be established.

In addition, he does not say anything about just how large a confederate republic might become. He did, however, say that even a monarchy must remain only of "medium size,"[24] and one might infer a similar limitation on the size of a confederate republic.

Not surprisingly, Americans devoted to commerce and liberty, as they were, did not embrace classical republicanism of the sort described by Montesquieu. That said, the rhetoric of classical republicanism as well as many parts or elements of the ancient republics did appeal to Americans. The Antifederalists, in particular, were attracted by the closeness between rulers and ruled, the jealousy of power, and popular participation in the ancient republics. These attractions showed themselves in their preferences for states' rights, reliance on a militia, a fear of and distaste for policies that increase economic inequality, and efforts to rein in the less democratic branches of government. As the party conflicts of the 1790s would show, this stream of thought blended nicely with the liberal republicanism of Madison, Jefferson, and Paine and with the new political economy of Adam Smith that promised to combine liberty and peace while, at the same time, avoiding dangerous concentrations of power in a national government. Hamilton severely criticized all three strands of thinking: the Montesquieuian account of the ancient republic, the American adaptation of Montesquieu, and the new liberal republican thought.

To Hamilton's mind, if the principle of the ancient republics was virtue, then it was singularly ineffective. Hamilton truly admired the occasional brilliance of these republics, but still their instability, weakness, and injustice filled him with sensations of "horror and disgust."[25] Those republics that had exhibited stability—Sparta, Rome, and Carthage—owed their success to institutional factors such as representation and the presence of a senate. If the principle of virtue was ineffective in ancient times, it was even clearer that it was wholly out of place in modern circumstances. When making the case for adequate compensation for those engaged in public service, Hamilton remarked with typical pungency that

> We may preach till we are tired of the theme, the necessity of disinterestedness in a republic, without making a single proselyte. . . . There is a total dissimulation in the circumstances, as well as the manners, of society among us; and it is as ridiculous to seek for models in the simple ages of Greece and Rome, as it would be to go in quest of them among the Hottentots and Laplanders.[26]

Hamilton's argument did not deny the possibility that real virtue, "stern virtue" as he termed it in *Federalist* 73,[27] will be found in a few, but he did believe that the expectation that one could make it a principle of government was a fanciful one. The expectation made for good speeches but not much more. Characteristic of the confusion on the Antifederalist side of the debate was the particular and, perhaps, opportunistic error in their analysis of identifying the existing American states with Montesquieu's small republics. Hamilton pointed out that the states as they existed were many times larger than the kind of city-states Montesquieu had in mind when he spoke of republics. The logical implication of this Antifederal argument would be the breakup of even the small states. In his speeches, letters, and writings, Hamilton tried to provide an analysis of the American situation that went beyond wishful theories and romantic stories.

Hamilton favored the idea of a confederate republic. Indeed, he believed Montesquieu's comments on the advantages of a confederate republic contained a "luminous abridgement of the principal arguments in favor of the Union." Hamilton focused, however, on the ability of a federal system to "repress domestic faction and insurrection," an advantage also stressed by Montesquieu, but not by the Antifederalists.[28] Two large questions remained: first, left unresolved in the *Spirit of the Laws* was the general issue of the precise internal structure of this union and, second, there was the particular American problem of the vast size of the union. Hamilton was emphatic that one could solely rely on neither a sense of the common interest, as the experience under the Articles had demonstrated, nor on a Smithian "invisible hand" to reconcile the potential sources of conflict among the states. To put the basic problem in Montesquieuian terms, given the particular circumstances of the American federal republic, how could it identify and pursue the common good?

Hamilton was unhappy with the Constitution that came out of the convention in Philadelphia in 1787. At the convention he had, with little prospect of success, proposed a senate and executive to serve during good behavior. His objective was to establish one or more fixed points in what he thought would be a fluctuating, turbulent, and essentially democratic system. Hamilton found cause for optimism, however, in the fact that Washington would likely be at the head of the new government. Washington's immense popularity would add strength to the government and, more importantly, he would likely choose able men for his administration, thus ensuring a "good administration" that would "conciliate the confidence and affections of the people and perhaps enable the government to more consistency than the proposed constitution seems to promise for so great a country."[29]

The new Constitution, in Hamilton's understanding of it, made the executive power the key to ensuring a good administration. He saw the executive as necessarily having a national outlook and as having something of a popular foundation. At the New York Ratifying Convention, Hamilton said the president will be "the representative of the people."[30] Both at the convention and afterwards Hamilton sought to rest the executive on the "shoulders of the people" at large.[31] But Hamilton did not have in mind the kind of thoroughly democratized presidency that Croly urged. Hamilton's purpose was not to make the institution more democratic but rather to secure its independence from the other branches of government, particularly Congress. An independent executive rather than a merely democratic executive would be able to do the people's business. As Hamilton put the matter in *Federalist* 71, the people "commonly *intend* the PUBLIC GOOD" but they do not necessarily "*reason right* about the *means* of promoting it."[32] One function of the executive was to do this reasoning in the people's stead by recommending measures to Congress, preparing plans of finance, and when necessary exercising the veto power.

We are now in a position to state more precisely what is meant by "Hamiltonian ends." Hamilton's goal was to make republican government compatible with liberty. This required that the institutions of government be made capable of identifying and pursuing the common good. The key supplement Hamilton envisaged to the process of deliberative democracy was an energetic executive. In this regard, he envisaged the executive as the most national of the national institutions. A corollary to this public philosophy was the necessity of establishing the authority of national institutions and policies. With these two major Hamiltonian ends in mind, let us turn to the matter of Hamiltonian means.

Hamiltonian Means

Hamilton's famous June 18 speech at the convention of 1787 considers the forces or springs of action that may serve as the basis of a government's authority and policies. The speech represents an intense effort to think through the problem of establishing good government in a large republic. In what is in effect a disaggregation of Montesquieu's three main regime principles, Hamilton identifies five springs: interest, opinion, habit, influence, and force (of laws and arms). A national government capable of establishing good government would not only have to be able to discern the common good, but it would have to be able to utilize these springs of action in such a way as to accomplish the common good and establish the authority of the Constitution.

As Hamilton explained in *The Federalist,* in the circumstances of the United States, the state governments had the decided advantage in utilizing these fundamental springs of human behavior. It is a "fact in human nature that its affections are commonly weak in proportion to the distance or diffusiveness of the object." As a result of this "fact," citizens are likely to be more attached to the state and local governments. Furthermore, the states controlled many "minute interests" that could be used to influence citizens. Last, and most important, the states retained the "transcendent advantage" of administering the civil and criminal justice systems. The national government was at a disadvantage because of its distance from the people and because of the limited scope of its objects. Having said this, he believed "as a general rule, that [the people's] confidence in and obedience to a government, will commonly be in proportion to the goodness or badness of its administration."[33] There were strong reasons to believe that the national government's administration within its assigned area would be superior to that of the states.[34] If it were to establish a successful administration, the national government would be in a position to bring about a shift, probably a substantial one, in the attachment of the people away from the states and to the national government.

What precisely were Hamiltonian means? What were the set of policies that could utilize the various springs of human conduct? Hamilton's program moved at two levels: at the first (or vertical) level Hamilton sought to attach the people to their government, and at the second (or horizontal) level Hamilton sought to unite the nation in certain limited but fundamental ways. These two axes are not independent in any strict mathematical sense but they provide a useful way to conceptualize Hamiltonian means.

Along the vertical axis Hamilton tried to appeal—through "interest" and "influence"—to individuals and groups of individuals. The difference between interest and influence would seem to turn on the directness of the connection between the government and the individual. Influence implies a much more direct connection, say, for example, than between a government and a government employee. His first and most conspicuous effort was his attempt to cement the authority of the new government while at the same time remedying the nation's financial ills. Most famously, through his program to restore public credit he sought the support of the financial interest of society. The assumption of the state debts, the funding system, and the creation of a national bank effectively nationalized the American financial system, thereby making the financial interest vitally concerned with the success of the national government and its policies. In view of the great controversy associated with this program at the time and the debate it has provoked since, it is important to point out the sheer necessity involved in this policy: if a nation is going to have a *modern* financial system it cannot do so without the support of the financial interests. Some of Hamilton's policies, the implementation of an excise tax, for example, also had the effect of increasing the national government's workforce. As he explained with characteristic frankness in "The Continentalist," such expansions "create in the interior of each state a mass of influence in favour of the Federal government."[35] However threatening such suggestions may have sounded to the advocates of state power, Hamilton saw it as essential for the government to expand its presence across the nation.

In addition to establishing these particular areas of support, Hamilton's policies aimed to create a broad, even universal foundation of support for the government. Hamilton hoped that a visibly efficient and successful administration, especially if it was to establish a widely *felt* prosperity, would be critical for establishing confidence in and support for the government. In addition to this connection through "interest," Hamilton's desire to see the new government utilizing where possible the powers granted to it was in part motivated by a desire to familiarize the people with their new government. Making the government visible, even in controversial matters, such as the excise, was a high priority. As he warned in *Federalist* 27, "A government continually at a distance and out of sight can hardly be expected to interest the sensations of the people."[36] The "sensations" Hamilton had in mind went beyond interest to include respect and familiarity. Multiplying the frequency of such sensations would increase the likelihood of securing obedience to national laws. In both cases mentioned, the goal of a good administration was to shift *some* of the attachments of the people from their state and local governments, which "human nature" would ordinarily lead them to favor, to the national government. In other words, the goal was to break down one of the critical components of virtue in the small republic, namely, the closeness and familiarity that citizens feel for one another and their local communities. This was a process that Hamilton understood to be already well advanced in the states but it is important to realize that his policies were conceived as a conscious alternative to republican virtue, as defined by Montesquieu and partially embraced by the Antifederalists.

On what I have called the horizontal axis—that relating to relationships among citizens—Hamilton's policies had two major goals. The first goal was the creation of a national market that would link citizens together through ties of mutual interest. As noted above, Hamilton did not think this would come about through the operations of an "invisible hand." Hamilton argues at length in *Federalist* 6–8 that commerce is likely to be a cause of controversy and conflict among loosely connected states. Hamilton's program, though not fully implemented, aimed at integrating the various sectors of American society. This required the opening of new fields of enterprise and endeavor, connecting the agricultural South with the commercial North through "internal improvements" and by keeping the westward expansion of the nation at a pace compatible with national cohesion. This last point indicates the substantial difference between Hamilton's idea of a practical sphere of government and Jefferson's idea of an expanding empire of liberty and reflects Hamilton's continuing fear that the nation was so vast that governing it would be extremely difficult whatever the form of government.[37]

The second horizontal dimension to Hamilton's policy program was his efforts to shape "opinion." Public opinion is obviously an outgrowth of individual opinions, but it is just as obviously the product of and reinforced by shared opinions in a community. There were two critical opinions Hamilton sought to foster. The first was a favorable opinion about the effectiveness of the national government. For this to solidify it was essential that policies be effective and be seen to be effective. A second opinion Hamilton sought to foster was a respect for law in general and the new Constitution in particular. Hamilton stressed again and again the centrality of establishing the rule of law. As he remarked in his "Tully" letters during the tense period of the Whiskey Rebellion, "If it were to be asked, What is the most sacred duty and the greatest source of security in a Republic? The answer would be, An inviolable respect for the Constitution and Laws—the first growing out of the last."[38] Hamilton's belief in a broad construction of the Constitution sometimes distracts from the emphasis he placed on establishing fidelity to the Constitution. Indeed, the importance of this goal seemed to rise in his estimation as the character of

American political life became clearer to him. Increasingly, it seems, he came to see the Constitution as the nearest thing to the fixed point in the governmental system that he had searched for at the convention of 1787.[39] Again Hamilton's belief that respect for the law is the essence of republicanism reflects a very different understanding of republicanism and republican virtue than Montesquieu, who had emphasized a competitive devotion to the common good as the core of republicanism.[40] It is also worth noting that what Hamilton seems to have had in mind—a shared opinion or perhaps even "faith" in the law—is precisely what Croly criticized in both *The Promise of American Life* and *Progressive Democracy* as American's superstitious reverence for the Constitution.

Conclusion

Our review of Croly's Hamilton and Hamilton himself allows for some closing reflections on the course of progressive liberalism over the twentieth century. An examination of Hamilton's thinking reveals that Croly's understanding is not so much inaccurate as it is partial or incomplete. This leads him to give an unbalanced portrait of Hamilton. Croly, for example, exaggerates the extent to which the Washington administration was an embodiment of pure Hamiltonianism. Croly neglects the extent to which Hamilton pursued second- or third-best policy alternatives and the extent to which his policies were frustrated by his rivals or simply by the failure of some of his policies to meet their objectives. Almost as if to compensate, Croly understates the extent to which Hamiltonianism was embedded in a political science that was much more than simply a manifestation of an English political heritage. It is possible that Croly was using Hamilton's "Englishness" as a kind of shorthand for such an argument. But Croly's mischaracterization of Hamilton's thinking spills over into his account of the way in which Hamilton used constructive legislation to pursue his national principle. One consequence of the underestimation of Hamilton's *thinking* about politics was that Croly too hastily assumed that the Hamiltonian method or means might be decoupled from Hamiltonian ends or goals. Put otherwise, Hamilton's "national principle" encompassed within it both ends and means and thus Hamiltonian means are not simply extendable or transferable to non-Hamiltonian ends.

Hamilton's national principle is certainly more modest and, therefore, more attainable than Croly's. His objectives were to attach the people to their government and to bind the people together in a national market. Good laws and policies, well executed—a wise administration—were the key to meeting these goals. Hamilton's theory of administration was conceived as a result of a recognition of the fundamental insufficiency of republican virtue, especially over a vast nation and not simply out of a fear of democracy, as stressed by Croly. Administration is a necessary supplement to and sometimes even a sufficient substitute for republican virtue. In retrospect, then, we ought not be surprised that the grander elements of Croly's project to enhance "popular reasonableness" outlined in *The Promise of American Life* and *Progressive Democracy* failed to materialize. Administration simply cannot do what Croly wanted it to do. Hamiltonian means are not simply transferable to Jeffersonian ends. In light of this, it is not surprising that government efforts to reduce inequality evolved into entitlements. Nor is it surprising that as government programs expanded in size and scope, the public came to question the effectiveness of government and lose faith. It is worth mentioning here that Hamilton envisaged a national government that confined itself to the great objects of government: commerce, finance, diplomacy, and war.[41] We might add that these are the areas where government could be effective and be seen to be effective. Thus, it is not enough to say, as Michael Sandel does, that later progressive liberals abandoned Croly's emphasis on character formation in making the shift to what Sandel calls "procedural liberalism."[42] The shift was foreshadowed in the fundamental incoherence of Croly's program of combining Hamiltonian means and Jeffersonian ends.

Furthermore, one wonders whether the success of Croly's program in its fullest sense would not have had grave implications for liberty since it is hard to imagine its realization in circumstances other than a democracy engaged in a war for its very survival, as the Union was under Lincoln. Perhaps the greatest problem with the failure of Croly's project is that it has contributed to the discrediting of the national principle itself. Conservatives have long been skeptical of the idea of a national community and the administrative state that supports it, but even now on the left-liberal side of politics there is considerable disenchantment with the idea of a national community, as exemplified in Sandel's *Democracy's Discontent*.[43]

Yet it is not enough to say simply that Hamilton shows greater realism than Croly.[44] We can see the inadequacy of this view by considering the "conception of the person"—the foundation of a public philosophy, according to Sandel—entailed by Hamilton's program. It is true that Croly and Hamilton had profoundly different conceptions of the person underwriting their public philosophies. The fundamental point of difference was Hamilton's adherence to the idea of abstract or natural rights. Croly had little time for such notions which, among other things, seemed to limit individual and social possibilities. He preferred instead to speak of the rights and duties of "historic individuals," that is, of the rights of beings living in history.[45] Hamilton, in contrast, saw and, one must add, personally experienced the natural rights philosophy as liberating. Despite these foundational differences, there are certain profound similarities between Hamilton and Croly. Just as Croly hoped that a new democratic faith would bind the nation together and, at the same time, provide avenues for the emergence of a higher individualism, Hamilton also had hopes that binding the nation together in a national market under a constitution would provide outlets for certain types of higher individualism. Hamilton's outlook had much in common with the likes of Adam Smith and especially David Hume, both of whom argued that civilized society characterized by a division of labor would give rise to and foster a sophisticated and polished individualism. This kind of thinking by Hamilton is clear in two respects. First, Hamilton's economic writings argue for multiplying the number of outlets for human ingenuity. This could be done by fostering the growth of a manufacturing sector in the United States to balance the dominant agricultural sector. This would necessitate the growth of cities and all the diversity that accompanies urban life. Under such conditions a higher individualism would have a chance of flourishing. As he comments in the "Report on Manufactures," "minds of the strongest and most active powers" fail to achieve their completion if they are denied appropriate outlets.[46] Second, Hamilton envisaged a scope for statesmanship under the new constitution. In *Federalist* 72 he famously speaks of those moved by the love of fame, "the ruling passion of the noblest minds," who might be induced to undertake extensive and arduous projects for the common good.[47]

In certain decisive respects, however, Hamilton's expectations were disappointed in both areas. His economic plans were accepted only in part. He was successful in pushing ahead with dramatic changes in the American financial system, but he did not gain acceptance for his goal of beginning the process of fostering manufactures. It is clear, furthermore, that at the political level the course of American politics in the 1790s was a severe disappointment to him. There was something more involved here than the mere failure of a few of his policies. It was a recognition that at some fundamental level he had misjudged the possibilities inherent in American political life. Writing to a Scottish relative, Hamilton reflected on public service in America:

> Public Office in this country has few attractions. The pecuniary emolument is so inconsiderable as to amount to a sacrifice to any man who can employ his time with advantage in any liberal profession. The opportunity of doing good, from the jealousy of power and the spirit of faction, is too small in any station to warrant a long continuance of private sacrifices. The enterprises of party had so far succeeded as materially to weaken the necessary influence and energy of the Executive Authority, and so far diminish the power of doing good in that department as greatly to take the motives which a virtuous man might have for making sacrifices. The prospect was even bad for gratifying in the future the love of Fame, if that passion was to be the spring of action.[48]

In a similar but more emotional vein Hamilton remarked to Gouverneur Morris that "Every day proves to me more and more that this American world was not made for me."[49] These reflections have a highly personal character to them, but they are just the same penetrating insights into the shape of American politics, insights that would be later confirmed by acute observers like Tocqueville.[50]

What are we to conclude from these second thoughts on Hamilton's part? They surely constitute, as with the fate of Croly's program, a caution to all those who hope that a "higher individualism" might be made to sit easily with a modern democracy. That said, was Hamilton's dark pessimism justified? A full answer to this question would take us beyond the scope of our present topic, but the benefit of hindsight gives us a peculiar perspective. In one respect, at least, we can say he was too pessimistic. Hamilton wrote, in the conclusion to his "Continentalist" essays, that "[t]here is something noble and magnificent in the perspective of a great Federal Republic, closely linked in the pursuit of a common interest, tranquil and prosperous at home, respectable abroad."[51] When we see that the United States, notwithstanding the dominance of progressive liberalism, is at the beginning of the twenty-first century conspicuously Hamiltonian, with its dominant military, dynamic economy, and powerful central government holding peaceful sway over a vast and diverse land, it is clear that this much of the nobility and magnificence Hamilton envisioned has been realized.

What does the future hold for the progressive liberal synthesis of Hamiltonian means and Jeffersonian ends? There are many clear signs that the time is overdue for rethinking this synthesis. Our consideration of Croly and Hamilton has made clear that any synthesis involves sharp tensions and trade-offs between ends and means. The success of any future synthesis will in no small part depend on awareness of how deeply these conflicts are rooted in the politics of a large republic.

NOTES

1. "Public philosophy" is a term that has come back into vogue. Michael Sandel, in his influential book, *Democracy's Discontent: America in Search of a Public Philosophy* (Cambridge, MA: Harvard University Press, 1996), 4, defines public philosophy as "the political theory implicit in our practice, the assumptions about citizenship and freedom that inform our public life." See also James W. Ceaser, "What Is the Public Philosophy?" *Perspectives on Political Science*, 30, 1 (Winter 2000): 9–20, for a critical discussion of the idea of public philosophy.

2. Herbert Croly, *The Promise of American Life* (hereafter *PAL*) (New York: Macmillan, 1909).

3. See Eric Goldman's classic, *Rendezvous with Destiny* (New York: Knopf, 1952), ch. 9, and, more recently, Edward A. Stettner, *Shaping Modern Liberalism: Herbert Croly and Progressive Thought* (Lawrence: University Press of Kansas, 1993). Stettner provides an impressive account of the evolution or, perhaps, unraveling of Croly's thought over time.

4. *PAL*, 29.

5. Herbert Croly, *Progressive Democracy* (hereafter *PD*), intro. Sidney A. Pearson (New Brunswick, NJ: Transaction, [1914] 1998). Pearson's fine introduction was extremely helpful for the present essay. Pearson observes that what is at stake between the Founders and Croly is not the existence but the "character of the national community." Pearson's suggestion that the founders, especially Hamilton, had in mind a "community of 'commercial' interests more than 'passion'" is true but incomplete (xxi). I expand upon it in what follows.

6. *PAL*, 198, 45, 38, 39, 44.

7. *PAL*, 69.

8. *PAL*, 41, 44, 40, 193.

9. *PD*, 54–55.

10. *PAL*, 42.

11. *PAL*, 207.

12. *PD*, 338–39.

13. *PAL*, 168, 169, 173, 175.

14. For a general discussion see Kevin C. O'Leary, "Herbert Croly and Progressive Democracy," *Polity* 26:4 (Summer 1994): 533–52.

15. *PAL*, 410, 407, 452, 453; see also *PD*, 424–25.

16. One might find here the intellectual influences of William James and Josiah Royce and the example of the Union under Lincoln's leadership. For useful discussions, see Stettner, *Shaping Modern Liberalism*, 45–48; O'Leary, "Croly and Progressive Democracy," 547; and John Patrick Diggins, "Republicanism and Progressivism," *American Quarterly*, 37 (Fall 1986): 572–98 at 580–82.

17. *PAL*, 454.

18. *PD*, 34–39.

19. *PD*, 38.

20. This republican dimension of Croly has been most fully explored by Diggins, "Republicanism and Progressivism," and O'Leary, "Croly and Progressive Democracy."

21. See his remark at the Constitutional Convention as recorded by Madison: "[Hamilton] professed himself to be as zealous an advocate for liberty as any man whatever, and trusted he should be as willing a martyr to it though he differed as to the form in which it was most eligible"; June 26, 1787, *Papers of Alexander Hamilton* (hereafter *PAH*), 26 vols. (New York: Columbia University Press, 1961–87), 4:218. I have discussed some of the issues that follow in *Political Economy and Statesmanship: Smith, Hamilton, and the Foundation of the Commercial Republic* (DeKalb: Northern Illinois University Press, 1998), especially 106–12, 139–43.

22. The critical books are IV–IX. All references are to Charles de Secondat, Baron de Montesquieu, *Spirit of the Laws*, trans. Anne Cohler, Basia Miller, and Harold Stone (Cambridge, UK: Cambridge University Press, 1989).

23. *Spirit of the Laws*, VIII.16.

24. *Spirit of the Laws*, IV.17.

25. *The Federalist*, No. 9, *PAH*, 4:333.

26. "The Continentalist," No. VI, July 4, 1782, *PAH*, 3:103.

27. *PAH*, 4:618.

28. The Federalist, No. 9, *PAH*, 4:337.

29. "Conjectures about the New Constitution," September 17–30, 1787, *PAH*, 4:275–76.

30. June 21, 1788, *PAH*, 4:38.

31. Letter to Bayard, April 6, 1802, *PAH*, 25:588.

32. *PAH*, 4:608. See also New York Ratifying Convention, June 24, 1788, *PAH*, 4:82–83.

33. *The Federalist*, No. 17, *PAH*, 4:371–72. At the New York Ratifying Convention, June 21, 1788, Hamilton remarked that support for the government would be obtained by ensuring a "train of prosperous events." *PAH*, 5:39.

34. *The Federalist*, No. 27, *PAH*, 4:435.

35. No. 6, July 4, 1782, *PAH*, 3:105.

36. *PAH*, 4:437.

37. Hamilton's reluctance to expand too rapidly the boundaries of the United States is most evident in his comments on the Louisiana Purchase. Hamilton

favored the acquisition of the port of New Orleans, by force if necessary, but he was concerned that rapid expansion beyond this might lead to the dismemberment of the Union. July 5, 1803, *New York Evening Post, PAH,* 26:129–36. Hamilton had expressed similar reservations when, as Treasury Secretary, he worried that faulty economic policies might hasten the pace of westward expansion. See his "Defence of the Funding System," July 1795, *PAH,* 19:39–41.

38. No. III, August 28, 1794, *PAH,* 17:159.

39. On this point, see his letter to Bayard, April 16–22, 1802, *PAH,* 25:602.

40. Colleen Sheehan argues persuasively that Hamilton's theory of public opinion is essentially passive, whereas Jefferson and Madison had a more active theory of public opinion in which the public opinion plays a vigorous role in the actual operations of government. "Madison v. Hamilton: The Battle over Republicanism and the Role of Public Opinion," this volume, 165–208.

41. See *The Federalist,* No. 17.

42. Sandel, *Democracy's Discontent,* 226–27.

43. For an influential conservative argument against the idea of a national community, see William A. Schambra, "Progressive Liberalism and American 'Community,'" *Public Interest* 80 (Summer 1985): 31–48.

44. This is essentially the view of Wilfred M. McClay, "Croly's Progressive America," *Public Interest* (Fall 1999): 57–63, and Sidney A. Pearson, "Herbert Croly and Liberal Democracy," *Society* (July/August 1998): 62–72. Note, however, that they speak of the founders in general, not Hamilton in particular.

45. Croly writes that "An individual has no meaning apart from the society in which his individuality has been formed" (*PAL,* 263).

46. December 5, 1791, *PAH,* 10:255.

47. *PAH,* 4:613.

48. Letter to William Hamilton, May 2, 1797, *PAH,* 21:78.

49. February 29, 1802, *PAH,* 25:544.

50. See *Democracy in America,* vol. I, part 2, ch. 2, on the decline of the Federalist Party after 1800 and vol. I, part 2, ch. 7, on the power of the majority in American democracy.

51. No. 6, July 4, 1782, *PAH,* 3:105. Sandel is clearly incorrect to say that national glory was the motivating force behind Hamilton's program (*Democracy's Discontent,* 138).

CHAPTER 11

Epilogue

Alexander Hamilton, Abraham Lincoln, and the Spirit of Capitalism

JOHN PATRICK DIGGINS

*I*N the study of American history, Abraham Lincoln is frequently treated as an exponent of Thomas Jefferson and the doctrines of liberty, democracy, equality, and popular sovereignty. On Fourth of July occasions Lincoln did indeed hail Jefferson, and in the debates leading up to the Civil War he invoked again and again Jefferson's Declaration of Independence to refute the argument for slavery and its expansion into the territories. But a further look at Lincoln's political mind and the values he stood for would place him closer to Alexander Hamilton and the values he expressed and the vision he had for America. Although a half-century separates Lincoln from Hamilton, and although the two thinkers read different intellectual sources and, in addition, had different attitudes toward democracy and equality, nonetheless their respective mind and thought had many affinities. Perhaps they ended up having a similar outlook on society and government because they started out on roughly the same basis. Whether or not the child is father to the man, the childhood of both figures made the past a prologue to the present and shaped their outlook.

Hamilton was an illegitimate orphan, born on Nevis in a penniless environment where he worked there and at St. Croix as a clerk at the age of twelve before escaping to America at sixteen. Lincoln was born to illiterate parents and worked with hand and shovel on neighbors' lands for little or no pay. Surviving the harsh conditions of youth without nurturing parents, both Hamilton and Lincoln would value opportunity and their lives would become part of the legendary American success story. Perhaps more importantly, both looked to ambition as the driving force that makes a difference in life, and both believed that special human beings aspire to honor and recognition and that an overweening ambition represents a danger that needs to be checked. Hamilton thought that the desire for glory was the "deepest passion" of exceptional people, and Lincoln envied the Founders for enjoying the "fame" and "glory" denied to subsequent generations of American political leaders; he wondered how the republic could survive if such "ruling passions" go ungratified. Humankind faced Hamilton and Lincoln as an economic creature and social animal, determined by interest and desiring distinction.[1]

In light of this common background of deprivation, it is hardly surprising that Hamilton and Lincoln would look to the economic sphere of life as liberating. Hamilton became involved in politics, of course, but his earlier efforts went toward establishing the republic on a sound financial basis and, as the first Secretary of Treasury, he conceived the new republic as an enterprise in rapid economic development. Unlike Jefferson, he had no reservations about a modernization that would leave the rural past behind. If a political thinker and actor is to be judged by his sense of the direction of history, Hamilton perhaps more than any other founder knew where America was heading.

Lincoln follows this same pattern of sensing that America would be determined by its future in a world of rapid change and development. He may have taken great satisfaction in the life of politics, and, from reading the accounts of his contemporaries, he was a natural-born politician; yet it is telling that he rarely mentions politics and government service as a proper goal for young Americans. Unlike Theodore Roosevelt, who encouraged youths to go into politics and take politics away from the politicians, or Max Weber, who wrote a famous address on "Politics as a Vocation," Lincoln rarely dwelled on the subject or expressed any fulfillment in the wheeling and dealing involved in political transactions. Both Hamilton and Lincoln had no instinct for what would come to be known as ward politics and the organization of political machines. While Lincoln may have urged citizens to respect the Constitution and the rule of law, he never thought of politics, as did ancient classical authors and even some of our academics today, as the main activity of the noble life. What Hamilton and Lincoln did have in common was a commitment to the integrity of government and its necessary functions. And this commitment, in the course of American history, transcends party identity. In Hamilton it expresses itself in the Federalist Party; in Lincoln, in the Whig-turned

Republican Party; in Theodore Roosevelt, in the Republican-turned Progressive Party; and in Franklin Roosevelt in the Democratic Party that ushered in the welfare state and modern liberalism as we know it—or, given recent political developments, as we used to know it.

In addition to believing in the positive role of the nation-state, Hamilton and Lincoln were also nationalists at periods in American history when most loyalties were local and regional. Again this common affinity may have much to do with both figures being born in circumstances that were far from stable and permanent. Young Hamilton went from island to island in the Caribbean before heading to New York; Lincoln went from state to state before settling in Illinois. Neither had roots in any particular part of the country, and thus both thought of the Republic as a whole, never doubting that the whole was greater than its parts. The doctrine of states' rights and state sovereignty that Jefferson and James Madison invoked in the Kentucky and Virginia resolutions made little impression on Hamilton, and in his First Inaugural Address Lincoln set out to refute such principles that South Carolina had used as the grounds for secession. Both Hamilton and Lincoln were devoted to the national good, and each believed it was the responsibility of the central government to take the lead in the economic development of the country, whether through banks and the availability of credit or railroads and the availability of transportation.

But the nationalism shared by Hamilton and Lincoln also confronted them with a common problem when it came to liberty and the right of revolution. In *The Farmer Refuted* (1775), Hamilton, defending the case of the colonies against the mother country, insisted that for authority to be legitimate it must rest upon the consent of the people, otherwise they have a right to rise up against their oppressors. "The nations of Turkey, Russia, France, Spain, and all the other despotic kingdoms in the world, have an inherent right, whenever they please, to shake off the yoke of servitude (though sanctified by the immemorial usage of their ancestors); and to model their governments on the principles of civil liberty."[2]

Significantly, Lincoln uses not only the same reasoning but even the same expressions when opposing America's war against Mexico and defending Hungary's uprising against tsarist Russia and imperial Austria. Lincoln had all along thought expansion into the Southwest an effort on the part of the South to extend the slave system, and he chastised President Polk for acting unconstitutionally. Believing that both Texas and Mexico had been exercising their proper jurisdictions over their respective territories, Lincoln believed it legitimate to oppose with force and violence any intrusions upon one's own land: "Any people anywhere, being inclined and having the power, have the *right* to rise up, and shake off the existing government, and form a new one that suits them better. This is a most valuable, a most sacred right—a right which, we hope and believe, is to liberate the world."[3]

But Hamilton and Lincoln, after having declared that people have a right to "shake off" an existing regime, had to back down when, in the first instance, the French rose up in 1789 and took the revolution to the streets in the 1790s, and when, in the second instance, the South seceded from the Union in 1860 in the name of the right of revolution guaranteed by the Declaration of Independence. Jefferson defended with indiscriminate enthusiasm the French Revolution, and the southern Jeffersonians defended the right of secession. Hamilton seriously doubted that the French Directory would expand the dimensions of human freedom, and Lincoln felt the same about the southern Confederacy.

Another parallel between our two figures is professional. Hamilton and Lincoln were also lawyers, and both, having read Blackstone, knew how to think legally and logically, always resting their case on principles and premises as well as precedent. Both thinkers were masters of reasoning by method of classification and definition. To be sure, both had a sardonic skepticism about how law was practiced in America. Perhaps they would have been amused to have read Alexis de Tocqueville claiming, in *Democracy in America,* that attorneys would serve as an aristocracy in America, a profession with a capacity for memory and a commitment to objectivity. Hamilton complained of the "cavilling petulance of an attorney," wondering if lawyers were interested in real evidence or instead simply offering persuasion in the guise of proof. Lincoln warned lawyers of his generation to avoid litigation and cease stirring up strife simply to put money in one's pockets. Ultimately, however, both had faith in the legal process in reconciling liberty with rules and distinguishing coercive power from consensual authority. Hamilton was fond of quoting David Hume to the effect we must start out with the assumption that everyman is a "knave"; Lincoln advised young Americans: "Choose some other occupation, rather than one in the choosing of which you do, in advance, consent to being a knave."[4]

In his vast speeches and writings, Lincoln cited Hamilton only twice, once to defend the prerogatives of the executive office, the other to categorize Hamilton, together with Dr. Franklin and Gouverneur Morris, as an example of the founders who opposed the slave trade and advocated restrictions against its advancement into the northwest territory. The latter citation raises the question of slavery and Hamilton and Lincoln's response to it. Here again, I would suggest, the early background of both figures may have shaped their critical attitudes toward an institution that scarcely concerned most Northerners while it came to be stoutly defended by almost all Southerners.

The islands of Nevis, St. Kitts, and St. Croix where Hamilton grew up were heavily populated with African slaves. Young Hamilton, a poor white boy sometimes finding himself in the same room with black slaves in a leisure-class plantation society, knew firsthand the potential for blacks to be capable of tasks if given proper education and opportunity. To John Jay he wrote in the midst of the American Revolution: "I have not the least doubt that the Negroes will make very excellent soldiers." Frequently told that he was wrong and that blacks were "too stupid" to be effective fighters, Hamilton replied: "This is so far from appearing to me a valid objection, that I think their want of cultivation (for their natural faculties are as good as ours) joined to the habit of subordination which they acquire from a life of servitude, will enable them to soon become better soldiers than our white inhabitants." Slavery is "fatal to religion and morality" and it "debases the mind, and corrupts the noblest springs of action," wrote Hamilton elsewhere. "I might shew, that it relaxes the sinews of industry, clips the wings of commerce, and introduces misery and indigence in every shape." Hamilton helped organize the Society for the Manumission of Slaves and proposed that its members free their own slaves. His resolution went nowhere. But he expressed himself further in signing a petition against the slave trade as "repugnant to humanity" and he believed that Virginia would remain decadent and stagnant as long as slavery remained and the slaves' "injured humanity" would lead them to "hate their masters."[5]

Lincoln's views were similar. He once told a friend that, while in the South, the sight of slaves in chains left him in "eternal torment." Although Lincoln never grew up amid blacks, he did know what it was like to work without remuneration. His father would hire him out to labor on neighbors' farms and the old man would take the hard-earned wages from the lad's pocket. His father told him that he had to work and showed him how to do chores, Lincoln mused, but he "never taught me how to love work." Lincoln hated slavery, and while he was willing to tolerate its existence in the South for the sake of preserving the Union, he never once uttered a thought that suggested blacks were inferior, even though a bigoted white society assumed so and Lincoln never openly challenged that prejudice since he needed votes to win office. White society "assigns" the superior position to itself, he observed. A most revealing term; to use "assigns" indicates he did not believe it to be true but only that society assumes itself superior, that social conventions are contingent and constructed expediently and have nothing to do with the natural order of things. But Lincoln's truest feelings on the subject are expressed in a letter to James Conkling written after the Emancipation Proclamation. Like Hamilton, Lincoln thought of arming blacks, only to be told that Northerners are not fighting to free slaves but to preserve the Union, and there was even some rumbling about rescinding the Emancipation Proclamation. Is it not the case, Lincoln replied, that blacks fighting on the Union side will help our cause? "Does it appear otherwise to you? But negroes, like other people, act upon motives. Why should they do anything for us, if we will do nothing for them? If they stake their lives for us, they must be prompted by the strongest motive—even the promise of freedom. And the promise being made, must be kept." And if not kept? Imagine, Lincoln, advised, what black soldiers would feel when told that the Proclamation is being withdrawn and the promise of freedom has been betrayed. "There will be black men who can remember that, with silent tongue, and clenched teeth, and steady eye, and well poised bayonet, they have helped mankind on to this great consummation; while, I fear, there will be some white ones, unable to forget that, with malignant heart, and deceitful speech, they have strove to hinder it."[6]

A curiosity, perhaps even a riddle, arises when we compare Hamilton and Lincoln on the issue of slavery. Hamilton believed African Americans would make good soldiers not only because they were accustomed to taking orders but also because their "natural faculties" could match that of white people. Lincoln denounced slavery as a violation of the Declaration of Independence, and he had no hesitation citing Jefferson's "all men are created equal" again and again when debating Stephen Douglas. He regarded the Declaration as the "sheet anchor" of the republic and the "moral emblem" for humanity everywhere in the world. Hamilton, like many Federalists, looked with skepticism upon the Declaration and instead valued a social order that would be aristocratic and hierarchical. Yet Hamilton no less than Lincoln condemned slavery. Why? If he did not do so because he believed in the doctrine of equality, what accounts for his aversion to America's "peculiar institution"? A comparison of Hamilton and Lincoln may help resolve this riddle.

In his very last days Lincoln advocated suffrage for blacks in Louisiana and elsewhere. But even more than political rights, Lincoln envisioned an America undergoing economic development to be accessible to blacks as well as whites. In championing an economic system open to all, Lincoln shared Hamilton's dream of a republic of workers and entrepreneurs, a culture that rewarded ambition and extended to people of all colors the right to rise.

Although the term "capitalism" did not exist in Hamilton's era and only began to make its appearance in Lincoln's, both political leaders had it in mind when thinking about the future of America. Both also understood that economic development would go hand in hand with scientific innovation. Hamilton planned a Society for Establishing Useful Manufactures that would be located in a park close to the Passaic Falls near Paterson, New Jersey. Hamilton sought to raise capital in order to construct the machines that would be applied to producing paper, sail cloth, blankets, clothes, and cotton and linen goods. The scheme proved to be unsuccessful, and one of Hamilton's partners was accused of fraudulent fund raising. But Hamilton knew that technology and scientific research would be the pivotal force behind the economy.

Today, in our age of globalization, there is much speculation as to why a few countries gallop ahead into a brave new world of material abundance and most others fall behind or never even leave the gate. The economic historian David S. Landes addressed this issue in his book, *The Wealth and Poverty of Nations: Why Some Are So Rich and Some So Poor.* At the turn of the last century, Max Weber addressed a similar issue in *The Protestant Ethic and the Spirit of Capitalism.* Weber sought to demonstrate that the religion of Calvinism left the Puritans in a state of agony about the salvation of their souls, and hence they threw themselves into a strenuous life of hard work, frugality, and self-denial, thereby starting the seeds of capital accumulation. Landes's explanation is less theological than technological. Certain cultures, he points out, have the daring to explore and reach out into the unknown, a willingness to determine change instead of simply responding to it, a capacity for curiosity even if it goes against convention. Both Weber and Landes emphasized the motives behind human action, one probing the needs of the soul in search for spiritual fulfillment, the other the needs of the mind in search for scientific mastery. Curiously, Abraham Lincoln presages both Weber and Landes.

In an important but rarely read address delivered in 1859, "Discoveries and Inventions," Lincoln discusses progress and scientific breakthroughs as a result of "observation," "reflection," and "experiment." He described how for centuries human beings had watched boiling water raise the lids of containers "with a sort of fluttering motion," but since no one had thought to ask why hot water could lift a pot lid, and since no one had bothered to experiment with the phenomenon, the principle of steam power had remained undiscovered. Lincoln then explains the method of scientific thinking as a method of posing questions. It is as though the material of the natural world cries out "Try me," and the curious investigator does try, and the resulting "trial gives the world control" over elemental forces.

To Lincoln, scientific progress is an aspect of culture, and he has no difficulty stating it is peculiar to the Western, secular world. He even goes so far as to suggest that other cultures, like the original Adam, lack curiosity and remain reluctant to penetrate into the reason of things, to make an effort to "Try me" and thereby eat of the forbidden fruit even at the cost of losing the state of grace and innocence. Invention requires the habit of observation:

> But for the difference in habit of observation, why did yankees, almost instantly, discover gold in California, which has been trodden upon, and over looked by indians and Mexican greasers, for centuries? Gold mines are not the only mines overlooked in the same way. There are more mines above the Earth's surface than below it. All nature—the whole world, material and moral, and intellectual—is a mine; and in Adam's day, it was a wholly unexplored mine. Now, as it was the destined work of Adam's race to develop, by discovery, inventions, and improvements, the hidden treasure of this mine. But Adam had nothing to turn his attention to the work. If he should do anything in the art of invention, he had first to invent the art of invention—the instance at least, if not the habit of observation and reflection. As might be expected he seems not to have been a very observing man at first; for it appears he went about naked a considerable length of time, before he even noticed the obvious fact. But when he did observe it, the observation was not lost upon him; for it immediately led to the first of all inventions, of which we have any direct account-the fig-leaf apron.[7]

Lincoln's passage is biblical and profane at the same time. Cultures unwilling to invent are like Adam before the Fall; they are unwilling to break with God as the first step toward the right to know. The will to inquire and know occurred in European society before it arrived in America to transform the environment with the turbine engine. First sin, then steam. It may be pointed out, in regard to Lincoln's marvelous phrase "Try me," that in German the word try and attempt are one in the same, as is to be tempted and temptation itself. Capitalism has its origins in the sinful temptation to disobey God, and so to the birth of freedom. Both were born in defiance of God's will since they came into existence by the sweat and stress of human striving and a heroic rebellion against divine authority. Herewith a quandary. Would a free culture of capitalism submit itself to any form of authority?

In his "Report on Manufactures" Hamilton addresses this question, and he touches on it in the earlier "Report on Public Credit." In the latter document, Hamilton found himself in the awkward position of defending paying off the state debts occurred during the Revolution at current, inflated value, thereby benefiting those speculators who had bought the securities. Hamilton justified his plan on the grounds that a national funding of the debt will bring coherence and stability to the country and endow the new economic system with confidence, as would funding a national bank. A nation's debt, Hamilton argued, almost in anticipation of John Maynard Keynes, is no curse if used for economic growth and with the will to face it in prosperous times and pay it off, hence "the creation of the debt should always be accompanied with the means of extinguishment." Establishing a system of public credit would help the moral condition of America since it would reinforce the sanctity of contracts and put the national government in the position of looking out for the republic's general welfare.[8]

Hamilton's "Report on Manufactures" called for the immediate development of productive enterprise and the end to all trade restrictions. He politely questioned, without mentioning his name, Jefferson's conviction that the "cultivation of the earth" is the most reliable endeavor in sustaining human subsistence and political freedom. Borrowing from Adam Smith's *The Wealth of Nations,* Hamilton also praised the many-sided benefits of the division of labor, noting the efficiency and "economy of time" that derives from specialization. Work that involves the tasks of manufacturing will also prove attractive to immigrants. Hamilton could well have used Karl Marx's wonderful phrase "the idiocy of rural life" when he spelled out why urban work more than farm labor "stimulates the activity of the human mind, by multiplying the objects of enterprise," and he believed that manufacturing would help the country overcome its diverse sectional interests. "Mutual wants," Hamilton observed, "constitute one of the strongest links of human connection," and the extent of such connections "bears a national proportion to the diversity in the means of mutual supply."

> In the proportion as the mind is accustomed to trade the intimate connection of interest, which subsists between all parts of a society united by the *same* government—the infinite variety of channels which serve to circulate the prosperity of each to and through the rest—in that proportion will it be little apt to be disturbed by the Solicitude and Apprehensions which originate in local discriminations.[9]

While commerce and manufacturing might tie the country together, what would hold the people themselves to standards of morality and probity? From his early years working in a store on St. Croix, Hamilton had no use for the creatures of capitalism, those who sought profit and profit alone. Later, observing the behavior of some compatriots during the time of the Revolution, Hamilton wrote to John Laurens: "In perfect confidence I whisper a word in your ear. I hate money-making men." Those who made a bundle during the war by cornering the market on certain goods increased Hamilton's disgust. In his "Publius" letters, Hamilton wrote:

> When avarice takes the lead in a State, it is commonly the forerunner of its fall. . . . There are men in all countries, the business of whose lives it is, to raise themselves above indigence, by every little art in their power. When these men are . . . influenced by the spirit I have mentioned, it . . . might be expected, and can only excite contempt. When others, who have characters to support, and credit enough in the world to satisfy a moderate appetite for wealth, in an honorable way, are found to be actuated by the same spirit, our contempt is mixed with indignation. But when a man appointed to be the guardian of the State, and the depository of the happiness and the morals of the people—forgetful of the solemn relation, in which he stands —descends to the dishonest artifices of a mercantile projector, and sacrifices his conscience and his trust to pecuniary motives; there is no strain of abhorrence . . . nor punishment . . . which may not be applied to him, with justice.[10]

When Hamilton read Adam Smith he doubted the Scottish philosopher's belief in the superior productive capacity of agriculture and his regarding labor as a source of value. But even more troublesome is the fact that Smith would be unmoved by the concerns that anguished Hamilton in the passage above. Smith saw economic phenomenon as natural, automatic, spontaneous, and, above all, self-regulating. And with Smith's sense of the irony of unintended outcomes, he need not worry about avarice, since in an unregulated market operating under the mysterious "invisible hand," behavior that is privately motivated produces public benefits, and thus vice somehow passes over into virtue. Hamilton would have none of this faith in the fetish of the competitive market. In "Report on Manufactures" he insisted that an economy on automatic pilot would remain stagnant, so much are people governed by habit and imitation that they would fail to imagine the simplest improvements and innovations. As would Lincoln years later, Hamilton believed that workers and producers would be accustomed to stick to their ordinary occupations and routines unless some of them, perhaps the enlightened few, were moved by curiosity and daring. Government must provide this stimulus, encourage commercial development and give the entrepreneur confidence. Government must also exercise a modicum of surveillance since America cannot count upon unrestrained egotism producing a just society. "There is, at the present juncture," wrote Hamilton in 1791, "a certain fermentation of mind, a certain activity of speculation and enterprise which, if properly directed, may be made subservient to useful purposes, but which, if left entirely to itself, may be attended with pernicious effects."[11]

Abraham Lincoln's economic philosophy could well suggest continuity from the Federalist Party to the Whig Party. He too was a nationalist and saw the American economy as a unifying force. He too believed in the drive of ambition and the imperative of hard work and the dream of upward mobility. Just before Lincoln came upon the political scene in America, Tocqueville saw everywhere in the country the impetus of "enlightened self-interest," and Lincoln partook of that ethos. Like Hamilton, Lincoln saw a role for government in the country's economic development, and he was a supporter of state-financed internal improvements from canals to railroads. Although Lincoln could be called an exponent of capitalism and self-help individualism, he recognized that there were limits to solitary striving and thus he acknowledged that America cannot wholly rely upon the people themselves to move the country ahead, lead honest lives, or advance their own position in society without a helping hand. In a "Fragment on Government," written privately to himself, possibly in 1854, Lincoln put it this way:

The legitimate object of government, is to do for a community of people, whatever they need to have done, but can not do, *at all,* or can not, *so well do,* for themselves—in their separate, and individual capacities.

In all that the people can individually do as well for themselves, government ought not to interfere.

The desirable things which individuals of a people can not do, or can not do well, for themselves, fall into two classes: those which have relation to *wrongs,* and those which have not. Each of these branch off into an infinite variety of subdivisions.

The first—that in relation to wrongs—embraces all crimes, misdemeanors, and non-performance of contracts. The other embraces all which, in its nature, and without wrong, requires combined action, as public roads and highways, public schools, charities, pauperism, orphanages, estates of the deceased, and the machinery of government itself.

From this it appears that if all men were just, there still would be *some,* though not *so much,* need of government.[12]

The last passage comes close to James Madison's dictum that if all men were "angels," no government would be necessary. Like Hamilton and the *Federalist* authors, Lincoln believed government was necessary to uphold law and order and guide the economy but he also wanted it to engage in deeds of social welfare and nation building. Moreover, in upholding the authority of the nation-state against the doctrine of state sovereignty and the right to secession, Lincoln was taking his stand with Hamilton against Jefferson and the Jeffersonian tradition. Such a perspective is far from the orthodox way of writing American intellectual history. In his three-volume *Main Currents in American Thought,* Vernon L. Parrington suggests that Lincoln came out of the same environment that bred Jefferson's presumed successor, Andrew Jackson. To Parrington, everything good in American history must be seen as emanating from Jeffersonianism and Ralph Waldo Emerson, and everything bad from Calvinism and Alexander Hamilton. Hence, "Whatever party name he may call himself by, in his love for justice and his warm humanity, Lincoln was essentially Jeffersonian."[13]

Such a conclusion cannot go unchallenged. Jefferson had no theory of the role of government, and even though he provided America with a foundation in natural, inalienable rights, he offered no institutional means of realizing and protecting such rights. Ironically, it was the very Supreme Court that Hamilton promoted and Jefferson opposed that turned out to be the agency that expanded civil rights for all citizens.

Because of the Dred Scott decision, Lincoln lost his respect for the Supreme Court, but years earlier, in the important Lyceum Address of 1838, he exhorted Americans to make respect for the Constitution and its laws the "political religion" of the nation. "Let reverence for the laws be breathed by every American mother to the lisping babe that prattles on her lap—let it be taught in schools, in seminaries, and in colleges—let it be written in primers, spelling books, and in almanacs—let it be preached from the pulpit, proclaimed in legislative halls, and enforced in the courts of justice."[14]

In writing the Constitution, Hamilton and Madison doubted that respect for the law would be sufficient to perpetuate the republic; hence the need for the "auxiliary precautions" of the Constitution's checks and controls. In could be said that Lincoln had greater faith in the popular masses than did Hamilton, and a "government of the people, by the people, and for the people" placed him closer to Jefferson in trusting the many rather than the few. Jefferson may have had aristocratic tastes and prejudices, but Hamilton was also an elitist who at times had doubts that the Constitution would survive the democratic pressures that would converge upon it. He believed in the class rule of the wealthy and talented not so they might exploit and oppress others but rather that they would steer the country in the right direction by promoting the public good. Hamilton could openly scorn the masses just as Lincoln, in his Second Inaugural during the Civil War, could scold them for the sin of slavery. Jefferson, as always, curried to their conceits.

There is one important matter on which both Hamilton and Jefferson cannot readily be considered as predecessors of Lincoln; neither subscribed to a labor theory of value. Lincoln spelled out that theory in his First Annual Message to Congress. Before the country's elected representatives, he rejected the idea that capital has precedence over labor: "It is assumed that labor is available only in connexion with capital; that nobody labors unless somebody else, owning capital, somehow by the use of it, induces him to labor. This assumed, it is next considered whether it is best that capital shall *hire* laborers, and thus induce them to work by their own consent, or *buy* them, and drive them to work without their consent." Such a relation of capital and labor Lincoln dismissed as spurious. On the contrary, "Labor is prior to, and independent of, capital. Capital is only the fruit of labor, and could never have existed if labor had not first existed. Labor is the superior of capital, and deserves much higher consideration."[15]

Alexander Hamilton would no doubt question this argument. But imagine what might be Hamilton's response to a speech Lincoln gave in New Haven in March 1860, at a time when a shoemaker's strike had taken place:

> What is the true condition of labor? I take it that it is best for all to leave each man free to acquire property as fast as he can. Some will get wealthy. I don't believe in a law to prevent a man from getting rich; it would do more harm than good. So while we do not propose any war upon capital, we do wish to allow the humblest man an equal chance to rise with everybody else. [Applause] When one starts out poor, as most do in the race of life, free society is such that he knows that he can better his condition; he knows that there is no fixed condition of labor, for his whole life. I am not ashamed to confess that twenty five years ago I was a hired laborer, mauling rails, at work on a flat boat just what might happen to any poor man's son! [Applause] I want every man to have the chance—and I believe a black man is entitled to it—in which he *can* better his condition—when he may look forward and to be a hired laborer this year and the next, work for himself afterward, and finally to hire men to work for him! That is the true system.[16]

It would not be too much of a stretch to imagine the young, small Alexander Hamilton, standing tip-toed looking out over the audience, the dust of the sandy Caribbean islands still on his ragged shoes, applauding along with the rest of the crowd.

NOTES

1. Abraham Lincoln, "Lyceum Address," in *Lincoln: Selected Writings and Speeches,* ed. Don. Fehrenbacher (New York: Library of America, 1989), 2 vols., I, 28–36. It should be noted that although Hamilton believed in glory and honor, he realized they are rare qualities, "the growth of few soils." *Federalist,* No. 1, 22, 57, 73. On the framers and the issue of human motivation, see John P. Diggins, *The Lost Soul of American Politics: Virtue, Self-Interest, and the Foundations of Liberalism* (New York: Basic Books, 1984); still the best analysis of this issue is Arthur O. Lovejoy, *Reflections on Human Nature* (Baltimore: Johns Hopkins University Press, 1961)

2. Hamilton, "The Farmer Refuted," in *The Papers of Alexander Hamilton* (hereafter *PAH*), ed. Harold C. Syrett, 27 vols. (New York: Columbia University Press, 1961–87), 1: 81–165.

3. Lincoln, "Spot Resolution," "Speech on Mexican War," in *Lincoln,* ed. Fehrenbacher, I, 158–59, 161–71; "Resolutions on Hungarian Independence," in *The Political Thought of Abraham Lincoln,* ed. Richard Current (Indianapolis: Bobbs-Merrill, 1967), 45–47.

4. Lincoln, "Notes on the Practice of Law," in *Lincoln,* ed. Fehrenbacher, I, 245–46; on Hamilton and Hume, see Diggins, *The Lost Soul of American Politics,* 64–68.

5. Alexander Hamilton to John Jay, Mar. 14, 1779, *PAH,* 2: 17–19.

6. "Fourth Lincoln-Douglas Debate," Sept. 18, 1858, in *Lincoln,* ed. Fehrenbacher, I, 637–51; Abraham Lincoln to James C. Conkling, Aug. 26, 1863, in *Lincoln,* ed. Fehrenbacher, II, 495–99.

7. Lincoln, "Discoveries and Inventions," in *Lincoln,* ed. Fehrenbacher, II, 3–11.

8. Hamilton, "Report on Public Credit," *PAH,* 6: 106.

9. Hamilton, "Report on Manufactures," *PAH,* 6: 230–96.

10. Hamilton, "Publius Letter, I," Oct. 16, 1778, *PAH,* 1: 562–63.

11. Hamilton, "Report on Manufacturers," *PAH,* 6: 296.

12. Lincoln, "Fragment on Government," in *Lincoln,* ed. Fehrenbacher, I, 301–2.

13. Vernon L. Parrington, *Main Currents in American Thought: An Interpretation of American Literature from the Beginnings to 1920,* 3 vols. (New York: Harcourt, 1927), II, 152–60.

14. Lincoln, "Lyceum Address," in *Lincoln,* ed. Fehrenbacher, I, 30–36.

15. Lincoln, "Annual Message to Congress," in *Lincoln,* ed. Fehrenbacher, II, 279–97.

16. Lincoln, "Speech at New Haven," in *Lincoln,* ed. Fehrenbacher, II, 132–50.

Contributors

DOUGLAS AMBROSE is the Sidney Wertimer, Jr., Associate Professor of History at Hamilton College. His publications include *Henry Hughes and Proslavery Thought in the Old South* (Louisiana State University Press, 1996).

JOHN PATRICK DIGGINS is Distinguished Professor of History at the Graduate Center of the City University of New York. His many writings include *The Lost Soul of American Politics: Virtue, Self-Interest, and the Foundations of Liberalism* (Basic Books, 1984), *On Hallowed Ground: Abraham Lincoln and the Foundations of American History* (Yale University Press, 2000), and *John Adams* (Times Books, 2003).

STEPHEN KNOTT is Associate Professor and research fellow at the Miller Center of Public Affairs, University of Virginia. His book, *Alexander Hamilton and the Persistence of Myth*, was published by the University of Kansas Press in 2002. He is also the author of *Secret and Sanctioned: Covert Operations and the American Presidency* (Oxford University Press, 1996).

DANIEL G. LANG is Professor of Political Science and Dean of the School of the Humanities and Social Sciences at Lynchburg College. He is the author of *Foreign Policy in the Early Republic: The Law of Nations and the Balance of Power* (Louisiana State University Press, 1986) and co-author, with Frederick C. Mosher and W. David Clinton, of *Presidential Transitions and Foreign Affairs* (Louisiana State University Press, 1987). His essay "Human Rights and the Founding Fathers" can be found in *Moral Reasoning and Statecraft*, edited by Reed Davis (University Press of America, 1987).

ROBERT W. T. MARTIN is Associate Professor of Government at Hamilton College. He is author of *The Free and Open Press: The Foundation of*

Modern American Democratic Press Liberty, 1640–1805 (New York University Press, 2001) and articles in *History of Political Thought, Political Research Quarterly, The Journal of the Early Republic,* and *Polity.*

ROBERT M. S. MCDONALD is Associate Professor of History at the United States Military Academy. The author of several essays and journal articles, he is editor of *Thomas Jefferson's Military Academy: Founding West Point* (University of Virginia Press, 2004).

PETER MCNAMARA is Associate Professor of Political Science at Utah State University. He is the author of *Political Economy and Statesmanship: Smith, Hamilton and the Foundation of the Commercial Republic* (Northern Illinois University Press, 1997). He is the editor of *The Noblest Minds: Fame, Honor, and the American Founding* (Rowman and Littlefield, 1999), which includes his essay, "Alexander Hamilton, the Love of Fame, and Modern Democratic Statesmanship."

JAMES H. READ is Professor of Political Science at the College of St. Benedict and St. John's University. He is the author of *Power versus Liberty: Madison, Hamilton, Wilson, and Jefferson* (University Press of Virginia, 2000).

CAREY ROBERTS is Assistant Professor of History at Arkansas Tech University. He has presented and written widely on eighteenth- and nineteenth-century American history, particularly on the development of southern conservatism and conflicting patterns of early nationalism.

BARRY ALAN SHAIN is Associate Professor of Political Science at Colgate University. He is the author of *The Myth of American Individualism: The Protestant Origins of American Political Thought* (Princeton University Press, 1994).

COLLEEN A. SHEEHAN is Associate Professor of Political Science at Villanova University and a former member of the Pennsylvania House of Representatives. She is co-editor of *Friends of the Constitution: Writings of the Other Federalists 1787–1788* (Liberty Fund, 1998) and author of numerous articles on the American founding and the ethics of Jane Austen. Professor Sheehan is currently working on a book on the political thought of James Madison.

Index

In this index AH is used in place of Alexander Hamilton in the subentries.